THE LOW BLOOD SUGAR COOKBOOK

MARGO BLEVIN AND GERI GINDER

FOREWORD BY HERBERT B. GOLDMAN, M.D.

DOUBLEDAY & COMPANY, INC.
GARDEN CITY, NEW YORK

ISBN: 0-385-05174-3
Library of Congress Catalog Card Number 72–79378
Copyright © 1973 by Margo Blevin and Geri Ginder
Printed in the United States of America

This book is dedicated
to the memory of Jimmy Peer.

ACKNOWLEDGMENTS

We want to give our special thanks to Dr. Lloyd Grumbles, M.D., who inspired us to write this book.

We would also like to thank the following people, without whose help and encouragement the book would not have been written:

Dr. Herbert Goldman, M.D., Dr. Alvin Krakower, M.D., Marilyn Light of the Hypoglycemia Foundation, Inc., Wilbert Ginder, Joan Peer, Denise Kane, Carole Schirmer, Tom and Theresa Tonkinson, Helen Ware, Alicia Keenan, Shirley Rubenstein, Pat Sweeney, Toni Heavener, Gail Abbatemarco, Faye Sander, Fritz Hirschberger, Joan Babbage, Tom Genné, Peggy Gordon, Wendy Geisler, Bonnie Horowitz, and all the Blevins and Ginders who were such intrepid tasters.

CONTENTS

FOREWORD

More and more doctors are now becoming aware of the problems faced by hypoglycemic patients. Rarely will you find a doctor nowadays who tells you to eat sugar and candy for hypoglycemia. Patients with hypoglycemia should be on a diet high in protein, moderate in fat, and low in carbohydrates. Of course, the diet is not the entire treatment for hypoglycemia, but it is a very important aspect of it.

Many patients have been told to follow a high protein diet with no specific instructions as to what they should eat. They have no conception of what proteins are; they have no idea that they can eat other foods in addition to steak and salads. They feel that their choice of foods is limited.

Geri Ginder and Margo Blevin have now not only given them hundreds of selections and combinations, but have explained things simply, so that the diet is easily understood.

For those doctors interested in the problems of the hypoglycemic patient, and their treatment, the task is made lighter by this book.

HERBERT B. GOLDMAN, M.D.

INTRODUCTION

Let us suppose that you have just been told that you have hypoglycemia (low blood sugar). As part of your treatment, your doctor has placed you on a rigid limited diet, which lists all the foods you can never eat again. You have been told that you must completely eliminate all sugars, starchy foods and alcoholic beverages, and that you must make other drastic changes in your eating habits. You find yourself bewildered, confused, and after the first few weeks, thoroughly tired of the foods you are allowed.

We (the authors of this book), who both have hypoglycemic families, were lucky to be close friends. We were able to help each other out with new ideas for meals and treats; whenever one of us was tempted to go on a "binge" with some forbidden food, the other friend was there to talk her out of it, or help with a new idea for a recipe.

Over the course of several years our families had visited back and forth, entertaining each other at dinner or sharing in birthday celebrations, Christmas and other occasions which seemed to center more and more on food. Swapping and inventing recipes came to be something of a game, and our meals became more and more elaborate, as we tried to outdo ourselves inventing sugarless versions of our favorite foods. When we finally realized that we had developed hundreds of recipes, we felt that we should compile them to help others who were struggling with the diet.

Years ago, people suffering from hypoglycemia were told to eat candy bars every few hours. Most doctors now feel that this is the worst possible treatment. The diet which is now recommended is a high-protein, medium-to-high-fat diet, with small amounts of slowly assimilated carbohydrates from fruits and vegetables. It requires that you eat small but frequent meals, with snacks of protein between meals. Besides eliminating sugar, you must do away with potatoes, rice, bread, wheat, corn, beans, and most canned, frozen and prepared foods (most of which contain sugar or starches). On the following pages, you will find detailed lists of all the foods allowed and not allowed, and many other suggestions which can help you adjust to this diet. We have even included the brand names of those few ready-to-eat products which do not contain sugar, and suggestions on where to buy them.

The foods allowed on the hypoglycemic diet *can* be delicious and varied, especially if you make a real effort to try out ideas for substitutions. Whenever we serve one of our low-carbohydrate "concoctions" to a guest, our first question is "What do you think of it?" and very often the answer is "Not bad! But it will never replace 'real' apple pie (or spaghetti or ice cream)." Our second question is always "But suppose it *had* to replace it?" And faced with a choice between going without a favorite food forever or eating a slightly different substitute, we think the answer would be "Very good indeed."

Hypoglycemic cooking is essentially replacement cooking; we substitute high-protein foods for starches and eliminate sugar completely. The object is to allow us to live as much as possible like anyone else. We don't think that the average person eats a sufficient variety of foods; but on the other hand, it is hard to change long-established habits. Ask anyone who lives with a meat-and-potatoes man how difficult it is to introduce new foods to her family.

Our method, which has worked on every husband or four-year-old we've ever encountered, is to make the food appear first in a familiar form, and as closely as possible follow meal patterns which are tried and true, gradually easing in a new dish every now and then. Hence you find candied squash listed as "mock sweet potatoes," and baked soybeans simply called "baked beans." We have always found that if you serve baked soybeans without any explanations, no one ever asks "What *is* this stuff?" They just eat it and ask for seconds.

And that, in a nutshell, is the real objective of this book.

THE HYPOGLYCEMIA DIET

The original anti-hypoglycemia diet, as devised by Dr. Seale Harris, is very brief. We are including it here as a basic guide which is easy to memorize. Then on the following pages, we have expanded the diet to give you a full day's schedule of meals and snacks, followed by a sample menu for a typical day. We call this schedule the "unit plan," and have broken it down into units of food to make meal planning easier. Keep in mind that this is a suggested guide, and is not to be confused with the diabetic's rigid counting of grams; it is merely a guide to make the diet more workable and more flexible until you are accustomed to it. The lists of foods allowed and not allowed and the amounts considered to be one unit can be found on the following pages.

THE DIET

Eat small meals: snacks of protein every two hours in between meals.

FOODS ALLOWED

Meats, fish and seafood, poultry
Dairy products (eggs, milk, cheese)
Nuts (in moderation)
Fats (butter, etc.)
Most vegetables
Most fruit (in moderation)
Oatmeal, oat flour (in moderation)
Sanka, weak tea, herb teas
Sugarless sodas (except colas)
Soybeans and soybean products
Artificial sweeteners, herbs, spices, vinegar, dill pickles
Unsweetened gelatin

FOODS NOT ALLOWED

Sugar in any form (honey, syrup, etc.)
Foods containing sugar of any kind
Potatoes, corn, rice, beans
Wheat, flour, starch
Bread, cereal, rolls
Macaroni, spaghetti, noodles
Dried fruit, bananas, watermelon, grapes, cherries, blueberries, raisins, prunes
Coffee, strong tea, cola drinks
Alcoholic beverages
Sweet pickles
Jams, jellies
Desserts made with sugar (ice cream, pies, cakes, candy, cookies, puddings, etc.)

"UNIT PLAN" DIET

Breakfast	1 unit fruit or juice 2 units protein (or more) 1 unit carbohydrate (optional) 1 serving fat Free beverage 1 unit milk (optional)
Snack, 2 hours later	1 unit protein and/or 1 unit milk or nuts
1 hour before lunch	1 unit tomato juice (optional)
Lunch	2 units protein (or more) 1 serving low-carbohydrate vegetable (or more) 1 serving medium-carbohydrate vegetable (optional) 1 serving fat Free beverage 1 unit carbohydrate or 1 unit fruit or ½ unit of each Free dessert or dessert using one of the above
2 hours later	1 unit protein and/or 1 unit milk or nuts
1 hour before supper	1 unit tomato juice (optional)
Supper	Soup (optional; if serving cream soup, count as a milk unit) 2 to 3 units protein (or more) 1 to 2 servings low-carbohydrate vegetables 1 serving medium-carbohydrate vegetable or 1 serving high-carbohydrate vegetable 1 serving fat

"UNIT PLAN" DIET

Free beverage
1 unit milk (optional)
Dessert:* 1 unit carbohydrate or
1 unit fruit or
½ unit of each

Every 2 hours   1 unit protein and/or
until bedtime   1 unit milk or nuts

Total milk for the day should not exceed 3 units.
Total fruit for the day should not exceed 3 units.

Carbohydrates and fruit allowed are subject to your doctor's preference, and should be eliminated or reduced if you find you can't tolerate them in these amounts.

SAMPLE MENU

To understand how the unit plan is used, here is a typical day's menu, using the simplest everyday foods:

Breakfast, 7:00 to 8:00   4 ounces orange juice
2 fried eggs
2 slices smoked bacon
½ cup oatmeal, light cream
1 cup Sanka

Snack, 10:00   8 ounces milk

Snack, 11:00   ½ cup tomato juice

* In making desserts, use discretion; don't combine fruit, milk and carbohydrate in one recipe, or if you do, then adjust the amount you eat in one serving. For instance, apple pie with ice cream contains all three; you might have a serving with ½ unit of fruit, ¼ unit of carbohydrate and 1 unit of milk, or some similar combination.

Lunch, 12:30–1:00	4 ounces tuna fish ¼ cup cottage cheese 2 leaves lettuce, 1 stalk celery, 2 olives 2 ounces tomato slices 2 tablespoons sugarless mayonnaise 1 cup herb tea 1 small apple
Snack, 3:00	2 ounces Cheddar cheese
Snack, 5:00	½ cup tomato juice
Supper, 6:00	1 bowl chicken broth 6 ounces broiled chicken 4 ounces French-style green beans 2 ounces tossed green salad Oil and vinegar dressing 4 ounces cooked carrots 1 bottle diet ginger ale 1 tangerine
Snack, 8:30	8 ounces milk 1 ounce almonds 1 slice American cheese
Snack, 10:30	1 cup tuna salad (leftover from lunch)

Total milk for the day: 2 units
Total fruit for the day: 3 units

PROTEINS

Amount: 1 unit protein=1 egg or
                  1 ounce cheese or
                  ½ cup cottage cheese or
                  2 ounces farmer cheese or
                  2 ounces cooked meat, seafood or poultry
1 unit=the *minimum* amount for a snack. For meals, 2 to 3 units are best.

PROTEINS ALLOWED

Bacon, smoked: not sugar-cured: *see* Brand Names

Beef: all cuts

Beef, dried: only sugarless, in jars: *see* Brand Names

Bologna, sugarless: these are extremely hard to find. Try all the different stores in your area, as well as small specialty shops and butchers. Some of the sugarless lunch meats we have found are: some salamis, a Polish loaf, a chopped ham loaf and a few brands of bologna. Check the label whenever you buy, as formulas can change from one store to another, even within the same brand!

Broth, clam: also some chicken and beef broths can be found without sugar. These contain some protein, but not enough to be used as a protein unit.

Cheese: any kind, so long as it contains no sugar, wine, etc.

Cheese spreads: any kind, so long as it contains no sugar, wine, etc.

Eggs: any style

Frankfurters, sugarless: always check the labels: *see* Brand Names

Gelatin, unflavored: can be used in any amount, but don't count it
    toward your protein units
Ham, smoked only
Heart, kidneys, liver: other organ meats, if prepared without sugar
Lamb
L.P.P. (Liquid Predigested Protein): *see* Brand Names
Lunch meat: *see* bologna, above
Mutton
Pork: fresh, smoked or cooked without sugar; *not* cured
Poultry
Sausage: only homemade or sugarless: *see* Brand Names
Seafood: all kinds if without breading or sauce
Soybeans: prepared without sugar. Also soy grits and soy flour
Veal: except breaded

MEDIUM PROTEIN FOODS TO BE USED IN MODERATION

These are foods high in protein which also contain some carbohydrate. They may be used as protein snacks, but do not exceed the
amount suggested.

Milk: whole, skim or buttermilk	1 unit=8 ounces
Milk, non-fat dry	1 unit=⅓ cup
Yoghurt, plain	1 unit=1 cup
Nuts: all kinds allowed, but	1 unit=1 ounce, or 10–12 nuts
peanuts and cashews are least	1 unit=1 ounce
good	
Seeds: sunflower, pumpkin,	1 unit=1 ounce
sesame, fresh coconut	

PROTEINS NOT ALLOWED

Cheese spreads containing wine, sugar, rarebits, fondue (except
    homemade by you)
Cottage cheese with fruit
Most cold cuts or lunch meats: *see* Brand Names

Pickled or spiced meats such as pastrami, corned beef, sauerbraten

Bacon, sugar-cured

Sausage, kielbasa, frankfurters unless the label specifically says no sugar

Turkey roll, chicken roll, southern fried chicken

Ready-made salads, such as egg salad, chicken salad, tuna salad

Fish cakes, deviled crabs, breaded fish, prepared shrimp cocktail

Breaded veal

Glazed baked ham

Canned ham

Meat with flour-thickened gravy

Presweetened or flavored yoghurt

Prepared chocolate milk

Dry-roasted or canned nuts which contain sugar

FRUITS

Fruit on the diet is needed for its natural sugar content, and should be spread out through the day as suggested in the unit plan. You may have fruit and other carbohydrates at the same meal, but you should cut the amount of each in half. Use a variety of fruit to prevent boredom; many delicious recipes can be found in the Dessert section and also under Preserves. You may use fresh, frozen "loose" in plastic bags without sugar or syrup or canned fruit (dietetic canned without sugar, "nutritive sweeteners" or grape juice; or canned in its own juice, such as Dole unsweetened pineapple).

FRUITS ALLOWED

	1 unit=
Apple	1 small or ¾ medium or ½ large
Apple juice (unsweetened)	4 ounces or ½ cup
Apple cider (unsweetened)	4 ounces or ½ cup
Apricot (fresh or diet-canned)	2 medium or 3 small
Blackberries	½ cup crushed or ¾ cup whole
Black raspberries	½ cup crushed or ¾ cup whole
Boysenberries	1 cup
Cantaloupe	½ medium
Crabapples	2 small
Cranberries	4 ounces or ½ cup
Cranberry sauce (homemade)	2 tablespoons
Damson plums	2

Fruit cocktail (sugarless, sold in bottles in the refrigerator section in supermarkets)	½ cup
Grapefruit	½ small
Grapefruit juice (unsweetened)	½ cup or 4 ounces
Honeydew melon	1 wedge, 2 by 7 inches
Kumquats	½ cup
Lemons	2
Lemon juice	4 ounces
Limes	1
Loganberries	½ cup
Mandarin orange (dietetic)	⅓ cup
Muskmelon	½ medium
Nectarine	1 small or ¾ medium
Orange	1 small
Orange juice (unsweetened)	4 ounces
Papaya	½ cup
Peaches (fresh or diet canned)	1 or ½ cup
Pear	1 tiny or ½ medium
Pineapple (fresh)	⅛ medium
Pineapple (canned, unsweetened or diet)	½ cup
Pineapple juice (unsweetened)	4 ounces or ½ cup
Plums	1 large or 2 small
Raspberries	½ cup
Strawberries (fresh or loose frozen)	1 cup whole
Tangerine	1½ medium
also:	
Rhubarb (cooked with artificial sweetener)	½ cup
Tomato juice	8 ounces

FRUITS NOT ALLOWED

Applesauce containing sugar

Jams, Jellies, Preserves: except homemade or sugarless. Be wary of so-called "diet" jams; many contain sugar or "nutritive sweeteners"

Bananas
Blueberries
Dried and Preserved fruit: figs, dates, raisins, prunes, stewed fruit
Cherries and cherry juice
Fruit cocktail with sugar or syrup
Grapes in any form
Lemonade, limeade containing sugar (only homemade with artificial
  sweetener)
Guava
Mangoes
Plantain
Prunes, prune juice
Raisins
Watermelon
Canned pie filling
Canned fruit with sugar or syrup
Frozen fruit with sugar or syrup

VEGETABLES

There are three types of vegetables allowed on the diet:

(a) Low-carbohydrate, which may be eaten in large amounts: suggested portion, 4 to 10 ounces total per meal; these contain 3 to 6 per cent carbohydrate.

(b) Medium-carbohydrate, which should be limited to a total of 4 to 6 ounces per meal; these are 10 per cent carbohydrate.

(c) High-carbohydrate, should be limited to a total of 4 ounces or ½ cup at dinner; these are 15 per cent carbohydrate. If you are having a 15 per cent vegetable, eliminate or cut down on fruit or carbohydrate.

LOW-CARBOHYDRATE VEGETABLES ALLOWED

Asparagus
Bamboo shoots
Bean sprouts
Beet greens
Broccoli
Cabbage, raw
Cauliflower
Celery
Chard
Chickory
Chinese cabbage
Chives

Collard greens, raw
Cucumbers
Dandelion greens
Eggplant
Endive
Escarole
Fennel
Kale
Leeks
Lettuce
Mustard greens
Mushrooms

Okra
Olives, green and black
Onions, cooked
Parsley
Pea pods (snow peas)
Peppers, green and red
Peppers, chili, hot, cherry, etc.
Pickles, sour and dill
Pimientos
Radishes
Rhubarb
Sauerkraut

Spinach
Scallions
String beans, French-style
Summer squash (yellow,
crookneck, etc.)
Tomato
Turnip, white
Turnip greens
Water chestnuts
Watercress
Wax beans, French-style
Zucchini

MEDIUM-CARBOHYDRATE VEGETABLES ALLOWED

Artichoke
Brussels sprouts
Cabbage, cooked
Carrots
Celeriac
Collard greens
Chervil
Green beans, whole or cut

Kohlrabi
Onion, raw
Rutabaga (yellow turnip)
Soybeans (larger portions
allowed because of high protein
content)
Tomato purée
Wax beans, whole or cut

HIGH-CARBOHYDRATE VEGETABLES ALLOWED

Beets
Jerusalem artichokes
Parsnips
Peas
Tomato paste (see Brand
Names)

Pumpkin
Salsify
Squash, winter
(acorn, butternut, etc.)

VEGETABLES NOT ALLOWED

Baked beans
Barley
Beans
Canned vegetables in sauce
Canned vegetables containing
   sugar
Chick peas
Chili beans
Corn
Dried peas
Hominy
Vegetables, canned
   or frozen in sauce
   (butter sauce, etc.)

Vegetables,
   frozen prepared (creamed
   spinach, etc.)
Lentils
Lima beans
Kidney beans
Potatoes
Rice
Sweet potatoes
Sweet pickles
   (and bread and butter pickles,
   etc.)
Pickled tomatoes
Yams

CARBOHYDRATES (STARCHES)

Carbohydrates must be rationed strictly according to the unit plan. All carbohydrates are to be eaten subject to your doctor's approval. If you find you have a reaction to one, stop using it or cut down on the amount. Remember, milk and fruit are also high in carbohydrate, and should not be eaten at the same time as carbohydrate foods unless you cut down the amounts.

CARBOHYDRATES ALLOWED

Bread: If your doctor allows you to have some wheat in your diet there are a few brands of bread which would be better than others. However, after trying the diet with and without "real" bread, it has been our experience that the protein breads are definitely too high in carbohydrate, and should be used only rarely, if at all. If you are able to tolerate them and are allowed to have a slice occasionally, you can find a list of the recommended brands under Brand Names.

Bread, homemade (*see* Breads)	1 thick or 2 thin slices
Oat flour	2 tablespoons
Oatmeal, cooked	½ cup
Oatmeal, uncooked	2 heaping tablespoons
Soy grits, cooked	1 cup or more as tolerated
Soy grits, uncooked	½ cup or more as tolerated
Soy flour	unlimited

Wheat germ if allowed by your   ¼ cup
  doctor and tolerated by you.
Noodles, Jerusalem artichoke: if   ½ cup cooked
  some wheat is allowed by your
  doctor, these may be used on
  occasion. They may be bought
  in health food stores (*see*
  Brand Names).
Noodles, homemade (*see* Breads,
  Pasta and Noodles).

CARBOHYDRATES NOT ALLOWED

Most bread and rolls
Breaded foods
Crackers
Cake
Candy
Cookies
Cereal (except oatmeal)
Biscuits
Corn bread
Corn meal
Desserts (except those in this
  book)
Dietetic cookies,
  candies, ice cream
Diabetic cookies,
  candies, ice cream
Dumplings
Flour
Gluten flour and gluten bread
Jell-O

Jam, jelly, etc.
Ice cream (except those in this
  book)
Kasha (buckwheat)
Matzoh and matzoh meal
Noodles
Muffins
Pancakes
Pasta
Pastries
Pie
Pudding
Rice
Rice flour
Rice pudding
Rye flour, rye bread
Tapioca
Tortillas
Wheat, whole wheat, wheat flour
Waffles

Peanut butter (except sugarless: *see* Brand Names)

Sugar in any form: honey, syrup, corn syrup, molasses, raw sugar, cane sugar, brown sugar, confectioners' sugar, sucrose, lactose, glucose, fructose, dextrose, dextrins, mannitol, sorbitol, corn syrup solids, nutritive sweeteners, natural sweeteners, maple syrup, maple sugar, heavy syrup, syrup, invert syrup, caramels, malt, maltose, sorghum, sorghum syrup, refined sugar. Also, if package says sugar cured or cured or mild cured.

Starch in any form: starch, corn starch, modified starch, potato starch, arrowroot, etc.

ARTIFICIAL SWEETENERS

ARTIFICIAL SWEETENERS ALLOWED

At the time of writing, several brands of artificial sweeteners are allowed. These are listed in Brand Names. However, your best protection is to form the habit of reading labels every time you buy. Those sweeteners which are safe to use are:

Saccharin

Crystallose

Saccharin-based liquid sweeteners which do not contain any of the sugars listed above

Saccharin-based sprinkle-type sweeteners which do not contain any of the sugars listed above

ARTIFICIAL SWEETENERS NOT ALLOWED

Weight Watchers brand

Sweeta

Sweet 'n Low

Most sprinkle-type sweeteners

Any other sweetener containing sugar in *any* form

BEVERAGES

BEVERAGES ALLOWED

Sugarless diet sodas: any, except cola flavors or those containing
  sugar or caffeine
Seltzer, club soda
Weak tea
Herb teas, all kinds: *see* Beverages
Decaffeinated coffee
Sugarless bouillon and homemade broth
Sugarless lemonade, weak
Cider, fruit juices: count as fruit units: *see* Fruits for amounts
Milk: actually a limited protein: *see* Proteins
Tomato juice, V-8 juice: count as fruit units: *see* Fruits

BEVERAGES NOT ALLOWED

Wine, beer, hard liquor, cordials or any other alcoholic beverages
  (this includes cooking wine in food as well)
Colas or other sodas containing caffeine
Regular sodas, except club soda
Lemonade
Grape juice
Tea, strong or regular
Instant tea mix
Punch
Coffee

Postum
Ovaltine
Chocolate milk
Hot chocolate
Kool-Aid-type drinks
Orangeade, orange drink, breakfast drinks, such as Tang, fruit
  drinks

CONDIMENTS AND SEASONINGS

Any herb or spice can be used, provided it is packaged without sugar. Most of the "combination" spices, such as seasoned salts, contain sugar. *See* Brand Names for those which are safe to use (at the time of writing). Always remember to check the label to be sure.

CONDIMENTS AND SEASONINGS ALLOWED

Prepared mustard: most brands, yellow or brown
Kikkoman soy sauce: the only brand we've found to be sugar-free
Herbs: marjoram, oregano, basil, chervil, thyme, parsley, bay leaves, etc.
Spices: pepper, cloves, cinnamon, paprika, ginger, curry, chili powder, etc.
Salt, plain or sea salt: not iodized
Onion powder, onion flakes, etc.: also onion salt, but check the ingredients
Garlic powder or flakes
MSG (monosodium glutamate, Ac'cent)
Seeds: mustard, caraway, sesame, poppy seeds, etc.
Dry mustard
Celery salt
Dehydrated lemon peel and orange peel
Sugarless seasoning mixtures: *see* Brand Names

Vinegar, white, cider or herb vinegar
Horseradish, white or red
Sugarless mayonnaise: homemade or *see* Brand Names
Sugarless salad dressings: *see* Brand Names
Capers
Hot Pepper sauce (check label for sugar)

CONDIMENTS AND SEASONINGS NOT ALLOWED

Most combination herb seasonings: meat loaf seasoning, gravy mixes, etc.
Chili sauce
Ketchup
Marinades
Smoke flavoring
Seasoned salts containing sugar (including lemon salt, butter-flavored salt, etc.)
Bottled salad dressings, unless no sugar is specified on label: *see* Brand Names
Mayonnaise-type salad dressings
Dijon or hot French mustard
Most soy sauces
Steak sauce
Cocktail sauce for seafood
Barbecue sauce
Meat tenderizers
Mayonnaise
Prepared dips
Worcestershire sauce
Most bouillon cubes and packets
Wine vinegar

FATS

Fats are to be used in moderate amounts with every meal. Use whichever ones you prefer and mix saturated with unsaturated fats so that you get equal amounts of each.

FATS ALLOWED

Butter, margarine
Crisco, Spry, etc.
Cream (heavy)
Salt pork
Homemade gravy and pan drippings
Mayonnaise, sugarless: homemade or bought (*see* Brand Names)
Sugarless peanut butter: *see* Brand Names
Oil
Lard
Cream cheese
Chicken fat, rendered
Sour cream

FATS NOT ALLOWED

Butter whipped with honey
Imitation dairy products for coffee, powdered or liquid. Warning: when served cream in restaurants, ask for milk instead; if not you

are probably using non-dairy creamer, which contains large amounts of sugar

Mayonnaise, unless specified sugarless

Prepared salad dressings in restaurants, etc., unless you can check the label

MEDICATIONS

There are many types of medications which affect your blood sugar. Whenever taking a drug, whether prescription or non-prescription, make sure the doctor knows you are hypoglycemic, and ask specifically for medication that doesn't contain stimulants or depressants. Following are some of the medications that you should avoid using:
Aspirin compounds containing caffeine: Anacin, Empirin, A.P.C. etc. (plain aspirin is all right to take, also buffered aspirin is fine).
4-Way cold tablets
Trigesic
Fiorinal
Medications containing alcohol, such as cough medicines
Cough drops and cough syrups containing honey, sugar, syrup, alcohol, codeine, etc.
No Doz
Midol
BC tablets

SUGGESTED READING LIST

Body, Mind & Sugar, by E. M. Abrahamson, M.D., and A. W. Pezet. A Pyramid Book published by Pyramid Publications, a division of the Walter Reade Organization, Inc., 444 Madison Avenue, New York, New York 10022

"Composition of Foods," Agriculture Handbook No. 8. Agriculture Research Service, United States Department of Agriculture, Washington, D.C.

"Hypoadrenocorticism," by Dr. John Tintera, M.D. Published by the Adrenal Metabolic Research Society of the Hypoglycemia Foundation, Inc.

"The Hypoglycemia of Hypoadrenocorticism," by Marilyn H. Light, executive director, the Adrenal Metabolic Research Society of the Hypoglycemia Foundation, October 1968, as delivered to a meeting of the Manhattan-Westchester Chapter of Health Frontiers Foundation, Inc.

Let's Eat Right to Keep Fit, by Adelle Davis. A Signet Book published by the New American Library, Inc., 1301 Avenue of the Americas, New York, New York 10019

Making Your Own Baby Food, by Mary Turner and James Turner. Published by Workman Publishing Company, New York, New York

Low Blood Sugar and You, by Carleton Fredericks, Ph.D. and Herman Goodman, M.D. Published by Constellation International, 51 Madison Avenue, New York, New York

Natural Health, Sugar and the Criminal Mind, by J. I. Rodale. A Pyramid Book published by Pyramid Publications, a division of the Walter Reade Organization, Inc., 444 Madison Avenue, New York, New York 10022

Prevention magazine, published monthly by RODALE Press, Inc., Emmaus, Pennsylvania 18049

The Stress of Life, by Hans Selye, M.D. McGraw-Hill Book Company, 1221 Avenue of the Americas, New York, New York 10020

For further information, literature can be obtained from:

The Adrenal Metabolic Research Society of the Hypoglycemia Foundation, 98 Fleetwood Avenue, Mt. Vernon, New York 10552

The Hypoglycemia Foundation, Inc., 98 Fleetwood Avenue, Mt. Vernon, New York 10552

IDEAS TO HELP YOU LIVE WITH LOW BLOOD SUGAR

READING LABELS: A GUIDE TO EASIER FOOD SHOPPING

Be prepared for a shock when you begin examining the labels on food products you are accustomed to buying. You will find, with few exceptions, that nearly all prepared, canned and convenience frozen foods contain sugar in one form or another. This includes not only the obvious items, such as desserts, but such unexpected items as iodized salt, canned soup, lunch meats, canned vegetables, baby food, bouillon cubes, frozen turkeys and almost every category of food. At first you will find it difficult and frustrating to shop, as one by one you find your favorite food items joining your growing list of "forbidden" foods. But as you gain shopping experience, and by searching through all the supermarkets and small grocery stores in your area, you will find in most categories at least one brand which doesn't contain sugar. Stock up on these items, and you will greatly simplify your shopping. The farther the store is from your home, the larger the quantity you should buy (providing of course, that the item can be stored).

We will mention from time to time in the recipe section some sugarless item you might be able to find in stores near you. Keep in mind, however, that manufacturers do change their formulas, and these suggestions may not always be valid. Also, a particular brand name may be made with sugar in one part of the country and without sugar in another. Your best protection is a sharp eye; read the labels front and back, and when in doubt, or if the ingredients aren't listed, don't buy it. At the present time manufacturers of such items as mayonnaise, vanilla extract, canned tomatoes, ketchup and other food products are not required to list their ingredients; all of these are products which usually contain some sugar. If you would like to buy a product which does not list its ingredients, or if you think you may be having a reaction to some product you have been buying, write to the manufacturer (preferably on your physician's stationery, to insure receiving an answer), and ask him to list his ingredients or to indicate whether or not his product contains some form of sugar.

Another factor which you may find confusing is the way in which sugar appears on labels. A manufacturer of "diet" foods who doesn't want to frighten off potential buyers may list in his ingredients "nutritive sweeteners." This is just another word for sugar. In fact, most "dietetic" or "diabetic" products contain sugar; a careful reading of the label will reveal this. If you have been in the habit of using these products, you may find a dramatic difference in the way you feel once they are eliminated from your diet. Many "diet" products which state "no sugar added" on the front label, list ingredients such as dextrin, sorbitol and mannitol on the back or side label (all of which are sugars). There are of course some genuinely sugar-free diet products, and we have listed as many of these as we were able to find. But even these are subject to change, and you must acquire the habit of checking and rechecking your labels each time you shop.

All products containing the following ingredients have sugar: sugar—raw sugar—turbinado sugar—invert sugar—brown sugar—refined sugar—cane sugar—maple sugar—dextrose—dextrins—glucose—sucrose—fructose—lactose—maltose—syrup—corn syrup—corn syrup solids—invert syrup—maple syrup—heavy syrup—glucose syrup—maltose syrup—sorghum syrup—honey—molasses—blackstrap molasses—natural sweeteners—nutritive sweeteners—caramel—caramel coloring—mannitol—sorbitol. Also, if package says: cured—sugar cured—mild cured.

Besides sugar, you should not buy any products which contain: starch—malt—corn starch—modified starch—potato starch—arrowroot—tapioca—flour—wheat—rice—rice flour—corn—corn meal—bread crumbs—coffee—caffeine—wine—carob.

CHANGING YOUR EATING HABITS

"If I have to look at one more hamburger, I'll . . ." Sooner or later, on any diet, you will hit a period of boredom and will begin looking with yearning at bakery windows; you will find yourself salivating at the mention of french-fried potatoes. Remember when this happens that it is your mind which craves these foods, not your body. If you hadn't acquired a taste for high-carbohydrate foods early in life you never would have missed them. This is why it is so important, if you suspect that your children may be hypoglycemic, to put them on the diet as early as possible, while their tastes are still forming. Your whole family will benefit from a low-carbohydrate regimen at home, even those who eat "normal" food away from home.

The craving for sweets, which is so widespread in our country, is not natural. It is an acquired taste or habit, resulting from the constant bombardment of our taste buds by sugar and starchy foods. Think, if you will, of the first days of a baby's life. Except for the lucky baby who is breast-fed, what is the first food a child is given, just hours after being born? A solution of water and glucose, or "sugar-water"; no doubt this custom started in the modern hospital, with its strict feeding schedules. What better way to quiet a roomful of hungry babies than with liquid candy? From this he moves on to formulas containing large amounts of sugar, and he has learned that first, important association in his mind of food: appeasement of hunger=sweet flavor. Next he is given strained baby foods (containing sugar and starch), baby cereal (starch, sugar and malt), and naturally we conscientiously give our baby his daily vitamin C, in the form of orange juice, made especially for babies with sugar added. Then there are the teething biscuits, baby cookies, not to mention pacifiers containing jelly, and the latest addition, exotic desserts for babies, such as blueberry cobbler. Is it any wonder that we grow up preferring sweet foods? After such a start, we have to struggle to disguise the flavor of vegetables and meats so that they will be palatable to sugar-oriented taste buds.

Now you are told that, for you, sugar is a poison. You *may* feel that eliminating sugar, candy and desserts will be an easy task; perhaps you are one of those people (of whom we are in awe) who can "take sweets or leave them." It would be natural for you then to assume that this diet would have very little impact on your way of life. You would be very wrong, because of the one fact that you had either forgotten or never known: *almost everything* we eat or buy today contains additives of sugar or starch. In fact the average person consumes over a hundred pounds of sugar a year, much of it without his knowledge. To illustrate this, let us look at a typical day's menu, of the type that the average housewife would feed her children:

For breakfast, she'd begin with an instant fruit drink (sugar), presweetened cereal (sugar, starch) with milk, toast (starch, sugar) with jam (sugar), and perhaps a cup of cocoa (sugar). Then on to lunch: a can of soup (sugar, starch), a sandwich of bologna (sugar, corn syrup solids, dextrose), two pieces of bread (starch, sugar) and mayonnaise (sugar). Milk or soda (sugar, and possibly caffeine) just wouldn't taste right unless accompanied by cookies (starch, sugar) and possibly canned fruit (in thick sugar syrup). Dinner might consist of some frozen fish cakes (starch, sugar), tartar sauce (sugar), spaghetti (starch, sugar), sweet pickles (sugar), salad with bottled salad dressing (sugar) and canned peas (sugar). Don't even mention dessert; it's about 90 per cent sugar, whatever it is. Later, there will be TV snacks of popcorn (starch), pretzels, (starch) and candy for "energy" or reward.

In short, almost every food which you have taken for granted is now going to be denied you. About all that you are left to eat is a small list of foods guaranteed to bore you after a few months. There is, however, a very simple solution to lift you out of the mealtime doldrums time after time: that is, variety. You *must* make sure that you are using the full range of foods which you are permitted to have; not just the one you were accustomed to eating before you were placed on the diet, but new foods, new spices and herbs, new recipes.

Begin by following the unit plan to the letter, using the simplest foods: raw and plain cooked vegetables, meats broiled or baked, raw fruit for desserts, milk or nuts or cheese for snacks. After a week, start using one new recipe every day, but don't overdo it. You shouldn't have the feeling that you are spending all your time cooking or you will become discouraged. If someone else is preparing your food, have them choose whichever recipes they think they would enjoy cooking. If they like to bake, for instance, have them try a new dessert every day, or some homemade bread. After you have found a recipe you especially enjoyed, repeat it and try a new one in addition. Once a week buy and use a vegetable which you rarely eat, or even one totally new to you; try it two or three different ways to see if you can find one you like. Stop eating your five favorite foods until you have found others you like equally well, then rotate them periodically so you won't become bored. Use a full range of vegetables: not just canned, but frozen and fresh, cooked and raw. Serve a hot and a cold vegetable at each lunch and dinner; another way to force yourself to vary your vegetables is to serve a green and a red (or orange) vegetable at each meal. Try some of the dessert recipes in this book, then see if you can vary them each time you make them, for most of them are basic recipes which can be altered in many ways. Make an extra effort to balance your menus and to make your food look as appetizing as possible. Prepare extra portions to freeze in TV dinner trays for those "tired of cooking" days. If there is a particular forbidden food you crave, such as ice cream or spaghetti, try the various substitutes until you hit one that pleases you. You'll soon forget what the "real thing" tastes like, and you'll find that you enjoy the substitute just as much. It's amazing how good Chinese food can taste without the rice, or Italian food minus the pasta. Try an entire week without beef; this will force you to try other forms of protein. Once you break the beef habit, you'll never go back to that dreary steak-roast beef-hamburger routine again. For good health and to insure against boredom, serve fish and organ meats, such as liver, at least once a week. If your family "hates" fish, try other forms of seafood, such as shrimp salad, sardine dip or clam chowder. Perhaps you don't like liver; try the chopped chicken liver dip, or Chinese chicken livers sweet and pungent. Treat yourself like "company" once a week, with some canapes or appetizers, a soup course, and one really elaborate dessert. Try to avoid restaurants until you're very familiar with the diet; there are few things you can order safely, and you'll have far more variety if you can eat at home or carry a lunch to work.

The final change in your eating habits will be one which will come about gradually, almost without your noticing it. After being on this diet for a year or more you will find that you will not need or want the amount of carbohydrate you craved in the past. If you are following the diet properly, and of course not smoking, drinking alcohol or using drugs, you will begin to find that you can eat correctly almost without thinking about it. You can help yourself to bring this about by being strictly honest in measuring your carbohydrate units; if you have a tendency to nibble a little more than your share, cut down on the amount you allow yourself. If you have been a compulsive eater of sweets, or even a mildly heavy eater of desserts, use few sweet recipes, so that you can rid yourself of the habit of eating these foods. At first this will be hard, and we would rather see you eat a sugarless dessert once or twice a day than to go on a sugar-eating binge in desperation; but gradually, you will feel the time arrive when you can start cutting down on your saccharin intake; when this happens you will be much better off. If you are cooking for young children, don't let them form the habit of having sweet-tasting food every day; even if you are not using real sugar, the taste of sweetened food will have more appeal to them and they will find it harder to keep from "cheating" when they grow up and are on their own. In fact, for some people the mere taste of saccharin triggers the same response they would have to sugar, and for these people the desserts and candies should be completely eliminated until they are well enough to handle them.

Always remember, the *most* important thing to you must be, not just eating well, but feeling well. That means eating as much protein as you need, as often as you need it. And if you follow the diet carefully, you will feel so full of new energy that it will be well worth the extra time and trouble involved in preparing meals.

PACKING A LUNCH PAIL

Packing a lunch is no trouble once you break the habit of sandwich—fruit—cookies, which is what most of us think of as an average lunch. To help maintain variety (and this is important for lunches eaten at home as well), plan your meals so that you will have leftovers appropriate for a lunch box. For instance, double your meat loaf recipe whenever you make it, and you will have snacks and cold lunches taken care of for a week. Or you could freeze some extra meat loaf in individual slices, with double sheets of wax paper between each slice. When there's nothing else to pack, wrap a slice or two, still frozen, and by lunchtime it will be thawed out and ready to eat.

Sandwiches can still be used, and we have included some which are appropriate for a packed lunch under Sandwiches. There are so many foods which can be carried easily, that you really should not have to rely on sandwiches. . . . All you need is a good supply of various size containers, some plastic forks and spoons and a little imagination.

There is one problem you may run into which requires a little ingenuity: that is, conformity. Children and teen-agers hate to be different; they usually want their lunches to look like everyone else's. Since it's important, when dealing with a hypoglycemic youngster, to remove the stress situations from their lives, it would be best to go along with their wishes. They can carry a lunch which resembles the other children's, and still be fooled in several ways into eating the correct amount of protein. You can make sandwiches, using homemade breads which are fairly low in carbohydrates, such as all-star bread, which allows them two slices, or soy bread, which is almost unlimited and, in fact, can be counted as a protein snack by itself. If you prefer the higher carbohydrate, or yeast-rising breads, such as Thomas' protein bread, chill the bread well, then slice thinly with a serrated knife. Always fill a sandwich with as much protein as possible, even if it means leaving out the lettuce to do so. For fillings or spreads such as tuna salad, you can't use thin toast, or you'll have a mess. In that case, use the soy bread or other egg breads. Add a Thermos of milk or milk shake with an egg blended in (*see* Beverages), a very small piece of fruit, some high-protein candies (*see* Candies) or a small bag of sunflower seeds or nuts, and you're all set. Eventually you will be able to add more adventurous foods as the child becomes adjusted to the diet, and soon you will be able to eliminate the bread altogether.

You should also see to it that your school-age youngster has a protein snack at midmorning and another the minute he arrives home at midafternoon. The midmorning snack of milk and cookies or fruit is standard now in most classrooms. Speak to the child's teacher, and you will surely be allowed to send a protein cookie or pancake-and-peanut-butter sandwich every day. For very young children it might be more practical to give the teacher several cans of nuts or seeds at the beginning of the year to be given to the child one ounce at a time when the other children are having their cookies. She could even tell the other children why your youngster can't have cookies, so they won't try to share theirs with him. An even simpler solution for all concerned is for the child to be told that he is "allergic" to sugar; all kids understand that explanation, and it doesn't sound so "different." Birthdays and parties in school are also handled quite easily with a little forethought (*see* Children's Parties).

Men and women who carry a lunch or dinner to work usually have their preferences as well. Go along with these, but add your own touches gradually. Avoid drippy foods, salads which wilt, cheese which is unattractive at room temperature (such as pasteurized process cheeses, American cheese), and leaky containers. Hot foods should be at a comfortable temperature . . . especially if the lunch break is a short one. Don't include anything too pungent; save the garlic and onions for dinner. Wrap each item individually.

To wrap peeled hard-cooked eggs, plums or anything crushable, wrap loosely in waxed paper, then again in heavy-duty aluminum foil. If no salt is available at the lunchroom or office, Sterling Salt puts out very tiny salt shakers which can be used several times, but won't break your budget if they're lost after one use.

Salads, cold leftovers and cold "finger foods" can be packed in good plastic containers. "Freezettes," made by Republic Molding Corp., are great because the tops screw on firmly and won't leak. Tupperware products are also excellent, but check the tops for leaks each time they're used. Glass containers should be avoided for obvious reasons. An excellent throwaway container for meats, fragile sandwiches, cake, etc., is a paper plate folded in half and stapled together, then wrapped in foil.

Insulated containers come in all shapes and sizes and can be used for hot or cold foods. Thermos brand is the best known, but there are others which are similar, such as Aladdin, as well as the Styrofoam type. If you pack a lunch or dinner every day, consider investing in a stainless steel Thermos bottle. The initial cost is high (about $13 to $15), but in the long run they pay for themselves, as they insulate better, are easier to clean and are guaranteed not to break. Hot soups and stews can be carried in wide-mouth Thermos jugs which come in several sizes. Milk shakes and eggnogs can be carried in wide-mouth bottles, or in regular Thermos bottles, to be eaten directly from the bottle with a long plastic straw.

Disposable plastic forks and spoons are cheap and hold up well for salads and soft foods. You may want to buy the heavier re-usable-type plastic forks and knives for meat and fish, or else try using toothpicks to spear the precut pieces. You might also include a paper napkin, paper plate and a Wash 'n Dri when taking finger foods.

Be sure to pack some extra protein snacks, such as nuts or seeds, which can be eaten unobtrusively at midmorning and midafternoon.

Small medicine vials and plastic bottles can be saved and used for seeds, mustard, homemade ketchup and other dressings, and dips for vegetables.

Carry your lunch in an insulated bag or a metal or plastic lunch box or even an attaché case. To insulate cold and hot foods you can wrap each container in newspaper, which also helps guard against leaks and breakage. Be sure to include a small re-usable container of frozen material, such as Hamilton-Skotch Corp.'s

"Skotch Ice" or "Freezit" made by Stanbel Inc., to keep food from spoiling in warm weather.

Here are a few suggestions for lunch ingredients:

Meats: broiled or baked pork chops (trim and cut into bite-sized chunks), cold hamburgers, tiny meat balls, meat loaf, sugarless liverwurst in sandwiches with homemade bread or pancakes, ham, uncooked hot dogs; broiled or fried sliced turkey and chicken (sliced or pieces).

Seafood: hot or cold fish cakes (homemade only); fish salads such as tuna, crab, etc.; canned fish with a wedge of lemon (tuna, salmon, sardines); smoked fish; broiled or fried shrimp.

Eggs: hard-boiled, deviled or stuffed, egg salad; in eggnogs, cake.

Cheese: semisoft, individually wrapped (such as Swiss Knight, Laughing Cow, etc.); sticks (Kraft 2-ounce Cheddar sticks); chunks or slices; spreads on pancakes.

Cottage cheese: in containers, plain; with cinnamon and sweetener; with vegetables, fruit or as a dip for celery, etc.

Yoghurt: with sugarless jelly or fruit, with vanilla extract and sweetener.

Nuts: peanuts, almonds, pecans, etc. Nut butters on pancakes, celery, etc.

Seeds: toasted sunflower seeds, pumpkin seeds; roasted soybeans.

Vegetables: raw (radishes, carrots, etc.); salads and slaws; pickles; hot cooked vegetables in wide-mouth Thermos jars.

Fruit: raw; cooked (stewed, baked); stuffed (with cream cheese, etc.).

Miscellaneous: Homemade soup, hot stews and casseroles fit into Thermos containers, as do bouillon, sodas (do not fill to top), milk, eggnogs, Sanka, herb tea and iced Sanka.

YOUR EMERGENCY KIT

Whenever you are away from home for more than a few minutes, you should have an emergency supply of protein near at hand. You may find you use it often, or you may never have to use it, but it's a good habit to have it along just in case. Here are some of the emergency items we have found useful to have around:

CAR EMERGENCY KIT

This is not meant to be a daily snack pack, but rather a box of emergency items kept in a cardboard box, or better yet, a waterproof container, in your trunk or under the seat of your car. It might be used in case you are ever in an accident and feel faint, or when you're stranded on the road, or even when you are in an unfamiliar area and can't find a store or restaurant when you need a snack:

Canned fish
Can opener
Fork, knife, spoon
Vitamin C tablets
Vacuum-packed can of nuts
Protein tablets (check label: must be at least 90 per cent protein)
1 or 2 cans fruit juice
small bottle of "LPP": Liquid Predigested Protein, in a pleasant sugarless syrup; does not need refrigeration; 1 ounce=9 grams or 1½ units protein.

POCKET (OR PURSE) EMERGENCY KIT:
This should be carried on you at all times:

a small vial of saccharin tablets
protein tablets or a ten-cent bag of nuts

PLACE OF BUSINESS (OR SCHOOL LOCKER)

Same as car emergency kit; if you like, you can also add a small jar of Sanka, a plastic cup, a small electric hot water heater, individual packets of non-fat dry milk (Weight Watchers makes these), a few herb tea bags.

VACATION EMERGENCY KIT
(also good for salesmen and people who travel a lot):

canned tuna, salmon, chicken
sugarless peanut butter
small jar of ReaLemon
small cans of vegetables
small cans of evaporated milk
saccharin and sprinkle-type sweetener
jar of instant Sanka
can opener, bottle opener
unbreakable cup
fork, knife, spoon
paper towels, Wash 'n Dris
small electric hot water heater
small plastic container for leftovers
homemade soy bread, cake, cookies, etc.
re-usable ice, such as Skotch-Ice cans
cans or packets of nuts
cans of fruit juice
cans of sugarless packed fruit

cans of diet soda
packet of instant non-fat dry milk
herb tea bags
protein tablets, vitamins
small amount of protein bread, wrapped well
insulated picnic basket
paper or plastic plate
onion powder, salt and pepper
wide-mouth Thermos jug for ice
any pills, vitamins you usually take, wrapped well
copies of prescriptions for any medications you take
name and phone number of your doctor in your purse or wallet
card explaining that you are hypoglycemic, and should not be given
    sugar or glucose in an emergency

It may seem rather paranoid, but we recommend anyone, even those people who *never* travel, to carry the last three items in their wallets. There have been many incidents in which someone fainted or was injured and was given glucose with disastrous results. Carrying a card is no guarantee against this happening, but it might help.

ENTERTAINING GUESTS

Naturally you want guests in your home to feel comfortable, and you can hardly make others feel comfortable if you are uncomfortable yourself. So we feel the primary rule of entertaining for a person on the hypoglycemia diet, or anyone else, is to look out for your own comfort and well-being first. This means not only taking the time to eat your snacks at regular intervals, but also having plenty of low-carbohydrate "goodies" on hand so that you don't feel left out if your company is eating forbidden foods. While it's not at all necessary, you might want to consider serving *only* low-carbohydrate food, so that you can relax and eat as much as you like along with your company. With the exception of alcoholic beverages, you can serve any kind of party food, from canapés to desserts, and nobody need know that he is eating "special" food. . . . Many recipes suitable for party food are given throughout this book, and if you don't make a big point of telling everyone about the diet, your guests will never suspect. Another way of taking pressure off yourself (or your hypoglycemic family members) would be to serve both allowed and not-allowed dishes, making sure that your family is briefed ahead of time as to what they may have and how much.

The other rule to remember when entertaining is "easy"; let's make life easier, not more complicated. If your hypoglycemic family member can't have wine vinegar, why use it at all? Use cider or malt vinegar for everyone. The same is true of all spices and condiments. You can avoid unintentional mistakes by simply buying the sugar-free brands only. We don't believe in duplicating everything we prepare. First of all, it's too much work; second, you're liable to get confused in serving two versions of everything and end up eating the wrong one.

Many of the desserts, such as cookies or ice cream (*see* Desserts) can be made quickly, or, if you prefer, made ahead of time and frozen. We prefer not to freeze canapés because of the danger of spoilage. However, you might try freezing some of the ingredients, ready to make when company comes.

If you entertain often and informally, keep on hand enough staples so that a good meal could be whipped up without much shopping. You have enough to do between preparing snacks and sugarless extras; why make life more complicated by having to dash around to six different stores to buy ingredients for your favorite recipe? If you have a spare shelf in your kitchen or cellar, use it to store two or three of each of your hard-to-find staples, such as sugarless peanut butter, and replenish it from time to time so that you're not caught short.

Many of the recipes we have included in this book can be made quickly, then kept warm, as for a buffet. Whenever a short cut can save you steps without sacrificing flavor or nutrition, use it. After all, why slave for twelve hours over a meal which will be eaten in a half hour? Try our recipes for quick soups, or some of the casseroles which can be prepared early and left to cook all day untended.

Most of the time, "company" means having a few friends over for coffee and cake. Whether the invitation has been issued well in advance, or on the spur of the moment, there is no need to panic. You can, of course, keep cakes and cookies containing sugar in the house for such occasions. But we prefer not to for several reasons. Sometimes it's hard to keep a child away from sweets if he knows they're around. Or you may be new to the diet and find your will power vanishes at the sight of leftover cake (a whole uncut cake, well wrapped and hidden in the back of your refrigerator or freezer is bad enough, but the sight of a half-eaten slice of cake left on someone else's plate can be devastating!) Also, you may find that it goes against your grain to serve food loaded with sugar to someone you like. The same is true of coffee and tea; we usually serve Sanka or herb tea, and we find that our company enjoys them while our conscience is appeased. Once you realize the harm that sugar, coffee and tea have done to your system, you hate to inflict them on your friends. We find that people think Sanka is delicious if made properly (*see* Beverages) and can't be distinguished from "real" coffee. If you must serve real tea, be sure to make it weak.

In addition to Sanka and tea, you might serve home-baked bread with a tub of whipped butter, cream cheese or some simple spread (*see* Appetizers), or a bowl of fresh fruit and a platter of cheeses. Also popular are the toasted pumpkin seeds called "pepitas," which can be found in the gourmet section of supermarkets, and assorted shelled or unshelled nuts. If you like dips, you'll find many in the Appetizer section, along with suggestions for low-carbohydrate foods to dip into them.

Here is a list of some items we keep on hand as an emergency kit for unexpected guests; you'll want to add your own favorites to it as you find more recipes to your liking:

EMERGENCY KIT FOR ENTERTAINING

canned smoked oysters
Knorr-Swiss onion soup and dip mix
canned anchovy fillets with capers
unshelled nuts
evaporated milk (for ice cream, etc.)
vacuum-packed nuts
canned soybeans
assorted cheeses, unopened, in refrigerator
Hebrew National cocktail franks, in freezer
toothpicks
nut crackers and picks
unflavored gelatin (for desserts)
pumpkin seeds, sunflower seeds
frozen loaves of homemade bread
plus a variety of staples needed for preparing meals, so that it would
    be fairly easy to cook for a few more people than you usually
    feed.

CHILDREN'S PARTIES

"What's a birthday without cake and ice cream?" moans the mother of a hypoglycemic four-year-old. There's really no problem easier to solve: make your cake and your ice cream too! With a little foresight and planning, a hypoglycemic child can take part in any social situation, from birthday parties to barbecues.

When giving a birthday party, the emphasis should be on wholesome food, clever decorations, good entertainment and small gifts rather than candies.

First, choose a theme for your party, and carry it out in your decorations. Excellent themes and party ideas can be found at your library; make your own decorations or favors, or choose from the clever, but rather expensive, matched decorations put out by Hallmark and other companies. These can include the party invitations, tablecloths, plates, cups, napkins and even the centerpiece. However this isn't necessary, for children will appreciate any decorations you make yourself, even if yours are long on imagination and short on skill. Some suggestions for party themes are: fireman, cowboy, pirate, holiday, Alice in Wonderland, Winnie-the-Pooh, flowers, Chinese, Hawaiian, space flight, etc. If you can, have your food tie in with the party's theme.

The food you serve will depend on the time of the party and the ages of the children. If you aren't planning to serve a meal, give each child on arriving a paper bag. This can contain a small plastic bag with snacks, such as cheese cubes, ham cubes, carrot sticks and nuts. Write each child's name on his bag so that he can use it for all his party "loot"; also include, if you wish, his party hat, a favor to carry out the theme of the party and a few balloons. Later you can serve the cake and ice cream. You can either serve a "sugar" cake and a sugarless version resembling it, or cupcakes using the same arrangement. Or you can bake a sugarless cake and serve it to everyone; this is up to you. The same is true of ice cream; personally, we prefer to serve all of the children the sugarless version. It's simpler, and they won't know the difference. We recommend the coconut cake or the soy nut cake with whipped cream and garnished with strawberries, and for ice cream, the fudge pops or the vanilla ice cream in individual ice-cream pop molds. There are many other recipes in this book which are suitable (see Desserts), but remember to keep the menu simple, especially for very young children.

At the table, in place of the usual cup of candy, give each child a paper cup, decorated if you wish, filled with nuts, and top with a small inexpensive toy, such as a tiny ball, toy car, pencil and fancy eraser or toy ring. Or you might buy a large container of assorted crayons, divide it equally, and wrap each bunch of crayons with a pretty ribbon. Place a bundle at each child's plate, along with a plain paper place mat to draw on.

Serve a light well-balanced meal, with a good amount of protein and lots of "finger food." Don't serve anything your child can't eat; if you choose your menu well the other children will enjoy it too. In fact, don't be surprised if a child whose mother calls him a picky eater devours two or three portions of your low-carbohydrate food.

Use paper plates and cups; make sure that the plates are grease resistant and strong enough to hold hot foods if you are serving any. Paper cups should have a wide enough base that they don't tip over easily; the best designed cups from this standpoint are the paper hot cups with handles. Use the heavy re-usable-type plastic spoons and forks. Toothpicks are good for spearing food, also some wooden french-fry skewers from your local hamburger joint.

Some foods your children and guests will enjoy are:

Hebrew National cocktail franks with toothpicks
Pineapple chunks and ham chunks speared with toothpicks
Chunks of cheese (American, Cheddar)
Pancake and peanut butter sandwiches (see Sandwiches)
Hot dog "nibble sticks"
Hamburger "satellites"
Mock "potato salad"
Fresh fruit salad
Fried chicken pieces

Cottage cheese head with features made of vegetables (carrot eyes, etc.)
Baked chicken pieces, cold
Beverages: diet soda, milk
Sugarless bologna, rolled up
Carrot and celery sticks
Pepper rings
Tomato wedges
Tiny dill pickles
Deviled eggs

Your guests will be much better behaved if they eat soon after arriving. Arrange some fairly quiet games for the first hour after eating. For instance, a drawing contest; or you could divide the children into teams, give each team a jigsaw puzzle and give a prize to the team which finishes first. To insure a good time for your child, keep the sound level down, and don't invite too many children. Be present to calm down any noisy or overstimulating situation with a distraction or suggestion for a new game. If there is a child who is too badly behaved or disruptive, take him aside quietly and explain that your child isn't supposed to get too excited or he will get sick. If this doesn't work, sit the child in front of a TV set until it's time for him to leave. Be casual and informal; it's only a children's party. If you are tense or up-tight about every little thing, your child will be tense too. The party is for him; see that he relaxes and enjoys it.

If your child is in kindergarten or nursery school, you may wish to have a little party for him in school. Rather than send the usual cupcakes and lollipops, send a paper bag for each child containing some nuts (shelled), a balloon and a small shiny apple. The children will be delighted and so will the teacher.

When your child is invited to a party, call ahead of time and explain the situation to the mother. If you prefer, tell her he's "allergic" to so many foods, you'd rather bring your own. Don't outline the diet and trust her to follow it unless she's your best friend and has fed your child before. Find out exactly what she's serving and give your child an insulated bag with as similar food as possible. If you wish, take the food to the mother before the party, so that your child won't feel conspicuous. If cake and ice cream are being served, bake your own cake, or pack some of the child's favorite sugarless cookies. Prepare the ice cream in individual ice-cream pop molds. When frozen remove from the mold, wrap in plastic wrap, then in aluminum foil. Ask the hostess to place it in her freezer and remind her to send the plastic "stick" home after the party. If your child becomes overexcited easily, don't allow him to stay at the party too long.

SPECIAL PROBLEMS
OF TEEN-AGERS

When a child reaches adolescence, he is subject to so many stress situations from adults, school, his own changing body, that it's a wonder that every teen-ager isn't severely hypoglycemic. Probably a great percentage of adolescents are, temporarily, as their endocrine systems are taxed more than at any other time in their lives, except perhaps during pregnancy. The adrenal cortex, working together with the pituitary, thyroid and other glands, must meet the challenge of greatly increased growth and the change in the body's shape and functions, from those of a child to those of a mature adult, in a short period of time. When the overtaxed adrenal cortex is also forced to cope with the teen-ager's customary high-starch, high-sugar diet, as well as the introduction of caffeine, cigarettes and alcohol, it becomes depleted and no longer can function properly. It's possible that all the problems of teen-age rebelliousness, his lack of integration into society, his sudden inability to cope with life, his touchiness, his need to show off, to commit crimes, all these may be caused by this combination of overworked endocrine system and a high-carbohydrate diet. Since this book deals with the person who has already been diagnosed as hypoglycemic, we hesitate to give symptoms which would lead you to feel your teen-ager should be following the diet; your physician can best be the judge of that. But we would urge you if you suspect that your teen-age youngster is hypoglycemic, to have him take a five- or six-hour Glucose Tolerance Test, and to have the test results interpreted by an endocrinologist or other doctor specializing in the treatment of hypoglycemia.

Your teen-age and pre-teen-age child must be told in detail what causes hypoglycemia and how and why the diet works. If he has just been placed on the diet, curtail some of his social activities, especially the very active ones, until he begins to show improvement. Then you can allow him to participate again, as long as he promises to adhere strictly to the diet. He himself will recognize a change in his feelings about himself and the world around him, and he should become more and more co-operative as his health improves. He must begin forming the habit of eating a protein snack every two hours, and oftener if he feels his symptoms returning. Point out to him something he can look for as a sign that his sugar level is dropping; is he, for instance, staring into space, or craving a cigarette? Or perhaps he is feeling anger without real cause, or grinding his teeth. Then he knows that he must eat at those times and the feeling will go away. Emphasize to him how much this diet will help him to improve his grades and enlarge his social life. If he is stubborn, urge him to give the diet a trial period of two months without "cheating" and set up some sort of reward for good behavior. Reinforce his determination by preparing our low-carbohydrate versions of his favorite treats, and don't keep food around that he is not allowed to have.

Young people often find themselves in a group where they are expected to chip in to share a pizza, or where they feel pressured to eat what the others are eating. If your child feels conspicuous in this type of situation, there are several ways you can suggest he handle it. He can order what everyone else is ordering, nibble his protein snack from home in the men's room or at the table unobtrusively, then give his plate to a buddy, saying, "I'm not so hungry after all." Don't think about the money wasted with this approach; it is a temporary ploy. As he becomes more comfortable with the diet he will no longer care so much about what the others might think and will be willing to carry and eat his snacks openly. You can also help him by pointing out all the foods he can safely order in restaurants; if he is worried about a particular eating place, call up and inquire in advance as to whether they serve Sanka and other allowed foods.

Boys and girls in school should carry a high-protein lunch and several snacks. For a complete list of suggestions for lunch boxes *see* Packing a Lunch Pail.

On dates, at sport or social events, and whenever the youngster is going to be away from home more than one hour, he *must* carry a snack for every two hours he plans to be away. This means that for a six-hour date, he should carry three separate snacks. These can consist of small hamburgers, which are odorless and resemble cookies, a 1-ounce cube of hard cheese, a pancake sandwich, several high-protein cookies (*see* Desserts), a small package of nuts, etc. Any of these can fit into a pocket or purse, and be popped unobtrusively into his mouth. If he is going to be drinking Sanka, be sure he carries saccharin tablets in a small pillbox or medicine vial. In the summer he should carry salted nuts or salt tablets, and carry snacks in an insulated bag with a can of frozen ice, such as Skotch Ice.

If he is going out for a meal with his friends, he can order: a cheese sandwich and leave the bread on the plate; a hamburger without roll, a steak, broiled fish or fried chicken (so long as it isn't honey-dipped) and cut off the breading (usually it slides right off). For a beverage, there is milk, Sanka, weak tea or Fresca. Don't chance other "diet sodas," unless they can be ordered by brand name and you can read the ingredients.

Have him wear a watch at all times so that he knows what time he must eat his snack.

An older teen-ager who is with others who are drinking can order a club soda with a twist of lemon or a glass of tomato juice.

Emphasize to him that he is not going to seem peculiar by adhering to his diet. Many teen-agers are weight- and complexion-conscious, and diets are a way of life for quite a few of them, girls as well as boys. A reassuring trend we have noticed in teen-agers is a growing awareness of food and nutrition. They are interested in preventive medicine and often they know more about food than their parents. A teen-ager who eats wheat germ and yoghurt is far less likely to be made fun of by his peers than an older person. We find this a hopeful sign for the future.

WHAT TO ORDER IN RESTAURANTS

No matter how successful you are in following the diet at home, you may be thrown for a loop the first time you attempt to eat out. Gone are the days of french fries, Roquefort dressing, cakes and pies, ketchup and all the other goodies that are part of the American scene. Gone also is the bacon, lettuce and tomato sandwich at the lunch counter, the corned beef on rye at the delicatessen and the hot dog and orange drink at Nedick's. What then can you eat away from home?

There are two answers to that question. First, you can dine out for pleasure, choosing a restaurant which, although a little more expensive, will have a greater selection of foods you can eat. Second, there will be times when you must eat in restaurants of necessity, in which case you order what you can and carry the rest of the meal with you. Whatever the reason, if you are prepared for emergencies you can salvage a filling high-protein meal out of almost any situation.

First, know in advance if possible where you will be eating. Call the restaurant and ask if they have the items you would like to order. Plan your order at home, with alternate choices in case they don't have your first choice. Be sure to take your saccharin tablets in a pillbox or small plastic vial, plus a small protein snack for emergencies. Also, carry a small bag of nuts to nibble after eating in case you crave dessert.

Some of the things you can order in an average-to-expensive restaurant are:

Appetizer: shrimp cocktail, no sauce; oysters or clams with lemon or melted butter, no sauce; tomato juice; ½ grapefruit (crush 2 saccharin tablets with your spoon and sprinkle on); slice of melon (*see* Fruits for amount allowed).

Soups: should be avoided, as they usually contain sugar or seasoning containing sugar; don't ask the chef it there's sugar in it: he's not about to admit that his rich beef broth comes from a bottle. The same is true of gravy in a restaurant. Even *au jus* gravy usually has beef flavoring with sugar added.

Salad: any tossed salad is fine; ask for oil and vinegar separately and add them yourself. Do not use their dressing, or coleslaw.

Vegetables: few vegetables are safe, unless you can be sure that they are freshly cooked and not canned. Even so, sugar is often added, so these are best avoided. Order an extra salad, a side dish of lettuce and tomato, a small dish of cottage cheese as a side dish, sauerkraut or dill pickle.

Entrée: seafood, baked without sauce, broiled or boiled, such as shrimp or lobster. Melted butter or lemon may be used. Any meat allowed on the diet is fine, so long as it is baked or broiled without sauce, breading or gravy. If a gravy is specified on the menu, ask the waiter to bring yours without it; he will be glad to do so. Also specify no potatoes, etc. Many restaurants will give you a choice of substitutes so that you don't have to pay extra for salad or cottage cheese, but if they don't you can save by ordering what you want à la carte.

Dessert: if you had no fruit for an appetizer, you can order melon or grapefruit for dessert. Don't chance the fresh fruit cup, it usually is sweetened. At many restaurants you can order cheese for dessert or even fruit and cheese, which is marvelous. Sanka or weak tea are also good for ending the meal. If the other diners are lingering over a huge dessert, you can always munch your emergency bag of nuts.

Beverage: club soda, milk, water, Sanka, weak tea. You could carry an herb tea bag and ask for hot water; diet soda can be ordered if you can specify the brand name or see the label on the bottle (*see* Brand Names).

If, out of preference or necessity, you find yourself at a "fast food"-type restaurant, you can order several things, depending on what they have to offer: hamburgers or cheeseburgers without rolls (order at least two), milk, Sanka, fried chicken (remove the breading before eating); our favorite is a special that we always order at the kind of place that sells fifteen- or twenty-cent hamburgers: we ask for a double cheeseburger with the cheese in the middle. To eat, slide the meat up so that the roll acts as a holder and absorbs all the grease; eat only the meat and cheese, and discard the rolls when finished. This probably offers the most protein for the money. Supplement this, if you wish, with a small bag of carrot sticks, celery and a pickle brought from home and a small piece of fruit, and you have had a meal.

Special restaurants such as Chinese or Italian restaurants will no longer be much fun for you; you'll have to satisfy your "yen" for these foods with the foreign recipes you make yourself (*see* Foreign and Regional). If you should find yourself unavoidably in this type of restaurant, you can always order a steak or sandwich, American style (don't forget to leave the bread). Again, when in doubt, call ahead, or carry an emergency kit with you.

Health food restaurants are fine—for other people. There is no advantage for you in eating in one, and we doubt if you would find many items you could order safely. If you do visit this type of restaurant, order plain yoghurt and fresh fruit, unsweetened or fresh fruit juice, vegetable juice, nuts or seeds.

Kosher-style delicatessens will usually have sugarless frankfurters, but don't assume so. Memorize the brand names of those frankfurters you are allowed to have and insist on seeing the label before you order. If they are sugarless, you can have several without rolls, as well as sauerkraut and dill pickles.

If you are on a trip and unfamiliar with the local eating places, read the menus wherever you go before you decide to stay and order. Keep an emergency kit in your car or suitcase, and if there hasn't been enough protein in your meal, you can nibble something afterward in your car.

Most important, this diet shouldn't be allowed to interfere with your social life; there are more important reasons for going out than just the food; friends, conversations, atmosphere, a change in scenery—all are important parts of a full and active life. Staying at home out of fear is not going to help you, and in the long run, you will come to resent the diet for restricting your life. From there it is a logical step to cheating on the diet out of self-pity. So pocket your little bag of nuts and eat out as often as you like.

HINTS FOR STRETCHING YOUR FOOD BUDGET

At first you will be horrified by the increase in the amount of money you are spending on protein. If you will notice, though, you are actually saving money on this diet. By taking the money you used to spend on convenience foods and non-nutritious food items, you are only paying for the foods your body needs and uses. Useful foods are foods which contribute to your health, build up your body and do not have to be stored. Sugar and starches are empty calories, useful only for burning or storing in the form of fat. They do not contribute to the body-building process. Neither do all the fillers and food additives used in packaged food. They are simply there to enhance the appearance of the food, to disguise the flavor, or as preservatives. So you can see that the normal bag of groceries contains a large amount of useless food which serves only to fill the stomach. This money can be considered wasted, even though you derive pleasure from the food it buys.

On the diet, you are buying mostly proteins, fruit and vegetables, and such staples as soy products, nuts and seeds. Extras that are less necessary are spices and luxuries, such as fresh mushrooms, which you can cut down on if you are trying to save money. Diet sodas and other special dietetic products are always more expensive than their non-dietetic counterparts. There are substitutes which you can make to save money; iced herb tea is a good substitute for diet soda, and by using frozen vegetables you will avoid having to buy special brands of vegetables such as peas or carrots. If you have a large freezer, you can buy in quantity when items are cheap; fresh fruit frozen in the summer can last all winter so that you don't have to buy the expensive diet-packed canned fruit. If you have no freezer you might try canning some fruits in the summer; it's not too difficult and can be done using any of the jam or preserves recipes in this book (*see* Preserves).

Non-stick Teflon pans can cut down greatly on your butter and margarine costs; instead of buying bouillon, we have given an easy way to make your own beef or chicken stock using the pan drippings from your roasts and steaks (*see* Soups).

Save on nuts, seeds and other special products by buying them in bulk from health food companies or wholesalers in your nearest large city. Usually raw seeds are cheaper than toasted seeds, and you can always toast them yourself if you prefer them that way.

The most expensive item on your grocery list is meat and other protein. So many people eat meat as their main dish at every lunch and dinner meal, but actually for economy, variety and good health, this is not desirable. There are many delicious main dishes which use eggs, cheese, soybeans and seafood; you should try to find those which are acceptable to you and your family.

To compare the prices of various forms of protein, you should remember to compare the price per gram of protein, not the price per pound of the item. Buy a good small booklet giving the amount of protein, fat and carbohydrate in foods. If you look up a few of your staple protein foods, you will be able to compare how high in protein each one is, then see how much you are paying for that amount of protein. For instance: hot dogs (the sugarless kosher style) might cost $1.35 per pound and lean chopped sirloin $1.29 per pound; but the hot dogs contain only about 3½ grams of protein per ounce, while the ground sirloin contains about 6 grams of protein per ounce. Therefore, the hot dogs are twice as expensive as the hamburgers. The same is true of any prepared meat, such as sugarless sausage, liverwurst or bologna. So use these for variety and flavor, but remember that you are paying twice as much money as their protein content is worth. Nuts are also expensive for the amount of protein they contain and can be used only for taste or as convenient snacks when other proteins are too difficult to carry around.

The cheapest protein foods you can buy are eggs and fish, especially frozen fish fillets. Fresh fish is always higher in cost, and shellfish is usually very expensive. Cheese is excellent, and the domestic cheeses such as Cheddar are just as high in protein as the expensive imported cheese; use it often and in combination with other proteins. Soybeans are an excellent source of protein. If you buy the yellow soybeans in bulk and cook and freeze them in quantity, they are very inexpensive to use, as compared to the very expensive (and hard-to-locate) canned soybeans, which should just be used in emergencies. Liver is an excellent budget-saving meat. Although calf's liver is expensive, good baby beef liver, cut thin and cooked properly, tastes just as good. If you aren't fond of the taste or texture of liver, you might find one of the liver spreads to your liking (*see* Appetizers and Foreign and Regional).

In buying poultry, you will save money with the more expensive cuts. Chicken breasts are economical as they contain almost no waste, while whole chicken or chicken parts are much more expensive. That is because you are paying for the bones and skin, neither of which contributes much in the way of protein. The same is true of meats containing fat and bones. They are much more expensive per gram of protein than lean trimmed meat, even though they are cheaper per pound. If you do buy meat or poultry with the bones in, be sure to use all the drippings for bouillon or gravy, and the bones for soup (*see* Soups).

You can use the same rule in buying vegetables. When you buy canned vegetables, you are paying for the water in the can and the convenience of precooked food. But if you count the wasted vitamins (as most of the vitamin content in canned vegetables is in the liquid) the cost per can is enormous. So, using this yardstick, the frozen and fresh vegetables in season are many times cheaper than canned. If you are cooking for only one or two people, you can buy frozen vegetables in handy plastic bags and shake out only the amount needed, thus making them even more economical than canned vegetables. If you do use canned vegetables, check the labels carefully and save the liquid to be used in soups, etc.

Milk need not be a big expense on this diet. As it contains carbohydrates, the amount of milk allowed on the diet is limited. Instead of drinking whole milk each time, you can use non-fat dry milk in cooking, baking and in frozen desserts. Also, you can use soy powder, which is about twice as high in protein as milk, although it costs a little more.

If all this seems confusing, just remember this concept: at first it may seem as though you are spending more money, but you will quickly see the difference in the improved health of your family as they stop eating up "empty calories."

BRAND NAMES ALLOWED
And Where to Buy Hard-to-Find Ingredients

Many of the ingredients and ready-to-eat products that we can use are difficult to find. We include here a partial list, with some of the sugarless products given. Keep in mind, however, that all of these products are subject to change, and there is no product on this list which is guaranteed to be safe. You must acquire the habit of checking labels automatically every time you buy.

Many of these items are available in supermarkets and grocery stores. Those that you have difficulty finding might be found in gourmet or cheese stores or small independent grocery and specialty shops. Health food stores carry many products that are difficult to find, but you may have to visit several to find all the products on the list. If there is an item which you are unable to find, write to the manufacturer, being sure to include your name and address. They can give you a list of stores in your area which sell that particular item.

Many items are available through the mail from health food companies, which are always glad to send you their catalogues. Just remember that there are many items in these catalogues that we can't have; read the descriptions carefully, especially on the prepared item such as nut butter. If you should order an item and find that the label lists sugar as an ingredient, they usually will take it back and give you credit or refund your money. Most companies prefer their orders prepaid. Some, like the Natural Sales Company, will pay your postage, no matter how heavy the order. Before ordering, write to the various companies for their catalogues. Keep in mind when comparing prices that one price may include postage, and another will have postage added.

CATALOGUE SHOPPING

1. Walnut Acres, Penns Creek, Pa. 17862. Large catalogue specializes in unsprayed fresh fruits and vegetables. Some of the products we can use are: seeds for sprouting (mung beans, sesame, oat grains, etc.), oatmeal, steel-cut oats, oat flour, peanut flour (raw or roasted), pumpkin seeds, sesame seeds, soy flour, soy grits, soybeans, instant soy milk powder, soy granules (precooked for cereal), squash seeds, sunflower seeds and sunflower meal, wheat germ (raw or toasted), herb teas, cheese in bulk, goat cheese, yoghurt cultures, dried vegetables, pure vanilla and other extracts, herbs and spices, vegetable gelatin, coconut, unsweetener (coarse, medium and fine grinds), gelatin, nuts, raw peanuts, roasted seeds and soybeans, unsweetened peanut butter, coconut-peanut butter, various kinds of oil, bread pans, seed sprouter, yoghurt incubator.

2. Cellu, Chicago Dietetic Supply, Inc., Box 40, La Grange, Ill. 60525. Sells products for allergy diets. Some dietetic canned fruits and vegetables, but many contain sugar or grape juice. Cellu oat flour, Cellu soybean flour.

3. Natural Sales Company, Box 25, Pittsburgh, Pa. 15230. No postage needed, very prompt and reliable service. Specializes in natural vitamins, also has a prescription drug service. Sunflower seeds and meal, toasted soybeans, yellow soybeans, toasted and salted sunflower seeds, onion-flavored sunflower seeds, sesame seeds, sea salt, soy flour, soy grits, oat flour, rolled and steel-cut oatmeal, sugarless mayonnaise, unsweetened peanut butter, coconut meal, canned nuts, herb teas, including rose hips tea in tea bags, various kinds of oil.

Health food stores: Look for the same items as in the above lists, plus others that you may find, such as powdered vegetable seasoning, roasted yellow soybeans, and Jerusalem artichoke products, if tolerated (De Boles brand). Read labels carefully, especially on any baked product, protein tablets, tea bag mixture or dietetic products.

Gourmet and cheese shops: Look for such items as soups without sugar or starch, Knorr-Swiss and other sugarless bouillon cubes, bulk cheeses, etc.

The following is a list of some of the ready-made products which do not, as of this writing, contain sugar. Although you can't buy directly from the manufacturers, we are including the addresses as listed on the labels; if your local store does not carry any of these products, you might be able to get the store manager to order them. Also, if you write to them, many companies will supply you with the name of a store near you which carries their products.

SAUCES AND CONDIMENTS

McCormick Salad Supreme with Bleu Cheese
McCormick & Company, Inc.
Baltimore, Md. 21202

McCormick Season Salt
McCormick & Company, Inc.
Baltimore, Md. 21202

French's Hickory Smoke Salt
The R. T. French Company Manufacturers
Rochester 9, N.Y.

Kikkoman Soy Sauce
Kikkoman International, Inc.
San Francisco, Calif. 94115

Cresca Dijon Mustard
Cresca Company, Inc.
Bronx, N.Y. 10454

Chelten House Mayonnaise
Chelten House Products, Inc.
Pennsauken, N.J. 08110

Bernstein's Vinaigrette French Dressing
Bernstein's of Long Beach, Inc.
Seal Beach, Calif. 90740

Girard's Original French Dressing
Early California Foods, Inc.
Los Angeles, Calif. 90024

Porky Manero's Steak House Garlic Dressing
Porky Manero's Steak House
Westport, Conn. 06880

Virginia Dare Garlic Sauce
Virginia Dare Extract Company, Inc.
Brooklyn, N.Y. 11232

Virginia Dare Onion Sauce
Virginia Dare Extract Company, Inc.
Brooklyn, N.Y. 11232

Ashley's of Texas Taco Sauce
Ashley's, Inc.
El Paso, Tex. 79925

Aunt Millie's Spaghetti Sauce
Aunt Millie's Sauces, Inc.
Hawthorne, N.Y. 10532

Del Monte Tomato Sauce (plain)
Del Monte Corporation
San Francisco, Calif. 94119

Maggi Seasoning
The Nestle Company, Inc.
White Plains, N.Y. 10605

Knorr-Swiss Bouillon Cubes (chicken and beef)
Knorr Food Products Company Ltd.
Thayngen, Switzerland Plant Control ⅍61

Knorr-Swiss Onion Soup Mix and Dip
Knorr Food Products Company Ltd.
Thayngen, Switzerland Plant Control ⅜61

Barnett Pure Bouillon Cubes (chicken)
Barnett Spices, Inc.
Jersey City, N.J. 07307

Hain's Vegetable Seasoned Salt (health food stores)
Hain's Pure Food Company, Inc.
Los Angeles, Calif. 90012

Golden Harvest Natural Kelp Seasoning (mail order and health food
    stores)
Natural Sales Company
Box 25
Pittsburgh, Pa. 15230

Adolph's Sugar Substitute (sprinkle-type)
Adolph's Ltd.
Burbank, Calif. 91503

Sucaryl No-Calorie Food Sweetener
Consumer Products Division, Abbott Laboratories
North Chicago, Ill. 60064

Sweet-10 Non Caloric Food Sweetener
The Pillsbury Company
Minneapolis, Minn. 55460

Crystallose Saccharin Sodium U.S.P.
Distributed by Jamieson Pharmacal Company, Inc.
New York, N.Y.

Durkee Extracts and Flavorings: imitation brandy extract, black
    walnut flavor, strawberry extract, etc.
Durkee Famous Foods
Cleveland, Ohio

Ideal Extracts and Imitation Flavorings: peppermint extract, imitation sherry, cherry extract, imitation maple, peach extract, almond extract, imitation coconut flavor, orange extract, imitation rum flavor, imitation butter flavor, imitation banana flavor, raspberry extract, strawberry extract, vanilla extract, etc.
Brooke Bond Foods, Inc.
Lake Success, N.Y. 11040

BEVERAGES

Slim-Ette No-Calorie Cooler Beverage Mix (fruit flavors only)
Chelten House Products, Inc.
Pennsauken, N.J. 08110

No-Cal Flavorings: raspberry, strawberry, blackberry
No-Cal Corporation
Brooklyn, N.Y. 11206

Floridagold Unsweetened Grapefruit Juice from Concentrate
Lykes Pasco Packing Company
Dade City, Fla. 33523

Shop-Rite Low-Calorie Artificially Flavored Soda: ginger, black cherry, orange, lemon
Shop-Rite Supermarkets
Wakefern Food Corporation
Elizabeth, N.J. 07207

No-Cal Diet Sodas: red-pop, grapefruit, citrus, ginger, orange, black raspberry, etc.)
No-Cal Corporation
Brooklyn, N.Y. 11206

Cott Diet Sodas: ginger, strawberry, cherry, etc.
Cott Corporation
New Haven, Conn. 10513

Fresca
Coca-Cola Bottling Company of New York
New York, N.Y. 10016

DESSERTS

D-Zerta Low-Calorie Gelatin Dessert
General Foods Corporation
White Plains, N.Y. 10602

FLOURS, NOODLES, BREADS, ETC. (only if tolerated or allowed by physician)

Oat flour, soy flour, peanut flour (*see* also Catalogue Shopping)
Walnut Acres
Penns Creek, Pa. 17862

Oat flour, soy flour, soy grits (*see* also Catalogue Shopping)
Natural Sales Company
Box 25
Pittsburgh, Pa. 15230

Oat flour, soybean flour
Cellu Products
Chicago Dietetic Supply, Inc.
Box 40
La Grange, Ill. 60525

Jolly Joan Oat Mix
Ener-G-Foods, Inc.
Seattle, Wash. 98134

De Boles Imitation Spaghetti and Macaroni
Manufactured for the Anthony Alphonse De Boles Company, Inc.
American Artichoke Products
290 E. Jericho Tpke.,
Mineola, N.Y. 11501

Jane Parker Protein Bread
A & P Stores
The Great Atlantic & Pacific Tea Company, Inc.
New York, N.Y. 10017

Thomas' Protein Bread
S. B. Thomas, Inc.
Totowa, N.J. 07512

Thomas' Rite-Diet Bread
S. B. Thomas, Inc.
Totowa, N.J. 07512

FRUIT

Comstock Pie-Sliced Apples
Borden, Inc.
Newark, N.Y. 14513

Dole Pineapple Chunks, Crushed Pineapple and Sliced Pineapple in
    Pineapple Juice (unsweetened)
Dole Company, Division of Castle & Cooke, Inc.
Honolulu, Hawaii 96801

Shop-Rite Pineapple in Unsweetened Pineapple Juice
Shop-Rite Supermarkets
Wakefern Food Corporation
Elizabeth, N.J. 07207

Diet Delight Unsweetened Grapefruit Sections
California Canners and Growers
San Francisco, Calif. 94106

Sherman's Arcadia Bartlett Pears, water-packed
Sherman Foods, Inc.
Bronx, N.Y. 10454

Sherman's Arcadia Apricots, water-packed
Sherman Foods, Inc.
Bronx, N.Y. 10454

Mott's Natural Style Apple Sauce
Duffy-Mott Company, Inc.
New York, N.Y. 10017

Featherweight Mandarin Orange Sections, water-packed
Chicago Dietetic Supply, Inc.
La Grange, Ill. 60525

Polaner's Artificially Sweetened Jams (also marmalade)
M. Polaner Company
Roseland, N.J. 07068

MEATS

Beardley Sliced Dried Beef
Carson Packing Company
Philadelphia, Pa. 19148

College Inn Chicken Broth
R.J.R. Foods
New York, N.Y. 10017

Cresca French Smoked Goose Pate
Cresca Company, Inc.
North Bergen, N.J. 07047

Underwood Liverwurst Spread
William Underwood Company
Watertown, Mass. 02172

Oscar Mayer Potted Meat Food Product
Oscar Mayer & Company
Chicago, Ill.

Swanson Boned Chicken with Broth
Campbell Soup Company
Camden, N.J. 08101

Banquet Boned Chicken
Banquet Foods Corp.
St. Louis, Mo. 63101

Jones Liver Sausage
The Jones Dairy Farm
Ft. Atkinson, Wis. 53538

Jones Link Sausage
The Jones Dairy Farm
Ft. Atkinson, Wis. 53538

Jones Hickory Smoked Bacon
The Jones Dairy Farm
Ft. Atkinson, Wis. 53538

Hebrew National All Beef Frankfurters
Hebrew National Kosher Foods, Inc.
General Offices
Maspeth, N.Y. 11378

Ballpark All Meat Franks
Hygrade Food Products Corporation
Executive Offices
Detroit, Mich. 48219

Reese Danish Cocktail Sausages
Reese Finer Foods, Inc.
Chicago, Ill. 60614

Northland Queen Tiny Cocktail Franks
Reese Finer Foods, Inc.
Chicago, Ill. 60614

Esther Rachel's Old-Fashioned Chopped Chicken Liver, Eggs and
    Onion
Reese Finer Foods, Inc.
Chicago, Ill. 60614

Reese Italian Antipasto Appetizer
Reese Finer Foods, Inc.
Chicago, Ill. 60614

PREPARED SEAFOODS

Cross & Blackwell Anchovy Paste
Cross & Blackwell Company
Division of the Nestle Company, Inc.
White Plains, N.Y. 10605

Beardsley Shredded Salt Codfish
J. W. Beardsley's Sons
New York, N.Y. 07114

Cresca Rolled Fillets of Anchovies, Fancy Cherrywood Smoked
  Baby Clams, Escargots, Fancy Cherrywood Smoked Oysters
Cresca Company, Inc.
North Bergen, N.J. 07047

Cresca Mussels in Hot Sauce, Smoked Cocktail Mussels in Olive Oil,
  Pickled Mussels
Cresca Company, Inc.
Bronx, N.Y. 10454

Also: most brands of sardines, except those packed in tomato sauce.
Also canned tuna, salmon, clams in broth, shrimp, crab meat, anchovies and caviar

BABY FOODS

Gerber Strained Meats: beef, veal, pork, turkey, chicken
Gerber Products, Inc.
Fremont, Mich. 49412

Gerber Strained Green Beans, Strained Squash, Strained Beets,
  Strained Carrots and Peas
Gerber Products
Fremont, Mich. 49412

Gerber Oatmeal Cereal for Babies
Gerber Products
Fremont, Mich. 49412

Beech-Nut Chicken with Vegetables, Vegetables & Liver, Vegetables
& Lamb, Turkey & Rice, Green Beans
Beech-Nut Inc.
New York, N.Y. 10022

VEGETABLES

Hain's Soy Beans (canned)
Hain's Pure Food Company, Inc.
Los Angeles, Calif. 90061

Loma Linda Green Soy Beans (canned)
Loma Linda Food Company
Riverside, Calif. 92505

Hollywood Canned Cooked Soy Beans
Hollywood Health Foods
Los Angeles, Calif. 90061

Chun King Chow-Mein Vegetables (packed in water only; check
label)
R.J.R. Foods Inc.
General Offices
New York, N.Y. 10017

Ashley's of Texas Whole Jalapenos (chilies)
Ashley's Inc.
El Paso, Tex. 79925

Old El Paso Green Chilies
Mountain Pass Canning Company
Anthony, Tex. 88021

Progresso Sweet Fried Peppers with Onion
Progresso Foods Corporation
Jersey City, N.J. 07305

Progresso Olive Condite Olive Salad
Uddo & Taomania Company
Vineland, N.J. 08360

Schorr's Famous Quality Cucumber Garden Salad
Schorr-Stern Food Corp.
Brooklyn, N.Y. 11212

NUTS AND NUT PRODUCTS

Peter Pan Diet Spread Peanut Butter
Derby Foods, Inc.
Chicago, Ill. 60632

Elam's Natural Peanut Butter
Elam Mills
Broadview, Ill. 60153

Pernuts Toasted Soy Beans
Flavor Tree Foods, Inc.
Melrose Park, Ill. 60160

Fisher's Sunflower Nuts
Fisher Nut Company
St. Paul, Minn. 55106

Beatric's Bacon-Flavored Soy Bits
Fisher Nut Company
Division of Beatrice Foods Company
St. Paul, Minn. 55101

MISCELLANEOUS

Liquid Predigested Protein
Twin Laboratories Inc.
Freeport, N.Y. 11520

LIST OF REPLACEMENTS
FOR BREAD CRUMBS

If you have a recipe to adapt which calls for bread crumbs (fried chicken, for example), you can either make your own or experiment with the following:

1. Homemade bread crumbs: use homemade bread, toasted or slightly stale. Break into several pieces and grate in the blender, one slice at a time. Store in the refrigerator until needed. If your doctor allows bought bread, such as Thomas' protein bread, you can make bread crumbs using it in the same way. To make bread crumbs without a blender, place the toasted bread in a paper bag and roll over it with a rolling pin until well crumbed.

2. Non-fat dry milk: use on broiled fish, toppings for casseroles. Best when broiled or baked; do not use in recipes where food is first dipped in egg.

3. Ground nuts: patties, croquettes, heavy batters. Try filberts, Brazil nuts, almonds; grind in the blender at medium high speed and use like flour.

4. Soy grits: use as is, or grind in the blender and use like corn meal; swells when wet.

5. Seed meal: you can buy sunflower seed meal, sesame seed meal and pumpkin seed meal in health food stores, or grind your own in the blender.

6. Whole seeds: keeping in mind the flavor you want, you can use sesame seeds, poppy seeds, and even caraway seeds as breading and toppings where bread crumbs are called for. Sesame seeds are

particularly good as they are so bland. Buy them in quantity (*see* Brand Names) and they are relatively inexpensive.

7. Instant-type oatmeal: sprinkle on fish fillets, meat balls; use in croquettes, loaves, etc.

8. Allowed flour: soy and oat. Also, small amounts of gluten flour if tolerated.

9. Grated American or Parmesan cheese: the dry type in the shaker containers. Sprinkle on vegetables and casseroles when recipes call for bread crumb toppings.

10. Crumbled bacon: fry, drain and crumble fine. Marvelous on vegetables, casserole toppings, loaves, bland meats.

11. Grated carrots: grind raw carrots in the blender at high speed until finely ground (for best results, slice thinly, blend only about half a carrot at a time). Use in loaves and stuffings.

12. Onion flakes: or minced dehydrated onion; roll food in flakes, or dip first in egg, then roll. Deep-fry, pan-fry, pan-broil or broil, but not too close to the heat source.

13. Combinations: make up a container of bread crumbs, grated cheese, sesame seeds, and seasoning (or any other combination you prefer) and store in an airtight container, to be used as needed for broiling or frying.

UTENSILS USED IN THE RECIPE SECTION

*=strongly recommended

**=*very* strongly recommended

Garlic press

Small grater for nutmeg, cheese

*Broiler rack and pan

Colander

Ricer

Gelatin molds

Pepper mill

Muffin pan

Casseroles and ovenproof pans

*Cake pans, layers, loafs, square

*Pie plates

Spring-type tube pan

Fondue pot and fondue forks

*Bread pans, at *least* one

Pastry tube

Skewers

Wire whisk

Teapot

Cutting board

Tea strainer

Deep-fat fryer

*Large grater or shredder

Pressure cooker

*Good knives and a knife

Rolling pin

sharpener

*Electric mixer

**Rubber spatulas

Bread board

*Cookie sheet, preferably
Teflon-lined

**Blender: You could conceivably cook without one, but we've long since forgotten how. With all the snacks and extras that you are cooking, a good blender is not a luxury but a necessity. We recommend buying the model with the heaviest duty motor you can find, preferably with six to ten speeds and a five-cup container with a wide base, such as an Osterizer.

Insulated jars and bottles (Aladdin, Thermos, etc.)

*Stainless-steel insulated bottles: These are guaranteed unbreakable, they insulate better and there are never any expensive glass liners to replace. Made in pint and quart sizes by Thermos and other companies.

Plastic containers for leftovers: Freezettes are excellent, won't spill or come apart easily. Others are Tupperware, etc.

**Food scale or postage scale: Should show weight in ounces up to 16 ounces.

Glass jars for storage of pickles, jams, etc. (Pyrex canisters, Mason jars, etc.)

*Teflon-lined pans: Will save you time, cook better, be easier to clean.

Seed sprouter: (Beale's Seed Sprouter, Walnut Acres, Penns Creek, Pa., makes fresh bean sprouts in seven to ten days.)

**Measuring cups: One- and two-cup sizes.

**Measuring spoons: Assorted sizes, preferably with a rack for hanging.

Canisters: For storage of non-fat dry milk, soybeans, etc.

*Ice pop molds: Ice Tups by Tupperware Company, any others.

**Ice Crusher: Any kind or ice cube trays which automatically make chipped ice, such as "Magic Touch Ice Chipper," by Magic Touch Company.

100 SUGGESTIONS FOR QUICK PROTEIN SNACKS

These are just some suggestions to prove that snacks need not be boring; you could use three of these snack ideas a day and not repeat yourself for a month. You probably can come up with many more of your own. We suggest that you keep a list, so that from time to time you can glance at it and make sure that you are not falling into a rut. These are almost all snacks that you can grab and eat right from the refrigerator or cupboard, or fix in a few minutes. (The word "cold" indicates leftovers.)

1. Filberts
2. Almonds
3. Brazil nuts
4. Walnuts
5. Pignolia nuts
6. Peanuts
7. Sunflower seeds
8. Pumpkin seeds
9. Toasted soybeans
10. Milk
11. Buttermilk
12. Vanilla milk shake
    See Beverages
13. Vanilla eggnog
    See Beverages
14. Chocolate eggnog
    See Beverages
15. Health drink
    See Beverages
16. Cottage cheese
17. Cottage cheese with fresh pineapple
18. Cottage cheese with Spanish olives
19. Cottage cheese salad
    See Salads
20. Cheese blintz
    See Foreign and Regional
21. Rich vanilla ice cream
    See Desserts
22. Cheddar cheese
23. Edam cheese
24. Gouda cheese
25. American cheese

26. Swiss cheese
27. Muenster cheese
28. Wispride Spread on pancake
See Breakfast Foods
29. Plain yoghurt
30. Plain yoghurt with fresh fruit
31. Hard-cooked egg
32. Deviled eggs
See Eggs
33. Egg salad
See Salads
34. Cold soufflé
See Eggs
35. Carrot soufflé
See Vegetables
36. Tuna salad
See Salads
37. Salmon salad
See Salads
38. Crab meat salad
See Salads
39. Sardines
40. Smoked oysters
41. Canned clams
42. Oyster stew
See Soups
43. Boiled shrimp
44. Cold lobster tail
45. Cold fish cakes
See Seafood
46. Clam broth
47. Clam chowder (Manhattan)
See Soups
48. New England clam chowder
See Soups
49. Cold fried fish fillets
See Seafood

50. Tuna chunks with lemon
51. Lox and cream cheese on pancake
52. Sugarless bologna
53. Sugarless salami
54. Sugarless hot dogs
55. Sugarless liverwurst on pancake
56. Hamburger
57. Minute steak
58. Cold meat balls
See Foreign and Regional
59. Cold roast beef
60. Leftover pot roast, heated
61. Cold sliced pork
62. Cold pork chops
63. Cold spare ribs
See Meats
64. Baked ham chunks
65. Boiled ham, sliced
66. Ham and cheese on soy bread
See Sandwiches
67. Ham and peanut butter on pancake
68. Broiled lamb chop
69. Sliced lamb
70. Cold meat loaf
See Meats
71. Cold ham loaf
See Meats
72. Chef salad with cheese and ham
See Salads
73. Cold broiled chicken
74. Chicken salad
See Salads
75. Sliced turkey
76. Cold turkey leg or wing

77. Chicken soup
See Soups
78. Cold fried chicken
See Meats
79. Soy grits cookies and milk
See Desserts
80. Peanut butter chews
See Candies
81. Almond paste candies
See Candies
82. Coconut chews and milk
See Candies
83. Vanilla pudding
See Desserts
84. Sponge Cake
See Desserts
85. Cheesecake
See Desserts
86. Chocolate pudding
See Desserts
87. Buttermilk meringue pie
See Desserts
88. Soy bread
See Breads, Pasta and Noodles
89. Soy grits bread
See Breads, Pasta and Noodles

90. Soy bread, peanut butter
and sugarless jelly sandwich
91. Cream cheese and olive
sandwich on soy bread
92. Baked soybeans
See Vegetables
93. Cold chili
See Vegetables
94. Leftover wax bean lasagna,
heated
See Foreign and Regional
95. Leftover stuffed cabbage,
heated
See Casseroles
96. Egg drop soup
See Foreign and Regional
97. Chinese egg rolls
See Foreign and Regional
98. Cold stuffed peppers
See Casseroles
99. Leftover beef stew, heated
See Casseroles
100. Leftover turkey soup,
heated
See Soups

A MONTH OF BREAKFAST MENUS

These are some suggested breakfasts to show you how to balance your proteins and carbohydrates. Naturally, you wouldn't cook like this every week; but it is possible, as we have shown, to make a different dish for breakfast every day for a month. Unless noted, beverages can be Sanka or herb tea.

1. Oatmeal pancakes — *See* Breakfast Foods
   Jones sausage links — *See* Brand Names
   Homemade apple butter — *See* Preserves
   Milk

2. 2 slices smoked bacon — *See* Brand Names
   2 fried eggs
   Onion bread — *See* Breads, Pasta and Noodles
   ½ baked apple — *See* Desserts

3. Cheese blintzes — *See* Foreign and Regional
   Apple syrup — *See* Sauces and Dressings
   Milk

4. 2 poached eggs on asparagus tips — *See* Eggs
   Soy grits bread — *See* Breads, Pasta and Noodles
   Orange juice
   Milk

5. Grilled cheese sandwich on oatmeal bread — *See* Breakfast Foods / *See* Breads, Pasta and Noodles
   Strawberries and cream
   Mint tea

6. Lox and cream cheese   *See* Breads, Pasta and Noodles
    Bagel
    Tangerine
    "Gossip tea"   *See* Beverages
7. Health drink   *See* Beverages
    Small lamb chop, broiled
8. Swiss cereal with milk   *See* Breakfast Foods
    Baked eggs   *See* Eggs
9. Mushroom omelette   *See* Eggs
    All-star bread   *See* Breads, Pasta and Noodles
    Small fresh peach
10. 2 hard-cooked eggs (warm)
    Strawberry cheesecake   *See* Desserts
    Café au lait   *See* Beverages
11. Shirred eggs
    Scrapple   *See* Meats
    Stewed fruit   *See* Foreign and Regional
12. Eggs Benedict on oat   *See* Eggs
      muffins   *See* Breads, Pasta and Noodles
    Apple sauce   *See* Desserts
13. "Mary-Jane egg"   *See* Eggs
    Smoked ham slice, fried
    Small orange
    Chocolate milk   *See* Beverages
14. ½ cup oatmeal with milk   *See* Breakfast Foods
    2 soft-boiled eggs
    Cantaloupe
15. French toast with plain   *See* Breakfast Foods
      yoghurt
    Baked bacon   *See* Breakfast Foods
    ½ baked pear   *See* Desserts
16. Cheese omelette   *See* Eggs
    Toasted oatmeal bread   *See* Breads, Pasta and Noodles
    Homemade strawberry jam   *See* Preserves
17. Breakfast burger   *See* Breakfast Foods
    Wedge of Gouda cheese
    Hot chocolate   *See* Beverages
    Tomato juice
18. Fruity flapjacks   *See* Breakfast Foods
    Frizzled ham   *See* Breakfast Foods
    Milk

19. Huevos rancheros   *See* Eggs
    Mexican chocolate   *See* Beverages
    Apple juice
20. Buttermilk pancakes with   *See* Breakfast Foods
       "maple syrup"   *See* Sauces and Dressings
    Sliced ham
    Honeydew melon
21. Whitefish, smoked sturgeon,
       with lemon wedge
    "Corn meal" muffins with   *See* Breads, Pasta and Noodles
       chive cheese
22. Soy grits cereal with   *See* Breakfast Foods
       blackberries and milk
    Assorted cheeses
23. Homemade sausage   *See* Meats
    Scrambled eggs   *See* Eggs
    Oat biscuits   *See* Breads, Pasta and Noodles
    Canned sugarless pineapple *See* Brand Names
24. Cheese and eggs   *See* Eggs
    "Corn meal" bread   *See* Breads, Pasta and Noodles
    Grapefruit juice
25. Peanut butter pancakes   *See* Breakfast Foods
    Banana eggnog   *See* Beverages
26. Cheese "Danish"   *See* Breakfast Foods
    Strawberry eggnog   *See* Beverages
27. Scrambled eggs with herbs   *See* Eggs
    Fried coffee cake   *See* Breakfast Foods
    Pineapple juice
28. Jelly roll eggs   *See* Eggs
    Soy muffins   *See* Breads, Pasta and Noodles
    Milk
29. Almond pancakes   *See* Breakfast Foods
    Fresh fruit cup   *See* Desserts
    Milk
30. Coddled eggs   *See* Breakfast Foods
    Cinnamon toast   *See* Breakfast Foods
    Fancy morning fruit juice   *See* Beverages
31. Apple pancakes with   *See* Breakfast Foods
       whipped cottage cheese
    Rose hips tea

SUGGESTIONS FOR CHILDREN'S LUNCHES

Here are some menus for you to use as guidelines in preparing meals for children. Notice that there is a limitation on the amount of milk, and where ice cream is given, milk can be eliminated. Wherever a sandwich is indicated, it should be on homemade bread or pancakes (*see* Sandwiches).

1. Chicken soup — *See* Soups
   Ham sandwich
   ½ deviled egg — *See* Eggs
   8 ounces milk
   Fruit gelatin — *See* Desserts
2. Vegetable soup — *See* Soups
   Sugarless bologna sandwich — *See* Brand Names
   Dill pickle
   Peanut butter fudge — *See* Candies
   6 ounces milk
3. Sugarless hot dogs — *See* Brand Names
   Sauerkraut
   Baked soybeans — *See* Vegetables
   8 ounces milk
   Applesauce — *See* Desserts
4. Tuna fish salad — *See* Salads
   Pickled beets — *See* Preserves
   Cottage cheese
   4 ounces milk
   Walnuts

5. Oyster stew .... *See* Soups
   Peanut butter (sugarless) ...... *See* Brand Names
     and jelly (homemade) .... *See* Preserves
     sandwich
   Chunks of ham on toothpicks
   Punch .... *See* Beverages
6. "Spaghetti" and meat balls ... *See* Foreign and Regional
   Lettuce and tomato salad
   8 ounces milk
   Fresh peach (small)
7. Manhattan clam chowder ...... *See* Soups
   Cheeseburger on soy bread
   Sugarless soda .... *See* Brand Names
   Vanilla ice cream .... *See* Desserts
8. "Satellites" .... *See* Meats
   String beans
   8 ounces milk
   Orange ice pop .... *See* Desserts
9. Grilled cheese sandwich ...... *See* Breakfast Foods
   Coleslaw .... *See* Salads
   Chocolate milk .... *See* Beverages
   Peanut butter cookies .... *See* Desserts

FOODS OF OTHER LANDS

For those who are afraid they will miss their favorite foreign cuisine on the diet, we recommend several menus that can be made using recipes in various sections of this book:

4 CHINESE MEALS

1. Egg drop soup — *See* Foreign and Regional
   Oriental pork balls — *See* Meats
   Sub gum chicken chow mein — *See* Foreign and Regional
   Papaya tea
   Almond macaroons — *See* Desserts
2. Chinese egg roll with Chinese — *See* Foreign and Regional
      mustard and duck sauce — *See* Sauces and Dressings
      (plum sauce) — *See* Sauces and Dressings
   Sweet and pungent pork — *See* Foreign and Regional
   Violet leaf tea
   Fruit ice — *See* Desserts
3. "Fried rice" — *See* Foreign and Regional
   Pepper steak — *See* Foreign and Regional
   Weak Chinese green tea (if
      tolerated)
   Candied pineapple — *See* Foreign and Regional
4. Won ton soup — *See* Foreign and Regional
   Chicken egg foo yung — *See* Foreign and Regional
   Rose hips tea
   Coconut custard — *See* Desserts

4 ITALIAN MEALS

1. Antipasto — *See* Foreign and Regional
   Pizza with meat crust — *See* Foreign and Regional
   Eggplant parmigiana — *See* Foreign and Regional
   Lemon sherbet — *See* Desserts
2. Eggplant appetizer — *See* Appetizers
   Homemade soy noodle linguini with clam sauce — *See* Breads, Pasta and Noodles / *See* Sauces and Dressings
   Chicken cacciatore — *See* Foreign and Regional
   Cappuccino — *See* Beverages
3. Minestrone — *See* Foreign and Regional
   Veal parmigiana — *See* Foreign and Regional
   Garlic bread — *See* Breads, Pasta and Noodles
   Tossed salad with French dressing — *See* Sauces and Dressings
   Spumoni — *See* Foreign and Regional
4. Steamed clams
   Stuffed peppers — *See* Casseroles
   Artichokes with garlic butter — *See* Vegetables
   Rum cake — *See* Foreign and Regional

4 JEWISH-STYLE MEALS

1. Scrambled eggs with onions — *See* Eggs
   Lox and cream cheese
   "Bagel" — *See* Breads, Pasta and Noodles
   Lettuce, tomato, slice of Bermuda onion
   Milk
   Stewed fruit — *See* Foreign and Regional
2. Chopped liver on celery — *See* Foreign and Regional
   Tzimmes — *See* Foreign and Regional
   Mock "potato latkes" — *See* Foreign and Regional
   Sponge cake — *See* Desserts

3. Borscht   *See* Foreign and Regional
   Spinach soufflé   *See* Vegetables
   Cottage cheese with   *See* Cheese
     vegetables
   "Potato" blintzes with sour   *See* Foreign and Regional
     cream
   Weak tea with lemon and
     saccharin
   "Raisins" with almonds   *See* Candies
4. Golden chicken soup and   *See* Foreign and Regional
     knaidlach
   Roast beef (brisket)
   Baked water chestnuts   *See* Vegetables
   Mock "potato kugel"   *See* Foreign and Regional
   Rogelach   *See* Desserts

4 MEXICAN MEALS

1. Avocado salad   *See* Salads
   Chili con carne   *See* Casseroles
   Tacos   *See* Foreign and Regional
   Mexican chocolate   *See* Beverages
2. Vegetable soup   *See* Soups
   Enchiladas   *See* Foreign and Regional
   "Frijoles" refritos   *See* Foreign and Regional
   Apple soda   *See* Foreign and Regional
3. Guacamole   *See* Foreign and Regional
   Tortillas   *See* Foreign and Regional
   Huevos rancheros   *See* Foreign and Regional
   Fresh prickly pear
   Caffè espresso   *See* Beverages
4. Bean dip with raw vegetables   *See* Appetizers
   Tostadas   *See* Foreign and Regional
   "Frijoles" with chili   *See* Foreign and Regional
   Flan   *See* Foreign and Regional

HOLIDAY MENUS

NEW YEAR'S EVE PARTY

"Bloody Mary"   *See* Beverages
Cheddar balls   *See* Appetizers
Stuffed walnuts   *See* Appetizers
Green onion dip with raw   *See* Appetizers
   vegetables
Beef fondue   *See* Meats
Chili sauce   *See* Sauces and Dressings
Raspberry whip   *See* Desserts
Sponge cake   *See* Desserts
Punch   *See* Beverages

NEW YEAR'S DAY BRUNCH

Quiche Lorraine   *See* Cheese
Dill-spiced green beans   *See* Preserves
Caesar salad   *See* Salads
Mulled cider   *See* Beverages
Chocolate mousse   *See* Desserts

VALENTINE'S DAY PARTY

Deviled eggs	*See* Appetizers
Lemon-broiled chicken	*See* Meats
Fresh steamed asparagus	
Cranberry-pineapple juice	*See* Beverages
Jelly "hearts"	*See* Candies
Peanut butter fudge	*See* Candies

EASTER DINNER

Celery stuffed with olive spread	*See* Appetizers
Baked ham with jelly glaze	*See* Meats
Curried egg casserole	*See* Eggs
French-fried parsnips	*See* Vegetables
Waldorf salad	*See* Salads
Layer cake with whipped cream icing (shape like an egg and trim)	*See* Desserts
Marzipan eggs	*See* Candies

FOURTH OF JULY PICNIC

Sugarless frankfurters, no rolls	*See* Brand Names
Hamburgers, no rolls	
Barbecue baked soybeans	*See* Vegetables
Bread and butter pickles	*See* Preserves
Mock "potato" salad	*See* Salads
Coleslaw	*See* Salads
Piccalilli	*See* Preserves
Cold diet soda	
Chocolate ice cream (made in ice cream freezer)	*See* Desserts
Coconut cup cakes	*See* Desserts

HALLOWEEN SUPPER AND TREATS

Tomato stuffed with tuna salad	*See* Salads
Grilled cheese and bacon sandwiches on soy bread	*See* Sandwiches *See* Breads, Pasta and Noodles
Pickled cauliflower	
Apple brown Betty	*See* Desserts
Pumpkin ice cream	*See* Desserts
Sesame chews	*See* Candies
Seven-sweets confection	*See* Candies
"Pumpkins" (orange jelly candies)	*See* Candies

THANKSGIVING DINNER

Mock split pea soup	*See* Soups
Roast turkey with giblet stuffing	*See* Meats
Mashed "potatoes" (cauliflower)	*See* Vegetables
Creamed peas and onions	*See* Vegetables
Cranberry-orange relish	*See* Sauces and Dressings
"Sweet potato" pudding	*See* Vegetables
Olives	
Celery sticks	
Cider	
Pumpkin pie (2 hours after meal)	*See* Desserts

CHRISTMAS EVE SUPPER

Clam dip with raw vegetables and soy chips	*See* Appetizers *See* Breads, Pasta and Noodles
Super scrambled eggs	*See* Eggs
Cold sliced meat platter	
Pickled pears	*See* Preserves
Hot cocoa	*See* Beverages
Almond candy wreaths	*See* Candies

CHRISTMAS DINNER

Eggnog	*See* Beverages
Consommé (basic beef stock)	*See* Soups
Roast duckling à l'orange with sage stuffing	*See* Meats *See* Sauces and Dressings
Broccoli with lemon butter	*See* Vegetables
Candied carrots	*See* Vegetables
Dill pickles	
Vanilla ice cream	*See* Desserts
Hot gingerbread	*See* Desserts
Holiday fruitcake (2 hours after meal)	*See* Desserts

RECIPES

APPETIZERS

The recipes in this chapter are intended to be used as hors d'oeuvres and appetizers, but many of them would be suitable for protein snacks, side dishes or sandwich spreads. For variety, include some in a lunch pail; encourage children to use the dips with their vegetables, and you will add extra protein to their diet without their knowing it.

Many of the appetizers can also be used as "finger food" at parties or buffets. There are spreads and dips for crisp vegetables, crackers and tiny pancakes. There are stuffed foods which can be picked up easily, balls which can be picked up with the fingers or skewered with toothpicks, and classic canapés, or tiny open-face sandwiches. We have also included some of the hot appetizers most likely to be seen at a buffet or served as a meal's first course.

Canapés can be served on homemade low-carbohydrate bread, on homemade Melba Toast (*see* Breads, Pasta and Noodles) or on Pancakes (*see* Breakfast Foods). Our favorite base for canapés and spreads are "Pennies." These are tiny pancakes which can be made from freshly made or leftover pancake batter; simply fry tiny pancakes on an oiled griddle. Use these also for dips.

Dips can be used with Soy Chips (*see* Breads, Pasta and Noodles), which are like small tortillas; or with any of the allowed fruits and vegetables.

In planning your meal remember to take into consideration the amount of carbohydrates consumed before the meal. If you are serving high-carbohydrate hors d'oeuvres such as crackers and spreads, then cut down on the amount of carbohydrates and fruit in the rest of the meal.

In addition to the recipes in this section, many recipes in other sections of the book can be used as appetizers. *See* Salads for such ideas as Marinated Artichoke Hearts, Shrimp Cocktail and others. For more spreads, *see* Sandwiches.

Vegetables, etc., for dipping
Green Onion Dip
Sour Cream Dip
Sardine Dip
Clam Dip
High-protein "Sour Cream"
Blue Cheese Dip
Olive Dip
Guacamole
Bean Dip
Bacon Spread
Cheddar Spread
Pickle Spread
Chili Spread
Olive Spread
Basic Sweet Creamy Spread
Turkey Pâté
Liver Pâté
Cheese Ball
Sardine-stuffed Eggs
Deviled Eggs
Stuffed Walnuts
Stuffed Pickles
Stuffed Celery
Soybean Balls

Tiny Meat Balls
Liverwurst Balls
Cheddar Cheese Balls
Eggplant Fondue
Cheese Fondue
Swiss Fondue
Beef Fondue
Cheese Bubbles
Anchovy-mushroom Surprises
Cocktail Franks
Water Chestnuts Supreme
Eggplant Appetizer
Clam Canapés
Anchovy Canapés
Ham and Cheese Roll-ups
Chopped Liver Canapés
Pimiento Canapés
Classic Caviar Canapés
Smoked Salmon Canapés
Toasted Pumpkin Seeds
Curried Pumpkin Seeds
Stuffed Cabbage: *see* Casseroles
Egg Rolls: *see* Foreign and
    Regional
Chive Egg Rolls: *see* Eggs

VEGETABLES, ETC., FOR DIPPING

To be used with suitable dips, in place of potato chips or crackers.

Carrot sticks
Celery sticks
Slivers or wedges of green pepper
Diagonally cut carrot slices

Raw cauliflower flowerettes
Raw cabbage (center section)
Raw red cabbage
Cherry tomatoes
Short pieces of thick-sliced bacon, baked and drained
Whole small radishes
Chunks of lettuce hearts
Sticks of firm Cheddar cheese
Hard-cooked egg whites, quartered
Raw mushroom caps
Whole cooked mushrooms
Cucumber slices
Cucumber sticks (remove seeds)
Pancakes, cut into squares or rounds
Coin-sized pancakes ("pennies")
Chunks of avocado (dipped in lemon juice)
Chunks of apple (dipped in lemon juice)
Chunks of raw pineapple
Scallions
Cooked shrimp
Pitted black olives
Small Spanish olives
Slices of raw pear, not too ripe
Sliced water chestnuts
Chunks of soy bread
Chunks of soy grits bread
Cubes and sticks of ham
Chunks and sticks of chicken
Bite-sized chunks of lobster
Firm pickles

GREEN ONION DIP

2 cups tangy small curd cottage cheese
3 scallions, minced fine, with tops
½ cup sour cream or plain yoghurt
Dash of dill weed
¼ teaspoon onion powder
¼ teaspoon salt or to taste

Mix all ingredients and salt to taste. Refrigerate at least 1 hour, preferably overnight. Serve with any firm raw vegetables for dipping. Makes 2½ cups.

SOUR CREAM DIP

1 teaspoon oil or bacon drippings
½ an onion, minced fine
2 cups sour cream
1 sprig parsley, minced fine
½ teaspoon onion powder
Salt, pepper to taste

Heat the oil or bacon fat in a frying pan and sauté the onion until crisp and brown (even a little bit burned). Drain on a paper towel, and allow to cool. Combine the onion with the remaining ingredients and mix well. Serve with firm dipping vegetables, especially strong-flavored ones. (For a firmer dip, chill.) Makes 2¼ cups.

SARDINE DIP

1 can sardines in oil, drained
2 hard-cooked eggs
¼ cup allowed or homemade mayonnaise
1 teaspoon lemon juice
1 teaspoon dry mustard
½ teaspoon parsley flakes
½ teaspoon tarragon
2 scallions, chopped, with tops

Place all ingredients in blender. Blend until mixed. Serve with vegetables or tiny pancakes. Makes ¾ cup.

CLAM DIP

1 6-ounce can minced clams
4 or 5 drops Tabasco sauce
1 cup cottage cheese
½ teaspoon salt
1 teaspoon minced onion
1 tablespoon juice from the clams

Drain the clams and reserve the juice. Place all ingredients in blender. Blend until smooth, adding more juice as needed. Makes 1½ cups.

HIGH-PROTEIN "SOUR CREAM"

1 cup cottage cheese
1 tablespoon lemon juice

Place ingredients in blender, and blend until smooth. Use as is, or in place of sour cream in any recipe where you want to increase the protein content. Makes 1 cup.

BLUE CHEESE DIP

1 cup sour cream or 1 cup High-Protein "Sour Cream" (*see* above)
3 ounces blue cheese, crumbled (Roquefort, Gorgonzola, etc.)
Dash of garlic powder
Salt to taste

Place all ingredients in blender, blend until smooth. Makes 1½ cups.

OLIVE DIP

1 cup sour cream
½ cup chopped stuffed olives
1 cup cottage cheese

Combine all ingredients, mix well by hand. Or blend until smooth if preferred. Makes 2½ cups.

GUACAMOLE

1 ripe avocado
1 tablespoon lemon juice or lime juice
3 scallions, minced, including tops
Salt, pepper to taste

Mash the avocado with the lemon juice. Add the remaining ingredients, and mash together until smooth. Insert the avocado pit in the bottom of the bowl and place plastic wrap on the top of the dip to keep the air out; it will prevent the dip from turning brown. Serve with vegetables, Soy Chips, shrimp, etc. Makes 1 cup.

BEAN DIP

1 tablespoon butter
4 to 6 mushrooms, sliced
1 cup leftover baked soybeans (any style: see Vegetables)
1 clove garlic, crushed
½ teaspoon chili powder
Tomato purée as needed

Melt the butter, and sauté the mushrooms until browned. Add the next three ingredients, plus a little water if needed to prevent burning. Stir until the beans are heated through. Pour into the blender and purée until smooth, adding tomato purée as needed for flavor and consistency. Correct seasoning. Serve hot with vegetables, hard cheese, fondue, Soy Chips, etc. Makes 1½ cups.

BACON SPREAD

4 strips bacon (not sugar cured)
1 3-ounce package cream cheese
Pinch of red pepper
½ teaspoon dry mustard
¼ teaspoon celery salt

Fry bacon until crisp. Drain on paper towels and place in the blender with the other ingredients. Blend briefly, pushing mixture down with a rubber spatula when the blades jam. (Can also be made by mashing in a bowl with a spoon.) This and other spreads can be served on celery, homemade bread, pancakes, etc. Makes ½ cup.

CHEDDAR SPREAD

4 ounces sharp Cheddar cheese, grated
2 tablespoons cream or evaporated milk
½ teaspoon dry mustard
½ teaspoon vinegar

Mash together all ingredients (cheese will be easier to mash if it is left at room temperature for an hour after grating). Spread on celery stalks (in the cavity), chill, then slice into 2-inch lengths. Or serve with pancakes or Soy Bread. Makes ⅔ cup.

PICKLE SPREAD

1 3-ounce package cream cheese, softened
1 sour pickle, chopped fine
½ teaspoon onion salt
Liquid from the pickle jar if needed

Mash the cream cheese, mix with the other ingredients, adding pickle juice until the mixture reaches desired consistency. (Can also be used as a dip by adding more liquid.) Makes ⅔ cup.

CHILI SPREAD

4 ounces sharp cheese, grated (Cheddar, Jack, etc.)
Dash of cayenne pepper
¼ cup minced red or green pepper
Salt to taste if needed
½ teaspoon chili powder
2 tablespoons cream or evaporated milk

Combine all ingredients, mash until blended and smooth. Makes ¾ cup.

OLIVE SPREAD

8 ounces farmer cheese
½ cup stuffed olives, chopped

Mash the cheese, mix with the olives and mash to the desired consistency. Makes 1½ cups.

BASIC SWEET CREAMY SPREAD

1 3-ounce package cream cheese, softened
½ teaspoon vanilla or strawberry extract
1 teaspoon liquid artificial sweetener or to taste
1 or 2 drops red food coloring

Mash the cream cheese, and add the other ingredients. Mix well until smooth; spread on pancakes or canapés. Can be spread on very thin pancakes, then rolled like a jelly roll. Chill, then slice. Makes ½ cup.

TURKEY PÂTÉ

2 cups cooked turkey meat and skin, ground or chopped in the blender
2 hard-cooked eggs, chopped fine
¼ cup finely ground filberts or Brazil nuts
¼ cup allowed or homemade mayonnaise
¼ sweet Spanish onion, minced fine
Dash Tabasco or pepper sauce (check label)
Salt, pepper to taste

Combine all ingredients, and mash to a stiff paste. Correct seasoning to taste. Pack tightly in an oiled mold and chill. Turn out of the mold; serve with small knives for spreading on Soy Bread, pancakes, etc. Makes 3 cups.

LIVER PÂTÉ

4 slices bacon
1 small onion, minced fine
1 clove garlic, split
1½ pounds pork liver
Pinch of basil
1 hard-cooked egg, mashed or riced
Pinch of thyme
Salt, pepper to taste

Fry the bacon until crisp, and set aside to drain. In the bacon fat, sauté the onion and garlic until translucent. Discard the garlic, and remove the onion to a bowl. Next, fry the liver in the bacon fat until just cooked through (do not overcook; liver is cooked properly when it has just lost the pink color all through). Mash the liver; add the onion, crumbled bacon and rest of the ingredients. Mash together, adding more fat if needed to form a stiff paste. Form into a ball or press into an oiled mold, and chill. Turn out of mold and serve with small knives for spreading and soy bread or pancakes. (For another version of liver pâté, see Chopped Chicken Livers.) Makes 3 cups.

CHEESE BALL

1 8-ounce package cream cheese
1 pound Cheddar cheese, grated
3 cloves garlic, crushed
½ cup chopped pecans
¼ cup finely chopped fresh parsley
2 tablespoons paprika

Soften the cheese at room temperature for 1 hour. Mash cheeses together, add the garlic and pecans. Mix thoroughly, then divide in half. Form each half into a ball. Roll one ball in the chopped parsley until completely coated; roll the other ball in the paprika. Chill; serve as is; or cut each ball carefully down the middle, and place half of a red ball together with half a green ball; press together gently, brushing the cut surfaces with a little hot water to make them stick. Serve as a spread at room temperature. (Excellent for Christmas buffets.) Makes 2½ cups.

SARDINE-STUFFED EGGS

4 hard-cooked eggs
1 can sardines in oil
1 tablespoon cream cheese, softened
¼ teaspoon dried chives
Salt, pepper to taste

Cut the eggs in half, scoop out the yolks and mash with the other ingredients. Stuff the egg whites with the mixture. Makes 8 stuffed egg halves.

DEVILED EGGS

6 hard-cooked eggs
¼ cup allowed mayonnaise
1 stalk celery, minced very fine
½ teaspoon onion powder
½ teaspoon prepared white horseradish
½ teaspoon prepared mustard
Salt, pepper to taste

Cut eggs in half and remove the yolks carefully. Mash the yolks with the rest of the ingredients. Scoop the mixture into the egg white halves, using a spoon or pastry tube. Sprinkle lightly with paprika. Makes 12 deviled eggs.

STUFFED WALNUTS

Cream cheese, chilled
Walnut halves (or pecans)

Slice the cream cheese ¼ inch thick. Place a 1-inch square between two halves of shelled nuts. Trim away the excess cream cheese. Chill.

STUFFED PICKLES

4 ounces cream cheese, softened at room temperature
2 large half-sour barrel pickles (kosher style) with pickle juice

Mash the cream cheese with a little pickle juice. Slice the ends off the pickles. Remove the seeds with an apple corer or long thin knife. Stuff the cavity with cream cheese. Chill, slice ½ inch thick with a very sharp knife. Serve as is, or with toothpicks. Makes 24 slices.

STUFFED CELERY

Celery is natural for stuffing; its bland taste, firmness and ready-made cavity make it easy to fill and useful with all sorts of flavors. Besides stuffings and dips given in the preceding pages, instant appetizers and snacks can be made by stuffing celery stalks with any of the following:

Anchovy paste
Cottage cheese
Liverwurst (check the label)
Allowed peanut butter
Roquefort cheese
Cream cheese (regular or whipped)
Chive cheese
Pimiento cheese (check the label)
Wispride and similar cheese spreads
Leftovers, such as tuna salad, etc.

SOYBEAN BALLS

1 cup leftover cooked or baked soybeans
1 egg, slightly beaten
4 slices crisp bacon, crumbled
Salt to taste if needed
¼ teaspoon chili powder
1 tablespoon tomato purée
1 tablespoon bacon drippings (optional)

Prepare beans, or use leftovers in freezer allowing time to defrost. Mash the beans with a fork, and add the remaining ingredients except bacon fat, until the mixture is the consistency of meat ball. Roll into balls, and bake at 325° until firm and brown; or fry in bacon fat until crisp and brown. Serve with toothpicks. Makes 8 to 10 balls.

TINY MEAT BALLS

1 slice allowed bread, toasted
1 pound lean ground round
¼ cup milk
¼ teaspoon garlic powder
Salt, pepper to taste
1 egg, slightly beaten
Dash of oregano or thyme
¼ cup Kikkoman soy sauce

Break the toast into small pieces, and whirl in the blender until finely crushed. Combine all ingredients except soy sauce and roll into small balls, about ½ inch. Brush with small amount of soy sauce, and broil on rack over pan until brown, turning once. Serve hot with toothpicks. If using bought bread, entire recipe contains 1 unit carbohydrate; each meat ball contains a trace of carbohydrate. Makes 20 meat balls.

LIVERWURST BALLS

¼ Bermuda onion
1 pound liverwurst (check label for sugar)
½ teaspoon prepared white horseradish
½ teaspoon hot German-style mustard or other brown mustard (check label for sugar)
Fresh parsley, chopped very fine

Cut the onion into ¼-inch cubes. Mash the liverwurst with the horseradish and mustard until soft. Scoop up a 1-inch ball of the liverwurst mixture, and form it around an onion cube. Roll in the parsley. Shake off excess parsley, repeat until all the liverwurst has been used. Chill until firm. Makes 10 to 16 balls.

CHEDDAR CHEESE BALLS

8 ounces sharp Cheddar cheese, grated
¼ tablespoon Kikkoman soy sauce
½ teaspoon vinegar
¼ teaspoon prepared mustard
½ cup finely ground almonds

Grate the cheese, allow to stand until it is room temperature. Add the seasonings and mash. Roll into small balls and roll the balls in the ground almonds until covered. Chill until firm.

Variation: Prepare as above, roll in lightly toasted sesame seeds. Makes 16 balls.

EGGPLANT FONDUE

1 egg, slightly beaten
½ cup soy flour
1 small eggplant, cut into ½-inch cubes
1 cup oil
Dash of freshly ground pepper
¼ teaspoon salt
Dash of oregano

Mix the egg and soy flour well, adding a little water if needed, to make a thick batter. Coat the eggplant cubes in the mixture, turning until evenly coated. Heat the oil in a fondue pot until hot but not smoking. Spear the cubed eggplant on fondue forks, sprinkle with the seasonings and place in the pot of hot oil. Leave the cubes in the oil until crisp and brown on the outside, tender on the inside. (Experiment to find the length of time you prefer.) Dip in Cheese Sauce, Spaghetti Sauce, hot Chili Sauce, or eat as is. Serves 4 to 6.

CHEESE FONDUE

8 ounces sharp Cheddar cheese, grated
Dash of cayenne pepper
1 cup light cream or half and half
1 tablespoon butter
Dash of garlic powder
Salt, pepper to taste
1 loaf homemade Soy Bread, Soy Grits Bread or other low-carbohydrate bread

Combine all ingredients except the bread in a fondue pot. Heat
until the cheese is melted, stir until well mixed. Cut the bread into
1-inch cubes and toast in the broiler, shaking or stirring occasionally, until browned. Spear the cubes of bread on fondue forks,
and dip into the sauce. For carbohydrates, see the bread recipe
used. Serves 4 to 6.

SWISS FONDUE

Same as Cheese Fondue: omit the Cheddar cheese, substitute
½ pound Gruyère cheese. Omit the cayenne and garlic powder; add
2 tablespoons minced onion flakes. Serves 4 to 6.

BEEF FONDUE

1 pound good lean steak, ¾ inch thick
Whole black peppercorns, crushed
¼ teaspoon MSG
¼ teaspoon garlic powder
1 cup oil
Salt to taste

Trim all visible fat and gristle from the meat, and cut the steak
into ¾-inch cubes. Place the peppercorns in a paper bag with the
other spices and roll repeatedly with a rolling pin to crush. Place
the beef cubes in the bag and shake to season evenly. Do not salt.
Heat the oil in a fondue pot until hot but not smoking. Spear the

cubes of meat on fondue forks and place in the oil until cooked to desired degree (experiment until you find the time you prefer); salt pieces individually after cooking. Dip into any preferred sauce (*see* Sauces and Dressings). Serves 4 to 6.

CHEESE BUBBLES

4 ounces sharp Cheddar cheese
1 3-ounce package cream cheese
2 egg yolks, slightly beaten
Pinch of basil, pinch of thyme
1 clove garlic, crushed
Salt, pepper to taste
4 slices Oatmeal Bread ※2 or other homemade bread

Grate the Cheddar cheese, let both cheeses stand until room temperature. Mash cheeses together, and add eggs and seasonings. Beat until well blended. Toast the bread lightly on both sides in the broiler. Cut slices into quarters. Spread thickly with the cheese mixture. Place in the broiler 4 to 6 inches from the heat until cheese is brown and bubbly. For carbohydrates, see the bread recipe used. Makes 16 canapés.

ANCHOVY-MUSHROOM SURPRISES

¼ pound raw mushrooms
1 can anchovy fillets wrapped around capers
1 tablespoon butter
1 tablespoon lemon juice
1 teaspoon finely minced fresh parsley

Remove the stems from the mushrooms and set aside for another recipe. Place the mushroom caps, cup end up, in a baking dish. Place one anchovy-wrapped caper in the center of each mushroom cap. Melt the butter in a small saucepan, add the lemon juice and parsley. Drizzle the mixture over the stuffed mushrooms. Place in a preheated 350° oven and bake until the mushrooms are cooked (45 minutes), basting occasionally with the pan liquids. For faster baking, cover the pan and bake at 375° for 20 to 30 minutes. Skewer with toothpicks, serve warm. Makes about 10 surprises.

COCKTAIL FRANKS

1 12-ounce package Hebrew National cocktail franks
1 package Jones smoked bacon

Place the franks in boiling water until warm, about 5 minutes. Partially fry or bake the bacon slices, until limp and transparent. Wrap one slice of bacon around each hot dog; place on a rack over a broiler pan. Bake or broil until the bacon is crisp. Serve with toothpicks and delicatessen-style mustard, slightly warmed. Makes 24 franks.

WATER CHESTNUTS SUPREME

1 can water chestnuts, drained
1 tablespoon butter, melted
2 tablespoons minced onion (instant)

Slice each water chestnut in half across the middle, making two wafers of each piece. Brush well with the melted butter, and sprinkle with the minced onion. Place on a foil-lined broiler rack and broil until the onion is crisp and brown. Skewer with toothpicks to serve. Makes about 20.

EGGPLANT APPETIZER

2 tablespoons olive oil
1 medium eggplant, minced
1 green pepper, minced fine
1 small onion, minced fine
2 cloves garlic, finely minced
8 to 10 capers
1 tablespoon lemon juice
1 8-ounce can Del Monte tomato sauce
¼ teaspoon salt
Pinch of oregano
Pinch of basil

Dash of liquid artificial sweetener
Dash of pepper

Heat the oil in a skillet, and sauté the vegetables (including the garlic), until soft and translucent. Add the rest of the ingredients; lower heat and cover. Simmer slowly until the eggplant is soft. Remove the cover, and continue to simmer on low heat until the sauce is very thick. Serves hot or cold as an appetizer, or cold as a relish. Makes 3 cups.

CLAM CANAPÉS

Pancakes, cut into squares or small rounds
Whipped butter or cream cheese as needed
1 can whole baby clams or 1 can smoked oysters, if preferred
1 small jar sweet roasted peppers or pimientos

Spread each pancake with the butter or cream cheese; top with a single clam or oyster and garnish with a thin sliver of pimiento.

ANCHOVY CANAPÉS

1 firm cucumber, unpeeled
Whipped butter as needed
Pancake "pennies" or squares
1 can anchovy fillets rolled around capers

Score the cucumber lengthwise with a fork all around; slice thin. For each canapé, butter 1 "penny" or pancake section. Add 1 slice cucumber, and top with an anchovy-wrapped caper. See pancake recipe used for carbohydrate units.

HAM AND CHEESE ROLL-UPS

4 ounces farmer cheese
½ teaspoon allowed mayonnaise
2 tablespoons finely chopped pimiento
2 tablespoons finely chopped sour pickle
8 ounces boiled ham, sliced fairly thick (or more as needed)

Mash the cheese and mayonnaise together until smooth and creamy; mix in the pimiento and pickle. For each canapé, spread the cheese mixture thickly on a slice of ham, and roll up tightly. Chill. Slice into convenient lengths for nibbling, such as 1 inch. Can also be sliced ¼ inch thick and placed on a round piece of pancake. Makes 2 dozen.

CHOPPED LIVER CANAPÉS

1½ cups chopped chicken liver (*see* Foreign and Regional)

Use as follows:
1. Chill in an oiled mold, turn out on serving plate; serve with plastic spoons.
2. Spread on pancake rounds, garnish with a slice of dill pickle.
3. Spread on a thick slice of firm cucumber, top with a small ring of sweet onion.
4. Toast any thinly sliced homemade bread. Spread chopped liver on one slice, top with the other slice; cut into quarters, top with half an olive and spear with toothpick.
5. Spread chopped liver in the cavity of a celery stalk; cut into 2-inch lengths, top each with a sliver of pickled red pepper.

PIMIENTO CANAPÉS

2 tablespoons chopped red Wonder peppers (pickled)
1 teaspoon vinegar from the pepper jar
1 3-ounce package cream cheese
4 thin pancakes

Mash together all ingredients, spread on thin pancakes; roll, slice and chill (to do this best, make the pancakes just before spreading so that they are still slightly warm and will roll without cracking). Or make a stack, alternating a layer of spread with a layer of pancake, beginning and ending with a pancake. Chill and cut into 1-inch cubes, skewered with toothpicks. Makes 16 to 20 canapés.

CLASSIC CAVIAR CANAPÉS

Red caviar:

2 slices homemade bread
Unsalted whipped butter as needed
1 jar red caviar

Toast the bread under the broiler for just a minute; do not brown. Allow the bread to cool. Butter heavily, and cut each slice into quarters. Place ½ teaspoon caviar on each piece. Makes 8 canapés; see bread recipe for carbohydrate units.

Black caviar:

Same as above, but use whipped cream cheese instead of butter and black caviar instead of red.

SMOKED SALMON CANAPÉS

Prepare bread as for Caviar Canapés. Spread each piece with whipped cream cheese, add a thin slice of cucumber (unpeeled). Top with a 2-inch square of smoked salmon (lox). Makes 8 canapés.

TOASTED PUMPKIN SEEDS

Spread shelled pumpkin seeds in a single layer in a hot oiled skillet. Fry until the seeds "pop," stirring. Sprinkle with salt and serve warm in a bowl as an appetizer or for nibbling.

CURRIED PUMPKIN SEEDS

¼ cup curry powder
1 clove garlic, crushed
¼ cup hot water
1 cup water
1 teaspoon salt
2 cups plain shelled pumpkin seeds
Melted butter

Combine the curry powder, garlic and hot water; mix until blended. Add 1 cup water and salt. Heat to a simmer, stirring constantly. Add the pumpkin seeds, and simmer for 5 minutes; drain. Spread the seeds on a cookie sheet, brush with a little melted butter and sprinkle with additional salt. Toast under the broiler until lightly browned. Makes 2 cups.

BEVERAGES

Despite that fact that coffee, tea and alcoholic drinks are not allowed on the diet, there can be great variety in the beverages you use. There are numerous brands and flavors of sugar-free sodas; there are milk drinks and dessert-type drinks, such as eggnogs and milk shakes. There are herb teas, which do not contain caffeine, and decaffeinated coffee. Juices can be classified as beverages, but they must be counted as units of fruit, according to the unit plan.

Also included under Beverages are party drinks to replace alcoholic drinks, quick and easy beverages to give your menus variety, hot and cold drinks to use in Thermos bottles for school lunches and others.

Coffee, of course, is never allowed, but Sanka and other decaffeinated coffees can be substituted. Keep in mind that Sanka contains some caffeine, and if you drink ten or twelve cups a day you are getting too much caffeine. Tea, which is high in caffeine, can be used occasionally, especially at social gatherings or in restaurants when no alternative is handy. Ask to have the tea bag brought separately from the water, and just dunk it once or twice for a little color; or if the tea has been brewed, pour only a half cup and dilute it with water or milk.

Diet sodas are wonderful, but should not be used constantly, as they reinforce the taste for sweet foods. Be sure to read the labels carefully, and use only those which are sugarless. Never use diet cola, even if it is sugarless, because of the caffeine it contains; use other "brown" sodas (root beer, cream soda) in moderation, as they contain a little caramel coloring.

We have listed many of the herb teas available in health food stores. You may have to experiment to find one to your liking. None of them tastes exactly like "real" tea, but they are refreshing and convenient, and can be used in any strength and amount. Some herb teas are sold in tea bags, and these can be carried in a pocket for a refreshing change from Sanka.

Vanilla Milk Shake (or eggnog)
Coffee Milk Shake (or eggnog)
Mocha Milk Shake
    (or eggnog)
Chocolate Milk Shake
    (or eggnog)
Banana Milk Shake (or eggnog)
Strawberry Milk Shake
    (or eggnog)
Peach Milk Shake (or eggnog)
Spice Milk Shake (or eggnog)
Holiday Eggnog
Pineapple Egg Punch
Health Drink
Chocolate Milk
Mocha Milk
Strawberry Milk
Banana Milk
Hot Cocoa #1
Hot Cocoa #2 (Instant)
Mexican Chocolate
Coffee

Iced Coffee
Caffè Espresso
Cappuccino
Orange-spiced Coffee
Spiced Viennese Coffee
Café au Rhum
Cinnamon Mocha
Café au Lait
Teas
Iced Rose Hips Tea
Gossip Tea
Pep-up Tea
Lime Tea
Fancy Morning Fruit Juice
Lemonade
Cranberry-pineapple Juice
Party Punch
Mulled Cider
Tomato Juice Cocktail
"Bloody Mary"
Clam-tomato Juice Cocktail
Hot Broth

VANILLA MILK SHAKE (OR EGGNOG)

All milk shakes can be made with or without eggs, as you prefer. The eggs, of course, make it suitable for use as a protein snack, or simply to add a little more protein to your meal; they also give a "thicker," richer flavor. However, if you prefer a more "milky" flavor and do not need the extra protein in your menu, you can omit the eggs. For all milk shake recipes, we will add "optional" for eggs; but we must recommend that you use the eggs more often than not, especially for children's drinks. All directions for milk shakes are for 2 people, and each portion=1 unit milk.

1 cup milk
⅓ cup non-fat dry milk
Dash of salt
Saccharin to taste (about 4 to 6 ¼-grain tablets)
1 teaspoon vanilla extract
2 eggs (optional)
1 cup or ½ tray chipped ice

Pour the milk into the blender, add dry milk and blend on low until mixed. Add the salt, saccharin and flavoring. Blend on high until the saccharin is crushed. Add the eggs for an eggnog; last, add the ice, cover and blend until ice is crushed and the shake is thick and smooth. Taste, and correct for sweetness. Leftover milk shake can be frozen and used for ice milk. Serves 2, approximately 2 cups each. Each serving=1 unit milk.

COFFEE MILK SHAKE (OR EGGNOG)

Same as Vanilla Milk Shake, plus one teaspoon freeze-dried Sanka.

MOCHA MILK SHAKE (OR EGGNOG)

Same as Coffee Milk Shake, plus one tablespoon unsweetened cocoa.

CHOCOLATE MILK SHAKE (OR EGGNOG)

Same as Vanilla Milk Shake, plus one heaping tablespoon unsweetened cocoa.

BANANA MILK SHAKE (OR EGGNOG)

Same as Vanilla Milk Shake, except:
Omit vanilla extract; substitute ½ teaspoon imitation banana flavor-

ing. Omit 1 cup milk; substitute 4 ounces evaporated milk, 4 ounces ice water.

STRAWBERRY MILK SHAKE (OR EGGNOG)

Same as Vanilla Milk Shake, but instead of crushed ice, use 1 cup loose frozen strawberries (packed without sugar). Thaw the berries just enough to separate them (about 5 minutes at room temperature), add to the milk shake last, and blend until smooth. Makes 2 portions; each portion=about 2 cups. Each portion=1 unit milk, ½ unit fruit.

PEACH MILK SHAKE (OR EGGNOG)

Same as Vanilla Milk Shake, except:
Omit 1 cup milk, substitute ½ cup evaporated milk. Omit vanilla extract, substitute ½ teaspoon peach flavoring, 1 small ripe peach, chopped. Add water as needed to blend. Each portion=1 unit milk, ½ unit fruit.

SPICE MILK SHAKE (OR EGGNOG)

½ cup evaporated milk
⅓ cup non-fat dry milk
½ teaspoon vanilla extract
Dash of allspice
Dash of ground ginger
Saccharin to taste (2 to 4 ¼-grain tablets)
12 ounces diet ginger ale, chilled
½ cup crushed ice or more as needed

Combine the evaporated milk and dry milk in the blender, blend on low until mixed. Add the seasonings, blend. Pour in the soda and blend on high until smooth, adding ice as needed until mixture reaches desired amount. Makes 2 portions; each portion=1 unit milk.

HOLIDAY EGGNOG

½ cup light cream
2 cups milk
½ teaspoon vanilla extract
¼ teaspoon freshly ground nutmeg
2 eggs (extra large)
1 teaspoon imitation rum flavoring
4 ¼-grain tablets saccharin

Mix all ingredients well in blender. Chill several hours, and serve cold, blending for a few seconds to mix before serving. Garnish with a little more nutmeg sprinkled on top of each cup. Serves 3 or 4. Recipe=2 units milk.

PINEAPPLE EGG PUNCH

1 cup canned pineapple (Dole sugarless, packed in its own juice, chilled well)
⅓ cup non-fat dry milk
2 eggs
Saccharin to taste if needed
4 ounces evaporated milk
Dash of salt
½ cup crushed ice

Make sure the pineapple is very cold, even partly frozen. Combine all ingredients and blend. Taste for sweetness after blending. Use the juice from the pineapple as needed until you reach the right consistency. Serves 2; 1 portion=1 unit milk, 1 unit fruit.

HEALTH DRINK

4 ounces orange juice
⅓ cup non-fat dry milk
1 cup crushed ice
Saccharin to taste (1 to 3 ¼-grain tablets)
2 eggs
¼ cup wheat germ
Dash of salt

Combine juice and dry milk in blender, and blend on slow until mixed. Add the rest of the ingredients and blend on high until liquefied. This can be used as a complete breakfast in a glass. Serves 1; 1 health drink=1 unit milk, 1 unit juice, 2 units protein, 1 unit carbohydrate.

CHOCOLATE MILK

8 ounces cold milk
1 teaspoon unsweetened cocoa
¼ teaspoon vanilla extract
1 or 2 ¼-grain tablets saccharin or to taste

Pour the milk into the blender, turn on low and gradually add the cocoa while the blender is running. Add the other ingredients, blend until smooth. Chill, or serve immediately. Serves 1; 1 portion=1 unit milk.

MOCHA MILK

Same as Chocolate Milk, plus ½ teaspoon instant or freeze-dried Sanka.

STRAWBERRY MILK

8 ounces milk
1 or 2 drops red food coloring
½ teaspoon imitation strawberry extract
2 tablets saccharin or to taste
Combine in blender, blend well. Chill, or serve immediately. Serves
1; 1 portion=1 unit milk.

BANANA MILK

4 ounces evaporated milk
¼ to ½ teaspoon banana flavoring
2 ¼-grain tablets saccharin or to taste
4 ounces ice water
1 or 2 drops yellow food coloring

Combine in blender, blend until smooth. Chill, or serve. Serves 1;
1 portion=1 unit milk.

HOT COCOA #1

1 teaspoon unsweetened cocoa
Dash of vanilla extract
Dash of salt
1 cup milk
2 ¼-grain tablets saccharin

Place all ingredients in blender, blend until smooth. Pour into saucepan, heat, but do not boil. Pour into the blender, blend again until
smooth. Drink while hot. Serves 1.

HOT COCOA #2 (INSTANT)

1 teaspoon unsweetened cocoa
2 tablespoons non-fat dry milk
¼ cup evaporated milk
Dash of vanilla extract
2 ¼-grain tablets saccharin
Dash of salt
Boiling water

Place the cocoa and dry milk in a large mug. Gradually add the evaporated milk, mixing to a paste. Add the vanilla and the saccharin, pour in the boiling water, stirring, until smooth. Add enough boiling water to fill the cup, mix and serve. Serves 1.

MEXICAN CHOCOLATE

Same as Hot Cocoa #1, plus ¼ teaspoon cinnamon. After heating, blend on high until very frothy. Serve in tall glasses, top with whipped cream (see Desserts) if preferred.

COFFEE

Very good coffee can be made using decaffeinated coffee, regular or instant. Follow directions on the label for freshly perked coffee. Instant decaffeinated coffee comes in two types: granulated, or powdered, and freeze-dried. The best we've ever had was made as follows:

¾ cup water per person
1 level teaspoon freeze-dried Sanka per person

Measure out the water and heat to a low boil. Add the Sanka in the pot. Cover, remove from heat, and steep for 5 minutes before serving. This is also good reheated if you don't heat it to boiling.

ICED COFFEE

1 rounded teaspoon freeze-dried Sanka
2 ¼-grain tablets saccharin
¼ cup hot water
6 ice cubes
¼ to ½ cup milk

Place the Sanka and saccharin in a large glass; pour in the hot water and stir until the saccharin is dissolved. Add the ice cubes and milk, stir. Fill the rest of the glass with water. Stir until ice cold and serve. Serves 1.

Variation: Make a large pot of Sanka, double strength, steeping in the pot (*see* Coffee above). Use about 5 cups water to 12 teaspoons freeze-dried Sanka. Pour into a pitcher and chill in the refrigerator until cold. Add 1 or 2 trays of ice cubes and 2 cups milk. If you wish to serve it already sweetened, add 10 to 12 ¼-grain tablets saccharin to the coffee when it is still hot. Or, if preferred, serve with liquid artificial sweetener on the side. Serves 12.

CAFFÈ ESPRESSO

4 ounces boiling water
1 rounded teaspoon freeze-dried Sanka
Twist of lemon peel
1 tablet saccharin (optional)

Pour the boiling water over the rest of the ingredients. Steep for 5 minutes before serving. Serves 1.

CAPPUCCINO

4 ounces milk
2 ounces water
1 heaping tablespoon non-fat dry milk
1 heaping teaspoon freeze-dried Sanka
1 or 2 ¼-grain tablets saccharin (optional)
Pinch of cinnamon
1 stick of cinnamon

Place the milk and water in a saucepan, sprinkle in the dry milk. Stir until mixed, then heat almost to boiling. Pour into blender container which has been rinsed with boiling water. Add the Sanka, saccharin and powdered cinnamon. Blend on high until frothy. Pour into a mug with a stick of cinnamon, serve immediately. Serves 1; 1 portion=1 unit milk.

ORANGE-SPICED COFFEE

2 cups water
4 whole cloves
2 or 3 ¼-grain tablets saccharin
Peel of 1 small orange
2 heaping teaspoons instant Sanka or 2 level teaspoons freeze-dried Sanka

Place all ingredients except Sanka in a saucepan. Heat until nearly boiling; simmer for 5 minutes. Strain, discarding the cloves and orange peel. Stir in the Sanka, steep for 1 to 2 minutes. Pour into cups, serve with cinnamon sticks (optional). Serves 2.

SPICED VIENNESE COFFEE

½ cup water
½ cup non-fat dry milk
¼ teaspoon ground nutmeg

¼ teaspoon cinnamon
½ teaspoon vanilla extract
6 to 8 ¼-grain tablets saccharin, crushed
6 cups strong brewed Sanka
1 teaspoon orange extract

Mix together the water and non-fat dry milk; pour into a shallow pan and freeze until ice crystals form on sides of pan. Remove to mixer bowl and mix at high speed until the mixture is the consistency of whipped cream. Add nutmeg, cinnamon, vanilla, and half the crushed saccharin. Whip until stiff. Combine the hot coffee, orange extract and remaining sweetener and pour into individual mugs. Top with the whipped milk mixture. If preferred, substitute whipped cream for the whipped milk. Serves 6.

CAFÉ AU RHUM

2 cups water
2 teaspoons freeze-dried Sanka
2 whole cloves
¼ teaspoon imitation rum extract
Saccharin to taste

Boil the water, stir in the Sanka and steep for 1 minute. Add the cloves and extract and 2 to 4 ¼-grain tablets saccharin if preferred. Cover and steep a few minutes more and serve. Serves 2.

CINNAMON MOCHA

2 cups milk
½ teaspoon vanilla extract
1½ teaspoons unsweetened cocoa
¼ teaspoon cinnamon
1½ teaspoons freeze-dried Sanka
4 ¼-grain tablets saccharin

Heat the milk to scalding; pour into blender with the rest of the ingredients. Blend until smooth. Serves 2; each portion=1 unit milk.

CAFÉ AU LAIT

Same as Cinnamon Mocha, but omit the cocoa, and increase the Sanka to 2 tablespoons. Serves 2; each portion=1 unit milk.

TEAS

Herb teas are made by pouring boiling water over the leaves, flowers, etc., of various plants. Some of them have medicinal and beneficial value: rose hips tea, for example, is extremely high in vitamin C. Whatever the reputed healing qualities the various teas may have, they are also a very good way to vary your menus to avoid boredom.

To brew herb teas: use 1 tea bag for every 2 cups water, or 1 heaping tablespoon loose tea. Bags can be placed in a cup with boiling water and steeped 5 minutes, or steeped in a tea pot. If you haven't got a good tea strainer, here is a method you can use:

Buy a package of coffee filters (special filtering paper). Measure the amount of tea you need into one of the filter papers. Fold the edges toward the middle and fasten with a stapler. Place your tea bag in the bottom of a tea pot, pour actively boiling water over it and steep at least 5 minutes. Pour into cups, add sweetener, milk or lemon to taste. Other additions to herb tea: orange juice, cloves, lemon peel, orange peel. The most common herb teas and the ones you will probably find easiest to like are rose hips and mint. There are many others; experiment until you find the ones you like best. Some of those available are:

Camomile tea	Red clover tea
Rose hips tea	Alfalfa tea
Oat straw tea	Alfalfa mint tea
Maté tea	Papaya mint tea
Sassafras bark tea	Sarsaparilla tea
Peppermint tea	Shave grass tea
Papaya tea	Spearmint tea
Fenugreek tea	Horse tail tea
Comfrey root tea	Comfrey leaf tea

Senna leaf tea
Slippery elm tea
Strawberry leaf tea
Violet leaf tea
Althea root tea
Anise seed tea
Blueberry leaf tea
Buck thorn tea
Burdock root tea
Catnip tea
Celery seed tea
Centaury herb tea
Cleavers herb tea
Corn silk tea
Couch grass tea
Dandelion leaf tea
Dogwood bark tea
Dulse leaf tea
Elder flower tea
Eucalyptus tea
Eyebright tea
Fennel seed tea
Gentian root tea
St. John's wort tea
Uva-ursi tea

Watercress tea
Yerba santa tea
Goldenseal herb tea
Hops tea
Horehound herb tea
Huckleberry leaf tea
Irish moss tea
Juniper berry tea
Kaffir tea
Knot grass tea
Laurel leaf tea
Lavendar flower tea
Licorice root tea
Linden flower tea
Mullein leaf tea
Parsley tea
Pink hibiscus tea
Plantago seed tea
Plantain tea
Princess pine tea
Rosemary leaf tea
Sage tea
Skullcap tea
White oak bark tea

This list was taken from the catalogue of the Natural Sales Company and does not include such ready-to-use blends as Cynopep, etc., which can be found in various health food stores. Many companies put out blends of herb teas, which are often more expensive than the individual herbs, but are very tasty.

Of all the herb teas, the most popular is rose hips tea, which is sweet, light in flavor and blends well with other flavors. You can brew rose hips tea and drink it hot, or use it in the following variations:

ICED ROSE HIPS TEA

Prepare a pot of rose hips tea, brewed strong (tea should be a deep pink). Chill in the refrigerator. Fill a glass with ice cubes, add 1 tablespoon lemon juice, 2 ¼-grain tablets crushed saccharin and fill to the top with the tea. Stir and serve.

GOSSIP TEA

1 cup hot water
½ teaspoon dehydrated orange peel
1 short stick cinnamon
1 teaspoon loose rose hips tea
2 or 3 whole cloves

Combine all ingredients in a saucepan over low heat. Simmer and brew for 5 minutes. Remove from the heat, strain and serve hot. Sweeten to taste. Serves 1.

PEP-UP TEA

1 cup boiling water
½ teaspoon camomile tea
1 teaspoon loose rose hips tea
½ teaspoon peppermint or mint tea

Pour into a teapot. Steep for 5 minutes. Strain and serve. Sweeten to taste. Serves 1.

LIME TEA

Combine a 4-cup pot of hot rose hips tea with 1 bag of mint tea and the juice of 1 lime. Steep, strain and serve. Sweeten to taste. Serves 4.

FANCY MORNING FRUIT JUICE

12 ounces orange juice
8 ounces unsweetened pineapple juice
Liquid artificial sweetener to taste if needed
Juice of 2 lemons
2 cups ice water

Mix together all ingredients and serve well chilled. Serves 5; 4 ounces=1 unit fruit.

LEMONADE

4 cups ice water
½ cup freshly squeezed lemon juice
Saccharin to taste (about 8 ¼-grain tablets saccharin) crushed and
    dissolved in 1 tablespoon hot water

Combine all ingredients, correct sweetener if needed. Chill. Serve with a sliver of orange or a sprig of mint. For pink lemonade, add a dash of strawberry extract and a drop of red food coloring. Serves 4.

CRANBERRY-PINEAPPLE JUICE

16 ounces unsweetened pineapple juice
Pinch of ground cloves
2 ¼-grain tablets saccharin
½ cup whole raw cranberries
Pinch of cinnamon

Combine ingredients in blender, blend until liquefied. Chill; serve over cracked ice or dilute with ice water if needed. Serves 4; 4 ounces=1 unit fresh fruit.

PARTY PUNCH

2 16-ounce bottles diet ginger ale
1 16-ounce bottle citrus diet soda (or grapefruit or Fresca)
1 cup lemon juice or ReaLemon
6 to 8 whole cloves
1 quart orange juice
1 cup unsweetened pineapple juice
Ice (freeze water in a square plastic box)

Chill all ingredients until very cold. Just before serving, combine all ingredients in a large punch bowl with 1 large block of ice. Makes 10 cups; 1 cup=1 unit fruit.

MULLED CIDER

1 quart cider (no sugar added)
1 stick cinnamon
3 or 4 whole cloves
Dash freshly ground nutmeg

Combine all ingredients; heat to simmering point for 5 minutes (do not boil). Strain or remove cloves and cinnamon. Serve hot. Serves 8; 4 ounces=1 unit fruit.

TOMATO JUICE COCKTAIL

1 quart tomato juice
1 teaspoon lemon juice
½ teaspoon prepared white horseradish
¼ teaspoon salt
¼ teaspoon white vinegar
¼ teaspoon celery seed

Combine all ingredients, shake or stir. Chill before serving. Serves 5; 6 ounces=1 unit juice.

"BLOODY MARY"

6 ounces tomato juice
Pinch of salt
Dash Tabasco sauce
1 or 2 drops Kikkoman soy sauce

Mix well, chill. Drink when others are drinking alcoholic beverages, or as a before-meal appetizer. Serves 1; 6 ounces=1 unit juice.

CLAM-TOMATO JUICE COCKTAIL

4 ounces clam juice or clam broth
Pinch of salt
4 ounces tomato juice
½ teaspoon lemon juice

Combine all ingredients and chill. Serves 1; 1 serving=slightly less than 1 unit fruit.

HOT BROTH

2 cups water
1 Knorr-Swiss beef or chicken bouillon cube
Pinch of minced parsley

Heat the water to boiling. Add the other ingredients, lower heat to simmer. Cover and simmer for a few minutes. Stir and serve in mugs. Serves 2.

BREADS, PASTA AND NOODLES

Although you can't use wheat flour, there are many breads and miscellaneous foods, such as crackers, which can be made using the foods allowed on the diet. Since conventional breads rely on starch for the yeast to work, we have devised several kinds of bread which use eggs as a base. The eggs will rise, giving the fluffiness and texture of bread, and enabling you to use the breads as protein foods. The flavor of an egg bread naturally will be a good deal different from a yeast bread. Think of it as being something like brown bread or date and nut bread, and you will have some idea of the type of bread we use; not at all bad, when you are used to it, and certainly a lot better than no bread at all. In addition, these breads are amazingly easy to make; they require no beating, kneading, rising, and the timing and oven temperature can vary quite a bit without their being ruined. You can probably bake several loaves a week in the time it would have taken you to make a standard cake from a cake mix.

Soy Bread (and its variations) is the "staff of life" on the hypoglycemia diet; it can be used in almost unlimited amounts. Although soy flour is about 12 per cent carbohydrate, it is so filling and so high in protein that it would be almost physically impossible to eat too much of it. Use it for sandwiches, toast, spreads and almost any other purpose for which you use bread. The only limitation we would put on it is that when eating soy breads you should cut down on your other carbohydrates slightly. And always remember that small but frequent meals are preferred to maintain a constant blood sugar level.

If you find the flavor of plain Soy Bread is too bland, there are many flavorings which can be added to it. Soy Grits Bread is also rather bland, but with flavorings added it rivals any corn meal or corn flour bread. This also is almost unlimited in amount, but is a little harder to digest and should be eaten in reasonable amounts, such as two thin slices in a sandwich or one nice thick hunk to sop up gravy. Both Soy Bread and Soy Grits Bread can be used as protein snacks because of the large amount of protein, although you will probably prefer to use them with spreads and sandwich fillings.

The other basic breads used in this section are the All-star Egg Bread and the Oatmeal Bread; these are both delicious and can be used in sandwiches, as long as other carbohydrates are not used at the same meal. While we have called these breads "high-carbohydrate," they are really far lower than any bread you have ever eaten and certainly much lower than the bought protein bread which many doctors allow. Since they are so easy to make and so delicious, we feel it is much better to eat these than to use protein breads, all of which contain large amounts of wheat flour. Therefore, don't be frightened off by the term "high-carbohydrate" by these recipes; it is merely used to show that these breads must be measured, as opposed to the other recipes which allow larger portions.

For those who have never made noodles, you are in for a pleasant surprise. We have found that most old-time recipes call for unnecessary extra steps and huge amounts of dough which make it difficult for the novice to make. The recipes we have given result in a very good "imitation" noodle which gives variety to your meals, and is, again, almost unlimited in quantity. We doubt that you could possibly eat enough of these noodles to exceed one unit of carbohydrate. Included are instructions for making spaghetti, macaroni and other variations, all from the same basic dough. The flavor is slightly different from that of a wheat-flour noodle, but the texture is good and chewy, and they can be used in any of your favorite recipes.

You don't need a great deal of equipment to make these breads; a rolling pin, a few bread pans and a slap-dash experimental approach will be of help if you are preparing these foods for the first time. You'll find that preparing low-carbohydrate breads and noodles our way is creative and, above all, fun.

Soy Bread

Onion Bread

Cinnamon Bread

Soy Nut Bread

Soy Grits Bread

Oatmeal Bread

All-star Egg Bread

"Corn Meal" Bread

Polenta (fried "Corn Meal" Bread)

Soy Muffins

"Corn Meal" Muffins

Oat Muffins

Oat Biscuits

"Jolly Joan" Biscuits

Garlic Bread

Garlic Sticks

Bread Sticks

Melba Toast

"Bagels"

Best Sandwich Pancakes

Tortillas

Soy Chips

Sesame Crackers

Basic Soy Gluten Noodles

Soy Noodles

Egg Noodles

Oriental Soy Noodles

Spaetzle (tiny dumplings)

Knaidlach (dumplings)

Almond Balls (for soup)

"Pretzels"

SOY BREAD (LOW CARBOHYDRATE)

6 extra large eggs

1 cup soy flour

½ cup milk

¼ teaspoon salt

Dash of liquid artificial sweetener

⅓ cup non-fat dry milk

Preheat the oven to 375°. Beat the eggs well with an electric mixer or blender. Add the rest of the ingredients and stir to mix. Grease a small loaf or bread pan and sprinkle lightly with soy flour; shake out the excess flour. Pour the batter into the pan. Bake at 375° for 10 minutes; lower the heat to 350°, and bake for 40 to 50 minutes longer, or until set. Allow to cool before cutting. Makes 1 loaf, approximately 14 slices.

Variation: Same ingredients as above: separate eggs, beat the yolks and combine with the other ingredients. Beat the whites until stiff; fold in, and bake as above; bread will be higher and lighter. This is a very filling bread, almost foolproof to make. Eat as much as you like because it is so high in protein.

ONION BREAD (LOW CARBOHYDRATE)

6 extra large eggs

1 cup soy flour

½ cup milk

¼ teaspoon salt
½ teaspoon onion powder
⅓ cup non-fat dry milk
1 teaspoon instant minced onion
½ teaspoon caraway seeds or poppy seeds

Prepare just as for Soy Bread; sprinkle the top of the bread with a few more seeds and a pinch of fresh onion, minced fine. Makes 1 loaf, approximately 14 slices.

CINNAMON BREAD (LOW CARBOHYDRATE)

Same as Soy Bread, plus the following ingredients:
1 teaspoon cinnamon
¼ cup melted butter
4 ¼-grain tablets saccharin, crushed

Prepare the batter as if for Soy Bread, and pour into the pan. Mix the remaining ingredients in a dish, and just before baking, cut the mixture through the batter with a knife. Save a little of the cinnamon mixture and sprinkle on top of the bread. Bake as above. Makes 1 loaf, approximately 14 slices.

SOY NUT BREAD (LOW CARBOHYDRATE)

6 eggs
½ cup milk
¼ teaspoon salt
½ teaspoon vanilla extract
4 ¼-grain tablets saccharin, crushed
1 cup soy flour
⅓ cup non-fat dry milk
¼ cup oil
1 cup nut meats, broken (walnuts, pecans)
½ teaspoon cinnamon

Combine all ingredients, mix well. Bake as for Soy Bread. Makes 1 loaf, approximately 14 slices.

SOY GRITS BREAD (LOW CARBOHYDRATE)

Exactly the same as Soy Bread and its variations, except:
Omit soy flour, and substitute 1 cup soy grits; increase the milk to
1 cup. Also, allow the batter to set for 20 minutes before pouring
into the pan and baking. In addition to the variations above, you can
add berries and other fruit to the batter before baking.

OATMEAL BREAD (HIGH CARBOHYDRATE)

2 cups old-fashioned-style oat cereal
1 cup hot water (but not boiling)
¼ cup oil
½ teaspoon salt
⅔ cup non-fat dry milk
1 ¼ -grain tablet saccharin, crushed
4 eggs
½ teaspoon baking soda
1 cup soy flour

Combine the oat cereal and the hot water in a large bowl. Mix well
until the oatmeal is softened. Add the remaining ingredients and stir
well until mixed. Grease a loaf pan, then sift in a little soy flour,
shaking out the excess after the bottom and sides are lightly coated.
Pour in the batter. Place in a preheated 375° oven for 15 minutes,
then bake at 325° for 45 minutes. Entire recipe=14 units carbohydrates. Divide as follows: mark off 14 units on the top with a
knife, but do not slice. Each section can then be cut into 1 thick or
2 thin slices for each unit of carbohydrate. Do not cut until the bread
is cool. Delicious with butter, spreads or in all kinds of sandwiches.
This bread will hold its shape and is excellent for lunch-box sandwiches, for toasting and any other use. Store in the refrigerator. To
freeze: allow the bread to cool overnight, loosely wrapped. Wrap
well with freezer paper or heavy aluminum foil, seal and freeze.
Makes 1 loaf, approximately 14 slices.

ALL-STAR EGG BREAD (HIGH CARBOHYDRATE)

6 eggs
1 cup oat flour
1 teaspoon salt
1 cup soy flour
½ cup non-fat dry milk
1 teaspoon baking powder
2 ¼-grain tablets saccharin, crushed
1 cup water
1 cup wheat germ
Sesame seeds as needed

Beat the eggs and set aside. In a large bowl sift together the dry ingredients, except for the wheat germ and sesame seeds. Gradually beat in the eggs, then the water. Last, mix in the wheat germ, mixing well. Grease a large loaf pan, then dust lightly with soy flour, shaking out the excess. Pour the batter into the pan, and sprinkle the top lightly with sesame seeds. Bake in a preheated 375° oven for 15 minutes, then lower to 325° and bake for 35 to 40 minutes longer. This is called All-star Egg Bread because we feel that it is the best combination of ingredients, giving the flavor of Oatmeal Bread with the low carbohydrates of Soy Bread, and the texture of real bread. This is very tasty, and can be sliced thin easily. It will not crumble in the toaster and can be used for sandwiches and spreads. Those who cannot use wheat germ can make the bread by eliminating the wheat germ and adding an extra cup of soy flour or oat flour, or ½ cup of both. Makes 1 loaf, approximately 14 slices. Entire recipe =14 units carbohydrate; measure same as for Oatmeal Bread.

"CORN MEAL" BREAD (LOW CARBOHYDRATE)

1 cup soy grits
1 cup milk
4 eggs
¼ teaspoon salt
1 teaspoon liquid artificial sweetener
3 tablespoons butter, at room temperature

Soak the grits in the milk for 20 minutes. Beat the eggs, add the grits mixture, salt, sweetener and 2 tablespoons of the butter. Spread thinly (about 1 inch deep) in a well-oiled casserole, or pour into a cast-iron corn bread stick pan. Bake at 325° for 30 minutes. Spread the top with the remaining butter; bake until crusty and lightly browned (15 to 20 minutes). Cut into squares and serve plain, buttered or with pan gravy. Use as a protein snack or supplement. Makes 1 loaf.

POLENTA (FRIED "CORN MEAL" BREAD) (LOW CARBOHYDRATE)

1 cup soy grits
1 cup milk
½ cup non-fat dry milk
2 eggs
½ teaspoon salt
¼ teaspoon pepper
1 ¼-grain tablet saccharin, crushed
2 tablespoons butter

Soak soy grits in the milk for 20 minutes. Add the dry milk, eggs and seasonings. Mix well. Pour into a buttered piepan and bake in a slow oven (300°) for 1 hour. Melt the butter in a large skillet. Carefully turn out the baked polenta into the skillet without breaking. Fry until brown and crusty; carefully turn and fry until other side is crusty. Cool slightly before serving so bread will be firm. Serve with butter, sour cream, tomato sauce, etc. Makes 1 loaf.

Variations: To the above batter, add 1 small onion, minced fine; or add 1 cup grated sharp Cheddar cheese.

SOY MUFFINS (LOW CARBOHYDRATE)

Prepare batter as for Soy Bread or Soy Bread variations. Pour into greased muffin tins. Bake at 350° for 30 to 40 minutes, or until high and browned. Makes 9 muffins.

"CORN MEAL" MUFFINS (LOW CARBOHYDRATE)

Prepare batter as for "Corn Meal" Bread; pour into muffin pans. Bake at 325° for 30 to 40 minutes. These can be made into blackberry muffins, by adding a few berries to each muffin in the pan before baking. Makes 9 muffins.

OAT MUFFINS (HIGH CARBOHYDRATE)

Prepare batter as for Oatmeal Bread; pour into muffin pans. Bake at 325° for 30 to 40 minutes. Serves 14. If you make 14 large muffins, each muffin=1 unit carbohydrate. For 21 medium muffins, 1½ muffins=1 unit carbohydrate.

OAT BISCUITS (HIGH CARBOHYDRATE)

¼ cup butter or margarine
1 cup oat flour
1 egg
1 cup milk or buttermilk
¼ teaspoon salt
½ teaspoon baking powder

Cut the butter into the oat flour. Add the remaining ingredients and mix. Preheat oven to 425°. Drop the batter by well-rounded table-spoons onto a greased cookie sheet (or for neater biscuits drop into greased muffin pans, ¼ inch thick). Bake 12 to 15 minutes or until lightly browned. Entire recipe=8 units carbohydrates; for ease in measuring, make into 8 large, 12 medium or 16 small biscuits. One unit carbohydrate=1 large, 1½ medium or 2 small biscuits. Serve with butter, sugarless jam.

"JOLLY JOAN" BISCUITS (HIGH CARBOHYDRATE)

1 egg, slightly beaten
½ cup milk
2 tablespoons oil or melted butter
1 cup "Jolly Joan" Oat Mix (*see* Brand Names)

Combine the egg, milk and shortening, and mix well. Add the oat mix, and stir until smooth. Pour the batter into greased muffin tins, ¼ inch to ½ inch thick. Preheat oven to 350°, and bake for 30 minutes or until lightly browned. For ease in measuring carbohydrates, see Oat Biscuits. Entire recipe=8 units carbohydrate. Makes 8 biscuits.

GARLIC BREAD

1 loaf any homemade bread (except sweet breads such as "Corn Meal")
Butter, softened to room temperature
Several cloves of garlic, crushed
Garlic powder

Slice the bread, spread the slices on a cookie sheet, and toast lightly on both sides to warm (do not brown). Remove from the oven. Spread the slices with butter thickly, sprinkle with garlic powder and smear with the crushed garlic. Place the slices back together, forming a loaf again. Preheat the oven to 400°. Wrap the loaf tightly in heavy-duty aluminum foil, sealing the edges. Bake for 10 minutes. For crisper bread, tear away the foil from the top of the loaf and bake an additional 5 to 10 minutes. Makes approximately 14 slices. For carbohydrates, see the recipe used.

GARLIC STICKS

4 slices bread
2 tablespoons oil or melted butter
Salt, garlic powder to taste

Cut slices of homemade bread. Cut each slice into 4 sticks. Set on an aluminum foil-lined cookie sheet. Brush with oil or melted butter and sprinkle lightly with salt and garlic powder. Place in the broiler and toast lightly, turning occasionally. For carbohydrates, see the bread recipe used. Makes 16 sticks.

BREAD STICKS

Same as above, but eliminate the salt and garlic powder.

MELBA TOAST

Slice any homemade bread paper thin with a serrated knife. Place on foil-lined pan and toast in broiler on both sides. Cool before using.

"BAGELS"

Cut thick slices of homemade bread. Cut a hole in the center of each slice. Place slices on foil-lined cookie sheet and toast in the broiler until lightly browned. Serve with the traditional lox and cream cheese, or any other spreads or fillings.

BEST SANDWICH PANCAKES

6 eggs
½ cup finely ground nuts (almonds, filberts, Brazil nuts)
1½ tablespoons oil
2 tablespoons soy flour or oat flour
½ cup milk
½ teaspoon salt

Combine all ingredients in the blender and blend until mixed. Heat a well-oiled skillet until sizzling. Pour in the batter to form a large thick pancake. If the batter is too thick, add a little more milk. Turn when the bottom is browned and bubbles appear all over the top. Remove when both sides are browned (do not burn). Repeat until batter is used up. To use for sandwiches, cut pancakes in quarters. Makes 3 large pancakes; 1 whole pancake=1 unit carbohydrate.

TORTILLAS (LOW CARBOHYDRATE)

1 cup soy grits
4 eggs
¼ teaspoon salt
2½ cups water
Oil as needed

Combine the grits, eggs, salt and water in blender; blend on medium until the grits are rather finely ground. Allow the mixture to stand 15 to 20 minutes until thickened. Heat a lightly oiled griddle or frying pan, lower the heat to medium and pour in enough of the grits mixture to make a flat pancake about 6 inches in diameter. If mixture is too thick, add more water as needed. Tortilla should bake, rather than fry. When able to turn, cook on other side just until tan. Remove, and repeat, adding a little more oil as needed, until entire batch is finished (for easier handling, place each tortilla between wax paper). Makes about 12 tortillas. For recipes using tortillas, see Foreign and Regional.

SOY CHIPS

1 cup soy grits
4 eggs
Dash of onion powder
2 cups water
1 teaspoon salt
Oil or shortening as needed

Combine all ingredients in blender, and blend on low until mixed. Let the mixture stand 15 to 20 minutes; blend again to mix. Heat ½ inch of oil or shortening in a frying pan or deep fat fryer. When the shortening is very hot, spoon the batter into the pan by the level tablespoon. Fry until crisp; remove and drain well on paper towels. Serve hot or cold, with dips. Salt is preferred. Can also be reheated in the oven.

Variations: Add chili powder, garlic powder or onion flakes to the batter. Serves 4 to 6.

SESAME CRACKERS (HIGH CARBOHYDRATE)

1 cup soy flour
½ cup gluten flour (if tolerated)
½ cup oil
½ teaspoon salt
2 tablespoons ice water
¼ cup sesame seeds

Combine the flours and stir in the oil until mixed. Add the remaining ingredients and mix well. Roll or pat between 2 sheets of wax paper until ⅛ inch thick. Cut into squares or rounds. Peel the crackers off the wax paper and place on a baking sheet. Sprinkle with additional salt if desired, or chili powder, onion powder or any other seasoning for variety. Bake in preheated 375° oven for 12 to 15 minutes. Entire recipe=6 units carbohydrate. Serves 6.

BASIC SOY GLUTEN NOODLES

¼ cup gluten flour
1¾ cup soy flour
2 extra large eggs
½ teaspoon salt

Combine the flours in a large bowl, make a well in the middle, and drop in the eggs. Stir gently, working the eggs into the flour with a spoon until the mixture forms a stiff dough. Add the salt, and turn out on a board or wax paper floured with soy flour. Knead the dough well until small pieces no longer drop off and dough is pliable. Flour the dough lightly with soy flour on both sides; place between 2 sheets of wax paper, and roll out thin with a rolling pin. Peel away the top sheet of paper, and cut the noodles into the desired shapes with a sharp knife. Peel the noodles away from the paper using the tip of the knife, and place loosely on a cloth dish towel to dry. These can be cooked immediately or dried for several hours until quite firm. Store in refrigerator until needed. To cook, drop into rapidly boiling salted water until tender (5 to 10 minutes, depending on the thickness). These are quite low in carbohydrates, despite the presence of gluten flour, and because they are so filling can be used in almost any amount, if gluten flour is tolerated. One recipe makes enough noodles for 4 to 6 servings.

Variations:
1. Slice the dough ⅛ inch wide for linguine.
2. Slice the dough ⅛ inch wide, allow to dry a little, then slice each strand in half again for thin spaghetti.
3. For soup noodles, slice ½ inch wide, then cut into 1-inch segments.
4. For macaroni, cut into ½-inch strips, then cut each strip into ½-inch segments. Roll each segment slightly, forming a cone, and pinch at one end. These will resemble shells when finished.

SOY NOODLES

If gluten flour is not allowed by your doctor, substitute an additional ¼ cup of soy flour. Prepare same as for Basic Soy Gluten Noodles; dough can be worked, but must be handled more carefully.

EGG NOODLES (MEDIUM CARBOHYDRATE)

4 eggs
2 tablespoons gluten flour (if tolerated; if not, use oat flour)
4 tablespoons water
¼ teaspoon salt

Beat the eggs slightly; add the remaining ingredients and beat until smooth. Heat a small frying pan, grease lightly and pour in a little batter, just enough to cover the surface of the pan. Cook only until set and golden on both sides. Keep the pancakes covered until all are baked. While still warm, cut into fine strips (one easy way to do this, is to roll the pancakes up tightly, then cut). Shake out on a dish towel and allow to dry. Add to boiling soup just before serving, or serve as a side dish with meat and gravy. Serves 4 to 6.

ORIENTAL SOY NOODLES

1 cup soy flour
1 egg yolk
Water as needed
Pinch of salt

Mix together the flour and egg yolk. Add a few drops of water until the mixture forms a thick pasty dough. Add salt and knead well. Allow to stand 1 hour. Roll out between 2 pieces of wax paper floured with soy flour. Peel away the top sheet of paper and cut into thin strips, about 4 inches long. Drop into sizzling hot fat or peanut oil, and deep-fry for only a few seconds. Remove immediately and drain on paper towels. Serve with chow mein, with dips, or as pretzel sticks. Serves 4.

SPAETZLE (TINY DUMPLINGS)
(MEDIUM CARBOHYDRATE)

¼ teaspoon caraway seeds
¾ cup boiling water
½ cup soy flour
½ cup oat flour
2 large eggs
Dash of salt, pepper
Large pot of vigorously boiling water, chicken stock or chicken soup

Soften the caraway seeds in the boiling water, and set aside. Combine the flours in a bowl and break in the eggs. Add salt and pepper and mix well. Slowly add the water from the caraway seeds, beating, until a thick batter is formed. Boil a large pot of water, stock or soup. Hold a slotted spoon or small colander over the boiling water, and slowly pour the batter through it, so that it runs through the holes into the boiling water. From time to time shake the spoon (or colander) to get rid of the batter clinging to the bottom. When the batter hits the boiling liquid it will form into little dumplings. Stir the liquid gently while cooking. Cook only enough to fill the top of the pot with one layer of dumplings. Remove dumplings when they rise to the surface, and continue until all the batter is used. Do not overcook. If using soup, serve the dumplings immediately with the soup. If cooked in water, drain, toss with melted butter and serve as a side dish or in stews, casseroles, gravies. Entire recipe= 4 units carbohydrate. Serves 4.

KNAIDLACH (DUMPLINGS)

1 thick slice homemade bread
1 extra large egg
Dash of freshly ground nutmeg
Salt, pepper to taste

Place the bread in a 325° oven and bake until dry and lightly browned. Shred the bread into the blender and whirl until blended into fine crumbs. Mix the bread crumbs with the egg and seasoning, and soak until softened. Drop the mixture by rounded tablespoons into rapidly boiling broth, bouillon or chicken soup. Cover, and simmer until the dumplings float on top (about 5 minutes). Serves 4.

ALMOND BALLS (FOR SOUP)

½ cup finely ground almonds
2 eggs, separated
¼ teaspoon salt
1 teaspoon grated lemon rind (fresh)
Pinch of nutmeg
Hot oil or fat

Mix the almonds with the egg yolks, salt and flavorings; beat well. Beat the egg whites until stiff and fold into the almond mixture. Drop by teaspoons into hot fat, deep enough to cover. Drain when the balls have finished frying (they will float on top). Serve in soup, or sprinkle with crushed artificial sweetener and serve as a cookie. Serves 6 to 8.

"PRETZELS"

Prepare dough as for Soy Noodles or Basic Soy Gluten Noodles. Roll out the dough rather thick, and cut into pretzel-sized sticks. Bake in preheated 350° oven until crisp and lightly browned. If salted pretzels are preferred, salt with coarse kosher salt before baking. Serves 4.

BREAKFAST FOODS

Under the unit plan, a good breakfast must provide a unit of fruit and a minimum of two units of protein. In addition, you may have one unit of milk, and one unit of allowed carbohydrate, although some people find this too much to eat and prefer to have the milk and carbohydrate later in the morning. It is also possible to have your unit of fruit on arising, then your protein, milk and carbohydrate for breakfast an hour or so later. In this way you can avoid having too much carbohydrate all at once. Suggestions for breakfast menus which are varied and well-balanced in the amount of carbohydrate allowed are listed under A Month of Breakfast Menus.

In this chapter, we have given recipes for substitutes for many other high-carbohydrate foods you are no longer allowed to eat. Many of these recipes contain bread, oatmeal, wheat germ and various flours. Before using these ingredients, check with your doctor, or try them in small amounts. There are some people who have a bad reaction to these ingredients and should not use them.

In all recipes where flours and other carbohydrates are used, we have given maximum amounts suggested for each portion. Use discretion, especially when combining carbohydrate units and fruit units; if you find the amount is too much for you, cut down, or spread it out to last for a meal and a snack later. Most of the pancake recipes will keep well in the refrigerator, so if you prefer you can make only as many pancakes at a time as you can eat. Keep in mind that if you eat only one pancake, made with one egg, you still need some other form of protein at that meal, such as an egg. Bacon can be used freely for flavor, but it does not contain enough protein to count as part of your protein requirement.

There are many spreads, jams and jellies in the Preserves section which you can use on your pancakes and homemade breads. There are also recipes for pancake syrups in the section entitled Sauces and Dressings. You will also find many ready-made spreads listed in the section on Brand Names. There is also a chapter on eggs.

Oatmeal
Wheat Germ
Soy Grits Cereal
Hot Soy Cereal
Cold Swiss Cereal
Bread Cereal, hot
Bread Cereal, cold
Oat Flakes
Presweetened Flakes
Sunflower Seed Cereal
Pumpkin Seed Cereal
Pignolia Cereal
Nut Meal
Milk Pancakes
Fruity Flapjacks
Bread Pancakes
Soy Pancakes
Soy Waffles
Almond Pancakes
Rich Egg Pancakes
Buttermilk Pancakes
Peanut Butter Pancakes
Apple Pancakes
Soy Grits Pancakes
Swiss Cereal Pancakes
Cottage Cheese Pancakes
Oat Pancakes
Oatmeal Pancakes

Sesame Pancakes
Instant Blintzes
Frizzled Ham
Baked Bacon
Sausage (Bought)
Grits and Sausage
Grits #2 (Fried Oatmeal)
Grilled Cheese (Broiled)
Grilled Cheese (Fried)
Breakfast Burgers
French Toast
Fried Breakfast Cake
Fried Coffee Cake
Instant Cheese Danish
Lazy Danish Pastry
Cinnamon Toast
Eggs, all styles: *see* Eggs
Scrapple: *see* Meats
Homemade Sausage: *see* Meats
Bagels: *see* Breads, Pasta and Noodles
Biscuits: *see* Breads, Pasta and Noodles
Blintzes: *see* Foreign and Regional
Health Drink (breakfast in a glass): *see* Beverages

OATMEAL

Any style of oatmeal can be used, from instant to rolled to old-fashioned-style. Instant oatmeal is the easiest to make, but the longer cooking types are more nutritious and better tasting. Try to prepare enough to give yourself and your family ½ cup cooked oatmeal per serving. Follow the directions on the box carefully, then measure with a ½-cup measure. Add any of the following to the finished cereal: a pat of butter, milk or cream (include in unit of milk for the meal), a dash of vanilla or maple extract, crushed saccharin or liquid artificial sweetener. For ease in cleaning up, simply soak pan and dishes in cold water for ½ hour; oatmeal will float right off. Use leftover oatmeal in dessert recipes, or as thickener in gravies and soups. One half cup cooked oatmeal=1 unit carbohydrate.

WHEAT GERM

For each serving: pour ¼ cup toasted unsweetened wheat germ into a small dessert dish. Add ½ cup milk or cream. Let it sit for 5 minutes to absorb the milk; add more milk as needed, and crushed saccharin or liquid artificial sweetener to taste. One quarter cup wheat germ=1 unit carbohydrate. *Note:* Always remember to keep wheat germ in the refrigerator, as it can easily turn rancid.

SOY GRITS CEREAL

1 cup soy grits
2 cups milk
1 teaspoon butter
Salt to taste

Place the soy grits and milk in a saucepan. Cover, heat slowly until the milk is absorbed and the grits are softened (20 to 30 minutes). For softer grits, add up to ½ cup more milk or hot water and continue cooking 10 minutes longer. Top with butter, salt lightly. Serve with milk or cream, crushed or dissolved saccharin to taste, and fruit if desired. Serves 3.

HOT SOY CEREAL

2 eggs
1 cup soy flour
½ cup milk
Pinch of salt

Dash of vanilla extract
Rapidly boiling water

Beat the eggs slightly, gradually stir in the soy flour, mixing to a paste. Add the milk slowly, mixing until smooth. Stir in the seasonings. Hold a large slotted spoon over a large pan full of rapidly boiling water; slowly pour the batter through it, so that it runs out of the holes into the water. From time to time shake the spoon to get rid of the batter clinging to the bottom. When the batter hits the water it will form little dumplings. Stir gently while cooking. When all the dumplings are cooked they will float on top of the pan. Drain immediately. Place in individual bowls and serve with milk or cream and sweetener to taste. Serves 2.

COLD SWISS CEREAL

¼ cup toasted wheat germ
1 ounce assorted nuts, coarsely chopped
2 tablespoons finely ground filberts
½ small apple, minced fine

Toss all ingredients together; add milk or cream to taste. Add crushed or dissolved saccharin to taste. Serves 1; 1 portion=1 unit carbohydrate, 1 unit fruit.

BREAD CEREAL, HOT

2 slices allowed or homemade bread
½ cup boiling water
1 tablesoon butter
½ teaspoon cinnamon
Dash of salt
Artificial sweetener to taste
½ cup cream or evaporated milk
2 egg yolks, slightly beaten

Crumble the bread into the boiling water. Stir in the butter and flavorings. Stir until smooth. Add the cream and egg yolks, stirring. Cook over low heat, stirring constantly, until thickened. Serve hot, with additional cream or milk, and additional sweetener if needed.

If using homemade bread, see recipe foı units of carbohydrate. If using bought bread such as Thomas' protein bread, 1 slice=1 unit carbohydrate. Serves 2.

BREAD CEREAL, COLD

Homemade bread (1 thick slice per serving—use Soy Bread or Oatmeal Bread ⚹2)
Butter, as needed
Cinnamon
Saccharin to taste, crushed

Slice the bread, and toast on one side under the broiler. Turn, and toast other side. Butter one side and sprinkle with cinnamon and saccharin. Place under the broiler again and toast until the butter is melted (do not burn). Remove and allow to cool. Break or cut into small pieces; place in a bowl. Add milk or cream to taste; serve immediately while still crunchy. For carbohydrates, see the recipe for the bread used.

OAT FLAKES

Prepare recipe for Oatmeal Bread ⚹1. Pour batter into a large flat greased pan or baking sheet, so that batter is about ¼ inch thick. Bake at 350° for 35 minutes or until brown. Remove from the oven, allow to cool, then break into small flake-sized pieces or crumble in blender. Store in an airtight container after cooling. To serve, pour into a bowl, add milk and liquid artificial sweetener to taste. Eat immediately. Makes 4 cups; ⅓ cup=1 unit carbohydrate.

PRESWEETENED FLAKES

Prepare any cookie recipe. Bake according to the recipe, then break into small pieces. Serve in a bowl with milk. For carbohydrates, see the individual cookie recipe. Those recipes best suited are: Peanut Butter Cookies, Oatmeal Wheat-germ Cookies, Soy Grits Cookies and Sesame Seed Cookies.

SUNFLOWER SEED CEREAL

For each serving, pour 2 ounces toasted unsalted sunflower seeds into a bowl; add milk or cream and sweetener to taste.

PUMPKIN SEED CEREAL

1 tablespoon butter or oil
1 cup shelled pumpkin seeds
Pinch of salt

Melt the butter in a frying pan. Stir in the pumpkin seeds and cover the pan. Heat over a medium heat, stirring occasionally, until most of the seeds have "popped." Salt slightly to taste. Serve with milk or cream, and artificial sweetener if preferred. Serves 2. Each serving =1 unit limited protein.

PIGNOLIA CEREAL

Pignolia nuts make an excellent dish for breakfast. Just pour 2 ounces of the nuts into a bowl, add milk or cream and crushed or dissolved saccharin to taste. The nuts resemble puffed rice, are high in fat, but lower in carbohydrates than many other nuts. If they are too rich for your taste by themselves, try a few sprinkled on other cereals for extra protein and a different taste. One serving=1 unit limited protein.

NUT MEAL

Take 2 ounces of any allowed nuts, especially those lowest in carbohydrates, such as Brazil nuts, filberts, pecans or walnuts; crack or chop coarsely. Add milk or cream and sweetener to taste, and eat as cereal. For an interesting flavor, blend the nuts in the blender to the consistency of wheat germ, then mix half and half with toasted wheat germ. Two ounces=approximately 1 unit carbohydrate.

MILK PANCAKES

½ cup milk
⅔ cup non-fat dry milk
4 eggs
½ teaspoon vanilla extract
Dash of salt
Dash of liquid artificial sweetener
1 or 2 teaspoons butter

Add the milk to the dry milk, mix well by hand or in the blender. Beat the eggs and add to the milk, mix until smooth. Add the remaining ingredients except butter and mix well. Melt butter in a frying pan. Pour in one third of the batter. Lower heat and cook until the top is covered with bubbles and rather dry. Turn; cook briefly until brown. Turn and repeat. Butter well and serve hot with sugarless jelly and sausage, ham or bacon. Makes 3 large pancakes; 1 pancake=slightly less than 1 unit milk, and 1 unit protein; or make 4 medium pancakes—2 pancakes=a complete breakfast.

FRUITY FLAPJACKS

1 tablespoon baking powder
1 cup soy flour
¼ teaspoon salt
¼ teaspoon mace
1 cup milk
¼ cup sour cream
1 extra large or jumbo egg
1 cup berries or 1 large apple, finely chopped
2 tablespoons oil
Additional oil as needed

Sift together the dry ingredients and set aside. Beat the liquids and egg together and add gradually to the dry ingredients; mix well. Fold in the fruit. Heat an oiled skillet. Drop with a large spoon on the hot skillet and cook until bubbles form and the edges appear dry. Turn and brown briefly on the other side. Serves 3 or 4.

BREAD PANCAKES

2 slices Thomas' Rite-Diet bread if tolerated (or else 2 slices
  homemade bread)
¾ cup milk
4 eggs
½ cup sesame seed meal
1 teaspoon baking powder
½ teaspoon vanilla extract
1 tablespoon oil
⅓ cup non-fat dry milk
¼ teaspoon salt

Place the bread in the blender, 1 slice at a time. Chop into bread
crumbs. Add the milk and eggs and blend on mix. Change to stir
or low, and blend in the remaining ingredients. Heat an oiled
skillet; pour in half the batter; heat until bubbles appear on the surface; turn, cook until brown. Makes 2 large (12-inch) pancakes;
1 pancake=2 units protein, 1 unit carbohydrate, just under 1 unit
milk.

SOY PANCAKES

1 cup soy flour
½ cup milk, plus more as needed
½ teaspoon vanilla extract
8 eggs
½ teaspoon salt
½ cup wheat germ (optional)
2 ¼-grain tablets saccharin
1 tablespoon oil

Combine all ingredients and mix well. Heat an oiled skillet, pour
in half of the batter to make a large pancake. If the batter is too
thick add more milk as needed. Heat until bubbles appear on the
surface; turn, heat on other side until brown. Repeat until all the
batter is used up. Makes 4 large pancakes; 1 pancake=2 units protein, ½ unit carbohydrate if wheat germ is used.

SOY WAFFLES

1 recipe Soy Pancakes (*see* above)
1 teaspoon baking powder
2 tablespoons oil

Prepare pancake batter, adding the baking powder and extra oil. Mix well. To bake, follow the directions for your waffle iron. For best results, use a Teflon-lined waffle iron. Top with butter, syrup (*see* Sauces and Dressings) or fresh fruit. Makes 4 large waffles.

ALMOND PANCAKES

½ cup almonds
6 eggs
⅔ cup non-fat dry milk
Dash of salt
½ cup soy flour
2 cups water
½ teaspoon almond extract
1 tablespoon oil

Place the almonds in the blender; blend on grate until finely ground. Mix together all ingredients. Heat an oiled skillet, pour in enough batter to make a thin pancake, tilting the pan to allow batter to run off at the sides. Bake until bubbles form, turn and brown on other side. Repeat until batter is used up. Makes about 6 to 8 thin pancakes. If 6 are made, each pancake=1 unit protein, ⅓ unit milk, a trace of carbohydrate.

RICH EGG PANCAKES

1 sliced allowed or homemade bread, toasted
2 eggs plus 1 egg yolk
Dash of salt
Dash of vanilla extract
1 tablespoon butter

Allow the toast to cool, then whirl in the blender until it turns to crumbs. Beat the eggs and egg yolk together, add the crumbs and rest of the ingredients. Heat the butter in a medium-sized pan until bubbly. Pour in the batter, lower the heat to medium, cook until brown and top is beginning to set. Turn and brown on other side. Dust with crushed saccharin or top with fruit or sugarless jelly. Makes 1 large pancake which=2 units protein, about 1 unit carbohydrate, depending on the bread used.

BUTTERMILK PANCAKES

6 extra large eggs
½ cup non-fat dry milk
½ cup wheat germ
1 cup buttermilk
1 teaspoon salt
2 tablespoons soy flour
½ cup sunflower seed meal or pumpkin seed meal
1 teaspoon vanilla extract
1 tablespoon oil plus more as needed

Beat eggs, blend in other ingredients until smooth. Heat 1 tablespoon oil or margarine in skillet; pour in one third of the batter. If thinner pancakes are wanted, add a little water. Turn when the bottom is brown and bubbles appear on the surface, remove when other side is browned. Repeat; makes 3 large pancakes or 6 small thin pancakes. One large or 2 small pancakes=about 1 unit carbohydrate, 2 units protein.

PEANUT BUTTER PANCAKES

6 eggs
½ cup wheat germ
¼ cup milk
½ teaspoon vanilla extract
4 tablespoons allowed peanut butter
½ cup non-fat dry milk
Dash of salt
Dash of liquid artificial sweetener

Combine all ingredients in blender; blend until smooth. Prepare as for other pancakes. Serve with butter or a scoop of peanut butter. Serves 3; each portion=2 units protein, not quite 1 unit carbohydrate.

APPLE PANCAKES

Same as Soy Pancakes, plus 1 cup blender-chopped apples, and 1 tablespoon cinnamon. Prepare as in Soy Pancake recipe. Makes 4 pancakes; 1 pancake=2 units protein, ½ unit carbohydrate, ½ unit fruit.

SOY GRITS PANCAKES

Same as Soy Pancakes, but use soy grits instead of soy flour, plus ½ teaspoon cinnamon. Prepare the batter, allow it to sit for 20 minutes after blending. Add more water if needed. For chewy consistency, blend very briefly on lowest setting, for smoother consistency, blend well on medium until smooth but grainy. Cook as for Soy Pancakes. If no wheat germ is used, these may be eaten in any amount.

SWISS CEREAL PANCAKES

See the recipe for Cold Swiss Cereal. Combine all ingredients with 6 eggs and 1 cup milk; blend very briefly on low until consistency of pancake batter, adding more milk as needed. See cereal recipe for carbohydrates. Cook as for other pancakes.

COTTAGE CHEESE PANCAKES

1 cup cottage cheese
Dash of salt
½ teaspoon cinnamon
4 eggs
2 ½-grain tablets saccharin

2 tablespoons oat flour
1 tablespoon oil

Combine all ingredients except oil in the blender. Blend until smooth, adding water or milk as needed for thin pancakes; leave as is for thick pancakes. Pour into hot oiled skillet, and cook as for other pancakes. Makes 2 large or 4 small pancakes; 1 large or 2 small pancakes=3 units protein, a trace of carbohydrate.

OAT PANCAKES

Same as Soy Pancakes, but use oat flour in place of soy flour. Omit wheat germ. Allow the batter to stand 5 minutes to thicken, then add more water as needed to achieve the right consistency. Makes 8 small pancakes; each pancake=1 unit protein, 1 unit carbohydrate.

OATMEAL PANCAKES

1 cup instant-style oatmeal
1 cup boiling water
2 tablespoons butter
6 eggs
1 cup non-fat dry milk
Dash of salt (omit if using salted butter)

Combine the oatmeal and boiling water in a bowl, stir to mix. Add the butter, mix until it melts. Beat together the eggs, dry milk and salt, and mix with rest of the ingredients. Cook as for other pancakes, adding a little milk if needed for thinner pancakes. Serves 4; each serving=1 unit carbohydrate, slightly less than 1 unit milk.

SESAME PANCAKES

6 eggs
1 cup milk
½ cup sesame seeds (or pumpkin seeds or sunflower seeds, shelled)
Dash of salt
1 tablespoon oil
½ cup soy flour
½ cup non-fat dry milk

Mix together all ingredients, then blend very briefly in the blender (seeds should not be liquefied). Cook as for other pancakes. Serves 3; each serving contains a trace of carbohydrate.

INSTANT BLINTZES

1 pancake recipe
2 cups cottage cheese
¼ cup butter
Cinnamon, sweetener as needed

Make any of the pancake recipes; make into small (6-inch) thin pancakes; brown on one side only, lowering the heat and cooking until the top is fairly dry and bottom is lightly browned; do not turn. Remove to a plate. Place ¼-cup cottage cheese along the center of each pancake; fold the left side toward the middle, then fold the right side to the middle until the edges of the pancake are overlapping. Carefully turn the blintz over, repeat until all the batter is used up. When all are completed, heat a large frying pan and melt ¼ cup butter until sizzling. Transfer the rolled blintzes to the pan, and fry until brown on both sides, turning carefully once. Sprinkle with liquid or powdered sweetener and cinnamon, and serve at once.

Variation: For even quicker blintzes, make the pancakes by frying them in butter on both sides, remove and fill; roll or fold, and serve without refrying. For carbohydrates, see the pancake recipe used. Serves 4 to 8.

FRIZZLED HAM

1 tablespoon butter or margarine
½ pound sliced boiled ham (not sugar-cured)
½ cup orange juice
Dash of ground cloves

Melt the butter in a skillet, tear the ham into pieces the size of a strip of bacon and add to the skillet. Stir and fry until the ham curls. Add juice and cloves. Cover and simmer on low for 5 minutes. Remove the cover and heat until the ham is browned. This is best made in a Teflon-lined pan, as the juice will burn as it evaporates. Top with poached or fried eggs, or serve with pancakes. Serves 2. This is a good high-protein substitute for bacon.

BAKED BACON

Use 1 pound thick sliced bacon. Be sure it is not sugar-cured. Place on a broiler rack over a pan, separating the slices. Place in pre-heated 400° oven; bake until slightly brown; turn the slices and continue baking until lightly browned. Remove to paper towels and drain. Although still limp when removed from the oven, the bacon will become crisp as it drains. This method is easy, gives you more bacon for your money, as there is less shrinkage, and it enables you to prepare your bacon without having to watch it. Usual time for baking is 20 to 30 minutes. For crisper bacon, turn again, and bake until crisp. Serves 4 to 6.

SAUSAGE (BOUGHT)

Use Jones sausage or any other brand you can find without sugar (there are very few). To get the most protein from the meat, cook at very low temperature, turning often. If package directions call for adding water and steaming, be sure that the temperature is low and that you add as little water as possible. Long slow cooking will give you the least amount of shrinkage and the least loss of protein. When sausage is finished, remove from pan and use the pan juices as gravy or for frying eggs.

GRITS AND SAUSAGE

½ cup soy grits
¾ cup beef stock or allowed beef bouillon, cold
8 ounces Jones sausage links
1 medium onion, diced
¼ teaspoon paprika

Combine the grits and bouillon and soak 30 minutes. Cut the sausage links into quarters; fry the sausage over medium heat until browned. Add the onion and sauté until the onion is translucent. Drain off most of the fat. Add the soy grits and bouillon. Stir until mixed, lower the heat and cover. Cook for about 15 minutes and uncover. Add paprika. Stir and fry until the grits are softened and the sausage is crisply browned.

GRITS #2 (FRIED OATMEAL)

2 tablespoons bacon drippings or butter
1 cup old-fashioned-style oatmeal (uncooked)
¼ cup water
Dash of salt

Heat the fat and stir in the oats. Stir and fry until the oats are slightly browned. Add the water and salt, cover and simmer until the water is absorbed and the oats are softened. Add more water to taste if necessary. Serve as a side dish with eggs or breakfast meat. Serves 4; each serving=1 unit carbohydrate.

GRILLED CHEESE (BROILED)

1 slice of allowed or homemade bread
3 ounces Cheddar cheese

Toast the bread lightly in the toaster, or under the broiler until light brown. Remove and place on a sheet of aluminum foil.

Shred or thinly slice the cheese and pile on the toast. Heat the broiler and place the open-face sandwich 4 to 6 inches from the heat. Broil to taste, either until the cheese is just melted or, if preferred, until the top is puffy and browned. *Note:* Excessive heat destroys much of the protein and vitamin content in cheese; for best result, cook less time and farther from the heat. Serves 1; each serving=2 units protein, 1 unit carbohydrate if using high-carbohydrate bread; if using soy bread, count as a trace of carbohydrate.

GRILLED CHEESE (FRIED)

1 slice Thomas' Protein Bread or 2 thin slices of any homemade
  bread
2 slices processed American cheese (2 ounces)
1 tablespoon butter

Toast the bread, remove from the oven or broiler; if using bought bread, split carefully through the center with a serrated knife, making 2 thin slices. Place the cheese between the 2 slices, toasted side out. Trim away the excess cheese, and pile it inside the sandwich. Melt the butter in a frying pan, and fry the sandwich on one side until the cheese begins to melt. Turn and brown on the other side. Serves 1; 1 sandwich=2 units protein, 1 unit carbohydrate if using bought bread; for homemade bread, see recipe used.

BREAKFAST BURGERS

1 cup quick-cooking oat cereal
1½ cups boiling salted water
½ cup toasted wheat germ
1 cup non-fat dry milk
½ teaspoon vanilla extract
½ teaspoon liquid artificial sweetener
2 eggs, slightly beaten
Oil as needed

Cook the oatmeal in the boiling water for 1 minute. Combine all ingredients except oil, adding the eggs last. Mix well. Heat ¼ inch of oil in a heavy frying pan. Spoon the batter into the hot oil in the shape of large patties. Turn when the bottoms are brown and crusty. Fry on the other side until firm and brown. Serve with bacon, or top with sugarless jelly or poached eggs. (Patties can also be used cold as a sandwich roll.) Makes about 6 patties. This is to be used as a carbohydrate, not as a protein unit. Two burgers=1 unit carbohydrate, 1 unit milk.

FRENCH TOAST

1 extra large egg
¼ cup milk
Dash of salt
2 slices allowed or homemade bread
Butter as needed

Beat the egg and milk together, and add salt. Place the bread in the egg mixture to soak, turning carefully several times, and adding more milk if needed, until both slices of bread are saturated on both sides. Heat a frying pan and melt 1 tablespoon of butter; when butter is bubbly, place the bread in the pan and fry on one side until the bottom is golden brown; turn and repeat for other side, adding more butter if needed. Serve with any sugarless or homemade jam or syrup. Serves 2; 1 piece=1 unit carbohydrate (or see bread recipe used).

FRIED BREAKFAST CAKE

2 tablespoons butter
1 cup cooked or leftover cooked oatmeal
3 eggs
1 cup non-fat dry milk
½ teaspoon vanilla extract
¼ teaspoon salt
½ teaspoon cinnamon
¼ teaspoon liquid artificial sweetener

Melt the butter in a frying pan; lower the heat to medium and continue to heat until the butter is brown. Combine all other ingredients in a bowl and mix well. Pour into the pan, patting down until evenly distributed in one large thick pancake. Fry until the edges are set. Cover pan, lower heat and cook until firm enough to turn. Cook on other side until light brown. Turn out on a platter, cut into wedges and serve with butter, cream cheese, whipped cream, etc. Cut into 8 pieces; 2 pieces=½ unit carbohydrate, about ½ unit milk.

FRIED COFFEE CAKE

1 cup oat flour
4 eggs
½ cup milk
½ cup sesame seeds
¼ teaspoon salt
1 teaspoon vanilla extract
½ cup non-fat dry milk
1 teaspoon baking powder
1 cup berries or diced fruit
2 tablespoons oil

Combine all ingredients except the fruit and oil. Mix well. Heat a large frying pan and pour in enough oil to coat the pan well. When the oil is hot, pour in the batter. Cover the pan, lower heat and cook until the top is beginning to set. Add the fruit and pat with a spoon until fruit sinks below the surface. Continue cooking until firm. Turn out on serving plate and serve as is, or split and butter like a muffin. Slice into 8 portions; each portion=1 unit carbohydrate, a trace of fruit.

INSTANT CHEESE DANISH

2 ounces cream cheese
1 slice Thomas' Protein Bread if tolerated (or 1 slice homemade bread)
1 tablespoon homemade jelly
Liquid or sprinkle-type sweetener to taste

Spread the cream cheese on the bread. Spoon the jelly into the center of the bread, and fold the bread in half diagonally, forming a triangular filled pastry. Secure the corners with toothpicks. Sprinkle the top with sweetener, toast under the broiler at least 6 to 8 inches from the heat. Serves 1; 1 Danish=1 unit carbohydrate (for homemade bread, see recipe).

LAZY DANISH PASTRY

1 slice homemade bread
½ teaspoon butter
¼ cup farmer cheese
1 ¼-grain tablet saccharin, dissolved in a few drops hot water
¼ teaspoon cinnamon

Toast the bread lightly on both sides in a toaster or broiler. Spread with the butter on one side, then spread thickly with the farmer cheese (for easier spreading, have the cheese at room temperature). Sprinkle with the sweetener, then with the cinnamon. Serves 1. For carbohydrates, see the bread recipe used.

CINNAMON TOAST

For each serving, toast 1 slice of allowed or homemade bread in the toaster or broiler. Spread thickly on one side with butter, using about 1 teaspoon for each slice of bread. Sprinkle with crushed saccharin and cinnamon. Place on aluminum foil-lined baking sheet under the broiler until the top turns brown and bubbly. Each slice=1 unit carbohydrate (or see bread recipe for exact units).

CANDIES

We have mixed feelings in giving these candy recipes, having stressed over and over the necessity for breaking old patterns of behavior. Eating candy is certainly part of those old patterns for many people.

Yet there are occasions which can occur when you will feel the need to have a sugarless candy recipe. Certain holidays are associated in our minds with sweets, and even though we would prefer to break these associations, we'll concede that we like to have a candy or two at Halloween or Easter time. Therefore, we have developed these recipes, *not* so that we can eat candy all the time, but to keep ourselves from being tempted to eat "real" candy on these few occasions when temptation strikes (we find those so-called "dietetic" candies hard to pass by at times, and they are almost as bad for you as candy made with sugar). Even though our recipes are low in carbohydrate, if you eat them often you are not breaking the candy habit. Limit all candies to a few pieces at a time because the high concentration of sweetener can sometimes cause a craving for sugar.

Marzipan (Almond Paste Candy)
Brazil Nut Surprises
Peanut Butter Sesame Bars
Sesame Seed Chews
Coconut-peanut Chews
Seven-sweets Confection
Peanut Butter Fudge
Walnut Fudge
Marzipan Fudge
Coconut Cream Cheese Gooies

Toasted Coconut Balls
Cream Cheese Fruit Balls
Cream Cheese Orange Balls
Cream Cheese Lemon Balls
Jelly Candies
Turkish Paste
Candied Pineapple Sticks
"White Raisins"
"Black Raisins"
Frozen Cauliflower Candies

MARZIPAN (ALMOND PASTE CANDY)

4 ounces blanched almonds, slivered or whole
½ cup unsweetened coconut meal, finely ground
⅓ cup non-fat dry milk
¼ cup evaporated milk
Pinch of salt
1½ teaspoons extract or flavoring or to taste (almond, rum, coconut, vanilla, maple, etc.)
2 tablespoons liquid artificial sweetener or crushed saccharin tablets to taste

Place the almonds, a few at a time, in the blender and blend to a fine flour (makes about 1 cup). Mix with the coconut meal and dry milk. Slowly add the evaporated milk, mashing and turning, until well mixed. Add the salt, extract or flavoring and artificial sweetener; correct the flavor to taste. Add a few drops of food coloring if desired, or divide into several parts and color each part differently. Knead until smooth and even in color. Allow to stand for 1 hour to dry slightly. Form the candy into shapes with your fingers; allow to dry overnight on a paper towel. Wrap loosely; keeps well. Contain some carbohydrates and milk; eat 1 or 2 pieces at a time. Makes 32 pieces.

Variations:
1. Make as above, omitting the coconut meal for smoother candies; form into balls.
2. Valentine's Day: color red, use almond extract; roll into ½-inch balls, then form into hearts.
3. St. Patrick's Day: color green, use peppermint extract with a little vanilla to taste; form into tiny shamrocks.
4. Halloween: color orange (yellow and red), use maple extract; form into pumpkins.
5. Christmas: color ¼ red, use rum extract; form into candy canes. Also color green, use coconut extract; form into trees.
6. Easter: leave uncolored, use vanilla extract; form into eggs. Paint designs on with food coloring and a small brush.

BRAZIL NUT SURPRISES

Shelled Brazil nuts
Sugarless peanut butter as needed
Finely ground nuts

Roll the Brazil nuts in the peanut butter until thickly coated, then roll lightly in the ground nuts. Chill until firm or place in the freezer until firm, but not long enough to freeze solid. Approximately 4=1 unit nuts for protein snack.

PEANUT BUTTER SESAME BARS

½ cup salted peanuts
1 cup sugarless peanut butter
1 tablespoon oil
1 cup non-fat dry milk
1 tablespoon liquid artificial sweetener or crushed saccharin to taste
½ cup sesame seeds

Rub the peanuts between two paper towels to remove some of the excess salt; chop coarsely with a food chopper. Combine all ingredients and mix well. Press into a square pan and chill. Cut into bars or squares, wrap in foil and freeze. These taste best if eaten while still frozen or partially frozen. If allowed to thaw, simply refreeze. Entire recipe=3 units milk. Limit to 1 or 2 2-inch squares at a time. Makes approximately 16 2-inch bars.

SESAME SEED CHEWS

½ cup sugarless peanut butter
2 tablespoons non-fat dry milk
½ cup sesame seeds
1 teaspoon liquid artificial sweetener or crushed saccharin to taste
1 tablespoon heavy cream or evaporated milk

Combine all ingredients; add a pinch of salt if needed. Mix well; roll into ½-inch balls. Roll the balls in a little extra sesame seeds. Freeze until firm. Makes 24 ½-inch balls.

COCONUT-PEANUT CHEWS

4 tablespoons allowed peanut butter
2 ounces non-fat dry milk
1 teaspoon milk
4 ounces chopped nuts
¼ teaspoon liquid artificial sweetener
Coconut meal as needed

Combine all ingredients except the coconut meal. Mix well with a fork; form into ½-inch balls. Roll in coconut meal. Chill or freeze until firm. Limit to 1 or 2. Makes 24 ½-inch balls.

SEVEN-SWEETS CONFECTION

1 tablespoon dehydrated orange peel
¼ apple, chopped fine
¼ cup sesame seeds
¼ cup unsweetened coconut meal
½ cup allowed peanut butter
¼ cup sunflower seeds
½ cup salted peanuts
Liquid or crushed sweetener to taste

Combine all ingredients and mix well with a fork. Roll into ½-inch balls, then flatten slightly with fork. Freeze or chill; limit to 1 or 2 at a time. Makes 48 ½-inch balls.

PEANUT BUTTER FUDGE

1 cup allowed peanut butter
1 cup non-fat dry milk
¼ teaspoon salt (omit if peanut butter is salty)
1 teaspoon vanilla extract
¼ teaspoon maple flavoring
1 teaspoon liquid artificial sweetener
Cream or evaporated milk as needed
¼ cup walnut meats, coarsely broken

Combine the peanut butter, dry milk and flavorings; mash well. Add the cream a little bit at a time until the mixture is stiff but pliable. Turn out on wax paper. Knead until well mixed; add the walnuts and knead until evenly distributed. Press with a rolling pin between two sheets of wax paper until ¼ to ½ inch thick. Remove the top sheet and allow to dry. Cut into squares, wrap in foil and freeze. High in milk and carbohydrate, limit to 2 or 3. Makes approximately 128 1-inch squares.

WALNUT FUDGE

2 cups walnut meats
1 cup non-fat dry milk
Dash of salt
1 tablespoon oil
Cream or evaporated milk as needed
1 tablespoon liquid artificial sweetener
1 teaspoon vanilla extract

Chop half of the walnuts coarsely and set aside. Place the rest of the walnuts in the blender and grind to a fine flour. Place the walnut flour, dry milk and salt in a bowl. Gradually add the oil and cream, and mash with a spoon until mixed and stiff. Add the sweetener and vanilla, knead, then knead in the chopped nuts. Continue as for Peanut Butter Fudge. Makes approximately 128 1-inch squares.

MARZIPAN FUDGE

4 ounces blanched almonds, slivered or whole
¼ cup cream or evaporated milk
1 tablespoon liquid artificial sweetener
Dash of salt
1 teaspoon melted butter
½ cup unsweetened coconut meal
½ cup non-fat dry milk
½ teaspoon vanilla extract
2 tablespoons unsweetened cocoa
1 cup chopped walnuts

Place the almonds a few at a time into the blender, and grind to a fine flour. Mix with the rest of the ingredients. If too thick, add a bit more cream. If too thin, add more coconut. Spread in a small pan about ½ inch thick. Allow to dry before eating (can also be frozen). Limit to 1 or 2. Makes approximately 128 1-inch squares.

COCONUT CREAM CHEESE GOOIES

1 8-ounce package cream cheese
1 teaspoon grated orange rind
1 tablespoon lemon juice
1 teaspoon liquid artificial sweetener
¼ cup chopped pecans
½ cup shredded coconut or coconut meal

Mash the cheese with fork until fluffy. Add all ingredients except the coconut and mix well. Form into balls and roll in coconut. Refrigerate. One ball=a trace of carbohydrate. Limit to 2 or 3 at a time. Makes 42 ½-inch balls.

TOASTED COCONUT BALLS

1 8-ounce package cream cheese
1 teaspoon coconut extract

1 teaspoon liquid artificial sweetener
¼ cup coconut meal
½ cup shredded unsweetened coconut, toasted lightly in the oven

Prepare as for Coconut Cream Cheese Gooies. Makes 42 ½-inch balls.

CREAM CHEESE FRUIT BALLS

1 3-ounce package cream cheese
1 teaspoon liquid artificial sweetener
½ teaspoon vanilla extract
½ cup finely chopped fruit (apple, pineapple, etc.)
1 or 2 drops red or yellow food coloring (optional)
Finely ground nuts or coconut meal

Combine all ingredients except the nuts or coconut. Mix well with fork. Form into balls, roll in the nuts or coconut. Limit to 1 or 2. Each ball contains a trace of fruit. Makes 24 ½-inch balls.

CREAM CHEESE ORANGE BALLS

1 3-ounce package cream cheese
¼ cup orange juice
¼ cup non-fat dry milk
¼ teaspoon dehydrated orange peel
¼ teaspoon orange extract
Crushed saccharin to taste

Mash the cream cheese and juice together until fluffy. Gradually add the dry milk, then the remaining ingredients. Chill until firm, then roll into balls. Chill again or freeze. Makes 20 ½-inch balls.

CREAM CHEESE LEMON BALLS

Same as Cream Cheese Orange Balls, but use lemon extract, lemon peel and 2 tablespoons lemon juice. Makes 20 ½-inch balls.

JELLY CANDIES

4 ounces apple juice
5 tablespoons unflavored gelatin
16 ounces diet soda (fruit flavors)
½ teaspoon vanilla extract
1 or 2 drops food coloring
10 to 15 ¼-grain tablets saccharin

Pour the juice into a bowl, and sprinkle in the gelatin to soften; set aside. In a saucepan, heat the soda until boiling. Pour the soda over the gelatin mixture, stirring. Add the remaining ingredients, and stir until the gelatin and saccharin are dissolved. Pour into two 8-inch square cake pans. Chill. When firm, cut into cubes, or cut into fancy shapes using cookie cutters or canapé cutters. Makes approximately 32 cubes.

TURKISH PASTE

½ cup orange juice
2 tablespoons lemon juice
½ cup non-fat dry milk
¼ cup light cream or evaporated milk
¾ cup water
5 tablespoons unflavored gelatin
10 to 12 ¼-grain tablets saccharin
½ cup walnuts, coarsely broken
1 or 2 drops red food coloring
Pinch of salt
½ teaspoon orange extract

Combine the orange juice, lemon juice, dry milk and cream. Mix to a paste; set aside. Pour the water into a saucepan, and sprinkle in the gelatin to soften. Heat, stirring, until the water is boiling and gelatin is dissolved. Add the saccharin and stir until dissolved. Pour over the orange juice mixture, stirring until smooth. Add the remaining ingredients; mix and pour into two 8-inch square cake pans. Allow to cool, then chill until thick and syrupy. Stir to distribute the nuts evenly, then chill until firm. Slice or cut into cubes. Each piece contains a trace of milk and a trace of fruit. Limit to 2 or 3 pieces. Make sure the walnuts are fresh, or the candy will have an "off" taste. (Use canned walnuts to be sure.) Makes approximately 30 1-inch cubes.

CANDIED PINEAPPLE STICKS

1 small ripe pineapple (test for ripeness by smelling; ripe fruit has a sweet smell)
2 tablespoons butter
4 ¼-grain tablets saccharin

Cut the outer peel from the pineapple. Slice ½ inch thick crosswise. Cut each slice into strips ½ inch wide. In a large frying pan, melt butter. Heat until the butter is frothy. Add the saccharin and stir until dissolved. Add the pineapple sticks and stir to coat evenly. Brown the pineapple, stirring to prevent burning. Remove from the heat and chill before serving. These can also be frozen and served frozen or partially thawed. Serve with toothpicks or forks. One slice of pineapple (about 6 sticks)=1 unit fruit. Makes approximately 20 sticks.

"WHITE RAISINS"

Peel and core 1 apple; slice ¼ inch thick. Dice into ¼-inch cubes. Spread on a cookie sheet and dry slowly in the oven on "warm" several hours, or until pieces are dry and chewy. Do not dry in the sun, as this causes a chemical change resulting in more sugar in the fruit. One apple=2 units fruit. Use as is, in recipes, or mixed with shelled nuts such as almonds.

"BLACK RAISINS"

Same as "White Raisins," but use 2 small purple plums.

FROZEN CAULIFLOWER CANDIES

1 package frozen or ½ head fresh cauliflower
1 cup water
1 teaspoon vanilla extract
¼ teaspoon imitation butter flavoring
10 ¼-grain tablets saccharin or to taste
½ cup non-fat dry milk
½ teaspoon cinnamon
1 teaspoon butter

Cook the cauliflower on a rack over the water until tender (do not salt water). Drain, saving the liquid for soups, etc. Mash the cauliflower; add the remaining ingredients and mash well together. Drop by heaping tablespoons onto aluminum foil-lined pan. Flatten slightly with a fork. Freeze until hard, and serve frozen (thaw 1 minute before eating). Each candy contains a trace of milk; limit to 2 or 3. Makes approximately 24 candies.

CASSEROLES

A casserole is any dish that contains all the elements needed for a complete meal (meat or cheese, vegetables, etc.). It usually can be prepared well before mealtime and then allowed to cook or bake by itself until needed. We think they're lifesavers.

All of the casseroles given here are fairly easy to prepare and can be cooked for longer times than indicated in the recipes simply by lowering the oven temperature. Casseroles are fine for using up odds and ends of vegetables, as well as leftover meat and bits and ends of cheese that have lost their appeal.

You will find other casserole dishes given throughout the book in chapters where they are more appropriate, such as Foreign and Regional, Cheese, and Eggs.

Deviled Sea Casserole

Hot Crab Salad

Tuna Casserole

Tuna Parmigiana

Salmon and Green Vegetable
    Casserole

Oriental Shrimp and Chicken

Polynesian Chicken

Chicken-stuffed Peppers

Turkey Hash

Beef-chicken Fricassee

Beef-stuffed Peppers

Eggplant Casserole

Stuffed Cabbage

"Spaghetti" and Meat Balls

Beef Stew

Hamburger Stew

Roast Beef Hash

Veal Hash

Veal and Peppers

Lamb and Eggplant Casserole

Frankfurter-cabbage Stew

Franks and Sauerkraut

Franks and Beans

Pork and Bean Bake

Chili con Carne

Ham and Bean Casserole

Ham Parisienne

Baked Ham and Asparagus
   Roll-ups
Ham and Cheese Casserole
Cheese-stuffed Peppers
Wax Bean Lasagna

Wax Bean Loaf
Mushroom Loaf
Onion Loaf
Onion Pie
Cauliflower Pie

DEVILED SEA CASSEROLE

½ pound scallops
½ pound shrimp, cleaned and deveined
3 scallions, chopped
3 ribs celery, sliced thin
4 tablespoons butter
1 teaspoon dry mustard
Dash of freshly ground pepper
¼ teaspoon garlic powder
½ teaspoon salt
½ cup cream
1 6½-ounce can crab meat, drained
1 slice homemade bread, crumbed coarsely

Cook the scallops and shrimp in boiling water to cover for 1 minute. Set aside 6 or 8 shrimp. Coarsely chop the remaining shrimp and scallops. Sauté the scallions and celery in 2 tablespoons of the butter until tender. Stir in the seasonings and cream. Combine with the chopped seafood and canned flaked crab meat, and place in a 1½-quart baking dish. Sprinkle with the bread crumbs. Melt the remaining 2 tablespoons butter and drizzle on top. Top with the shrimp in a decorative pattern. Bake at 350° for 30 to 45 minutes, or until brown and bubbly. If using high-carbohydrate bread, each serving=a trace of carbohydrate. Serves 4.

HOT CRAB SALAD

2 6½-ounce cans crab meat, drained
2 scallions, chopped
¼ teaspoon celery seed
½ teaspoon salt
¾ cup allowed or homemade Mayonnaise
4 hard-cooked eggs, chopped
2 ribs celery, chopped
1 tablespoon lemon juice
¼ teaspoon pepper
¼ pound bulk Parmesan cheese, freshly grated

Combine all the ingredients except cheese, and mix. Place in a well-greased casserole or divide into individual ovenproof bowls. Sprinkle evenly with cheese and bake in a preheated 350° oven for 30 minutes (or less if using individual bowls). If browner topping is desired, place under broiler for a few minutes until the cheese is brown and bubbly. Serves 4 to 6.

TUNA CASSEROLE

½ envelope Knorr-Swiss onion soup and dip mix (*see* Brand Names)
1 13-ounce can tuna, slightly drained
1 package frozen peas and carrots
⅓ cup non-fat dry milk
½ pint sour cream
1 large can French-style string beans
2 cups milk

Shake the envelope of soup mix vigorously before dividing in half. Combine all ingredients, including the liquid from the canned beans. Pour into a large casserole. Cover, and bake at 375° for 45 minutes. Remove the cover for the last 15 minutes to allow sauce to thicken. Serves 3; each serving=1 unit milk.

TUNA PARMIGIANA

1 cup homemade noodles, cooked partially until chewy (*see* Breads, Pasta and Noodles)
1 13-ounce can solid white meat tuna, drained and separated into chunks
1 cup evaporated milk
1 small can cut green beans
1 tablespoon dehydrated onion flakes
Salt to taste
1 allowed beef bouillon cube, crumbled (*see* Brand Names)
½ cup freshly grated Parmesan cheese
1 small can mushrooms
⅓ cup non-fat dry milk
Dash of paprika
Dash of freshly ground pepper

Cook the noodles as directed, and drain (do not rinse). Combine with the other ingredients in a large casserole. Top with a little additional cheese, and bake uncovered at 350° for 30 to 40 minutes. This will keep well and it also reheats well. Entire recipe=3 units milk. The same recipe can be made without the noodles, but you should drain the mushrooms and beans before adding to the rest or it will be too runny. Serves 3; each serving=1 unit milk (for carbohydrates, *see* noodle recipe).

SALMON AND GREEN VEGETABLE CASSEROLE

1 tablespoon lemon juice
½ medium green pepper, chopped
3 tablespoons chopped fresh parsley
Salt and pepper to taste
1 cup frozen peas
4 ribs celery, chopped
½ cup sour cream
Dash of nutmeg
½ cup milk
1 1-pound can red salmon, drained

Preheat the oven to 350°. Mix together all ingredients except the salmon. Gently fold in the salmon, breaking it into chunks. Pour into a greased casserole and bake uncovered for 30 minutes. Serves 3 or 4.

ORIENTAL SHRIMP AND CHICKEN

2 pounds raw shrimp
4 tablespoons peanut oil
2 cloves garlic, minced fine
½ pound fresh mushrooms, sliced
4 ribs celery, sliced
1 can bamboo shoots, thinly sliced
8 ounces cooked chicken, shredded
2 cups chicken broth or as needed to cover
Dash of liquid artificial sweetener
1 small onion, diced
Dash of MSG
1 can bean sprouts

Shell and devein the shrimp. Heat the oil in a large skillet, and sauté the garlic, shrimp, mushrooms and celery for 5 minutes, stirring, over high heat. Add the bamboo shoots and continue stirring until they are heated through. Add the chicken, broth and remaining seasonings; cover, lower heat and simmer 5 minutes. Drain the bean sprouts, pressing out most of the liquid between paper towels. Toss into the mixture, heat through and serve. This is one of the few casseroles which does not improve on standing, and should be made and served hot immediately. Serves 6.

POLYNESIAN CHICKEN

1 3-pound fryer chicken
1 cup water
1 tablespoon peanut oil
3 scallions, finely sliced
½ cup diced celery
¼ teaspoon cayenne pepper
3 tablespoons Kikkoman soy sauce
2 tablets saccharin or more to taste
¾ cup whole almonds
½ medium green pepper, diced
1 cup fresh pineapple chunks (ripe)
1 teaspoon salt
1 can bean sprouts, freshened with cold water

Place the chicken on a rack in a pressure cooker or steamer. Add the water, cover and pressure-cook or steam until tender (about 15 minutes). Remove the chicken and discard the bones and skin. In a large skillet, heat the oil, and sauté the scallions, celery and pepper until softened. Add the boned chicken, the water in which it was cooked and the rest of the ingredients, except the bean sprouts. Cover and simmer gently 10 minutes. Remove the cover and simmer 10 minutes longer. Heat the bean sprouts in a little water, drain and squeeze out the excess moisture. Pour the chicken mixture over the hot sprouts and serve. Serve 3 or 4; each serving=¼ unit fruit.

CHICKEN-STUFFED PEPPERS

1 recipe Basic White Sauce (see Sauces and Dressings)
2 cups diced cold chicken
6 medium peppers
1 small onion, chopped
3 or 4 black olives, sliced
¾ cup chopped celery
Salt, pepper to taste
Pinch of dried parsley
1 cup allowed chicken broth (see Brand Names)

Prepare the sauce according to the recipe. Blend the sauce in the blender until smooth. Combine the chicken, vegetables and sauce in a bowl, mixing well. Season to taste. Stuff the mixture into the peppers. Place in a small greased casserole. Pour the chicken broth around the peppers. Bake at 350° for 1 hour. Serves 3 as a main dish or 6 as a side dish.

TURKEY HASH

1 tablespoon butter
6 to 8 mushrooms, sliced
1 small onion, chopped
½ cup chopped celery
2 cups diced leftover turkey and turkey skin
1 slice homemade bread, cubed
2 cups turkey gravy, pan drippings or chicken bouillon (*see* Brand
   Names)
Pinch of sage
Salt to taste
¼ cup evaporated milk
1 cup frozen sliced carrots
1 teaspoon minced parsley
Dash of freshly ground pepper

Melt the butter in a large skillet. Sauté the mushrooms, onion and celery until soft. Add the remaining ingredients and correct seasoning. Cover, and simmer over low heat until the carrots are cooked (about 10 minutes). This can be served immediately, kept warm on a low heat or reheated as leftovers without spoiling the flavor. Serves 3 or 4.

BEEF-CHICKEN FRICASSEE

1 pound lean ground round
1 egg, slightly beaten
1 slice homemade bread, crumbed fine
6 to 8 pieces chicken wings and drumsticks
1 medium onion, diced
Salt, pepper to taste
1 tablespoon paprika
½ teaspoon onion powder
½ cup water or more as needed
½ cup old-fashioned-style oatmeal

Mix together the ground round, egg and bread crumbs. Shape into meat balls. Place in a large deep pan, preferably Teflon-lined (if not, use about ½ teaspoon butter to begin the meat frying). Cook the meat balls in their own fat over medium heat until browned. Add the chicken, onion and seasonings, and simmer uncovered until the chicken is browned. Add the water, cover and simmer for 30 minutes. When the chicken is tender, add the oatmeal, plus more water if needed, and simmer until the oats are cooked and the sauce is thick. The oatmeal should be of the consistency of soft wild rice when ready to serve. Serves 4; each serving=1 unit carbohydrate.

BEEF-STUFFED PEPPERS

2 pounds lean ground round
½ cup crumbed homemade bread
1 small onion, chopped
1 teaspoon oregano
Salt and pepper to taste
4 large or 8 small green peppers, cored, with top slice removed
1 large can tomato purée
1 large can mushrooms, drained
2 ¼-grain tablets saccharin, crushed

Mix together the meat, bread crumbs, onion and seasonings. Stuff the peppers with the mixture. Place in a large pot and cover with a sauce made of the purée, mushrooms and saccharin. Cover and simmer over low heat for 1½ to 2 hours. To thicken sauce, set the cover slightly ajar during the last ½ hour of cooking. Correct seasoning of sauce before serving. If high-carbohydrate bread is used, entire recipe=1 unit carbohydrate. Serves 4.

EGGPLANT CASSEROLE

1 large eggplant
1 medium Spanish onion
2 medium tomatoes
½ cup oat flour
½ teaspoon salt or more to taste
¼ teaspoon freshly ground pepper
2 tablespoons olive oil or more as needed
1 pound lean ground chuck
1 teaspoon oregano
¼ cup grated Parmesan cheese

Cut the eggplant into slices ½ inch thick (do not peel). Peel and slice the onion and tomatoes and set aside. Dredge the eggplant in the oat flour and season with the salt and pepper. Heat the oil in a large skillet, and brown the eggplant slices on both sides. Remove the browned slices and continue frying until all slices are finished. Set aside and add more oil if needed; sauté the meat and onion, stirring, until the meat has lost its pink color and is well crumbled. Fill a greased casserole with alternating layers of eggplant, onion and meat, and tomatoes. Sprinkle each layer lightly with the oregano, grated cheese and salt to taste. Finish with grated cheese, using more if needed. Bake in a preheated 350° oven for 45 minutes, or until the eggplant is tender. Serves 4; each serving=1 unit carbohydrate.

STUFFED CABBAGE

1 large head cabbage
2 pounds lean ground round
2 eggs
½ cup uncooked rolled oats
¼ teaspoon salt or more to taste
3 cups tomato purée
1 small onion, diced
½ cup cider vinegar
Juice of 1 lemon
¼ teaspoon ground ginger
6 to 8 ¼-grain tablets saccharin or more to taste
1 cup water

Parboil or steam the cabbage briefly to soften; cut out the core, then peel off the leaves and set aside. In a bowl mix together the beef, eggs, oats and salt. Knead well. Place about ¼ cup of the beef mixture on each cabbage leaf. Fold the leaf like an envelope carefully around the filling, and arrange carefully in a large deep casserole. In a saucepan combine the tomato purée, onion, vinegar, lemon juice, ginger, saccharin and water (include the water in which you cooked the cabbage). Heat until the saccharin melts, and pour over the cabbage rolls. Cover the pan and bake in a slow oven (300°) for at least 2 hours. To thicken the sauce, uncover the pan for the last ½ hour. During baking, correct flavorings to taste. Sauce should be pungently sweet and sour. Serves 4 to 6; each serving=about ½ unit carbohydrate.

Variation (10-Minute "Stuffed" Cabbage):
This version cooks as long as the regular Stuffed Cabbage, but takes only 10 minutes' preparation time:
Same ingredients as Stuffed Cabbage, but eliminate the eggs. Sauté the meat in a hot skillet, stirring, until it is lightly browned. Cut the cabbage into eighths, and cook in a pressure cooker for 1 minute. Reduce the pressure and remove. Place the meat and cabbage in a deep pan, add the remaining ingredients (include the fat from the pan in which you cooked the meat). Bake in a slow oven for at least 2 hours, or longer if you can.

"SPAGHETTI" AND MEAT BALLS

1½ pounds lean ground round
1 egg
1 slice homemade bread, crumbed
¼ teaspoon salt
Dash of freshly ground pepper
1 tablespoon olive oil
4 to 6 mushrooms, chopped
1 small onion, minced
¼ green pepper, chopped
1 large can tomato purée
Dash of oregano
1 clove garlic, minced fine
1 ¼-grain tablet saccharin
Dash of basil
2 cans bean sprouts, freshened with cold water and squeezed dry
  between paper towels
Grated mozzarella cheese (optional)

Mix together the beef, egg, bread crumbs, salt and pepper. Form into meat balls and fry in a dry Teflon-lined pan, or bake at 375° in the oven until brown all through. Heat the olive oil in a frying pan, and sauté the vegetables until soft. Add the tomato purée and seasonings, including the saccharin. Cover and simmer slowly for 30 minutes (or longer, if possible). Squeeze the bean sprouts dry, and place in a deep casserole. Add the meat balls and sauce. Heat together in a moderate oven until well heated (about 15 minutes); or, if you prefer, cover with grated mozzarella cheese and bake until the cheese melts. Serves 4 to 6.

BEEF STEW

1 tablespoon butter
1½ pounds lean beef chunks
1 package frozen peas and carrots
1 tablespoon onion juice
1 bay leaf, crushed
1 tablespoon Kikkoman soy sauce
Salt, pepper to taste
8 ounces tomato juice
1 small onion, diced
½ package frozen cut green beans
Dash of thyme
Dash of garlic powder

Melt the butter in a large pan, and sear the meat until it loses its pink color. Add the remaining ingredients. Cover the pan, lower the heat and simmer 1½ to 2 hours, or longer if possible, leaving the lid slightly ajar during the last ½ hour, to allow the sauce to thicken. Serves 4; each serving=1 unit high-carbohydrate vegetable.

HAMBURGER STEW

1 medium onion, diced
2 cloves garlic, minced
1 large green pepper, diced
1 teaspoon butter or oil
2 pounds lean ground beef (round, sirloin)
1 teaspoon salt
1 teaspoon dehydrated parsley flakes
1 package frozen cut green beans
2 cups tomato purée
¼ teaspoon pepper
2 ¼-grain tablets saccharin
Dash of dry mustard

Sauté the onion, garlic and green pepper in the oil until soft. Add the beef, stirring to break up into chunks. Brown lightly over medium heat (if ground chuck is used, pour off the extra fat as it accumulates). When the meat has lost its pink color, add the other ingredients. Cover, and simmer slowly 30 minutes or longer. Leave the cover slightly ajar to thicken the sauce. Serves 4.

ROAST BEEF HASH

½ cup drippings and fat trimmed from the roast (including the pan gravy)
1 onion, diced
1½ to 2 cups leftover roast beef, shredded
1 can water chestnuts, drained and minced
1 package frozen peas
½ teaspoon dehydrated parsley flakes
Dash of hot pepper sauce
1 Knorr-Swiss beef bouillon cube
¼ teaspoon black pepper
½ cup water plus more as needed

Heat the pan drippings; cut up the trimmed fat fine and render in the hot drippings until crisp. Add the onion and sauté until transparent. Add the remaining ingredients to the pan. Cover and simmer until the peas are just cooked (about 10 minutes). Uncover, and simmer, stirring, until thick. Water chestnuts should be golden brown. Serves 3 or 4; each serving=1 unit high-carbohydrate vegetable.

VEAL HASH

2 tablespoons butter
1 onion, diced
2 stalks celery, chopped
6 to 8 mushrooms, sliced
3 cups cooked veal, minced (use leftover roast veal, include some of the skin)
1 package frozen French-style green beans
1 cup veal stock, drippings and gravy
Salt, pepper to taste
1 tablespoon paprika
Dash of nutmeg
½ cup sour cream plus more to taste

Melt the butter in a large skillet. Sauté the onion until soft. Add the celery, mushrooms and veal. Stir and fry for 5 minutes. Add the green beans, stock and seasonings. Cover, lower heat and simmer until the green beans are slightly thawed. Separate with fork, cover and simmer until cooked. Stir in the sour cream, remove the cover and simmer until thick, stirring. Serve at once. Serves 3 or 4.

VEAL AND PEPPERS

¼ cup oil
2 pounds lean boneless veal, cut into 1-inch cubes
2 cloves garlic, split
2 large green peppers, cut into thin strips
2 tablespoons grated Parmesan cheese
½ teaspoon oat flour
1 teaspoon salt
¼ teaspoon rosemary
¼ teaspoon pepper
12 ounces tomato juice

Preheat the oven to 350°. Heat the oil in a frying pan and brown the veal cubes with the garlic. Transfer to a 2-quart casserole. Sauté the peppers in the frying pan until softened. Transfer the peppers to the casserole. Sprinkle with the cheese, flour and seasonings, and mix together. Pour in the tomato juice. Cover and bake for 45 minutes. Serves 4.

LAMB AND EGGPLANT CASSEROLE

1 small eggplant, diced
1 Bermuda onion, diced
⅓ cup oil
2 pounds ground lamb
1 teaspoon salt
¼ teaspoon rosemary
3 tablespoons chopped fresh parsley
¼ teaspoon pepper
4 ripe medium tomatoes, chopped
¼ cup grated American cheese (dry)

Preheat the oven to 350°. Sauté the eggplant and onion in the oil until tender. Remove from the pan and set aside. Mix the lamb with the seasonings and form into patties. Brown in the same frying pan, until browned on both sides. In a large casserole alternate layers of meat patties with layers of the tomatoes, parsley and the cooked vegetables. Sprinkle the top layer with the cheese. Bake uncovered for 45 minutes. Serves 4.

FRANKFURTER-CABBAGE STEW

1 pound allowed frankfurters (*see* Brand Names)
½ head of cabbage, shredded
8 ounces tomato juice
2 to 4 ¼-grain tablets saccharin, crushed
2 tablespoons vinegar
Dash of dry mustard
½ teaspoon salt

Slice the frankfurters crosswise, ½ inch thick. Combine all ingredients in a greased casserole and mix. Cover and bake at 375° for 1 hour. Remove cover and bake 15 minutes, or until thickened and frankfurters on top are browned. Serves 3 or 4.

FRANKS AND SAUERKRAUT

1 1-pound can sauerkraut, drained
1 pound allowed frankfurters
¼ teaspoon caraway seeds
1 teaspoon butter

Drain the sauerkraut, place in a greased shallow baking dish. Slice the frankfurters lengthwise into 4 thin strips and mix with the sauerkraut. Sprinkle with the seeds and dot with butter. Bake at 375° for 1 hour. Serves 3 or 4.

FRANKS AND BEANS

2 tablespoons oil or bacon drippings
1 onion, diced
1 pound allowed frankfurters
1 can cooked soybeans (*see* Brand Names)
1 cup tomato juice
½ teaspoon dry mustard
1 cup beef bouillon (*see* Brand Names)
2 ¼-grain tablets saccharin

Heat the oil or bacon drippings, and sauté the onion until soft. Slice the franks crosswise 1 inch thick and fry with the onion for 5 minutes. Add the remaining ingredients and mix. Cover, lower heat and simmer gently for at least 2 hours over low heat; or transfer to the oven and bake for 2 hours or more at 325°. Serves 4.

PORK AND BEAN BAKE

2 cups cooked soybeans
½ onion, minced fine
2 ¼-grain tablets saccharin or to taste
1 large apple, chopped
2 cups beef stock or bouillon
1 teaspoon prepared mustard
Salt to taste if needed
2 pounds pork chops or sliced pork loin

Combine all ingredients except pork in a large casserole. Place the pork on top. Cover and bake at 325° for 2 hours or at 300° for 3 hours. Uncover and bake an additional ½ hour or as needed to brown the meat. Serves 4; each serving=½ unit fruit.

CHILI CON CARNE

2 cups yellow soybeans
8 cups water
Salt to taste
1½ pounds lean ground beef
1 small can tomato paste
1 20-ounce can tomatoes
1 small can chili peppers
Freshly ground pepper
1 large onion, diced
2 tablespoons chili powder or more to taste
1 clove garlic, minced
1 tablespoon onion powder (optional)

Soak the beans overnight in the water (refrigerate). Pour the beans and the water in which they soaked into a large deep pan. Bring to a boil, lower heat and simmer at a low boil for 4 to 6 hours. Add the remaining ingredients, beginning with 1 teaspoon salt, and adding more later as needed. Cover and bake at 325° for 1 hour. Lower oven to 200° and bake overnight, or for at least 8 hours for best results. Add more salt, if needed, and onion powder before serving if flavor is too flat. For faster cooking, chili may be simmered on the top of the stove for 3 to 4 hours, but the longer and slower it cooks, the better it will taste. Serves 6 to 8.

HAM AND BEAN CASSEROLE

2 cups yellow soybeans
6 cups water
2 cups smoked ham leftovers, cubed
¼ cup fat from the ham or bacon drippings
1 tablespoon vinegar
1 large can Dole unsweetened pineapple chunks, packed without
   sugar
1 medium onion, diced
Salt to taste

Soak the beans in the water overnight. In the morning, pour the soaked beans and soaking water into a large deep pan; bring to a boil and simmer for 5 to 6 hours. Add the remaining ingredients including the juice from the pineapple and transfer to the oven. Bake at 325° for 3 hours; during the last ½ hour, uncover, stirring in more water if needed to prevent drying out. Serves 6 to 8. Each serving=about 1 unit fruit.

HAM PARISIENNE

1 bunch broccoli or 2 packages frozen whole broccoli
½ cup water
6 thick slices smoked ham
1 small can sliced mushrooms
Dash of salt, pepper
Pinch of paprika
1 cup grated Swiss or Muenster cheese

Preheat the oven to 325°. Steam or pressure-cook the broccoli in the water until just tender, but not mushy. (For pressure cooker, cook 2 minutes). Arrange the ham slices in a large shallow baking dish. Place the broccoli sections on top of the ham, sprinkle on the mushrooms and mushroom liquid, then the seasonings and the cheese. Bake for 30 minutes, or until the cheese is bubbly and slightly browned. Serves 4 to 6.

BAKED HAM AND ASPARAGUS ROLL-UPS

1 15-ounce can asparagus spears, drained
12 thin slices smoked ham
¼ onion, minced
½ green pepper, chopped
¼ teaspoon salt
½ cup evaporated milk
Dash of pepper
1 cup cheese, cubed (Swiss, American)

Preheat the oven to 350°. Place 1 asparagus spear on each slice of ham. Roll up and place side by side in a well-greased casserole.

Sprinkle on the onion and green pepper. Place the remaining ingredients in the blender and blend until smooth. Pour over the ham rolls. Bake for 30 minutes, or until the sauce is bubbly and slightly browned. Serves 4 to 6.

HAM AND CHEESE CASSEROLE

2 cans cut wax beans, drained
2 cups diced cooked ham
2 stalks celery, sliced
1 tablespoon dehydrated onion flakes
Salt, pepper to taste
½ teaspoon dehydrated parsley flakes
Dash of paprika
⅔ cup milk
1 pound Cheddar cheese, cubed
1 tablespoon butter

Preheat the oven to 350°. Pour the beans into a well-greased casserole. Toss in the diced ham, celery, onion flakes and seasonings. Pour in the milk. Sprinkle evenly with cheese, cubed small, and dot with butter. Bake uncovered for 30 minutes, or until the cheese is brown and bubbly. Serves 4.

CHEESE-STUFFED PEPPERS

4 large peppers, cored
1 pound ricotta cheese
1 cup diced ham
1 tablespoon dehydrated vegetable flakes
1 onion, finely chopped
1 egg, slightly beaten
Salt, pepper to taste
1 large can Del Monte tomato sauce
¼ cup water

Cut the peppers ½ inch from the stem end and discard the tops and seeds. Combine all other ingredients, except the tomato sauce, in a bowl. Mix well, and stuff the mixture into the peppers. Place the stuffed peppers in a baking pan and drizzle the tomato sauce over them. Add water to the tomato sauce in the pan. Bake covered at 325° for 30 minutes, or until the peppers are tender. Serves 4.

WAX BEAN LASAGNA

2 tablespoons olive oil
1 onion, diced
2 cloves garlic, minced fine
1 small green pepper, diced
2 cups tomato sauce (*see* Brand Names or Sauces and Dressings)
1 package frozen French-style wax beans
1 egg, slightly beaten
1 pound ricotta cheese
1 teaspoon dehydrated parsley flakes
¼ teaspoon salt
Dash of freshly ground pepper
2 tablespoons oregano
8 ounces whole milk mozzarella cheese, sliced or diced
¼ cup grated Parmesan cheese

Heat the olive oil in a pan; sauté the onion, garlic and green pepper until soft. Mix with the tomato sauce and set aside. Separate the beans by tapping the package before opening; spread beans out to thaw slightly on a paper towel. In a small bowl, mix together the egg, ricotta cheese, parsley, salt and pepper until smooth. Take a large deep casserole and arrange the ingredients in layers as follows: a layer of wax beans, then the ricotta cheese mixture, then tomato sauce. Sprinkle with oregano, then follow with a layer of mozzarella cheese. Repeat until all ingredients are used up, ending with a layer of mozzarella cheese. Sprinkle with the Parmesan cheese. Place in a preheated 325° oven and bake for 30 to 45 minutes, or until the cheese is brown and bubbly. Serves 4.

Variation: Prepare as above, plus 1 pound lean ground beef, which is sautéed with the vegetables and added to the sauce. This has a heavier flavor, and for some reason tastes less like "real" lasagna than the cheese version. Both are delicious and high in protein.

WAX BEAN LOAF

1 1-pound can French-style wax beans
1 slice homemade high-carbohydrate bread
2 tablespoons butter, melted
¼ teaspoon paprika
½ teaspoon salt
Dash of pepper
½ cup milk
½ cup non-fat dry milk
4 or 5 ounces Cheddar cheese, grated
Slivered almonds (optional)

Drain the wax beans and chop well. Crumble the bread and mix with the beans, butter, seasonings, milk, dry milk and half the cheese. Pour into a greased casserole, sprinkle on the rest of the cheese, and top with the almonds and a little extra paprika. Bake in a preheated 350° oven until the cheese is brown and bubbly. Serves 2. Each serving=½ unit carbohydrate. Or serves 4 as a side dish.

MUSHROOM LOAF

4 eggs, beaten
¼ cup non-fat dry milk
2 tablespoons dehydrated onion flakes
1 teaspoon parsley flakes
Salt, pepper to taste
¼ teaspoon paprika
1 8-ounce can mushrooms, sliced

Beat the eggs, milk and seasonings together until frothy (or blend in the blender). Mix in the mushrooms and pour into a loaf pan or bread pan. Bake in a preheated 375° oven for 15 minutes. Lower the heat to 325° and bake until set (about 30 minutes). Serves 2 as a main dish or 4 as a side dish.

ONION LOAF

¼ pound smoked bacon (*see* Brand Names)
2 large or 4 small onions, diced
4 eggs
½ cup evaporated milk
Salt to taste
Dash of freshly ground pepper

Fry the bacon until crisp. Drain and crumble. Fry the onions in the bacon fat until soft and yellow. Drain and set aside. Beat the eggs and milk together, add the seasonings, onions and the crumbled bacon. Mix gently. Pour into a well-greased loaf pan. Bake in a preheated 325° oven for 45 minutes, or until set. Serves 2 as a main dish or 4 as a side dish.

ONION PIE

1 unbaked pie shell (*see* Desserts)
1 egg white
3 tablespoons butter
1 large Bermuda onion, diced
3 eggs
½ cup evaporated milk
¼ teaspoon chervil
¼ teaspoon salt
Dash of freshly ground pepper
½ cup grated Swiss or Muenster cheese
1 small can anchovy fillets, drained (optional)

Prepare the pie shell according to the directions. Brush well with the egg white and refrigerate. Preheat the oven to 400°. In a pan melt the butter. Sauté the onion until soft and transparent. Blend in the blender with the eggs and milk until smooth. Add the seasonings, mix and pour into the pie shell. Sprinkle the cheese evenly over the pie, then spread the anchovies over the top in a decorative manner (if preferred, you can use sliced olives, or nothing at all). Bake at 400° for 10 minutes; lower heat to 325° and bake 35 to 40 minutes, or until set. Cool slightly before serving. For carbohydrates, see the piecrust recipe. Serves 6 as a side dish.

CAULIFLOWER PIE

1½ cups grated Cheddar cheese (8 ounces)
¼ cup wheat germ
¼ cup finely ground Brazil nuts or filberts
1 small head cauliflower
½ cup water
2 extra large eggs, beaten
½ teaspoon salt
Pinch of nutmeg
½ cup evaporated milk
4 strips bacon, partially fried

Combine the cheese, wheat germ and ground nuts. Press most of the mixture into a large pie plate, forming a bottom crust. Reserve some of the mixture for topping. Chill the shell until firm. In pressure cooker or steamer, cook the cauliflower in the water just long enough to cook, but not until mushy. Drain, and mash well. Add the eggs and seasonings and enough evaporated milk to make a smooth mixture (if preferred, blend until puréed). Pour into the pie shell; top with the bacon and sprinkle on the rest of the cheese mixture. Bake at 325° for 1 hour. Serves 4 to 6. Each serving=a trace of carbohydrate.

CHEESE

Cheese is one of the best and cheapest sources of protein. It adds variety to your menus and can be carried conveniently as a snack. There are as many kinds of cheese to choose from as anyone could wish for, from the inexpensive and easy-to-use American and pasteurized process cheese, all the way to the exotic imported cheeses sold in gourmet shops. There is a cheese to suit every taste and age; even those who are not ordinarily fond of cheese will eat cheesecake, cottage cheese, mozzarella and other cheeses when they are prepared well.

There are recipes using cheese in every section of this book, ranging from Coeur à la Crème in Desserts, to Cheese Sauce in Sauces and Dressings. In fact, it's hard to plan a menu using the recipes in this book without using cheese at least once.

The recipes in this section are those whose main ingredient is cheese, and which don't really fit in any other category. To find other cheese recipes, check the index.

Always remember in cooking cheese, it will become tough and stringy if not cooked properly. The simplest rule to remember is, either cook it very briefly at high temperature, as for pizza, or long and slowly at low temperatures. When broiling cheese, as in a cheeseburger, remove from the oven when melted and bubbly, as overcooking will not only make the cheese less palatable, but will destroy much of the vitamin content.

Cheese Patties
Cheese Puffs
Cheese Pancakes

Fried Cheese
Quiche Lorraine
Cheese Polenta

Cheese Lasagna
Cheese Soufflé
Ricotta Loaf
Cheese Pudding
Pineapple Cheese Pudding
Cheese Custard

Cottage Cheese Casserole
Grandma's Cheese and Noodles
Cottage Cheese Vegetable Salad
Cottage Cheese Fruit Salad
Cottage Cheese

CHEESE PATTIES

1 slice homemade Oatmeal Bread
8 ounces Velveeta or American cheese, grated
¼ cup toasted wheat germ
1 tablespoon butter at room temperature
½ teaspoon onion powder
½ teaspoon dry mustard
Salt, pepper to taste
1 egg, beaten

Toast the bread and blend in the blender to fine crumbs. Mix together all the ingredients and shape into patties. Fry in a lightly oiled pan over low heat until well browned on both sides. Serve hot. Serves 3; 1 portion (⅓ of the patties) = 1 unit carbohydrate.

CHEESE PUFFS

2 eggs, separated
½ cup evaporated milk
¼ cup soy flour
¼ cup oat flour
6 ounces extra sharp Cheddar cheese
1 tablespoon butter at room temperature
Salt, pepper to taste
Solid shortening (Crisco, etc.)

Combine the egg yolks and milk, and beat well. Mix in the flours and beat until smooth. Grate the cheese in the blender, then mix in with the softened butter. Cream together, then beat into the egg mixture. Season lightly; beat the egg whites until stiff but not dry.

Gradually fold in the cheese mixture, cutting in until mixed. Melt the shortening in a deep skillet over deep fat fryer, about 1 inch deep. When the fat is hot, drop in the cheese mixture by tablespoonfuls. Fry very briefly, just until crisply browned. Remove immediately and drain on paper towels. Continue until all the batter is fried. Serve puffs as a side dish with meats, seafood, or as a hot hors d'oeuvre. Entire recipe=about 3 units carbohydrate. Makes 6 to 8 puffs.

CHEESE PANCAKES

Same as Cheese Puffs, but fry in a lightly oiled skillet, turning when golden brown. Makes very unusual 2-inch pancakes. Serve as side dish, or with spreads or dips, or use in making canapés. Makes 6 to 8 pancakes. Entire recipe=3 units carbohydrate.

FRIED CHEESE

1 thick slice Oatmeal Bread
1 tablespoon butter or margarine
4 thick slices semi-soft cheese (Edam, Gouda, Muenster, etc.)
¼ cup soy flour
1 egg, salted and slightly beaten

Toast the bread, tear into pieces and blend in the blender into fine crumbs. Heat the butter in a frying pan. Coat each slice of cheese in the soy flour, dip in the egg, then coat thickly with the bread crumbs. Fry the breaded cheese slices in the hot butter until brown, turning once (do not crowd). Drain on a paper towel and serve at once. Each slice=¼ unit carbohydrate.

QUICHE LORRAINE

1 unbaked homemade pie shell (*see* Desserts, especially the Cream Cheese Crust)
1 egg white
½ pound bacon (sugarless or smoked)

4 jumbo eggs
1 cup milk
½ cup light cream
½ teaspoon salt
¼ teaspoon freshly ground nutmeg
¼ teaspoon pepper
1 cup grated Gruyère cheese

Preheat the oven to 400°. Prepare the pie shell according to the recipe used and brush with the egg white. Chill in the refrigerator until the egg white is dry. Bake the bacon in the oven on a rack until brown. Remove bacon, drain on paper towels and crumble. Beat together the eggs, milk, cream and seasonings. Sprinkle the bacon on the pie shell, then sprinkle in the grated cheese. Pour in the egg mixture, coating the cheese completely. Place in the oven for 10 minutes. Reduce the heat to 325° and bake until puffy and brown (35 to 45 minutes). Test with a knife, and continue baking until set. Cool slightly before serving. See the piecrust recipe used for carbohydrates. Serves 4.

CHEESE POLENTA

1 loaf Polenta (see Breads)
8 slices American cheese
½ pint sour cream (optional)

Prepare the Polenta according to the recipe; bake it, then fry it, as described in the directions. Split the loaf in half through the center, and spread 4 of the cheese slices in the bottom half. Replace the top of the loaf and spread the remaining 4 slices on the top of the loaf. Return to the oven and bake at 325° until the cheese is melted and bubbly. Serve each portion with a scoop of sour cream if desired. Serves 4 as a main dish or 8 as a side dish.

CHEESE LASAGNA

2 eggs
1 pound ricotta cheese
½ teaspoon parsley flakes
¼ teaspoon salt
Dash of freshly ground pepper
1 medium jar Aunt Millie's spaghetti sauce, or 2 cups homemade
spaghetti sauce
½ teaspoon oregano
4 tablespoons grated Parmesan cheese
8 ounces sliced or shredded mozzarella cheese
1 tablespoon olive oil

Beat the eggs, add the ricotta cheese, parsley, salt, pepper; mix well. Pour into an oiled baking dish and pat out 1 inch thick. Bake at 325° until set (about 30 minutes). Remove from the pan, and break or cut into 2-inch squares. Place the cheese squares, slightly apart, in a greased baking dish. Pour the spaghetti sauce over the cheese squares. Sprinkle with the oregano, then the Parmesan cheese. Top each square with a slice of mozzarella, then shred the rest and sprinkle it evenly over the entire dish. Drizzle the oil over the top. Bake in a medium oven (350°) until the top cheese is bubbly and melted. Serves 4.

CHEESE SOUFFLÉ

4 eggs, separated
1 cup milk
½ cup evaporated milk
2 tablespoons butter
2 cups cheese (for sharp flavor use Cheddar; for milder flavor use
American)
Salt and pepper to taste
Dash of paprika or cayenne

Separate the eggs. Beat the yolks and milks together. In a saucepan, melt the butter. Add the egg mixture, stirring. Grate the cheese in the blender and add to the pan. Cook over a low heat, stirring, until the cheese melts. Add the seasonings and set aside to cool slightly. In a bowl, beat the egg whites well until stiff but not dry. Slowly cut the cheese mixture into the egg whites, folding gently, until mixed. Carefully pour into a well-greased deep ovenproof dish. Bake at 325° for 10 minutes, lower the temperature to 300° and bake for 1 hour. Serves 3 or 4.

RICOTTA LOAF

2 eggs
1 pound ricotta cheese
¼ teaspoon oregano
¼ teaspoon garlic powder
Dash of freshly ground pepper
½ teaspoon parsley flakes
¼ teaspoon onion powder
½ teaspoon salt
6 ounces mozzarella cheese, diced
¼ cup grated Parmesan cheese

Beat the eggs, add the ricotta cheese, seasonings, and half of the mozzarella. Pour the mixture into a well-greased casserole or loaf pan, and sprinkle on the Parmesan cheese and the rest of the mozzarella. Bake at 325° for 1 hour. Serve hot, as a side dish with Chicken Cacciatore, Veal Scallopini, etc. Serves 4 to 6.

CHEESE PUDDING

2 cups cottage cheese
Dash of salt
6 to 8 ¼-grain tablets saccharin, crushed
4 eggs
2 large apples, peeled, cored, sliced thin
1 tablespoon cinnamon
½ teaspoon nutmeg
¼ cup coarsely chopped nuts
⅓ cup sour cream
Dash of liquid artificial sweetener

Combine the cottage cheese, salt, saccharin and eggs in the blender. Blend until mixed. Pour into a well-greased casserole. Arrange the apple slices on top. Sprinkle with the cinnamon, nutmeg and nuts. Spread with a layer of sour cream, and sprinkle with liquid sweetener to taste. Bake in a preheated 375° oven, for 15 minutes. Lower the heat to 300° and bake for 30 minutes longer. Serve hot, with milk or cream, or cold. Serves 4 to 8 as dessert. Entire recipe =4 units fruit.

PINEAPPLE CHEESE PUDDING

3 eggs
1 can Dole unsweetened pineapple chunks, packed without sugar
2 cups ricotta cheese
½ teaspoon salt
6 ¼-grain tablets saccharin, crushed
1 teaspoon cinnamon

Beat the eggs; drain the pineapple, reserving the juice for other uses. Mix together all ingredients except the cinnamon. Pour the mixture into a greased casserole. Sprinkle the top with the cinnamon. Bake covered in a slow oven (300°) for 30 minutes. Serves 6; each serving=½ unit fruit.

CHEESE CUSTARD

1 cup milk
4 eggs, slightly beaten
1 cup grated sharp Cheddar cheese
Dash of cayenne or paprika
¼ teaspoon salt

Pour the milk into a pan and heat until scalded. Beat the eggs and gradually add the scalded milk, stirring. Add the rest of the ingredients and mix well. Pour the mixture into well-greased custard dishes or a shallow baking dish. Place in a pan with 1 inch of hot water. Bake at 350° for 30 minutes, or until a knife inserted in the center comes out clean. Serves 2 for lunch or 4 as a side dish.

COTTAGE CHEESE CASSEROLE

2 cups cottage cheese
½ package Knorr-Swiss onion soup and dip mix (shake well before
  dividing in half)
1 teaspoon onion juice
1 cup sour cream
1 small can mushroom slices, drained
Minced parsley

Combine all ingredients except parsley, and mix well. Pour into a
well-greased casserole, garnish with minced parsley and bake at
350° for 30 minutes. Serve with frankfurters, sausage, etc. Serves 2
to 4.

GRANDMA'S CHEESE AND NOODLES

2 cups homemade noodles, cooked (*see* Breads)
1 tablespoon butter
1 pound pot cheese or farmer cheese, crumbled
4 ¼-grain tablets saccharin, crushed
1 teaspoon cinnamon or more to taste
Dash of nutmeg

Cook the noodles according to the directions in the recipe. Drain.
Toss with the butter until all the noodles are coated and the butter is
melted. Toss with the remaining ingredients until loosely mixed, as
in a salad. Sprinkle the top with a little more cinnamon and serve
hot. Serves 4. For carbohydrates, see the noodle recipe used.

COTTAGE CHEESE VEGETABLE SALAD

2 cups creamed cottage cheese
1 green pepper, minced
1 pimiento, minced
Salt and pepper to taste
1 large ripe tomato, diced
½ cucumber, peeled and sliced thin
2 scallions, chopped, including tops
½ cup sour cream (optional)

Combine all ingredients, and mix well. Salad may be served as a main dish for lunch, or as a side dish for dinner. Will keep well in the refrigerator for several days. Serves 2 to 4.

COTTAGE CHEESE FRUIT SALAD

2 cups soft-curd creamed cottage cheese
1½ cups fresh or sugarless canned fruit, diced (strawberries, pineapple, apples, peaches, plums, pears, etc.)
½ cup sour cream (optional)
Artificial sweetener to taste

Combine all ingredients, mix and chill. Entire recipe=approximately 3 units fruit. Makes 4 cups.

COTTAGE CHEESE

There are many ways in which cottage cheese can be used as a side dish, or even as a main dish for a light lunch. Some of the combinations are:

—a scoop of soft-curd cottage cheese, sprinkled with 1 ¼-grain tablet crushed saccharin and ¼ teaspoon cinnamon.

—½ cup cottage cheese, mixed with a dash of salt and ¼ teaspoon freeze-dried chives.

—a scoop of cottage cheese, mixed with 1 chopped tomato.

—a scoop of cottage cheese with Thousand Island Dressing drizzled over it (*see* Sauces and Dressings).

—a scoop of cottage cheese, mixed with finely minced parsley or dill, plus salt to taste.

—a scoop of cottage cheese, topped with a spoonful of sugarless jam.

—⅓ cup cottage cheese, mixed with 1 tablespoon homemade Ketchup and a little minced green pepper.

In addition to the above, see the following recipes:

Sage Cottage Cheese (*see* Salads)
Green Onion Dip (*see* Appetizers)
Cottage Cheese Pancakes (*see* Breakfast Foods)
Coeur à la Crème (*see* Desserts)
Cottage Cheese Omelette (*see* Eggs)

DESSERTS

Imagine being told that you can never have desserts for the rest of your life. The doctor who put this order on our printed diet sheet never realized what a challenge we would find in these words. Instead of the 3 or 4 desserts he listed, we have developed almost 150. These include many nostalgic and holiday-based desserts, without which life would seem a bit bleak. Now you can have your pumpkin pie, your favorite flavor of ice cream, and almost any dessert you might miss. Even cakes are included, all low in carbohydrates.

In order to fit these recipes into your unit plan, simply scan the ingredients. If a high-carbohydrate ingredient, such as oat flour, is listed, omit bread or noodles from your meal. If fruit is an ingredient, include it in your fruit allowance. And if milk is included, drink some other beverage with your meal.

We have given a large number of recipes because there are so many different categories of desserts. This doesn't mean that you should make a different dessert for every meal. In fact, we feel that you will be able to stay on the diet more easily if you break the dessert habit. A few times a week should be more than enough to satisfy your craving for desserts and keep the diet from being boring.

All the recipes given use as few steps and utensils as possible. All are easy to make and are practically foolproof, with the exception of some of the cakes which can be tricky. In any case, follow the directions exactly to avoid problems. Have fun making and eating them, but always remember: don't eat more than you are allowed within a given period.

ICES AND SHERBETS

Fruit Ice
Orange Sherbet
Lemon Sherbet
Pineapple Sherbet
Raspberry Sherbet
Orange Ice Pops
Peach Popsicles

ICE CREAM

Vanilla Ice Cream
Lemon Ice Cream
Maple Ice Cream
Coffee Ice Cream
Butter Pecan Ice Cream
Banana Ice Cream
Chocolate Ice Cream
Mint Ice Cream
Peanut Butter Ice Cream
Eggnog Ice Cream
Strawberry Ice Cream
Peach Ice Cream
Pumpkin Ice Cream
Pineapple Ice Cream
Fudge Pops
Frozen Milky-rich Bars
Apple Ice Cream
Lemon Peel Ice Cream
Orange Cream Pops
Milkshake Popsicles
Eggnog Popsicles
Frozen Yoghurt
Spumoni: *see* Foreign and
   Regional

GELATIN DESSERTS

Jiffy Gelatin
Orange Gelatin
Molded Fruit Salad
Raspberry Whip

Black Cherry Whip
Cranberry Whip
Raspberry Mousse

PUDDING AND CUSTARDS

Instant Vanilla Pudding
Instant Chocolate Pudding
Butterscotch Pudding
Banana Pudding
Eggnog Bavarian
Cooked Chocolate Pudding
Baked Custard
Apple Pudding
Bread Pudding
Soy Grits Pudding
Apple Oatmeal Pudding
Maple Oatmeal Pudding
Apple Brown Betty
Lukshen Kugel (Noodle
   Pudding): *see* Foreign and
   Regional
Flan: *see* Foreign and Regional

FRUIT DESSERTS

Apple Sauce
Baked Apples
Apple Snacks
Apple Cheese Wheels
Baked Pears
Brandy Pears
Party Pears
Baked Pineapple
Frozen Pineapple
Ambrosia
Baked Ambrosia
Fruit Cocktail
Stewed Rhubarb
Stewed Fruit: *see* Foreign and
   Regional
Candied Pineapple: *see* Foreign
   and Regional

COOKIES

Chocolate Macaroons
Almond Macaroons
Nut Macaroons
Sponge Cookies
Peanut Butter Cookies
Bread-crumb Cookies
Pumpkin Cookies
Oatmeal Wheat-germ Cookies
Soy Grits Cookies
Sesame Seed Cookies
Pecan Balls
Coconut Crescents
Rogelach
Pfefferneusse
Chocolate Mint Bars
Coconut Cookies
Oatmeal-spice Cookies

CAKES

Sponge Cake
Sponge Cup Cakes
Chocolate Meringue Cake
Angel Food Cake
Oatmeal Cake
Coconut Cake
Johnny's Apple Cake
Pound Cake
Mock Jelly Roll Cake
Ice Cream Cake
Whipped Cream Cake
Gingerbread #1
Gingerbread #2
Nut Cake
Five-minute Spice Cake
Yellow Cake
English Trifle
Blackberry Trifle
Charlotte Russe

Soy Nut Cake
Holiday Fruitcake
Italian Rum Cake: *see* Foreign
    and Regional
Fried Breakfast Cake: *see*
    Breakfast Foods
Fried Coffee Cake: *see*
    Breakfast Foods
Instant Cheese Danish: *see*
    Breakfast Foods
Lazy Danish Pastry: *see*
    Breakfast Foods

PIES: CRUSTS

Cheese Piecrust
Thirty-second Piecrust
Peanut Butter Piecrust
Three-flour Piecrust
"Jolly Joan" Piecrust
Cream Cheese Crust
Oatmeal Wheat-germ Piecrust
Crumb Crust
Nut-crumb Crust
Coconut Piecrust
Soy Grits Piecrust

PIES: FILLINGS

Coconut Custard Pie
Buttermilk Meringue Pie
Nesselrode Pie
Soufflé Pie
Apple Pie
Strawberry Pie
Carrot Pie
"Sweet Potato" Pie
Pumpkin Pie
Boston Cream Pie
Banana Cream Pie
Quick Coconut Custard Pie
No-crust Apple Pie

Pineapple Cheesecake
Frozen Cheesecake
Fruit Cheesecake

MISCELLANEOUS

Almond Cream Frosting
Maple Topping
Butter Frosting
Chocolate Icing

Baked Frosting
Whipped Cream Topping
Low-calorie Whipped Topping
Coeur à la Crème
Fruit Yoghurt
Fruit-flavored Yoghurt
Ice Cream Sodas
Ice Cream Sundaes
Geri's Chocolate Mousse

ICES AND SHERBETS

FRUIT ICE

½ cup orange juice or ½ cup unsweetened pineapple juice
1 tablespoon lemon juice
½ cup water
2 ¼-grain tablets saccharin or to taste
1 egg white, stiffly beaten

Combine the fruit juices, water and sweetener. Place in the freezer, stirring often while freezing. When almost frozen, fold in a stiffly beaten egg white and freeze. Serves 1; makes 1 unit fruit.

ORANGE SHERBET

1 small can frozen orange juice
⅔ cup non-fat dry milk
8 ounces milk
6 to 8 ¼-grain tablets saccharin, crushed
½ teaspoon orange extract
Crushed ice as needed (about 1 tray)

Defrost the frozen juice until it can be spooned from the can. Place all ingredients except the ice in the blender. Blend on low to mix. Add ice, turning the blender on and off, on high, until about 4 cups have been made. Taste, and add more sweetener or more ice to taste as needed. Stir with a rubber spatula to keep the sherbet moving. Freeze, stirring occasionally. Serves 6; 1 portion=1 unit fruit, ½ unit milk.

LEMON SHERBET

Juice from 3 lemons
1 cup milk
Dash of lemon extract
¾ cup non-fat dry milk
½ teaspoon liquid artificial sweetener
1 tray crushed ice

Prepare the same as Orange Sherbet.

PINEAPPLE SHERBET

1 large can Dole unsweetened pineapple, packed without sugar or
    syrup
1 cup non-fat dry milk
1 tray crushed ice
10 ¼-grain tablets saccharin or to taste

Purée the pineapple and juice in the blender. Add the dry milk and blend well. Add ice and sweetener gradually until the mixture=about 4 cups. Freeze. Serves 6; each portion=1 unit fruit, ½ unit milk.

RASPBERRY SHERBET

1 cup evaporated milk
1 tablespoon lemon juice
¼ teaspoon lemon rind
Pinch of salt
Saccharin to taste
1 cup fresh or frozen raspberries (without sugar or syrup)
½ teaspoon raspberry extract
1 cup crushed ice or more as needed

Place all ingredients except ice in the blender. Blend well. Add the ice, and blend, stirring with a rubber spatula. Correct flavoring. Serve immediately, or freeze. Serves 4; each serving=½ unit milk, ½ unit fruit.

ORANGE ICE POPS

16 ounces unsweetened orange juice
1 teaspoon orange extract
½ teaspoon artificial sweetener

Mix together, and pour into individual ice pop molds. Makes 8 2-ounce pops; 2 pops=1 unit fruit.

PEACH POPSICLES

3 large ripe peaches
½ teaspoon vanilla extract
12 ¼-grain tablets saccharin or to taste
1 tray crushed ice

Peel the peaches. Cut them up, discarding the pits. Place all the ingredients in the blender, and turn on and off repeatedly until the peaches and ice are chopped and slushy. Pour into ice pop molds. Freeze until hard. Entire recipe=6 units fruit.

ICE CREAM

VANILLA ICE CREAM

1 cup cream
3 eggs
2 cups milk
1⅓ cups non-fat dry milk
1 tablespoon vanilla extract
15 to 20 ¼-grain tablets saccharin
Crushed ice as needed

In the blender combine the cream, eggs, milk, dry milk and extract. Blend on low until mixed. Add the saccharin. Blend on high until the saccharin is crushed. Add the crushed ice, and blend until smooth, stirring with a rubber spatula and adding more ice until the desired flavor and sweetness is arrived at. Freeze in shallow trays or individual ice pop makers. Makes 5 or 6 cups. Entire recipe =6 units milk, so if you make 6 cups, 1 cup=1 unit milk.

Variations:

1. Soak a 2-inch section of vanilla bean overnight in the cream. Discard the outer peel and add the seeds to the recipe.
2. Omit the cream, and add 1 cup evaporated milk (reduce the dry milk to ⅔ cup).

LEMON ICE CREAM

Same as Vanilla Ice Cream, plus ½ teaspoon lemon extract.

MAPLE ICE CREAM

Same as Vanilla Ice Cream: omit the vanilla extract, substitute 1 tablespoon maple flavoring.

COFFEE ICE CREAM

Same as Vanilla Ice Cream, plus 1 heaping teaspoon freeze-dried Sanka.

BUTTER PECAN ICE CREAM

Same as Vanilla Ice Cream, plus ½ teaspoon imitation butter flavoring. After blending, add ½ cup pecans to the blender, and blend on low for a few seconds to chop.

BANANA ICE CREAM

Same as Vanilla Ice Cream, variation #2 (using evaporated milk). Omit the vanilla extract, substitute 1 tablespoon banana flavoring. Add 1 or 2 drops yellow food coloring, and ½ teaspoon imitation butter extract.

CHOCOLATE ICE CREAM

Same as Vanilla Ice Cream, plus 2 tablespoons unsweetened cocoa.

MINT ICE CREAM

Same as Vanilla Ice Cream, plus ½ teaspoon peppermint extract and 4 drops blue food coloring (combined with the yellow of the eggs, it will turn green).

PEANUT BUTTER ICE CREAM

Same as Vanilla Ice Cream, plus 2 tablespoons peanut butter (sugarless). After blending, toss in ¼ to ½ cup salted peanuts and blend briefly on low to chop.

EGGNOG ICE CREAM

Same as Vanilla Ice Cream: omit the vanilla extract, substitute 1 teaspoon rum flavoring.

STRAWBERRY ICE CREAM

1 cup cream
1 cup non-fat dry milk
1½ cups fresh or frozen strawberries (loose frozen without sugar or
   syrup)
3 eggs
Dash of salt
Dash of red food coloring
15 to 20 ¼-grain tablets saccharin
1 teaspoon strawberry extract
1 cup crushed ice

Combine the cream and dry milk in the blender. Blend on low
until mixed. Add the other ingredients. Chop, turning on and off
until the strawberries are chopped. Add more ice if needed. Eat
as is immediately for soft ice cream, or freeze in ice trays or shallow
pan. Count toward fruit units. Serves 3; each serving=1 unit milk,
½ unit fruit.

PEACH ICE CREAM

Same as Strawberry Ice Cream; use 6 halves of diet canned (without
sugar or syrup) peaches, or 3 fresh peaches, dipped in boiling water
and peeled.

PUMPKIN ICE CREAM

1½ cups canned pumpkin (plain)
4 eggs
1 cup evaporated milk
½ teaspoon vanilla
½ teaspoon ginger
¼ teaspoon ground cardamom
2 cups milk
½ cup cream

½ cup non-fat dry milk
1 teaspoon cinnamon
½ teaspoon ground cloves
15 to 20 ¼-grain tablets saccharin

Combine all ingredients in the blender and blend well. Freeze, stirring occasionally to mix the frozen and unfrozen portions. Serves 6; each portion=1 unit milk, ½ unit limited vegetable.

PINEAPPLE ICE CREAM

1 large can Dole unsweetened pineapple, packed in its own juice
    without sugar
1 cup cream
2 cups milk
1 teaspoon pineapple extract
Dash of salt
2 eggs
1 cup non-fat dry milk
10 to 15 ¼-grain tablets saccharin

Empty the pineapple, including the juice, into the blender. Purée. Add the other ingredients and blend well. Freeze, stirring occasionally. Serves 6; each portion=1 unit milk, 1 unit fruit.

FUDGE POPS

1 cup non-fat dry milk
2 cups milk
2 tablespoons unsweetened cocoa
10 ¼-grain tablets saccharin or to taste
½ cup heavy cream
½ teaspoon vanilla extract
3 eggs
1 cup crushed ice or more as needed

Place the dry milk and milk in the blender and blend on low. Add the cocoa and saccharin. Blend until well mixed. Add the other ingredients. Blend on high until smooth and thick, adding more ice if needed. Pour into individual ice pop molds, or use small plastic glasses with a plastic fork inserted in each. Freeze until firm, and unmold. Makes about 10 pops. Entire recipe=5 units milk; 1 pop =approximately ½ unit milk.

FROZEN MILKY-RICH BARS

1 cup heavy cream
1 cup milk
½ teaspoon vanilla
Dash of salt
1 cup non-fat dry milk
2 eggs
1 tablespoon unsweetened cocoa
10 ¼-grain tablets saccharin
½ cup broken walnut meats or more

Place all ingredients except the nuts in the blender. Blend until smooth. Stir in the nuts, mixing by hand. Pour into individual ice pop molds. Freeze until hard. Makes about 8 pops. Entire recipe=4 units milk; 1 pop=½ unit milk.

APPLE ICE CREAM

2 red-skinned apples, cored (not peeled)
2 tablespoons lemon juice
½ cup milk
1 cup heavy cream
12 to 15 ¼-grain tablets saccharin
½ cup non-fat dry milk
1 or 2 drops red food coloring
1 egg
¾ tablespoon cinnamon

Slice the apples into the blender. Add the lemon juice and milk. Blend until the apple is liquefied. Add the other ingredients and blend well. Pour into shallow pans and freeze. Makes about 12 pops. Entire recipe=4 units fruit; 3 pops=1 unit fruit.

LEMON PEEL ICE CREAM

1¼ cups buttermilk
½ cup non-fat dry milk
1 egg
2 tablespoons lemon juice
½ teaspoon lemon extract
1 teaspoon dehydrated lemon peel
6 ¼-grain tablets crushed saccharin or more to taste

Combine all ingredients, and mix or blend until well mixed. Pour into ice pop molds. Insert sticks and freeze until hard. Makes 6 2-ounce pops; each pop=½ unit milk.

ORANGE CREAM POPS

3 ounces frozen orange juice concentrate, slightly thawed
5 ounces water
½ cup non-fat dry milk
1 egg
6 to 8 ¼-grain tablets saccharin
¼ cup evaporated milk
1½ cups milk
1 teaspoon vanilla extract

Mix the juice and water together to make 8 ounces of juice. Put aside 4 ounces of the juice. Using the other 4 ounces, pour a little into the bottom of 12 popsicle molds. Swish the molds around a little to coat the sides with juice and freeze. Combine the remaining ingredients except for the juice. Place them in the blender and blend on low until the saccharin is completely dissolved. Pour into the pop molds over the frozen orange juice. Freeze until slightly frozen to the touch. Pour in the remaining orange juice and insert the popsicle sticks (or plastic forks). Freeze until hard. Makes 12 2-ounce popsicles; each pop=½ unit fruit, and ¼ unit milk.

MILK-SHAKE POPSICLES

Freeze leftovers of any milk-shake recipe (see Beverages), in popsicle molds. Turn out when frozen. For units of milk, see the original recipe.

EGGNOG POPSICLES

Freeze leftovers of any eggnog recipe (see Beverages).

FROZEN YOGHURT

1 cup plain unflavored yoghurt
2 tablespoons sugarless jelly (homemade or Polaner)
Liquid artificial sweetener as needed

Prepare fruit yoghurt by mixing yoghurt and jelly together. Sweeten to taste. Pour into individual ice pop molds or plastic cup and freeze until hard. Makes 1 serving, which=1 unit milk.

GELATIN DESSERTS

JIFFY GELATIN

1 16-ounce bottle diet soda (sugarless, any fruit flavor)
1 tablespoon or 1 envelope unflavored gelatin

Pour ½ cup of the soda into a bowl and sprinkle in the gelatin to soften. Pour the remaining soda into a saucepan and heat until boiling rapidly. Pour the hot soda over the gelatin mixture, stirring until dissolved. Pour into 4 individual bowls and chill until firm (or place in freezer for a short time, to chill more rapidly). Serves 4.

ORANGE GELATIN

Same as Jiffy Gelatin, but omit the soda, and use 16 ounces orange juice. Makes 4 ½-cup servings; each serving=1 unit fruit.

MOLDED FRUIT SALAD

1 16-ounce bottle fruit-flavored diet soda
1 tablespoon plus 1 teaspoon unflavored gelatin
1 large apple, peeled, cored and diced
1 large pear, diced
½ teaspoon orange extract

Pour ½ cup of the soda into a large bowl. Sprinkle in the gelatin to soften and set aside. Heat the rest of the soda in a saucepan until boiling. Pour the boiling soda over the gelatin mixture and stir until dissolved. Chill until syrupy and slightly thickened. Add the fruit and extract, stirring. Pour into a large mold or into individual dishes. Makes 4 servings; each serving=1 unit fruit.

RASPBERRY WHIP

1 bottle diet raspberry soda
1½ tablespoons unflavored gelatin
10 ¼-grain tablets saccharin
½ teaspoon raspberry extract
½ cup crushed ice
½ cup light cream, chilled

Pour ½ cup of the soda into a bowl. Sprinkle in the gelatin to soften. Heat the rest of the soda to boiling and combine with the gelatin mixture. Add the sweetener and extract and stir to dissolve. Stir in the ice. Chill until the thickness of egg whites. Chill the cream, and a large bowl and beaters. Beat the cream until stiff. Fold the cream into the thickened gelatin, and beat until thick and frothy. Chill until firm. Serves 4.

BLACK CHERRY WHIP

Same as Raspberry Whip, but using black cherry soda and extract. Also try strawberry soda and extract, etc.

CRANBERRY WHIP

2 cups cranberries
1½ cups orange diet soda
2 tablespoons gelatin
10 ¼-grain tablets saccharin or more to taste
¼ cup cream

Cook the cranberries in 1 cup of the soda until soft. Set aside. Dissolve the gelatin in the remaining soda. Add the hot cranberry mixture and saccharin and stir until the gelatin is dissolved. Chill until syrupy, then beat until foamy. Whip the cream separately, then fold into the cranberry mixture. Chill in parfait glasses until set. Entire recipe=4 units fruit. Serves 4 to 6.

RASPBERRY MOUSSE

1 cup heavy cream
1 tablespoon plus 1 teaspoon unflavored gelatin
1 16-ounce bottle raspberry diet soda (without sugar only, or any other flavor)
½ teaspoon raspberry extract
4 to 6 ¼-grain tablets saccharin or more to taste
Dash of red food coloring (optional)

Pour the cream into the blender container and sprinkle the gelatin on the cream to soften. Pour the soda into a pan and heat until simmering. Pour into the blender, add the other ingredients, cover the blender and blend on high. Mixture should be almost doubled in amount. Pour into a mold or individual dishes, and chill until firm. Serves 4.

PUDDINGS AND CUSTARDS

INSTANT VANILLA PUDDING

1 cup cream
2 eggs
1⅓ cups non-fat dry milk
1 tablespoon vanilla extract
¼ teaspoon imitation butter flavoring
12 to 15 ¼-grain tablets saccharin
1 or 2 drops yellow food coloring (optional)
2 tablespoons unflavored gelatin
1½ cups boiling water
1 tray crushed ice or as needed

Pour the cream and eggs into the blender. Add the dry milk and blend on low for a few seconds. Add the flavorings and sweetener and blend again. Sprinkle the gelatin on top to soften, and blend for a second on low to mix. Pour in the boiling water. Blend on low until well mixed. Add some of the ice, and continue blending and adding ice until the mixture=about 5 cups and is thick. Pour into dishes immediately, and let stand for 1 minute in the refrigerator to harden before serving. Entire recipe=4 units milk. If using evaporated milk instead of cream, entire recipe would=6 units milk.

INSTANT CHOCOLATE PUDDING

Same as Instant Vanilla Pudding plus 2 tablespoons unsweetened cocoa, which should be added with the dry milk.

BUTTERSCOTCH PUDDING

Same as Instant Vanilla Pudding, except: omit the vanilla extract and substitute ½ teaspoon maple flavoring, plus another ¼ teaspoon butter flavoring.

BANANA PUDDING

Same as Instant Vanilla Pudding: except omit the vanilla extract and substitute 1 teaspoon banana flavoring.

EGGNOG BAVARIAN

2 eggs
1 cup light cream
3 tablespoons unflavored gelatin
2 cups milk
20 ¼-grain tablets saccharin
¼ teaspoon nutmeg
1 teaspoon vanilla extract
1 teaspoon rum flavoring
Dash of salt
Dash of allspice
2 egg whites
½ cup heavy cream
1 cup frozen strawberries (sugarless)
1 cup coarsely chopped nuts

Combine the eggs and light cream in a bowl and beat well. Sprinkle in the gelatin to soften. In a saucepan heat the milk until almost boiling. Pour into the egg mixture and mix well. Add the sweetener, nutmeg and other seasonings. Stir until the saccharin and gelatin are dissolved. Chill until syrupy. Beat the egg whites until stiff. Whip the heavy cream. Carefully fold the cream and the egg whites into the gelatin. Pour into a mold or tube pan and chill until firm. Unmold on a plate. Thaw the strawberries slightly and purée in the blender, adding sweetener to taste. Pour over the mold or pour over individual servings. Garnish with chopped nuts. This tastes very rich, but the entire recipe contains only 2 units milk and 1 unit fruit. Serves 8 to 10.

COOKED CHOCOLATE PUDDING

1 square bitter chocolate (unsweetened)
4 eggs, beaten
1 cup evaporated milk or light cream
10 ¼-grain tablets saccharin
1 teaspoon vanilla extract
Dash of salt

Melt the chocolate over a double boiler. Slowly add the eggs, then the other ingredients. Stir and cook until the pudding is thickened. Pour into dishes, cool, then chill in the refrigerator. Serves 4. If evaporated milk is used, each serving=½ unit milk.

BAKED CUSTARD

4 cups milk
¼ teaspoon salt
15 ¼-grain tablets saccharin
4 extra large eggs
2 teaspoons vanilla extract
Dash of freshly ground nutmeg

Combine the milk, salt and saccharin in a pan and heat until scalded. Remove from the heat. In a bowl, combine the eggs and vanilla. Beat until mixed, and slowly beat in the scalded milk. Pour into a shallow baking dish. Sprinkle the nutmeg on top. Place the dish in a pan with 1 inch of hot water. Bake at 325° for 40 minutes, or until a knife inserted a few inches from the side of the pan comes out clean. Remove and allow to cool at room temperature. Serve as is, or chill in the refrigerator. Makes 4 large or 8 small servings. Entire recipe=4 units milk.

APPLE PUDDING

3 large tart apples
1 cup milk
3 tablespoons unflavored gelatin
20 ¼-grain tablets saccharin
2 eggs
1 tablespoon cinnamon
1 or 2 drops red food coloring
Pinch of salt
1 cup heavy cream

Core and slice the apples. Place in the blender, add the milk and blend to liquefy. Pour into a saucepan or double boiler. Sprinkle the gelatin on top of the apple mixture, add the saccharin and heat. Stir until the gelatin is dissolved, and the mixture is hot. Remove from the heat and chill until syrupy. Pour into the blender and while the blender is running on low, add the other ingredients, ending with the cream. Whip on high briefly until doubled in size. Pour into a mold and chill. To remove from the mold when firm, set the mold in a pan of hot water for a few seconds, then turn upside down on a flat plate. Serves 6; each serving=1 unit fruit.

BREAD PUDDING

4 eggs, slightly beaten
1 cup milk
2 thick slices homemade high-carbohydrate bread
10 ¼-grain tablets saccharin
Dash of freshly ground nutmeg
1 tablespoon vanilla extract
½ teaspoon cinnamon
¼ cup "White Raisins" (optional) (see Candies)

Beat the eggs and milk together. Tear the bread into pieces, and add to the egg mixture along with the remaining ingredients. Soak for 15 minutes, or until the bread has absorbed most of the egg. Stir in the "raisins" if you are using them. Pour into a well-greased pan. Sprinkle the top with a little more nutmeg. Bake at 350° for 45 minutes to 1 hour. Serves 4; each serving=½ unit carbohydrate, trace of fruit if using "White Raisins."

SOY GRITS PUDDING

1 cup soy grits
1 cup milk
½ cup water
2 eggs, beaten
10 ¼-grain tablets saccharin
1 teaspoon cinnamon
1 cup evaporated milk or light cream
1 tablespoon vanilla
Dash of nutmeg

Soak the grits in the milk and water for 30 minutes. Transfer to a saucepan, cover and cook over low heat until the grits are soft (about 45 minutes, adding more water if needed). Combine all ingredients and pour into a greased baking dish. Set in a pan of water and bake at 325° for 1 hour or until set. Serves 6 people; each serving=½ unit milk.

APPLE OATMEAL PUDDING

2 cups milk
½ cup old-fashioned-style oatmeal (uncooked)
2 small apples
½ cup non-fat dry milk
¼ teaspoon salt
1 teaspoon cinnamon
1 egg, beaten
1 tablespoon butter
10 ¼-grain tablets saccharin, crushed

Heat the milk in a double boiler and stir in the oatmeal. Cut up the apples. Combine all ingredients and pour into a greased casserole. Bake at 325° until set (about 45 minutes to 1 hour). Serves 4; each serving=1 unit carbohydrate, ½ unit fruit, ½ unit milk.

MAPLE OATMEAL PUDDING

2 cups cooked oatmeal
½ cup evaporated milk or light cream
2 tablespoons butter
2 eggs, slightly beaten
½ teaspoon maple flavoring
10 ¼-grain tablets saccharin

Cook the oatmeal according to the package directions for 4 servings. Combine with the other ingredients and mix. Pour into a casserole and bake at 350° until set (about 45 minutes). Serves 4; each serving=1 unit carbohydrate.

APPLE BROWN BETTY

½ cup soy grits
½ cup apple juice
1 thick slice homemade Oatmeal Bread
3 tablespoons melted butter
4 small tart apples, peeled, cored and sliced
½ cup nuts, ground fine to medium
1 tablespoon oil
¼ cup freshly ground nutmeg
1 tablespoon liquid artificial sweetener
2 teaspoons cinnamon

Soak the grits in the apple juice for 20 minutes. Toss together the cubed or crumbed bread and the melted butter and set aside. Arrange half the apples in a greased baking dish. Mix the other ingredients together. Add a layer of the soy grits mixture, a layer of apples, and soy grits. Top with the bread cube mixture. Sprinkle the top with additional cinnamon and sweetener to taste. Bake in a covered casserole at 375° for 15 minutes. Uncover and bake for 45 minutes at 325°. Serves 4; each serving=1 unit fruit.

FRUIT DESSERTS

APPLE SAUCE

6 medium tart apples
2 cups water
1 tablespoon cinnamon
Saccharin to taste
Red food coloring (optional)

Peel, core and slice several tart apples. Place them in a saucepan with the water. Cover the saucepan and cook until soft. Mash the pulp, add 1 tablespoon cinnamon and crushed saccharin to taste. Also add 1 drop of red food coloring (optional). Cool, then refrigerate. Makes 8 small servings; each serving=1 unit fruit.

BAKED APPLES

4 large baking apples
8 large strawberries (optional)
16 ounces red fruit-flavored diet soda
1 tablespoon cinnamon

Core the apples; do not peel. Cut the apples in half and place the halves in a baking dish, cut side up. Place 1 strawberry in the center of each apple. Pour the soda over the apples and sprinkle them with cinnamon. Bake at 325° for about 1 hour, or until the apples are soft but not mushy. The skins should be slightly wrinkled and soft to the touch. Each half apple=1 unit fruit. Serves 8.

APPLE SNACKS

1 large apple
Juice of 1 lemon
Sugarless peanut butter as needed
Coconut meal as needed

Core 1 large apple. Slice crosswise ½ inch thick. Dip the slices in lemon juice. Spread each slice with sugarless peanut butter and sprinkle with unsweetened coconut flakes or coconut meal. Serves 2; entire recipe=2 units fruit.

APPLE CHEESE WHEELS

6 small apples
1 3-ounce package cream cheese at room temperature
2 tablespoons lemon juice
½ teaspoon liquid artificial sweetener

Peel and core the apples. Mash the cream cheese with the juice and sweetener. Stuff the cheese mixture into the centers of the apples. Chill and slice the apples ½ inch thick, so that the cheese is in the center of each slice. Sprinkle with more lemon juice and powdered sweetener or crushed saccharin to taste. Chill and serve. Serves 6; each serving=1 unit fruit.

BAKED PEARS

3 large ripe Bartlett pears
1 bottle diet ginger ale
½ teaspoon cinnamon
½ teaspoon allspice

Split the pears and place them in a baking dish, cut side up. Pour the soda over the pears; sprinkle them evenly with the spices and bake at 350° until the pears are soft, turning occasionally (about 45 minutes). Serves 6; each pear half=1 unit fruit.

BRANDY PEARS

3 large ripe pears
4 ¼-grain tablets saccharin, crushed
½ teaspoon cinnamon
Dash of freshly ground nutmeg
½ teaspoon imitation brandy flavoring

1 or 2 drops red food coloring
2 tablespoons lemon juice
½ cup water

Core the pears and slice thinly (about 8 sections per pear). Combine the other ingredients and pour over the pears. Refrigerate for several hours. Serves 6; 4 slices=1 unit fruit.

PARTY PEARS

¼ cup salted Spanish peanuts
½ cup sugarless peanut butter
1 tablespoon lemon juice
2 fresh pears, peeled, cored and halved
½ teaspoon grated lemon rind
Sweetener to taste

Chop the peanuts coarsely. Mix them with the peanut butter and juice. Divide into equal portions and stuff the mixture into the cavities of the pears. Sprinkle lightly with sweetener and grated lemon rind. Serves 4; each pear half=1 unit fruit.

BAKED PINEAPPLE

1 medium pineapple, very ripe
1 bottle strawberry diet soda (sugarless)
½ teaspoon cinnamon
1 teaspoon strawberry extract

Remove the peel and stem from the pineapple. Split it in half, then slice. Arrange the slices in a baking dish and pour in the soda. Sprinkle in the cinnamon and extract and bake until the pineapple is soft and reddish (325° for 1 hour). Serves 8; each slice=½ unit fruit (makes 16 slices).

FROZEN PINEAPPLE

1 very ripe pineapple
Liquid artificial sweetener as needed

Peel and core the pineapple. Slice in half, then slice each half making a total of 32 thin slices (16 from each half). Place a sheet of wax paper on a baking sheet, and arrange the pineapple slices on it so that none are touching. Sprinkle the pineapple generously with the liquid sweetener. Place the baking sheet in the freezer, and freeze until hard enough to hold without bending. Eat as is. If not serving immediately, freeze hard, then thaw at room temperature for a few minutes when serving. Serves 8; each serving (4 slices)=1 unit fruit.

AMBROSIA

1 large apple
½ cantaloupe
1 orange (seedless)
1 large ripe pear
1 tablespoon liquid artificial sweetener or more to taste
1½ cups sour cream
½ cup freshly grated coconut (packed down)

Peel and dice the fruit. Toss with the sweetener. Add the sour cream, toss lightly and sprinkle with the coconut. Serves 6; each serving=1 unit fruit.

BAKED AMBROSIA

4 small apples, cored and sliced
½ lemon, sliced thin (including peel)
4 small oranges, peeled and sliced
1 cup water
1 cup walnuts, broken
20 ¼-grain tablets saccharin
1½ teaspoons cinnamon
½ teaspoon ground cloves
Dash of allspice
½ cup freshly grated coconut

Toss the fruit with the other ingredients except the coconut. Pour into a greased casserole. Sprinkle the coconut on top. Bake at 350°

for 30 minutes, or until the apples are soft. Eat as is, or top with plain yoghurt or sour cream. Entire recipe=8 units fruit. Serves 8.

FRUIT COCKTAIL

1 small apple
1 medium grapefruit
1 small orange (seedless)
1 teaspoon lemon juice
4 ounces orange juice
1 teaspoon liquid artificial sweetener

Peel the fruit and cut into small pieces. Toss with other ingredients and chill. Serves 4. Entire recipe=4 units fruit.

STEWED RHUBARB

1 pound fresh rhubarb
1 bottle strawberry diet soda
3 or 4 drops red food coloring
½ teaspoon strawberry flavoring
8 to 10 ¼-grain tablets saccharin or to taste

Trim the rhubarb and discard the leaves. Cut stalks into 1-inch pieces. Place in a saucepan, and pour in enough soda to cover. Cover the pan and simmer on low heat until soft. Add the other ingredients plus more soda if needed. Chill before serving. Serves 4.

STEWED FRUIT

4 tiny blue Italian plums
2 small apricots
1 medium pear, ripe
½ small lemon, sliced thin
2 cups water
Sweetener to taste

Cut the fruit in quarters, removing the pits and seeds. Combine all ingredients in a saucepan. Cover and bring to a boil. Lower the heat and simmer gently until the fruit is soft. Remove the cover and simmer for 1 hour on very low heat. Correct sweetness to taste. Serves 5. Entire recipe, including the juice=5 units fruit.

COOKIES

CHOCOLATE MACAROONS

2 squares unsweetened chocolate (2 ounces)
2 cups shredded unsweetened coconut (available at health food stores, or shred your own)
½ cup non-fat dry milk
1 teaspoon vanilla
1¼ cups evaporated milk
Crushed saccharin to taste
¼ teaspoon salt

Melt the chocolate over hot water. Add the other ingredients, including sweetener to taste. Drop by teaspoonfuls onto a greased cookie sheet. Bake in a preheated 325° oven for 15 minutes. Entire recipe=3 units milk. If you make 12 cookies, 4 cookies=1 unit milk.

ALMOND MACAROONS

4 egg whites
Pinch of salt
½ teaspoon cream of tartar
1 cup almonds, ground fine in the blender
2 teaspoons liquid artificial sweetener
1 orange rind, grated
1 teaspoon almond extract

Combine the egg whites, salt and cream of tartar in a bowl. Beat until stiff. Combine with the other ingredients, folding gently to mix. Drop by teaspoonfuls 1 inch apart on an oiled baking sheet. Bake in a preheated 300° oven for 15 minutes. Increase to 350°

and bake until lightly browned on top. Makes about 2 dozen cookies.

NUT MACAROONS

4 egg whites
10 ¼-grain tablets saccharin, crushed
1 teaspoon vanilla extract
¼ teaspoon cream of tartar
1 cup pignola nuts

Preheat the oven to 325°. Beat the egg whites, sweetener, vanilla and cream of tartar together until stiff. Sprinkle half the nuts over the mixture and fold in gently. Scoop carefully by rounded teaspoonfuls onto an oiled cookie sheet. Sprinkle the rest of the nuts onto the cookies. Bake for 15 minutes, or until lightly browned. Makes about 2 dozen cookies.

SPONGE COOKIES

8 eggs, separated, at room temperature
Pinch of salt
20 ¼-grain tablets saccharin, crushed
3 tablespoons hot water
¼ teaspoon lemon extract
1 tablespoon lemon juice
½ teaspoon dehydrated lemon peel
1 cup oat flour
1 teaspoon baking powder
Pecan halves as needed

Beat the egg whites and salt together until stiff but not dry. Beat the egg yolks separately until pale yellow. Add the sweetener, water and flavorings to the yolks and beat well. Sift the dry ingredients into the egg mixture gradually, beating until well mixed. Fold in the whites carefully. Pour into greased or Teflon-lined muffin tins until ½ inch high. Top each with a pecan half. Bake until golden brown. Entire recipe=8 units carbohydrate. If you make 16 cookies, 2 cookies=1 unit carbohydrate.

PEANUT BUTTER COOKIES

1 cup oat flour
½ cup sugarless peanut butter
1 teaspoon baking powder
4 tablespoons liquid artificial sweetener
1 egg, slightly beaten
1 tablespoon melted butter
½ cup milk
½ teaspoon salt

Mix all ingredients together until blended. Roll into 1-inch balls. Place 2 inches apart on Teflon-lined or oiled cookie sheet. Flatten the cookies with a fork, making a crisscross design. Bake in a preheated 400° oven for 12 minutes, or until brown. If you make 24 cookies, 3 cookies=1 unit carbohydrate. Entire recipe=8 units carbohydrate.

BREAD-CRUMB COOKIES

2 slices homemade high-carbohydrate bread, crumbled in the blender
1 cup ground almonds
¼ pound softened butter
2 eggs
¼ teaspoon vanilla
1 tablespoon cinnamon
1 teaspoon ground cloves
15 ¼-grain tablets saccharin, crushed
Whole almonds as needed

Mix all ingredients except the whole almonds. Form into balls and flatten with a fork on a greased cookie sheet. Press an almond into the center of each cookie, flattening them so that the almonds are well stuck. Bake in a preheated 325° oven for about 20 minutes. Makes 2 dozen cookies; entire recipe=2 units carbohydrate.

PUMPKIN COOKIES

½ medium can pumpkin (1 cup)
½ cup non-fat dry milk
½ stick butter, at room temperature
Liquid artificial sweetener to taste
2 teaspoons cinnamon
¼ teaspoon nutmeg
2 eggs
½ cup oat flour
1 tablespoon vanilla
¼ teaspoon salt
¼ teaspoon ginger
¼ teaspoon ground cloves

Combine all ingredients and mix well. Drop by heaping table-spoonfuls on a greased cookie sheet. Bake at 325° until firm and lightly browned. These cookies should be refrigerated, and will not keep too long. Entire recipe=4 units carbohydrate, 4 units limited vegetable. If you make 16 cookies, 4 cookies=1 serving.

OATMEAL WHEAT-GERM COOKIES

2 eggs, slightly beaten
1 cup old-fashioned-style oatmeal, uncooked
¼ cup oil
¼ cup soy flour
2 tablespoons vanilla extract
1 cup wheat germ
½ cup non-fat dry milk
¼ cup butter at room temperature
30 ¼-grain tablets saccharin, crushed
1 tablespoon cinnamon
½ teaspoon coriander

Combine all ingredients and mix well. Preheat the oven to 350°. Drop by teaspoonfuls onto a greased cookie sheet. Flatten slightly with a wet spoon. Bake 12 to 15 minutes. For crisper cookies, use only 1 egg. Makes about 4 dozen cookies; 4 cookies=approximately 1 unit carbohydrate.

SOY GRITS COOKIES

⅔ cup soy grits
¼ cup oat flour
1 teaspoon cinnamon
1 teaspoon vanilla
2 eggs, slightly beaten
¼ cup non-fat dry milk
¼ cup butter at room temperature
1 tablespoon liquid artificial sweetener

Mix all ingredients until well blended. Refrigerate for 20 minutes. Preheat the oven to 350°. Drop by tablespoonfuls 2 inches apart on a cookie sheet. Pat out flat with a spoon. Bake 10 minutes or until lightly browned. Makes 16 cookies; 4 cookies=½ unit carbohydrate.

SESAME SEED COOKIES

1 egg
¼ cup oat flour
½ teaspoon vanilla extract
¼ teaspoon salt
Artificial sweetener to taste
¼ cup sugarless peanut butter
¼ cup sesame seeds plus more as needed
¼ teaspoon baking powder
1 teaspoon oil

Mix all ingredients together. Roll each ball in additional sesame seeds until covered. Flatten slightly on an oiled cookie sheet. Bake in a preheated 375° oven for 12 minutes. Makes about 1 dozen cookies; 3 cookies=½ unit carbohydrate.

PECAN BALLS

½ cup butter at room temperature
1 cup finely ground pecans
1 cup oat flour
1 teaspoon vanilla
2 teaspoons liquid artificial sweetener
½ teaspoon almond extract

Cream the butter and mix in the other ingredients. Form into small balls. Bake in a preheated 375° oven until lightly browned (about 10 minutes). Refrigerate and serve cold. Makes 16 cookies; 2 balls= 1 unit carbohydrate.

COCONUT CRESCENTS

6 egg whites
1½ cups unsweetened coconut meal (available at health food stores)
Pinch of salt
½ teaspoon almond extract
Saccharin to taste

Beat the egg whites until stiff. Mix together the other ingredients and fold the mixture into the egg whites. Drop by teaspoonfuls 1 inch apart on a cookie sheet which has been covered with heavy brown paper. Bake at 300° for 30 minutes, or until lightly browned. Remove from the oven, and place a wet dish towel between the pan and the paper. The steam will allow the cookies to be removed. Cool on racks. Makes 3 dozen cookies.

ROGELACH

1 recipe cream cheese dough (see Cream Cheese Crust)
½ tart apple, minced fine
1 tablespoon cinnamon
½ cup ground walnuts
Crushed saccharin to taste

Make the dough according to the recipe. Chill until firm. Separate into quarters for easier handling and chill when not in use. Roll the dough out between two sheets of wax paper floured with a little oat flour. Using a 2½-inch glass, cut the dough into circles. Combine the other ingredients in a bowl and mix, moistening with a little water. Place ½ teaspoon of the filling in the center of each circle of dough. Fold two edges together overlapping in the center, with the ends open so that the filling is visible. Preheat the oven to 325°. Bake for 20 minutes, or until lightly browned. Makes 18 cookies; 6 rogelach=1 unit carbohydrate.

PFEFFERNUESSE

2 eggs
¼ cup butter, softened
30 ¼-grain tablets saccharin, crushed
¼ teaspoon anise flavoring
½ teaspoon each: ground cloves, allspice, coriander, dehydrated lemon peel
⅛ teaspoon freshly ground pepper
1 teaspoon cinnamon
Pinch of salt
1½ cups oat flour
½ teaspoon baking soda
1¾ cups finely ground almonds

Beat the eggs. Add the butter, sweetener, extract and spices, and beat together. Add the remaining ingredients and beat well. Chill the dough. When firm, shape the dough into small balls. Bake in a preheated 325° oven for 15 minutes, or until lightly browned. Remove when cool. Makes 3 dozen balls; 2 or 3 balls=approximately 1 unit carbohydrate.

CHOCOLATE MINT BARS

½ cup sweet butter, softened
30 ¼-grain tablets saccharin, crushed
2 eggs, slightly beaten
1 teaspoon peppermint extract
2 teaspoons vanilla
2 squares unsweetened chocolate, melted, or 2 envelopes Nestlé's
   Choco-Bake chocolate
½ cup oat flour
1 cup finely chopped walnuts
Dash of salt

Cream the butter until fluffy. Mix in the saccharin, eggs and extracts. Beat until smooth. Blend in the remaining ingredients and mix well. Pour into a greased 8-inch square pan. Bake at 350° for 20 minutes. Chill until firm, then remove from the pan and cut into 16 bars. Four bars=1 unit carbohydrate.

COCONUT COOKIES

½ cup evaporated milk
½ teaspoon coconut flavoring
⅛ teaspoon salt
4 tablespoons non-fat dry milk
4 tablespoons unsweetened coconut meal plus more as needed
1 tablespoon liquid artificial sweetener
⅓ cup soy grits

Combine all ingredients. Stir to mix well. Let the mixture stand 20 minutes. Add more milk if the mixture is too stiff. Drop by teaspoonfuls onto a greased cookie sheet. Sprinkle each cookie with a little additional coconut meal. Bake in a preheated 350° oven for 20 minutes. Cool slightly before removing. Makes 16 cookies.

OATMEAL-SPICE COOKIES

¼ cup oat flour
¾ cup old-fashioned-style oatmeal
¼ cup soy flour
1 teaspoon baking powder
1 tablespoon vanilla extract
1 teaspoon cinnamon
¼ cup oil
½ cup non-fat dry milk
2 eggs, slightly beaten
¼ teaspoon salt
1 tablespoon pumpkin pie spice
½ cup evaporated milk
20 ¼-grain tablets saccharin

Combine all ingredients. Mix well. Drop by tablespoonfuls onto a greased cookie sheet. Bake in a preheated 375° oven for 10 minutes. Makes 24 cookies; 3 cookies=1 unit carbohydrate.

CAKES

SPONGE CAKE

8 eggs, separated, at room temperature
Pinch of salt
40 ¼-grain tablets saccharin, crushed
3 tablespoons hot water
2 tablespoons lemon juice
¼ teaspoon lemon extract
½ teaspoon dehydrated lemon peel
1 cup oat flour
1 teaspoon baking powder

Beat the egg whites and salt together until they are stiff but not dry. Beat the egg yolks until pale yellow. Add the sweetener, water, juice and flavoring. Beat together. Sift the flour and baking powder

and add to the egg mixture gradually, beat until well mixed. Fold
the egg whites into the egg yolk mixture. Pour into a small greased
tube pan or large loaf pan. Bake in a preheated 300° oven for 1
hour. Makes 8 servings; each serving=1 unit carbohydrate.

SPONGE CUP CAKES

Prepare as for Sponge Cake. Pour into greased or Teflon-lined muffin
tins, until three quarters full. Bake until the cake springs back
when pressed. Turn out, pry gently apart and fill the center with the
desired filling (such as sugarless jelly) or ice the top with any given
icing. Makes 8 cupcakes; each cupcake=1 unit carbohydrate.

CHOCOLATE MERINGUE CAKE

6 egg whites
Pinch of salt
½ teaspoon cream of tartar
¼ cup unsweetened cocoa
½ cup sifted oat flour
40 ¼-grain tablets saccharin, crushed
½ teaspoon almond extract
1 pint heavy cream
1 teaspoon vanilla extract
½ cup slivered almonds

Preheat the oven to 350°. Beat the egg whites until they are stiff
but not dry. Add the salt, cream of tartar, and beat again. In a large
bowl, sift together the cocoa and flour. Add most of the sweetener
and the almond extract. Gently fold in the beaten egg whites.
Spread the mixture gingerly in two greased 8-inch cake pans, being
careful not to crush the mixture down. Bake for 30 minutes. Remove
from the oven and cool. When cool, remove from the pans and set
aside. Beat the cream, vanilla and the remaining crushed saccharin
until heavily whipped. Spread a thick layer of whipped cream between the layers and spread a layer on top of the cake. Sprinkle the
top with slivered almonds. Serves 8; each serving=½ unit carbohydrate.

ANGEL FOOD CAKE

1 cup oat flour
10 to 12 egg whites (1⅓ cups) at room temperature
¼ teaspoon salt
1¼ teaspoons cream of tartar
40 ¼-grain tablets saccharin, crushed
1 teaspoon vanilla extract
¼ teaspoon almond extract

Sift flour several times. Place the egg whites in a large bowl. Sprinkle in the salt and cream of tartar and beat until the whites are stiff but not dry. Beat in the artificial sweetener and vanilla with a wire whisk. Add the flour, folding gently until mixed. Pour into an ungreased tube pan. Bake at 300° for 1 hour, or until it springs back when pressed. Serves 8; each serving=1 unit carbohydrate.

OATMEAL CAKE

1½ cups boiling water
1 cup old-fashioned-style oats
½ cup non-fat dry milk
1 tablespoon vanilla extract
1 tablespoon cinnamon
¼ cup milk
1 teaspoon salt
1 tablespoon butter or oil
30 ¼-grain tablets saccharin, crushed
6 eggs

Preheat the oven to 375°. Pour boiling water over the oatmeal and stir. Add all the ingredients except the eggs and mix. Place the eggs in a mixing bowl and beat until more than double in size. Add the oatmeal mixture and beat until well mixed. Pour into two greased layer cake pans or a loaf pan. Bake for 5 minutes. Lower the heat to 325° and bake for 40 minutes. Makes 8 servings; each serving= 1 unit carbohydrate.

COCONUT CAKE

6 eggs
¾ cup oil
2 teaspoons vanilla extract
1 teaspoon liquid artificial sweetener
¾ cup milk
1½ cups oat flour
1 teaspoon baking powder
½ teaspoon salt
1½ cups coconut meal
½ cup chopped walnuts

Place the eggs, oil, vanilla and sweetener in the blender. Blend on high till almost double in amount. Add the milk if there is room and blend well. Pour into a bowl. Sift together the flour, baking powder and salt, and add them to the batter. Mix in the remaining ingredients, beat until well mixed and pour into a well-greased loaf pan. Bake in a preheated 400° oven for 15 minutes. Lower the heat to 325° and bake for 45 minutes longer. Can be served as is, with butter, or with icing or topping. Divide into 12 slices; 1 slice=1 unit carbohydrate.

JOHNNY'S APPLE CAKE

2 eggs, beaten
½ cup oat flour
¼ cup soy flour
1 tablespoon cinnamon
10 ¼-grain tablets saccharin, crushed
½ cup evaporated milk
2 tablespoons butter
Dash of salt
2 large tart green apples, cored and sliced

Combine all ingredients except apples and beat well. Pour half the batter into a round layer cake pan. Spread the apples evenly in the pan. Pour on the rest of the batter. Bake at 350° until firm and lightly browned. Serves 8; each serving=½ unit fruit, ½ unit carbohydrate.

POUND CAKE

5 eggs
15 ¼-grain tablets saccharin, crushed
Dash of salt
1 teaspoon vanilla
1 tablespoon grated lemon rind
¼ cup oat flour
¼ cup soy flour

Separate the eggs. Beat the whites until stiff and set aside. Beat the yolks well, and add the sweetener, salt, vanilla and lemon rind. Mix in the flours, then fold in half of the egg whites. Fold in well, then fold in the other half, very carefully. Preheat the oven to 400°. Pour into a greased loaf pan. Bake for 10 minutes. Lower the heat to 350° and bake until firm, about 40 minutes. Serves 8; each serving=a trace of carbohydrate.

MOCK JELLY ROLL CAKE

Prepare Pound Cake. Slice into 4 layers. Spread homemade or Polaner sugarless jelly between the layers and replace as they were.

ICE CREAM CAKE

Prepare Pound Cake. Slice into 4 layers. Spread homemade ice cream between the layers and replace as they were. Chill or freeze.

WHIPPED CREAM CAKE

Same as Ice Cream Cake, but fill with the following:
1 cup heavy cream, 1 teaspoon vanilla extract and 4 ¼-grain tablets crushed saccharin. Whip until the cream forms into peaks. Spread on

the cake and also spread some in swirls on top. Garnish with chopped nuts.

GINGERBREAD #1

1 cup instant oatmeal (dry)
2 eggs
¾ cup milk
½ teaspoon salt
1 teaspoon baking powder
1 tablespoon liquid artificial sweetener
1 tablespoon oil
1½ teaspoons cinnamon
1 tablespoon vanilla
1 tablespoon ground ginger
1 teaspoon mace
½ teaspoon anise flavoring

Mix all ingredients together. Pour into a greased 8-inch cake pan. Bake at 375° for 30 minutes. Serve hot with whipped cream. Divide into 8 servings; each serving=½ unit carbohydrate.

GINGERBREAD #2

1 cup oat flour
½ teaspoon baking soda
½ teaspoon cinnamon
2 teaspoons ginger (ground)
1 teaspoon allspice
⅓ cup soft margarine or butter
3 eggs, slightly beaten
20 ¼-grain tablets saccharin, crushed
½ teaspoon anise flavoring
½ cup buttermilk or milk

Preheat the oven to 350°. Sift the flour with the dry ingredients. Cream the butter and add the eggs and sweetener. Beat until light and fluffy. Add the other ingredients and mix. Pour into a greased loaf pan. Bake for 30 minutes. Serves 8; each serving=1 unit carbohydrate.

NUT CAKE

10 to 12 eggs
40 ¼-grain tablets saccharin, crushed
1 teaspoon vanilla extract
Pinch of salt
¾ pound nuts, grated fine in the blender (walnuts, pecans, filberts, almonds)

Separate the eggs and beat the whites until stiff and dry. Cream the yolks with sweetener, vanilla and salt. Add the nuts. Fold into the whites. Oil a tube pan or two 8-inch layer pans. Bake at 300° for 1 hour for a tube pan, 45 minutes for layers. Serves 8 to 12.

FIVE-MINUTE SPICE CAKE

4 slices homemade high-carbohydrate bread (*see* Breads)
4 eggs, separated
1 tablespoon oil
½ cup milk or more as needed
½ cup chopped nuts
½ cup non-fat dry milk
2 tablespoons liquid artificial sweetener
½ teaspoon each nutmeg, ginger, ground cloves, mace
Pinch of salt
1 tablespoon vanilla
1 teaspoon cinnamon

Preheat the oven to 375°. Crumb the bread in the blender until finely crumbed. Separate the eggs and beat the yolks and liquids together. Add the crumbed bread, nuts, dry milk, spices and flavorings. Mix well. Beat the whites until stiff and fold into the batter. Pour into a greased Teflon-lined loaf pan and bake at 375° for 40 minutes. Serves 8; each serving=½ unit carbohydrate. To make this cake even faster, crumb the bread, mix all the liquids including the eggs in the blender. Stir in the crumbs and other ingredients, and pour into the pan.

YELLOW CAKE

2 eggs separated, plus 2 egg yolks
½ cup oat flour
½ teaspoon baking powder
1 cup milk
1 tablespoon vanilla extract
½ teaspoon grated lemon rind
½ cup cream
½ teaspoon freshly grated nutmeg
20 ¼-grain tablets saccharin, crushed

Beat the 4 egg yolks until thick. Sift the flour and baking powder into the eggs. Add the other ingredients, except for the egg whites. Beat the whites until stiff and fold into the batter. Pour into a greased 8-inch pan and set in a pan of hot water. Bake in a preheated 350° oven for 45 minutes. Serves 8; each serving=½ unit carbohydrate.

ENGLISH TRIFLE

1 recipe any cake you prefer (Soy Nut Cake, Coconut Cake, etc.)
1 teaspoon brandy flavoring
¼ cup water
¼ cup homemade jam or Polaner black raspberry jam
2 egg yolks
1 cup milk
1 teaspoon vanilla extract
10 ¼-grain tablets saccharin, crushed

Bake the cake according to the recipe given. Allow to cool and cut lengthwise to make 4 large slices. Combine the brandy extract and water, and sprinkle them evenly over the cake slices. Set 2 of the slices into a well-greased cake pan, cut sides up. Spread the jam over the cake evenly. Lay the other 2 slices of cake on top of the jam, with the cut sides up. In a small saucepan combine the other ingredients, mixing. Heat, stirring, until just slightly thickened. Pour over the cake and bake at 325° until the custard has set. For carbohydrates, see the cake recipe. Serves 4.

BLACKBERRY TRIFLE

1 cup milk
3 eggs
¼ cup oil
1 level tablespoon baking powder
1 teaspoon cinnamon
1 teaspoon vanilla extract
¼ teaspoon salt
12 ¼-grain tablets saccharin, crushed
1 cup soy flour
¼ cup oat flour
3 cups blackberries (or other tart fruit, cut up into tiny pieces)

Mix or blend together the milk, eggs and oil. Add the baking powder, cinnamon, vanilla, salt and half the saccharin. Mix well. Add the flours, a little at a time, mixing, and adding more milk if needed. Mixture should be the consistency of pancake batter. Grease a 9-inch piepan, and drizzle about one third of the batter into the pan, covering the bottom and sides evenly. Add the fruit and shake on the remainder of the crushed saccharin. Drizzle the rest of the batter over the fruit until all of it is covered, forming a crust. Place in a preheated 325° oven and bake for 1 hour. If the top is browning too much, place a sheet of aluminum foil loosely on top of the cake. Serves 4; each serving=½ unit carbohydrate, 1 unit fruit.

CHARLOTTE RUSSE

1 recipe Sponge Cake
1 pint heavy cream, chilled
1 teaspoon vanilla extract
6 to 8 ¼-grain tablets crushed saccharin or to taste

Make the Sponge Cake in a loaf or square cake pan. After baking, divide it into about 8 squares. In a mixing bowl, chill the cream until almost starting to freeze (about 20 minutes in the freezer). Beat the cream with an electric mixer, adding the vanilla extract and saccharin until the cream is whipped stiffly. Do not whip too long or cream will turn to butter. When just stiff, scoop with a large spoon onto the individual servings of cake. With a knife, form each scoop of whipped cream into a tall peak. Serve immediately; or if that isn't possible freeze until ready to serve, then thaw slightly. For carbohydrates, see the cake recipe used. Serves 8.

SOY NUT CAKE

6 eggs
½ cup oil or butter at room temperature
1 cup milk
2 tablespoons vanilla extract
1½ cups soy flour
1 tablespoon baking powder
Pinch of salt
30 ¼-grain tablets saccharin
1 cup walnuts, broken coarsely

Break the eggs into the blender container. Add the oil and blend well. Add the milk and vanilla and blend until smooth. Gradually add the dry ingredients while the blender is running slowly, stirring occasionally with a rubber spatula to free the blades. After the ingredients have been mixed in and the batter is smooth, add half of the nuts and blend just until the nuts have been chopped. You may have to transfer half of the batter to a mixing bowl and blend in two stages, as the batter may not all fit at once in your blender. After all the batter has been blended and the nuts have been chopped, stir in the remaining unchopped nuts by hand. Pour the batter into a well-greased large loaf pan, or two 8-inch round cake pans. Place in a preheated 375° oven and bake for 15 minutes. Lower the heat to 325° and continue baking until the cake is set, about 30 minutes for layer cakes and 45 minutes for a loaf cake. Serves 8 to 12.

HOLIDAY FRUITCAKE

Batter as given for Soy Nut Cake, except: use half and half instead
of milk, plus
½ cup oat flour
¼ ripe pineapple, diced
1 large tart plum, diced
1 tablespoon dehydrated lemon peel
½ teaspoon orange extract
½ cup coarsely chopped pecans
1 large tart apple, peeled and diced
1 pear, diced
1 tablespoon dehydrated orange peel
1 teaspoon brandy flavoring

Prepare the batter as for Soy Nut Cake, adding the oat flour in the
blender. Blend in stages, pouring into a large mixing bowl, and then
mix all together by hand. Add the fruit and the rest of the ingredients,
mixing by hand. Grease a large tube or spring-form pan. Sprinkle a
little more oat flour into the pan, and turn the pan around until all
the sides are lightly coated with the flour. Shake out all the excess
flour. Pour in the batter, distributing it evenly. Preheat the oven to
400° and bake 15 minutes; lower the heat to 325° and bake until
lightly browned and a toothpick inserted comes out clean (about 1
hour). If the cake is becoming too brown, cover with a sheet of
aluminum foil laid loosely on top. Serves 8; each serving=½ unit
carbohydrate, 1 unit fruit.

PIES: CRUSTS

CHEESE PIECRUST

1 cup soy flour
1 teaspoon salt
1½ cups grated Cheddar cheese

4 tablespoons solid shortening
3 tablespoons ice water or more if needed

Mix the flour, salt and cheese lightly with a fork. Cut in the shortening. Sprinkle on the ice water and stir until little balls form. Pat into the bottom of a piepan and smooth with a spoon. Or place between two sheets of wax paper and roll with a rolling pin. Peel away the top layer of paper. Turn upside down on top of a pie plate and carefully peel away the other layer of paper. Fill and bake (use for Apple Pie, Cheesecake, etc.). Makes one 9-inch pie shell. Also can be used for main-dish pies, such as Quiche Lorraine.

THIRTY-SECOND PIECRUST

2 slices any homemade bread
½ stick melted butter or ¼ cup oil
Cinnamon as needed
Crushed saccharin as needed

Crumble the bread in the bowl. Mix in the melted butter or oil. Spread as evenly as possible in the bottom of a pie plate. Sprinkle lightly with cinnamon and sweetener. Fill and bake. For an unbaked filling, place the "crust" in a preheated 425° oven and bake for 10 minutes. Cool and fill. If using high-carbohydrate bread, entire recipe=2 units carbohydrate.

PEANUT BUTTER PIECRUST

Prepare dough as for Peanut Butter Cookies. Press by hand or with a spoon into a 9-inch pie plate. Flatten evenly with a fork or an 8-inch pie plate. Bake for 5 minutes in a preheated 375° oven. Fill with pie filling and bake as directed for filling. Or bake 12 to 15 minutes until brown, and fill with any unbaked filling (such as cream pie, gelatin, unbaked cheesecake, etc.). Entire crust=8 units carbohydrate.

THREE-FLOUR PIECRUST

1 cup oat flour
½ cup soy flour
½ cup nut flour (nuts finely ground in the blender, such as filberts, almonds, etc.)
1 teaspoon salt
1 teaspoon baking powder
¾ cup shortening (Crisco, lard, etc.)
4 tablespoons ice water or as needed

Combine and sift the dry ingredients. Cut in the shortening until it forms into tiny balls. Sprinkle in the water gradually. Place the mixture in a plastic bag and squeeze the bag, kneading slightly, until well mixed. Divide the dough in half and chill until firm. Place the dough between two sheets of wax paper and roll (*see* Cheese Piecrust for exact directions). Makes two bottom crusts or one 2-crust pie. Entire recipe=8 units carbohydrate.

"JOLLY JOAN" PIECRUST

¼ cup solid shortening
1 cup Jolly Joan Oat Mix (*see* Brand Names)
4 tablespoons ice water

Cut the shortening into the oat mix. Add the water. Work into a dough. Roll out between wax paper or pat with fingers into the bottom of a pie plate to a uniform thickness. Makes one bottom crust. Excellent for Pumpkin Pie, Custard Pie, etc. Entire recipe=8 units carbohydrate.

CREAM CHEESE CRUST

1 stick unsalted butter at room temperature
⅛ teaspoon salt
½ cup soy flour

1 8-ounce package cream cheese at room temperature
4 ¼-grain tablets saccharin, crushed
½ cup oat flour

Combine all ingredients and mash together. Chill in the refrigerator until firm. Roll or pat out. Do not handle long; if necessary, chill until ready to bake. This is an excellent sweet crust and can be doubled and used for a two-crust pie. Entire recipe=4 units carbohydrate. For an unbaked pie filling, prepare the pie shell and bake at 375° for 12 to 15 minutes.

OATMEAL WHEAT-GERM PIECRUST

Prepare the batter as for Oatmeal Wheat-germ Cookies. Press into a pie plate and bake at 350° for 15 minutes. Makes two small pie shells or one large pie shell.

CRUMB CRUST

½ cup soy grits
½ cup apple juice
1 thick slice homemade high-carbohydrate bread
2 tablespoons oil or melted butter
4 ¼-grain tablets saccharin, crushed
1 tablespoon cinnamon

Soak the grits in the apple juice for 15 minutes. Toast the bread and crumb finely. Combine all the ingredients and transfer to a 9-inch pie plate. Pat into place evenly to make a pie shell of even thickness. Bake at 350° for 15 minutes for an unbaked pie filling. For a baked pie, bake the shell alone at 350° for 5 minutes. Cool, then fill and bake. Entire recipe=1 unit carbohydrate.

NUT-CRUMB CRUST

Same as Crumb Crust; omit the soy grits and apple juice, substitute ½ cup finely ground Brazil nuts or almonds.

COCONUT PIECRUST

Prepare the batter as for Coconut Cookies and pat into a pie plate. Bake as for the cookies, being careful not to brown too much. Fill with custard, pudding, cheesecake or any other unbaked filling.

SOY GRITS PIECRUST

See recipe for Soy Grits Cookies. Prepare same as Coconut Piecrust.

PIES: FILLINGS

COCONUT CUSTARD PIE

2½ cups milk
½ cup cream
¼ teaspoon salt
1 teaspoon vanilla
40 ¼-grain tablets saccharin, crushed
1 cup unsweetened coconut meal (available at health food stores)
4 eggs
1 pie shell
½ cup cleaned and shredded fresh coconut

Pour the milk, cream, salt, vanilla, saccharin, coconut meal and eggs into the blender. Blend until smooth. Pour into a pie shell. Sprinkle the top with coconut flakes and some additional sweetener to taste. Bake at 425° for 10 minutes. Lower heat to 350° and bake until set, about 20 minutes more. For carbohydrates, see piecrust recipe used. Makes enough filling for one pie.

BUTTERMILK MERINGUE PIE

1 tablespoon oat flour
1 teaspoon butter
2 eggs, separated
1 cup buttermilk
1 teaspoon lemon extract
20 ¼-grain tablets saccharin, crushed
1 tablespoon lemon juice
1 pie shell
⅛ teaspoon salt

Cream the flour and butter together. Gradually add the egg yolks, slightly beaten. Add the buttermilk, extract, half the saccharin and lemon juice. Mix well and pour into an unbaked pie shell. Bake at 425° for 15 minutes, or until a knife inserted comes out clean. Make the meringue as follows: beat the egg whites, salt and remaining saccharin together until stiff (if the whites are not turning stiff, add a dash of cream of tartar). Cover the pie with the meringue, piling it on in peaks. Bake at 325° for 20 minutes. For carbohydrates, see piecrust recipe used. Makes enough filling for one pie.

NESSELRODE PIE

1 tablespoon unflavored gelatin
2 cups evaporated milk
3 egg yolks
Dash of salt
1 teaspoon rum flavoring
10 ¼-grain tablets saccharin, crushed
1 baked pie shell
½ cup walnuts, broken

Sprinkle the gelatin into the milk. Beat the egg yolks and stir into the milk mixture. Heat, stirring constantly, until the gelatin is dissolved and the mixture thickens. Stir in the flavorings and sweetener until well mixed. Pour the entire mixture into a baked pie shell and sprinkle on the nuts. Allow some to sink and some to float on top. Chill until firm. Entire pie=4 units milk. For carbohydrates, see the piecrust recipe used. Makes enough filling for one pie.

SOUFFLÉ PIE

1 pie shell
6 eggs, separated
⅓ cup butter, softened
2 teaspoons oat flour
1 tablespoon lemon juice
2 tablespoons liquid artificial sweetener
½ cup finely ground almonds
⅔ cup cottage cheese
1 tablespoon grated lemon rind
½ teaspoon salt

Make any pie shell. Bake 5 minutes and cool slightly. Pour all the ingredients except egg whites into the blender. Blend on low until smooth. Beat whites until stiff and fold into mixture. Pour into the pie shell and bake in a preheated 375° oven for 30 minutes, or until firm. For carbohydrates, see the piecrust recipe used. Makes enough filling for one pie.

APPLE PIE

1 recipe Three-flour Piecrust
4 large tart apples, peeled, cored and sliced thin
1 tablespoon cinnamon
6 to 8 ¼-grain tablets saccharin, crushed
4 ounces apple juice
1 tablespoon butter
2 tablespoons oat flour

Prepare piecrust according to recipe. Place the bottom crust in a 9-inch pie plate. Spread the apples around in the pan and sprinkle on the cinnamon and sweetener. Pour in the juice. Dot with butter and sprinkle evenly with the oat flour. Place the top crust on the pie, sealing the edges. Make several vents in the top. Bake at 375° for 15 minutes, then at 325° until the crust is lightly browned and the apples are cooked (30 minutes). Serves 8; each serving= 1 unit carbohydrate, 1 unit fruit.

STRAWBERRY PIE

2 cups fresh or loose frozen strawberries (packed without sugar or syrup)
3 egg yolks
8 ¼-grain tablets saccharin, crushed
Any pie shell, crumb crust or cheesecake

Mash the berries (thaw partially if frozen). Save a few for garnishing if desired. Beat the egg yolks well and mix with the berries and sweetener. Cook in a double boiler, stirring, until thickened. Pour into a pie shell or on top of a cheesecake. Chill until firm. Serves 4; each serving=1 unit fruit. For carbohydrates, see piecrust recipe used.

CARROT PIE

1 8-inch pie shell, unbaked
1 can sliced carrots (without sugar)
1 cup evaporated milk
1 teaspoon pumpkin pie spice or more to taste
½ teaspoon salt
2 eggs
1 tablespoon butter
25 ¼-grain tablets saccharin, crushed

Prepare piecrust. Drain the carrots and mash well. Combine with the rest of the ingredients. Beat well. Pour into the pie shell and bake at 400° for 45 minutes or until set. Cool, garnish with whipped cream. Contains 4 units high-carbohydrate vegetable. Makes enough filling for one pie.

"SWEET POTATO" PIE

1 Soy Grits Piecrust
1 package frozen winter squash (plain, puréed)
2 tablespoons butter
½ cup pecans, chopped in the blender
1 teaspoon maple flavoring
Pinch of salt
1½ cups evaporated milk
2 eggs, slightly beaten
⅛ teaspoon nutmeg
40 ¼-grain tablets saccharin, crushed
8 to 10 pecan halves

Prepare the crust according to the recipe and bake for 5 minutes at 350°. Remove and set aside to cool. Cook the squash according to the package directions in a very small amount of water. Drain and mix together with the other ingredients, except the pecan halves. Pour into the piecrust and garnish the top with the pecan halves. Bake at 325° until set (about 45 minutes). Entire recipe= 4 units high-carbohydrate vegetable. Makes enough filling for one pie.

PUMPKIN PIE

1 pie shell
1½ cups canned pumpkin (plain, puréed, without seasoning)
2 eggs, slightly beaten
1 teaspoon vanilla extract
Dash of salt
1 tablespoon cinnamon
½ teaspoon ground cloves
10 ¼-grain tablets saccharin, crushed, or more
1 teaspoon ground ginger
¼ teaspoon freshly ground nutmeg
1 cup evaporated milk
¾ cup heavy cream

Prepare the pie shell and chill in the refrigerator (we recommend the "Jolly Joan" Piecrust, but any other in the book will do too). Beat the pumpkin and eggs together until smooth. Add the flavorings and spices, then beat in the milk and cream. Mix by hand until smooth. Preheat the oven to 425°. Pour the pumpkin mixture into the pie shell (if there is any left over, pour it into a small ovenproof bowl and bake separately as a pudding). Bake for 15 minutes; lower the heat to 350° and bake until set (about 45 minutes). Cool slightly before serving. Serves 8; each serving=½ unit limited vegetable, 1 unit carbohydrate. Makes enough filling for one pie.

BOSTON CREAM PIE

Prepare any pie shell. Bake the crust, then set aside to cool. Prepare Instant Chocolate Pudding. Pour the pudding into the pie shell. Top with whipped cream. Makes enough filling for one pie.

BANANA CREAM PIE

Same as Boston Cream Pie, but use Banana Pudding.

QUICK COCONUT CUSTARD PIE

Same as Boston Cream Pie, but use Instant Vanilla Pudding (prepared with half and half in place of milk). Top with shredded unsweetened coconut or coconut meal.

NO-CRUST APPLE PIE

1 can Comstock pie-sliced apples (packed in water without sugar
  or spices)
1 tablespoon cinnamon
10 ¼-grain tablets saccharin, crushed
½ cup wheat germ
½ cup chopped nuts (walnuts, pecans)
2 tablespoons butter at room temperature
¼ teaspoon nutmeg

Pour the canned apples into a well-greased pie plate. Sprinkle on
half the cinnamon and half the saccharin. Stir to mix. In a bowl,
combine the remaining ingredients and mix. Crumble the topping
over the apples evenly. Bake in a preheated 325° oven until the
topping is browned (about 30 minutes). Serves 4; each serving=
1 unit carbohydrate, 1 unit fruit.

PINEAPPLE CHEESECAKE

1 pie shell or crumb crust (optional: a pie plate without any crust
  can be used)
1 large can Dole sugarless pineapple chunks (packed without sugar
  or syrup)
3 tablespoons gelatin
1 cup lemon-flavored diet soda
15 ¼-grain tablets saccharin
½ teaspoon vanilla
¼ teaspoon salt
2 cups cottage cheese
1 8-ounce package cream cheese, softened

Prepare pie shell if desired. Drain the pineapple and reserve the
juice. In a bowl, sprinkle the gelatin on the pineapple juice to
soften. Heat the soda and sweetener to boiling and pour on the
gelatin mixture. Stir until the gelatin is dissolved. Add the pineapple
chunks and chill until slightly thickened. Pour half the pineapple
mixture into the blender with the remaining ingredients. Blend until

smooth and pour into the pie shell or pie plate. Top with the rest of the pineapple mixture, arranging the pineapple pieces attractively around the edges. Chill until firm. Serves 6; each serving= 1 unit fruit. For carbohydrates, see piecrust recipe if used.

FROZEN CHEESECAKE

1 large can Dole unsweetened crushed pineapple (packed in its own juice)
2 cups cottage cheese
1 tablespoon lemon juice
1 cup sour cream
8 to 10 ¼-grain tablets saccharin

Drain the juice from the pineapple. Pour the juice into the blender; add all the ingredients except the pineapple. Blend until smooth. Pour into a pie plate. Stir in the crushed pineapple, mixing to distribute evenly. Freeze until firm. To serve, thaw slightly until a fork can be inserted. Place in a bowl of hot water and turn upside down to unmold. Serve immediately or refreeze. Serves 6; each serving=1 unit fruit.

FRUIT CHEESECAKE

1½ tablespoons unflavored gelatin
½ cup cream or evaporated milk
4 tablespoons water
4 tablespoons lemon juice
15 to 20 ¼-grain tablets saccharin, crushed
2 cups cottage cheese
1 teaspoon vanilla extract
1 cup fresh fruit, diced (except pineapple)

Sprinkle the gelatin into the cream or milk until softened. Add the water and lemon juice. Transfer to the stove and heat the mixture, stirring, until the gelatin is dissolved (do not burn). Add the saccharin and stir until dissolved. Set the mixture aside to cool. Place the cottage cheese in the blender with the vanilla extract, and blend until smooth. Add the gelatin mixture and blend well. Pour into a mold or cake pan and chill until partially set. Fold in the fruit, reserving some to decorate the top. Chill until firm. Serves 4; each serving=½ unit fruit.

MISCELLANEOUS

ALMOND CREAM FROSTING

½ cup blanched almonds
1 cup heavy cream, chilled
½ teaspoon almond extract
1 teaspoon vanilla extract
8 ¼-grain tablets saccharin
Slivered almonds (optional)

Grate the blanched almonds in the blender to a fine powder. Add the cream and flavorings. Blend on low until the consistency of thick whipped cream (do not blend for too long or it will turn to butter). Spread on cake or cupcakes. Garnish with a few slivered almonds if desired, and chill until firm. Makes approximately 2 cups of frosting.

MAPLE TOPPING

1 cup heavy cream
Pinch of salt
10 to 12 ¼-grain tablets saccharin, crushed
1 teaspoon nutmeg
1 teaspoon maple extract

Place all ingredients in a bowl. Beat until the cream is stiff, but not too long or it will turn to butter. Spread on cake or cupcakes, or heap on individual slices of cake. Makes approximately 2 cups of topping.

BUTTER FROSTING

1 cup heavy cream
1 teaspoon vanilla extract
½ teaspoon butter flavoring
Saccharin to taste
1 or 2 drops food coloring (optional)

Place all ingredients in a bowl. Beat until the cream is stiff and just beginning to turn slightly buttery. Add food coloring if desired. Use to ice cakes. Makes approximately 2 cups of frosting.

CHOCOLATE ICING

¼ cup unsalted butter
1 envelope Nestlé's Choco-Bake (unsweetened chocolate in liquid form) or 2 squares unsweetened chocolate, melted
¼ cup non-fat dry milk
Crushed saccharin to taste
1 teaspoon vanilla extract

Soften the butter at room temperature. Mix together all ingredients. Correct for sweetness and chill slightly before using. Use to ice cakes, cookies, cupcakes, etc. Makes enough to ice one 8-inch two-layer cake.

BAKED FROSTING

2 egg whites
¼ teaspoon salt
6 to 8 ¼-grain tablets saccharin, crushed
¼ cup chopped nuts or more as needed

Combine the egg whites, salt and saccharin in a bowl. Beat until stiff. Fold in the nuts. Spread over cake batter before baking in the cake pan. Bake as required for cake recipe. Makes enough frosting for a two-layer cake.

WHIPPED CREAM TOPPING

1 cup heavy cream, chilled
1 teaspoon liquid artificial sweetener or 4 to 6 ¼-grain tablets saccharin, crushed
½ teaspoon vanilla extract

Beat the cream, add the other ingredients, and continue beating until stiff, but not buttery. Use on puddings, gelatin desserts, etc. Makes approximately 2 cups topping.

LOW-CALORIE WHIPPED TOPPING

½ cup non-fat dry milk
1 teaspoon vanilla extract
Dash of fresh lemon juice
½ cup evaporated milk, chilled
1 teaspoon liquid artificial sweetener

Combine all ingredients, mix and chill. Beat with an electric mixer for at least 10 minutes at high speed until mixture forms peaks. Entire recipe=2 units milk. Makes approximately 3 cups topping.

COEUR À LA CRÈME

1 cup sour cream
1 pound cottage cheese
10 ¼-grain tablets saccharin
2 cups fresh strawberries

Place the sour cream, cottage cheese and saccharin in the blender. Blend on medium until perfectly smooth. Pour into a heart-shaped mold and chill. Unmold and surround with fresh fruit, sprinkled with additional crushed saccharin. Serves 4; each serving=½ unit fruit.

FRUIT YOGHURT

2 tablespoons sugarless jelly (homemade or Polaner)
1 cup plain unflavored yoghurt

Combine the jelly and yoghurt and mix until smooth. Makes 1
serving; which=1 unit milk, ½ unit fruit.

FRUIT-FLAVORED YOGHURT

1 cup plain unflavored yoghurt
1 or 2 drops food coloring
½ teaspoon fruit extract (strawberry, etc.)
2 to 4 ¼-grain tablets saccharin, crushed

Combine all ingredients and mix until smooth. Makes 1 serving;
1 unit milk.

ICE CREAM SODAS

Basic Ice Cream Soda:

½ cup crushed ice
8 ounces diet soda, well chilled
1 serving homemade ice cream
Whipped cream

Combine the ice and soda in the blender. Blend until the ice is
completely crushed. Add the ice cream and stir by hand. Serve with
a scoop of whipped cream. Makes 1 serving.

Variations:
1. Vanilla Ice Cream and diet cream soda.
2. Vanilla Ice Cream and root beer.
3. Vanilla Ice Cream and ginger ale.
4. Chocolate Ice Cream and cream soda.
5. Chocolate Ice Cream and cherry soda.
6. Strawberry Ice Cream and strawberry soda.
Plus any other variations you can think of.

ICE CREAM SUNDAES

Sundaes consist of ice cream, whipped cream and a topping. Try these combinations or invent your own:
1. Vanilla Ice Cream, chopped nuts and 1 tablespoon sugarless jelly.
2. Vanilla Ice Cream topped with 2 tablespoons semi-thawed orange juice concentrate.
3. Chocolate Ice Cream plus 2 tablespoons strawberry jelly (sugarless) mixed with two tablespoons water.
4. Any ice cream with Strawberry Syrup (*see* Sauces and Dressings)
5. Any ice cream plus Maple Butter Syrup (hot) (*see* Sauces and Dressings).
6. Any ice cream plus chopped nuts, wheat germ and sweetener.
7. Vanilla Ice Cream with unsweetened crushed pineapple.

GERI'S CHOCOLATE MOUSSE

1 pint heavy cream, chilled well
¼ teaspoon vanilla
2 tablespoons unsweetened cocoa
Saccharin to taste

Place all ingredients in the blender. Blend at medium speed until the cream is whipped (do not blend too long or it will turn to butter). Pour into a serving bowl or individual dishes. Chill until firm. This may also be frozen and eaten slightly thawed. Serves 4.

EGGS

There are so many ways in which eggs can be used in the diet that they might almost be called the "hidden proteins." There are recipes using eggs in every section of this book, and for those people who don't like to eat eggs, there are hundreds of ways to use eggs in a meal without their being detected. This section deals only with those main-dish recipes whose main ingredient is eggs. Others can be found under Casseroles, Beverages, and Desserts.

Most people use eggs for breakfast in the standard styles: fried, boiled or scrambled. There are many other ways of using eggs as your main dish, not only for breakfast, but for any meal. Incidentally, eggs are one of the least expensive forms of protein you can buy. So if you are concerned about your food budget, have eggs for dinner occasionally.

Eggs can be added to low-protein foods to boost the protein intake of picky eaters. Instead of milk, give your family a delicious egg-nog or a milk shake containing eggs (see Beverages) and egg-rich desserts such as puddings, custards and cakes. To add protein to salads and vegetables, garnish with riced egg yolks. To use up left-over hard-cooked egg whites, fill with cheese spreads and other spreads (see Appetizers).

A medium egg contains about 6 grams of protein, roughly the equivalent of a hamburger. The yolk contains 3 grams and the white contains 3 grams. The yolk is also very high in nutritional value, containing many vitamins and minerals needed for good health. One hard-cooked egg is an adequate between-meal snack and is easy to carry and eat away from home. If you find preparing protein snacks too time-consuming, make about a dozen hard-cooked eggs at a time and keep them in the refrigerator ready for nibbling. For variety, season with various spices or spread with allowed mayonnaise and other salad dressings.

Poached Eggs
Eggs Benedict
Coddled Eggs
Baked Eggs
"Mary Jane" Egg
Scrambled Eggs
Scrambled Eggs with Herbs
Scrambled Eggs with Onions
Super Scrambled Eggs
Cheese and Eggs
Seafood Scrambled Eggs
Pork Chop Scrambled Eggs
Huevos Rancheros
"Green Eggs and Ham" à la Dr.
    Seuss
Jelly-roll Egg
Chive Egg Rolls

Egg Cake
Cheese Omelette
Mushroom Omelette
Ham and Vegetable Omelette
Strawberry Tart Omelette
Cottage Cheese Omelette
Cheese Soufflé
Mushroom Soufflé
Deviled Eggs
Stuffed Eggs
Belgian Eggs
Curried Egg Casserole
Huevos Exquisitos
Eggs Provençal
Egg Salad: see Salads
Chicken Egg Foo Yung: see
    Foreign and Regional

POACHED EGGS

This is the easiest way we've found to poach eggs:

Heat a Teflon-lined frying pan. Melt 1 tablespoon butter over medium heat. Add ¼ cup water and gently break eggs into pan. Salt to taste, and add a little more water if needed. Cover, reduce heat to low and serve as soon as the eggs are set.

EGGS BENEDICT

Poach 2 eggs (above). Butter 2 thin slices homemade low-carbohydrate bread (see Breads, Pasta and Noodles). Place the poached eggs on the bread, and cover with Hollandaise Sauce (see Sauces and Dressings). Serves 1.

CODDLED EGGS

1 cup water
2 teaspoons butter
4 eggs

Pour the water into a large saucepan and heat to boiling. Into two small ovenproof bowls place 1 teaspoon butter. Break 2 eggs gently into each bowl. Set the bowls in the saucepan and cover the pan. Cook until the whites are set. Serve in the bowls or slice carefully onto toast or pancakes. Serves 2.

BAKED EGGS

Butter as needed
2 eggs
Salt to taste, dash of pepper
Grated cheese (Swiss, Parmesan, etc.)

Grease a small ovenproof dish generously with butter. Carefully break the eggs into the dish. Sprinkle on the seasonings to taste, then sprinkle generously with the grated cheese. Preheat the oven to 325°, and place the dish in the oven. Bake until the eggs are set (about 12 minutes). Serves 1.

"MARY JANE" EGG

1 tablespoon butter
1 slice homemade bread
1 jumbo egg
Salt to taste

Heat the frying pan and melt the butter until sizzling and slightly browned. Tear a hole in the center of the bread, leaving the outer part intact. Place the bread crust in the pan, and carefully break the egg into the center. Lower the heat and continue cooking until the bottom is set. Turn and fry on the other side until brown (do not overcook or the yolk will be too hard). Serves 1.

SCRAMBLED EGGS

2 or 3 eggs
1 ounce milk
1 tablespoon butter or margarine or bacon drippings
Salt, pepper to taste

Combine the eggs and milk in a bowl and beat well with a wire whisk or a fork. Heat a frying pan until hot. Melt the butter until sizzling. Pour in the egg mixture which should sizzle. Lower the heat to medium low; after a minute stir up the bottom, continue stirring slowly while the eggs cook. Remove from the heat while still glossy and moist. Season to taste. Serves 1.

SCRAMBLED EGGS WITH HERBS

Same as Scrambled Eggs (above): before pouring the egg mixture into the pan, add 1 or 2 teaspoons herbs which have been crushed by rubbing between the palms of your hands or with a mortar and pestle. Use any of the following or a combination of several: basil, chervil, parsley, marjoram, celery tops, thyme, etc.

SCRAMBLED EGGS WITH ONIONS

1 tablespoon butter
1 small onion, diced
4 to 6 eggs
¼ cup milk
Pinch of parsley flakes
Dash of paprika
Salt, pepper to taste

Heat the butter in a frying pan until melted and sauté the onion until yellow and translucent. Beat the eggs and milk and seasonings together in a bowl, and pour into the pan with the onion. Cook, stirring slowly, until eggs are cooked, but moist and glossy. Serve at once. Serves 2 or 3.

SUPER SCRAMBLED EGGS

5 eggs
1 tablespoon sour cream
½ teaspoon salt
½ teaspoon dill weed
Pinch of pepper
½ cup diced cooked chicken, shrimp or ham
1 4-ounce can mushrooms, drained
1 tablespoon butter

Beat the eggs in a bowl; add the sour cream and seasonings and beat until well mixed. Stir in the meat and mushrooms. Melt the butter in a frying pan and add the egg mixture; heat slowly and stir until eggs are cooked. Serves 2 or 3.

CHEESE AND EGGS

1 tablespoon butter
6 eggs
Salt, pepper to taste
4 ounces sharp Cheddar or American cheese

Melt the butter in a frying pan. Beat the eggs with the seasonings and pour into the pan. Dice or crumble the cheese and sprinkle over the eggs. Cook over low heat, stirring, until the eggs are set and the cheese is melted. Serves 3 or 4.

SEAFOOD SCRAMBLED EGGS

1 can king crab meat
4 ounces cooked shrimp
2 tablespoons butter
1 tablespoon oat flour
¾ cup milk
1 teaspoon chopped chives
8 eggs
½ teaspoon salt or more to taste
Dash of freshly ground pepper
1 or 2 drops Tabasco sauce

Drain and flake the crab meat and mix with the shrimp; set aside. Melt 1 tablespoon of the butter in a saucepan, and stir in the flour and milk. Bring to a boil, stirring constantly to prevent burning. Reduce heat and stir in the chives and seafood mixture; set aside. In a blender, combine the eggs, salt, pepper and Tabasco. Blend until frothy. In a large skillet heat the remaining butter. Pour in the egg mixture and cook over a low heat. Stir the eggs until partially cooked, then stir in the seafood mixture. Cook until the eggs are done, but not dry. Serves 3 to 6.

PORK CHOP SCRAMBLED EGGS

2 leftover cooked pork chops
1 tablespoon butter
6 eggs
A few drops of water
Salt, pepper to taste
Pinch of thyme

Cut the meat off the pork chops, discarding the fat and bones, and dice the meat. Heat the butter in a frying pan until melted. Sauté the diced pork until warm. Beat the eggs in a bowl with water and the seasonings. Pour into the pan with the pork. Scramble together over medium heat, stirring, until the eggs are set but still glossy. Serve immediately. Serves 2 to 4.

HUEVOS RANCHEROS

1 or 2 tablespoons oil
1 small onion, minced
1 clove garlic, minced fine
¼ cup minced green chili peppers
½ green pepper, diced
½ cup thick tomato sauce (homemade or Del Monte)
¼ teaspoon chili powder
½ teaspoon salt
1 tablespoon butter
6 eggs, beaten slightly

In a small pan, heat the oil. Sauté the onion, garlic and peppers until soft. Add the tomato sauce and seasonings, and heat 10 minutes. In a skillet, melt the butter; pour in the eggs and scramble, stirring, until set but not dry. Transfer the eggs to serving dish and pour the sauce over them. Serves 2 or 3.

"GREEN EGGS AND HAM" À LA DR. SEUSS

2 thick slices smoked ham
4 eggs, beaten
¼ cup milk or cream
¼ teaspoon salt
1 or 2 drops each green and blue food coloring
1 tablespoon butter

Cut the ham into cubes. Mix the first four ingredients together, adding green and blue food coloring until the desired shade is reached. Melt the butter in a pan, add the egg mixture and scramble, stirring, until eggs are set. This is strictly for children as a novelty; adults will enjoy it without the coloring. Serves 2 to 4.

JELLY-ROLL EGG

2 eggs
¼ cup non-fat dry milk
Dash of salt
2 teaspoons soy flour
Sugarless jelly or jam (*see* Brand Names or Preserves)

Combine the eggs, dry milk, salt and soy flour in the blender; blend until smooth. Heat a well-oiled skillet until hot. Pour in enough batter to form a large thin pancake. Tilt the pan to allow batter to run off at the edges. When the pancake is set and the top is almost dry, do not turn, but remove from the pan. Spread thinly with jelly and roll to form a jelly roll. Serve hot. Serves 1.

CHIVE EGG ROLLS

1 8-ounce package cream cheese at room temperature
1 teaspoon chives
6 eggs
4 tablespoons soy flour
2 tablespoons water
¼ teaspoon salt

Mash the cheese and chives together with a fork until smooth and spreadable; set aside. Beat the eggs, flour, water and salt together until smooth. Pour a third of the batter into a large hot well-oiled pan. Make a very large thin pancake. Turn when the bottom is set and the top is beginning to dry. Fry until the other side is lightly browned. Turn out onto a sheet of wax paper. Repeat until the batter is used up. Spread the pancake with the cheese mixture and roll as for a jelly roll. Serve hot; or wrap in wax paper and chill until firm. Unwrap and slice crosswise for snacks or canapés. If preferred, use 8 ounces chive cheese at room temperature and omit chives. Serves 3.

EGG CAKE

½ cup non-fat dry milk
½ cup milk
6 eggs
Dash of salt
1 teaspoon vanilla
6 ¼-grain tablets saccharin, crushed

Combine the dry milk with the milk and mix well. Add the eggs and flavorings and beat until smooth. Heat an oiled Teflon-lined pan. Pour in the egg mixture. Cover the pan and lower the heat. Cook slowly until the bottom and edges are cooked and the top is fairly dry. Turn and cook on the other side until set. To serve, sprinkle with crushed saccharin or spread with butter, jelly (sugarless), nut butter, etc. Serves 2 to 4.

Variations: Add any of the following to the batter: ¼ cup wheat germ, sesame seeds, sunflower seed meal, pumpkin seed meal, ground almonds, pignolia nuts.

CHEESE OMELETTE

2 ounces semi-soft cheese (Gruyère, Muenster, etc.)
4 small or 3 extra large eggs
¼ cup milk
¼ teaspoon salt
Dash of garlic powder
1 tablespoon butter
2 tablespoons light cream or evaporated milk

Shred the cheese and set aside at room temperature. Beat the eggs and milk together with a wire whisk or fork, and add the seasonings. Melt the butter in a small frying pan. When the butter sizzles, pour in the eggs. Lower the heat and cook without stirring until the bottom and edges are "set"; tilt the pan occasionally and lift the edge of the omelette, and sprinkle in the cheese on top. Cover the pan and continue cooking until the cheese is melted. Uncover, carefully fold the omelette in half and serve. Serves 2.

MUSHROOM OMELETTE

¼ pound fresh mushrooms, sliced
2 tablespoons butter
4 eggs
¼ cup milk or half and half
Pinch of onion powder
Salt, pepper to taste

Sauté the mushrooms in 1 tablespoon of the butter and set aside. Beat the eggs, milk and seasonings together. Add the rest of the butter to the skillet and pour in the eggs. Lower the heat, and cook until the top is beginning to "set." Add the sautéed mushrooms to the center and continue cooking until the egg is set but not dry. Fold in half and serve. Serves 2.

HAM AND VEGETABLE OMELETTE

½ cup diced cooked ham
4 scallions, minced
2 tablespoons butter
½ cup French-style green beans, cooked or canned and drained
6 eggs
Salt, pepper to taste
½ teaspoon Kikkoman soy sauce

Sauté the ham and scallions in the butter in a large skillet until the scallions are beginning to brown. Add the string beans and stir until heated. Set aside the mixture, and add a little more butter to the pan. Beat the eggs, seasonings and soy sauce together in a bowl and pour into the hot pan. Cook until the bottom is set and the top is beginning to dry. Add the ham and vegetable mixture to the eggs and fold the omelette in half. Serves 2 or 3.

STRAWBERRY TART OMELETTE

1 3-ounce package cream cheese at room temperature
4 eggs
Dash of salt
2 tablespoons water
1 tablespoon butter
¼ cup sugarless strawberry jam (*see* Brand Names or Preserves)
Crushed saccharin as needed

Mash the cream cheese. Place in blender, add the eggs, salt and water. Blend until smooth. Melt the butter in a heavy skillet. Pour in the egg mixture. Fry without stirring over medium heat, lifting the edges occasionally to allow the liquid to run off to the sides. Lower the heat to prevent browning. Cook until the center is set. Spoon the jam into the center, and fold the omelette in half. Gently slide onto a plate, and sprinkle the top with crushed saccharin. Serves 2.

COTTAGE CHEESE OMELETTE

1 tablespoon butter
4 eggs
1 cup cottage cheese
½ teaspoon salt
¼ cup milk
1 teaspoon chopped chives
Dash of freshly ground pepper

Melt the butter in a heavy skillet. Combine the rest of the ingredients in a bowl and beat until well mixed. Pour into the hot pan, lower the heat and cook until the bottom is brown. Cover the pan and continue cooking over a low heat until the egg is "set," or no longer runny. Turn carefully and brown on the other side. Or for a softer omelette, fold in half instead of turning and serve as is. Serves 2.

CHEESE SOUFFLÉ

6 eggs, separated
½ cup light cream or evaporated milk
½ teaspoon salt
¼ teaspoon paprika
¼ teaspoon freshly ground pepper
Pinch of garlic powder
1 pound sharp Cheddar cheese, grated

Beat the egg yolks, and beat in the cream and seasonings. Mix in the grated cheese. Beat the egg whites until stiff, and fold into the cheese mixture. Transfer to a well-greased casserole. Bake in a preheated 375° oven for 10 minutes, lower the heat to 325° and bake until set (about 20 minutes). Serve immediately, as soufflés have a tendency to fall as they cool. Serves 4.

MUSHROOM SOUFFLÉ

1 tablespoon butter
1 small onion, diced
2 cups sliced mushrooms
1 cup beef bouillon (see Brand Names) or beef stock
6 eggs, separated
Pinch of thyme
Salt to taste if needed

Melt the butter in a skillet, and sauté the onion and the mushrooms, stirring. When the onion is translucent, add the bouillon, cover and cook for 5 minutes. Beat the egg yolks; drain the cooked vegetables and add to the egg yolks; mix well. Beat the egg whites until frothy and stiff. Fold into the egg mixture. Correct seasonings. Preheat oven to 375°. Pour the mixture into a well-greased casserole and bake for 10 minutes. Lower heat to 325° and bake until set (about 15 to 20 minutes). Serve immediately. Serves 2 or 3.

DEVILED EGGS

4 hard-cooked eggs
1 tablespoon prepared German-type mustard (check label for sugar)
2 tablespoons cream or evaporated milk
1 teaspoon finely minced parsley or chives
Dash of freshly ground pepper
½ teaspoon paprika
Dash of cayenne pepper
½ teaspoon salt
Dash of liquid artificial sweetener

Slice the eggs in half carefully. Remove the yolks and mash them with the rest of the ingredients until smooth. Fill the whites with the mixture, sprinkle lightly with additional paprika. Serves 8 as appetizer or 2 as a main dish.

STUFFED EGGS

6 hard-cooked eggs
1 slice Oatmeal Bread
¼ cup milk
½ cup mashed cooked carrots
4 scallions, sliced thin
½ teaspoon thyme
½ teaspoon parsley
Dash of nutmeg
Salt, pepper to taste
1 tablespoon butter

Slice the eggs in half carefully. Place the bread in a bowl and pour in the milk. Soak 5 minutes. Add the egg yolks and mash. Add the carrots, scallions and seasonings. Place the egg whites in a well-greased casserole and stuff with the carrot mixture. Pour a little milk into the pan to about ¼ inch deep. Place in preheated 325° oven and heat for 25 to 30 minutes. Serves 2 as a main dish; each serving=½ unit carbohydrate, ½ unit high-carbohydrate vegetable.

BELGIAN EGGS

8 hard-cooked eggs
8 ounces cooked shrimp
4 ounces canned mushrooms, drained
½ teaspoon fennel
½ teaspoon thyme
½ teaspoon parsley
1 cup cream or evaporated milk
½ cup milk
2 tablespoons prepared mustard
½ teaspoon salt
¼ teaspoon pepper
1 ounce sharp cheese, grated
2 tablespoons butter

Preheat oven to 400°. Cut the eggs into slices and place in a buttered casserole. Cut the shrimp into bite-sized pieces and place in mixing bowl. Add the mushroom, herbs, cream, milk and seasonings. Mix well and pour over the eggs. Top with the grated cheese, and dot with the butter. Bake until browned (15 to 20 minutes). Serves 4.

CURRIED EGG CASSEROLE

6 hard-cooked eggs
2 tablespoons sugarless mayonnaise
¼ teaspoon dry mustard
½ teaspoon curry powder
¼ teaspoon salt
¼ teaspoon paprika
¼ teaspoon freshly ground pepper
Pinch of garlic powder
½ pint sour cream

Preheat the oven to 375°. Slice the eggs in half carefully and set aside the whites. Mash the yolks with the remaining ingredients, except the sour cream. Stuff the egg mixture into the egg whites. Place the stuffed eggs in a greased baking dish, and spoon the sour cream over them. Sprinkle lightly with additional paprika, and bake for 20 minutes. Serves 3.

HUEVOS EXQUISITOS

1 tablespoon butter
1 small green pepper, chopped
½ teaspoon onion powder
¼ teaspoon chili powder
Salt, pepper to taste
½ teaspoon oregano
1 cup tomato purée
½ cup evaporated milk or light cream
½ cup milk
6 black olives, chopped
Dash liquid artificial sweetener
2 ounces grated sharp white cheese (Jack or white Cheddar)
6 to 8 hard-cooked eggs (freshly made)

Melt the butter in a skillet. Add the green pepper and sauté until soft. Add the spices, herb, tomato purée, cream, milk and olives. Simmer gently, stirring, until well blended and hot. Correct seasoning to taste. Add the cheese, and simmer until the cheese is just melted. Slice the eggs on a serving platter, cover with the sauce and serve hot. Serves 3 or 4.

EGGS PROVENÇAL

1 egg, slightly beaten
2 tablespoons soy flour
Salt, pepper to taste
Pinch of basil
½ medium eggplant
2 tablespoons oil plus more as needed
1 clove garlic, mashed
6 jumbo eggs
1 cup allowed or homemade Spaghetti Sauce (see Brand Names or Sauces and Dressings)

Beat the egg, gradually add to the soy flour; add the salt, pepper and basil, and mix well. Slice the unpeeled eggplant to make 6 slices. Dip each slice into the batter, and coat evenly. Heat the oil in a large pan, and sauté the garlic for 1 minute. Fry the eggplant slices until golden brown on both sides. Cover the pan, lower heat and cook until the eggplant is soft inside (eggplant will turn a grayish-green inside when cooked). Remove the eggplant and set aside. Heat more oil if needed and carefully break the eggs and slip them into the pan. Fry gently over low heat until firm. Place the eggplant slices on individual plates, place a fried egg on each and top with a spoonful of hot spaghetti sauce. Season to taste with salt and pepper if needed, and serve immediately. Serves 3 to 6.

FOREIGN AND REGIONAL

When people hear the list of foods forbidden on the hypoglycemia diet, their usual reaction is, "Well, I could never live without spaghetti (or potato pancakes or chili con carne). It's not easy to convince them that there is almost no limit to the foods that can be adapted to a low-carbohydrate diet with a little ingenuity.

The diet should not work a hardship on any nationality, although we admit that it is easier to fit it into the eating habits of some regions than of others. For instance we can substitute soybeans for the starchier beans which are a staple food in the Southwest and Mexico, but there is a definite difference in the taste and texture of the foods. We think the difference is not great enough to discourage you from trying these dishes. After all, isn't it better to be able to eat a good substitute than to do without your favorite foods entirely? (Or worse, to "cheat" and eat the forbidden food.) Therefore, we will preface this chapter with a warning: be prepared for a slight difference in taste and consistency when you try your favorite recipe; you may be pleasantly surprised to find that you like the "imitation" better than the original!

CHINESE FOOD

Egg Drop Soup
Won Ton Soup
Quick Chicken Chow Mein
Sub Gum Chicken Chow Mein
Chicken Egg Foo Yung
Pepper Steak (Chinese Steak and Peppers)
Fried "Rice"
Sweet and Pungent Pork
Egg Rolls
Candied Pineapple
Chinese Mustard: *see* Sauces
Duck Sauce: *see* Sauces
Oriental Pork Balls: *see* Meats
Chinese Sweet Pork: *see* Meats
Sweet and Pungent Chicken Livers: *see* Meats
Ginger Shrimp: *see* Seafood

ITALIAN FOOD

Minestrone
Meat-crust Pizza
Eggplant Parmigiana
Chicken Cacciatore
Veal Parmigiana
"Spaghetti" and Meat Balls
Antipasto
Spumoni
Italian Rum Cake
Veal Scallopini: see Meats
Wax Bean Lasagna: see
    Casseroles
Stuffed Peppers: see Casseroles
Artichokes with Garlic Butter:
    see Vegetables
Salad with Italian Dressing: see
    Dressings

JEWISH FOOD

Borscht
Blintzes
"Potato" Latkes ⚹1
"Potato" Latkes ⚹2
"Potato" Kugel ⚹1 (Mock
    Potato Pudding)
"Potato" Kugel ⚹2 (Mock
    Potato Pudding)
Lukshen Kugel (Noodle
    Pudding)
Tzimmes (Pot Roast)
Chopped Liver
Golden Chicken Soup with
    Knaidlach (Dumplings)
Chicken Soup with Kreplach
Almond Balls (Mondlein): see
    Breads, Pasta and Noodles
Rogelach: see Desserts
Stuffed Cabbage: see Casseroles

MEXICAN FOOD

Tortillas ⚹1
Tortillas ⚹2
Tacos (Meat Tarts)
Tostadas (Sandwiches)
Enchiladas
"Frijoles" Refritos (Refried
    Soybeans)
"Frijoles" with Chili
Apple Soda
Montezuma Pie
Flan
Huevos Rancheros: see Eggs
Mexican Chocolate: see
    Beverages
Haddock Veracruzana: see
    Seafood
Chili: see Vegetables
Chili con Carne: see Casseroles
Guacamole: see Appetizers

MISCELLANEOUS

Sukiyaki
Shish Kebab
Sauerbraten
Spaetzle: see Breads, Pasta and
    Noodles
Southern Fried Chicken: see
    Meats
"Grits": see Breakfast Foods
Southern-style Beans with Ham
    Bone: see Vegetables
"Corn Meal" Bread: see Breads,
    Pasta and Noodles

CHINESE FOOD

Most oriental dishes can be made using low-carbohydrate substitutions. Chinese restaurants are very popular with many Americans, and the weekly visit to the local Chinese restaurant is a ritual in many families. You can make your own adaptations of Chinese dishes by using any good Chinese cookbook and substituting saccharin for sugar, bean sprouts for rice, oatmeal for corn starch, and of course you must omit wine, sherry, etc. We have given you some of the most popular Chinese dishes, in easy-to-make adaptations, eliminating some of the unnecessary steps. To make sure that your Chinese dishes taste authentic, cook the vegetables for as short a time as possible, so that they are cooked, but still crisp. Also, use fresh peanut oil whenever oil is called for.

EGG DROP SOUP

4 cups chicken broth (use homemade soup or *see* Brand Names)
3 or 4 mushrooms, sliced thin
2 eggs, beaten well
½ ¼-grain tablet saccharin
½ teaspoon MSG (optional)

Combine the soup and mushrooms and simmer until the mushrooms are cooked. Bring the soup to a rolling boil. Gradually stir in the beaten eggs while the soup is boiling. Remove from the heat, add saccharin and MSG and stir until the egg is cooked (a few seconds). Correct seasoning to taste, serve immediately. Serves 2 to 4.

WON TON SOUP

1 recipe soy noodle dough (*see* Soy Noodles in Breads, Pasta and Noodles)
¼ pound ground lean pork or beef
Dash of MSG
Dash of salt
1 egg white
4 to 6 cups chicken broth or chicken soup (*see* Egg Drop Soup)

Prepare the dough according to the recipe (or use any of the other dough recipes given in that section). Roll out very thin and cut into 2-inch squares. Mix the pork and seasonings, and knead until smooth. Place a teaspoonful of the pork in the center of each square. Brush the edges of the square with egg white. Fold the dough in half and seal the edges by pinching them together. Drop into the hot soup and simmer until the won tons are cooked, about 5 minutes (remove one and test to see if it is done). If your dough is not paper thin, cooking time will be 10 minutes or longer. Serves 4 to 6.

QUICK CHICKEN CHOW MEIN

1 large chicken breast, split
1 can College Inn chicken broth
2 tablespoons peanut oil
1 cup almonds (not blanched), sliced
2 or 3 scallions or 1 small onion, slivered
1 can Chun King chow mein vegetables packed in water (not in sauce), drained
1 can bean sprouts, drained
1 small can mushroom pieces
2 tablespoons Kikkoman soy sauce
Dash of MSG
½ teaspoon garlic powder

Cook the chicken breast in the soup until tender (about 20 minutes). Remove the chicken and discard the skin and bones. Shred the meat and set aside. In a large skillet, heat the oil. Fry the almonds, stirring until crisp. Remove and set aside to drain. Sauté the scallions until soft. Add the vegetables, chicken, soup and seasonings. Cover and heat 5 minutes. Pour into a bowl and garnish with the fried almonds. Serves 2 or 3.

SUB GUM CHICKEN CHOW MEIN

1 can College Inn chicken broth or 2 cups Knorr-Swiss chicken bouillon
1 large chicken breast, split
¼ cup peanut oil
2 or 3 large scallions, minced
4 large ribs celery, sliced
1 clove garlic, minced fine
½ cup red pepper or pimiento, minced
6 to 8 fresh mushrooms, sliced
⅓ package frozen snow peas (slice with frozen food knife, wrap and refreeze the unused portion)
1 can sliced bamboo shoots, drained
1 can bean sprouts, drained well
½ can water chestnuts, drained and sliced
2 tablespoons Kikkoman soy sauce
1 teaspoon MSG
1 tablespoon steel-cut or Scotch-style oatmeal
Fried Oriental Soy Noodles (see Breads, Pasta and Noodles)

Heat the soup in a small saucepan. Remove most of the skin from the chicken breast; cook the chicken in the soup until tender (about 20 minutes). Set aside. In a large skillet, heat the oil. Sauté the scallions, celery and garlic in the oil, stirring, until the vegetables are softened and translucent. Add the red pepper, mushrooms and snow peas. Stir and fry until the peas have thawed and the vegetables are well coated with oil. Pour in the soup in which the chicken was cooked. Add the drained canned vegetables, soy sauce and MSG. Lower heat, cover and simmer briefly to heat through; do not overcook. Vegetables should be almost crunchy. In the meantime, remove all the skin and bones from the chicken. Shred the chicken and add to the vegetables. Mix a little cold water with the oatmeal, and add to the mixture. Simmer until the oatmeal is dissolved and the sauce is thickened. Serve over crisp homemade fried Oriental Soy Noodles. This will be thinner than the Chow Mein you are accustomed to, but the flavor is the same. This does not contain enough protein to be used as the only dish, but should be accompanied by some other protein. For carbohydrates, see the noodle recipe. Serves 2 to 4.

CHICKEN EGG FOO YUNG

¼ cup peanut oil
½ cup diced celery
½ cup fresh mushrooms, sliced
½ cup frozen peas, separated
1 onion, sliced thin
6 eggs
2 ¼-grain tablets saccharin, crushed
½ teaspoon MSG
Dash of garlic powder
¼ teaspoon salt
1 cup cooked shredded chicken
1 can bamboo shoots, drained
1 cup beef gravy or beef stock
2 tablespoons oat flour
1 ¼-grain tablet saccharin

Heat half the oil in a large pan. Add the celery, mushrooms, peas and onion. Stir and fry until the vegetables are slightly softened and the onion is translucent. Do not overcook. Remove from the heat and set aside in a covered dish. In a large bowl, beat the eggs well. Add the seasonings, beat again. Add the chicken, bamboo shoots and the cooked vegetables. Heat the rest of the oil in the frying pan and pour in the egg mixture. Fry until the bottom is browned; cover the pan, lower heat and cook until the top is beginning to set. Fold as for an omelette. Transfer to a warm dish; heat the gravy or stock and stir in the oat flour and saccharin. Stir until thickened, maintaining a rolling boil. Pour over the omelette and serve. Serves 2 or 3.

PEPPER STEAK (CHINESE STEAK AND PEPPERS)

2 pounds lean steak (shoulder, etc.), frozen, then thawed slightly
2 tablespoons peanut oil plus more as needed
½ cup finely minced scallions
4 large green peppers, sliced lengthwise in thin strips
2 cloves garlic, minced fine
2 cups rich beef stock or allowed bouillon (see Brand Names)
½ teaspoon MSG
Freshly ground pepper to taste
2 tablespoons Kikkoman soy sauce
2 tablespoons oat flour
1 or 2 tablespoons cold water
Salt to taste
1 can bean sprouts, rinsed and drained
½ cup water or boullion

While the steak is still semi-frozen, slice it across the grain with a serrated knife. Slices should be paper thin and about 3 inches long. Set the slices aside to thaw, then dry on a towel. Heat the oil in a large skillet. Stir-fry the scallions, peppers and garlic in the oil until the scallions are transparent. Transfer to a warm plate. Pour more oil in the pan if needed; heat again and fry the steak, stirring, until it loses its pink color. Pour in the beef stock, add the vegetables and seasoning. Lower the heat, cover and simmer 5 minutes. Combine the soy sauce, flour and a little cold water, mixing to a paste. Add to the steak mixture, stirring, until the sauce is thickened. Season to taste with salt if needed. Do not overcook; the peppers should still be a bright green and a bit crunchy, not soft. If a thicker sauce is desired, transfer the steak and peppers to a plate, and simmer the sauce uncovered until reduced and thick (stir constantly). To serve, heat the bean sprouts in water or bouillon, drain and place on individual plates; spoon the pepper steak over them. Contains only a slight trace of carbohydrate per serving. Serves 4.

FRIED "RICE"

1 tablespoon peanut oil plus more as needed
2 scallions, minced, including tops
¼ green pepper, chopped
3 or 4 raw mushrooms, sliced
1 can bean sprouts, drained
Dash of MSG
Dash of salt
Dash of pepper
1 teaspoon Kikkoman soy sauce
1 egg, slightly beaten

Heat the oil in a large skillet. Add the scallions, peppers and mushrooms. Stir and fry until slightly softened, but not limp. Drain the bean sprouts and rinse with cold water and drain again (squeeze slightly). Transfer the sprouts to a cutting board, and mince with a sharp knife until the pieces are the size of rice. Add the minced sprouts to the cooked vegetables. Add the seasonings, mix and pour in the egg, scrambling as it cooks. Serve hot with a Chinese main dish. Serves 2 to 4.

Variations: Add 1½ cups minced roast pork, or 1½ cups sliced cooked chicken. May be used as a main dish.

SWEET AND PUNGENT PORK

¼ cup oat flour
2 eggs, slightly beaten
½ teaspoon salt
1 tablespoon water
2 pounds lean pork, cut into ½-inch chunks
Peanut oil as needed
1 ounce of carrot, thinly sliced
2 medium green peppers, cut into large chunks
1 large ripe tomato, cut in eighths
1 large can Dole unsweetened pineapple chunks, packed without
    sugar
½ cup white vinegar

¼ cup homemade sweet pickles (optional) (*see* Preserves)
½ teaspoon MSG
1 tablespoon Kikkoman soy sauce
2 ¼-grain tablets saccharin or to taste
Water to taste

Combine the flour, eggs, salt and the 1 tablespoon water. Mix to form a batter. Soak the pork cubes in the batter until well coated. Heat ½ inch of peanut oil in a large skillet. Fry the pork, turning to brown evenly for about 10 minutes, or until crisp and brown (don't crowd the pan, but fry a few at a time until all are done). Drain on paper towels and set aside. Pour the excess oil out of the pan. Stir in the carrots and peppers for 1 minute, then add the tomato and pineapple chunks, reserving the liquid. Stir and fry until the vegetables are lightly cooked, but still crisp. Pour in the juice from the pineapples and add the vinegar, pickles and other flavorings. Stir until flavors have mingled. Add the pork to the pan; correct flavoring, adding water if taste is too strong. Sauce should be sweet and sour, without either one dominating. Thicken the sauce as follows: transfer the vegetables, fruit and pork with a slotted spoon to a serving dish and cover. Simmer the sauce, stirring over medium-high heat until reduced and thick. Pour the sauce over the pork mixture and serve hot. Serves 4.

EGG ROLLS

2 eggs
¼ cup oat flour
Dash of salt
¼ cup water
Peanut oil as needed
2 scallions, minced, including tops
¼ cup chopped celery
¼ cup finely chopped cabbage
¼ cup bean sprouts, rinsed and drained well
½ cup small raw shrimp, peeled
Dash of liquid artificial sweetener
Dash of salt
Dash of MSG
Dash of Kikkoman soy sauce
1 egg white

Beat the eggs in a bowl. Mix in the oat flour and stir to a paste. Add the salt and water, and mix until smooth. Heat a large skillet and oil it lightly with a brush. Pour in enough of the batter to form a large very thin pancake, rolling the pan to allow any excess batter to run off to the sides. Heat over medium-low heat until the top is fairly dry. Do not turn; remove to a sheet of wax paper, and repeat until the batter is used up. Makes about 3 very thin pancakes. Cut the pancakes, dividing them into thirds (makes 9 pieces). Set aside.

Heat about 1 tablespoon of the oil in the frying pan. Add the vegetables and sauté, stirring, until slightly cooked (they should still be crunchy). Chop the shrimp and add to the pan, stirring. Add the seasonings, and stir and fry until the shrimp turn opaque (about 1 minute). Place a spoonful of the mixture in the center of each section of pancake. Brush the edges of the pancakes with the egg white. Fold the edges toward the centers, making 9 filled envelopes and pinch to seal. Heat ½ inch of peanut oil in the frying pan. Place the egg rolls, sealed sides down, in the hot oil, and fry until golden brown, turning several times to prevent burning. Makes 9 egg rolls. Entire recipe=2 units carbohydrate. Serve with Chinese Mustard and Duck Sauce (*see* Sauces and Dressings).

CANDIED PINEAPPLE

1 very ripe medium pineapple
¼ teaspoon ground ginger
1 bottle red fruit-flavored diet soda (sugarless)

Peel the pineapple and discard the top. Slice crosswise, making 8 large slices. Place the slices in a large baking dish. Sprinkle on the ginger and pour in the soda. Bake at 300° for 2 hours, or until the pineapple is cooked and the soda is reduced to a thick sauce. Remove from the oven and allow to cool. Chill before serving. Serves 8; 1 slice=1 unit fruit.

ITALIAN FOOD

Except for the various kinds of pasta, Italian food is fairly low in carbohydrate and can be very easily adapted. Use olive oil in cooking for authentic flavor. The tomato sauce you use can either be the homemade kind (*see* Sauces and Dressings) or a simpler one using tomato purée and seasonings. There are a few canned or bottled spaghetti sauces on the market which do not contain sugar (*see* Brand Names); but since companies often change their formulas, these might be changed at any time in the future. For this reason, we prefer not to rely on them, but to make our own sauces. There are Italian recipes in other sections of this book; if you prefer cooking Italian style, you should have no trouble adapting many of your favorite recipes. If you must use pasta, use De Boles Jerusalem artichoke products (very sparingly), if tolerated. If wheat is not tolerated, use the noodle recipes given in Breads, Pasta and Noodles.

MINESTRONE

½ pound salt pork, diced
2 quarts beef stock or Knorr-Swiss beef bouillon
2 cups canned tomatoes
1 carrot, diced
¼ small cabbage, shredded
1 large onion, chopped
Dash of basil
1 cup green beans, cut into 1-inch lengths
6 ribs celery, diced
¼ head of lettuce, shredded
1 small zucchini, diced
Dash of liquid artificial sweetener
½ cup homemade macaroni or artichoke noodles
Salt, pepper to taste
Grated Parmesan cheese

Combine the salt pork and stock. Boil for 15 minutes. Add the other ingredients, except the noodles, seasonings and cheese. Cover and cook gently for 1 hour. Add the macaroni or noodles and cook for another 10 minutes, or until the noodles are cooked. Season to taste and garnish with Parmesan cheese. Serves 6 to 8.

MEAT-CRUST PIZZA

1 pound extra lean ground beef
1 egg
2 thick slices homemade high-carbohydrate bread or 2 slices allowed
 bread, crumbed in the blender
¼ teaspoon salt
Dash of pepper
2 cups tomato purée
1 tablespoon dehydrated green pepper flakes
2 teaspoons dehydrated onion flakes
½ teaspoon garlic powder
1 teaspoon oregano
1 tablespoon olive oil
8 ounces mozzarella cheese, shredded
Any or all of the following: homemade Italian sausage, sliced thin
 (see Meats); sliced onions, anchovy fillets

Combine the meat, egg and bread crumbs in a bowl. Knead until
smooth. Season with salt and pepper. Press the meat mixture into a
large round pan or two pie plates, making one or two thin piecrusts.
Bake at 300° for 30 minutes. Remove from the oven. Pour off ac-
cumulated fat if any. In a saucepan, heat the tomato purée, pepper
flakes, onion flakes and garlic powder. Simmer, stirring until the
sauce is reduced and thick (or simmer on low while the crust is baking). When the sauce is thick, spread it on the crust. Sprinkle with
oregano and olive oil, then sprinkle on the shredded cheese until the
surface is covered. If you want to use any of the extra ingredients,
add to suit your taste. Preheat the oven to 400°. Bake briefly, just
until the cheese is melted and bubbly. Serve immediately. Serves 4;
entire recipe=2 units carbohydrate. 1 serving=½ unit carbohydrate.

EGGPLANT PARMIGIANA

1 egg, slightly beaten
¼ teaspoon salt
2 tablespoons soy flour

½ medium eggplant, sliced ½ inch thick
2 tablespoons olive oil
½ small onion, minced
1 clove garlic, minced fine
1 8-ounce can Del Monte tomato sauce (check the label)
½ teaspoon oregano
4 ounces of bulk Parmesan cheese, grated in the blender

Mix the egg with the salt and soy flour. Dip the eggplant slices into the mixture, turning until coated. Heat the oil in a large frying pan, and fry the eggplant until browned on both sides. Transfer to a casserole. Add the onion and garlic to the frying pan, and sauté briefly. Pour in the tomato sauce, add the oregano and stir to heat. Pour the sauce over the eggplant. Sprinkle on the grated cheese until evenly covered. Bake at 325° for 1 hour, or until the eggplant is tender. Serves 4 as a side dish.

CHICKEN CACCIATORE

¾ cup water
2 chicken breasts, split
1 tablespoon olive oil
1 small onion, minced
2 cloves garlic, minced fine
½ green pepper, chopped
2 cups tomato sauce (Del Monte, etc.)
1 ¼-grain tablet saccharin
Dash of basil (optional)
¼ cup grated Parmesan cheese

Combine the water and chicken in a small deep saucepan. Cover and steam until the chicken is cooked enough so that the skin can be easily removed. Skin and bone the chicken. In a large pan, heat the oil; sauté the onion, garlic and pepper until soft. Add the tomato sauce and saccharin. Season to taste, adding a dash of basil if needed. Place the chicken fillets in the pan. Spoon the sauce over the chicken so that it is covered. Cover the pan and simmer over low heat until the chicken is tender. Add the grated cheese and simmer uncovered until the sauce is thickened. Serve as is or with cooked homemade noodles or De Boles artichoke noodles if tolerated. Serves 4.

VEAL PARMIGIANA

1 slice homemade high-carbohydrate bread, crumbed in the blender
2 tablespoons dry grated Parmesan cheese
½ teaspoon salt
Dash of pepper
1½ pounds lean veal, sliced thin
1 egg, slightly beaten
2 tablespoons butter or oil
8 ounces bulk Parmesan cheese, grated in the blender
2 cups tomato sauce, homemade or Del Monte, heated

Mix the bread crumbs and the dry cheese together, and add the salt
and pepper. Dip the veal in the egg, then in the crumb mixture until
evenly coated. Heat the butter or oil in a pan and fry the veal, turning once, until both sides are well browned. Sprinkle the shredded
cheese on top of the veal. Cover the pan, lower the heat and continue cooking over low heat until the veal is tender and the cheese is
melted. Transfer the veal to a serving dish and surround with tomato
sauce. Or, if preferred, you can pour the sauce over the veal before
adding the cheese, then cover and cook as before. Entire recipe=1
unit carbohydrate. Serves 2 or 3.

"SPAGHETTI" AND MEAT BALLS

1 tablespoon olive oil
½ small onion, minced
1 clove garlic, minced
1 large can tomato purée
½ teaspoon salt
1 ¼-grain tablet saccharin
¼ teaspoon oregano
1 small can or 3 ripe fresh tomatoes
1½ pounds lean ground round
1 egg, slightly beaten
½ teaspoon parsley flakes
½ teaspoon salt

Dash of pepper
2 cans bean sprouts, rinsed with cold water and drained well
¼ cup dry grated Parmesan cheese

Heat the olive oil in a frying pan; sauté the onion and garlic until soft. Add the tomato purée, salt, saccharin and oregano. Lower the heat, cover and simmer. Peel the tomatoes (or, if canned, drain). Chop the tomatoes and add to the sauce. Simmer over low heat for at least 1 hour. Mix the meat, egg, parsley, salt and pepper together and knead until smooth. Form into meat balls. Place the meat balls in a baking pan and bake in a 325° oven for 30 minutes. Remove from the oven and add to the sauce. Drain the bean sprouts, rinse again with cold water and drain again. Squeeze the moisture from the sprouts until they are reduced to about half their original bulk. Place the sprouts in the pan with the sauce and simmer until the sprouts are cooked, about 5 minutes. Sprinkle with the grated cheese and serve. The bean sprouts will take the place of spaghetti, and, if drained properly, have no flavor of their own (also no carbohydrates). Serves 2 or 3.

ANTIPASTO

Assorted salad greens (romaine, chicory, endive) as needed, torn
   into chunks
2 ounces sharp white Cheddar cheese
2 slices ham
½ cup homemade pickled beets
1 large can chunk white tuna, drained and separated into chunks
1 can anchovy fillets, drained
1 large pickled pepper, cut into strips
6 to 8 pickled black olives
½ small sweet Spanish onion, sliced
1 clove garlic, crushed
3 tablespoons salad oil
2 tablespoons tarragon vinegar
Salt to taste

Arrange the greens on a large platter, using as much as you need for the number of people being served. Cut the cheese, ham and pickled beets in strips and arrange on the greens. Separate the tuna into chunks and add to the salad along with the anchovies, pepper, olives and onion rings. In a small bowl, crush the garlic and mash with the oil. Add the vinegar and salt and mix together, then drizzle over the salad and serve. This can be cut in half, doubled or changed freely to suit your own taste. Serve as an appetizer, salad course or main dish, as you wish. Serves 3.

SPUMONI

4 egg yolks
4 to 6 ¼-grain tablets saccharin or to taste
½ teaspoon rum flavoring
⅔ cup heavy cream, chilled
Chopped nuts (optional)

Combine the egg yolks, saccharin and flavoring in a small saucepan and heat, beating constantly with a hand beater, until warm. Transfer to an electric mixer and beat until cool. Set aside. In another bowl, whip the cream until stiff. Fold the whipped cream gently into the egg mixture. Pour into a mold or small individual dishes and freeze. Makes 2 to 4 servings. If desired, garnish the tops with a dusting of chopped nuts.

ITALIAN RUM CAKE

1 Sponge Cake (see Desserts)
½ cup warm water
1 teaspoon imitation rum flavoring
2 tablespoons Polaner sugarless red raspberry jam
1 cup heavy cream, chilled
¼ teaspoon vanilla extract
4 ¼-grain tablets saccharin, crushed

Make the cake according to the recipe in a tube or spring form pan. Allow the cake to cool. Combine the water and rum flavoring and sprinkle over the cake on the top, sides and bottom. Slice the cake across the center, dividing it into 2 layers. Sprinkle any remaining rum mixture over the cut edges; spread the bottom layer with the jam and replace the top layer. Combine the cream, vanilla and saccharin in a small mixing bowl and beat with an electric mixer until stiff (do not beat for too long or the cream will turn to butter). Pile the whipped cream on top of the cake in swirls. For units of carbohydrates, see the cake recipe.

JEWISH FOOD

There are really several styles of cooking which are "authentic" Jewish-style food. We have included some of those which are most familiar to anyone growing up in a Jewish home. Many of the dishes call for schmaltz, or rendered chicken fat. This gives the food its characteristic flavor, and is prepared easily as follows: save the hard yellow fat from several chickens or have your butcher sell you some. Place it in a pan with 1 onion, diced, and about ¼ cup of cut-up chicken skin. Simmer slowly until the fat is rendered to liquid and the onion and skin have turned to brown "cracklings" at the bottom of the pan (these can be drained and make delicious nibbling, hot or cold). Salt to taste and store in the refrigerator. Use as you would butter or any other shortening. Oil called for in recipes should be peanut oil, and always check to make sure that your peanut oil is not rancid.

Traditionally, meals are divided into two types: milk, or dairy meals, at which no meat or meat product is used, and meat meals, in which no dairy foods are used.

BORSCHT

4 to 6 beets
1 quart water
1 small onion, minced fine
2 tablespoons fresh lemon juice
½ teaspoon salt or more to taste
2 ¼-grain tablets saccharin or to taste
2 eggs, beaten
1 cup sour cream

Combine the beets and water in a saucepan and heat to boiling. Cover and simmer for 5 minutes; remove the beets and slip off the skins. Chop the beets and return to the pot. Add the onion, lemon juice and seasonings. Cover and cook slowly until the vegetables are tender, about 20 minutes. Correct the seasonings to taste. Remove from the heat and allow to cool. When cool, pour into the blender, add the eggs, and blend briefly. Chill in the refrigerator. Serve cold, with the sour cream stirred in or scooped on top. The sour cream can also be blended in at the same time as the eggs. Serves 4. Each serving=1 unit limited vegetable.

BLINTZES

3 jumbo eggs
¼ cup soy flour
¼ cup oat flour
½ cup water or as needed
¼ teaspoon salt
Oil as needed
3 tablespoons butter
1 egg white

Beat the eggs until well mixed. Stir in the flours, mixing to a thick paste. Add the water gradually, mixing until smooth. Salt and set aside for 15 minutes to thicken. Add more water if needed. Heat a small frying pan and oil lightly with a brush. Pour in a small amount of the batter and tilt the pan to allow the batter to spread out thin. Pour in only enough to make a very thin 6- to 8-inch pancake. Cook over moderate heat just until set. Do not turn. Remove from the pan and set aside on a sheet of wax paper. Oil the pan again and continue until the batter is used up. Prepare the filling. Place a heaping tablespoonful of the filling in the center of each pancake and fold the sides over the filling so that they overlap in the center. The blintz should form a filled tube, open at the top and bottom. Where the edges meet in the middle, brush with a little egg white and press to seal. Set aside until all are filled. In a large heavy skillet, melt the butter. When the butter is bubbly and slightly brown, gently place the blintzes, folded side down, in the pan. Lower the heat slightly and fry until golden brown on both sides. Serve hot and top with a scoop of sour cream or plain yoghurt. Entire recipe=3 units carbohydrate. Makes 6 blintzes.

Fillings:

1. Mock Potato Filling: Cook 1 package frozen cauliflower in ½ cup water until soft. Drain and mash. Mix with 1 teaspoon onion powder, ¼ teaspoon salt, a dash of freshly ground pepper and 1 small egg, beaten. Mix well and fill.

2. Cheese Filling: Place 8 ounces farmer cheese or 1 cup pot cheese in a bowl. Add ½ teaspoon salt and 1 small egg, beaten. Mix well and fill.

3. Fruit Filling: Beat 2 egg yolks until fluffy and lemon-colored. Stir in 1½ cups whole berries (strawberries, blackberries or raspberries) or diced fresh fruit, such as peaches or pears. Add 2 to 4 ¼-grain tablets of saccharin and heat in the top of a double boiler until the fruit is cooked and the mixture is thick and bubbly. Correct the sweetness to taste, and add a pinch of salt if needed. Fill the blintzes. Entire recipe=approximately 3 units fruit.

"POTATO" LATKES #1
(HIGH-CARBOHYDRATE VERSION)

1⅓ cups water
1 cup old-fashioned-style oatmeal
2 eggs
1 medium onion, cut up
½ teaspoon salt or to taste
Dash of pepper
Peanut oil as needed

Boil the water and slowly stir in the oatmeal. Reduce the heat to low, cover and simmer slowly, stirring often, until the water is absorbed (about 10 minutes). Break the eggs into the blender container and add the onion. Blend briefly on low until the onion is grated. Add to the oatmeal and mix well. Season to taste. Heat ½ inch of the oil in a heavy skillet. When hot, spoon the batter into the pan, forming 3-inch patties. Fry in the hot oil until the pancakes are crisp and golden on both sides. Drain on a paper towel. Repeat until all the batter is used. Serve hot with roast beef, pan drippings or other gravy, or with artificially sweetened applesauce. Entire recipe=4 units carbohydrate. Makes 8 patties; 2 patties=1 unit carbohydrate.

"POTATO" LATKES #2
(LOW-CARBOHYDRATE VERSION)

1 package frozen cauliflower
2 eggs, slightly beaten
2 tablespoons oat flour
½ teaspoon salt
½ teaspoon onion powder
Dash of freshly ground pepper
Peanut oil as needed

Separate the raw cauliflower, still frozen, into chunks. Place in the blender a few at a time. Grate, turning on and off, and emptying out the container into a bowl. Mix in the eggs, flour and seasonings. In a heavy skillet, heat ½ inch of oil. Spoon in the cauliflower mixture to form 2- to 3-inch patties. Do not crowd; fry a few at a time. Remove to a plate when crisp and golden brown on both sides. Drain on paper towels. Serve hot with sour cream, yoghurt, sugarless applesauce or roast beef gravy. Use the batter all at once; do not allow to thaw. Makes about 8 patties.

"POTATO" KUGEL #1 (MOCK POTATO PUDDING)

Same ingredients as for "Potato" Latkes #1
2 tablespoons rendered chicken fat

Combine the ingredients as for latkes, and mix with chicken fat. Pour into a well-greased casserole. Bake at 325° for 1 hour, or at 375° for 30 minutes. For browner crust, sprinkle with paprika and onion powder. Serves 4; each serving=1 unit carbohydrate.

"POTATO" KUGEL #2 (MOCK POTATO PUDDING)

2 packages frozen cauliflower or 1 small head raw cauliflower
2 eggs
1 medium onion, cut into pieces
½ teaspoon salt

¼ teaspoon paprika
½ cup water
Dash of freshly ground pepper
2 tablespoons oat flour
2 tablespoons rendered chicken fat

Break the cauliflower, still frozen, into flowerettes. Place a few pieces at a time into the blender and blend on low, turning on and off, until grated. Transfer the grated cauliflower to a bowl and repeat until all the cauliflower is grated. In the empty blender container place the eggs and onion. Blend on low until the onion is grated, but not liquefied. Combine with the cauliflower and mix. Add the remaining ingredients and mix well. Pour into a well-greased casserole. Bake at 375° until crusty and brown (about 30 minutes), or at 325° for 1 hour. Serves 4 to 6.

LUKSHEN KUGEL (NOODLE PUDDING)

2 cups salted water
1 cup uncooked homemade broad noodles (see Breads, Pasta and Noodles)
2 eggs
1 cup apple juice
6 ¼-grain tablets saccharin, crushed
2 tablespoons sweet butter
1 small apple, peeled and sliced
½ cup coarsely chopped walnuts
1 teaspoon cinnamon

Heat the water to boiling and cook the noodles for a few minutes, until soft but still chewy. Drain the noodles and pour into a bowl. Beat the eggs and stir into the noodles, tossing until coated. Add the apple juice and sweetener and butter. Grease a baking pan or casserole. Pour in some of the noodle mixture, then make a layer of apples, nuts and cinnamon. Add more of the noodle mixture, alternating and ending with noodles. Sprinkle the top with a little more cinnamon and some liquid sweetener. Bake at 325° for 1 hour. For carbohydrates, see the noodle recipe. Entire recipe=3 units fruit. Serves 3 to 6.

TZIMMES (POT ROAST)

1 teaspoon rendered chicken fat or oil
3 to 4 pounds first cut brisket of beef
2 tart plums or 4 tiny prune plums
2 small apples, peeled and cored
1 large carrot, sliced
¼ small butternut squash, peeled and cut in chunks
1 onion, diced
¼ teaspoon paprika
1 teaspoon salt
Water as needed

Melt the fat in a heavy frying pan. When the pan is hot, sear the meat on all sides until browned. Place the meat in a large deep casserole or baking pan. Arrange the fruit and vegetables all around and over the meat. Season; add about ¾ cup water to the pan in which the meat was seared. Mix with the pan drippings, then pour over the meat. Cover the pan tightly or seal with heavy aluminum foil. Bake at 325° for 2 hours. Remove the cover or foil, and bake for another hour, or until the gravy is thick and rich. Serve the meat with the fruit and gravy on top. Serves 4. Each serving=1 unit fruit, 1 unit high-carbohydrate vegetable.

CHOPPED LIVER

¼ cup rendered chicken fat
1 small onion, minced fine
1 pound fresh chicken livers
Dash of freshly ground pepper
1 teaspoon salt
4 ¼-grain tablets saccharin
½ teaspoon onion powder
2 or 3 hard-cooked eggs

Heat the chicken fat in a frying pan, and sauté the onion until it is tender, but not browned. Add the chicken livers and simmer in the fat until cooked (just until the liver loses its pink color all the way through). Place in a bowl with the seasonings and hard-cooked eggs. Chop well. Or, if you prefer, put the entire mixture through a grinder. (If you want to use a blender, blend only the livers; then add to the eggs and mash.) When well blended and smooth, press into a bowl to mold, and chill. Turn out onto a plate to serve. Eat plain, spread on homemade bread, or spread on celery. Serves 6 to 8.

GOLDEN CHICKEN SOUP WITH KNAIDLACH (DUMPLINGS)

1 recipe Basic Chicken Stock (*see* Soups)
1 recipe Knaidlach (*see* Breads, Pasta and Noodles)

Prepare soup according to recipe. When the soup is finished cooking, raise the heat until boiling. Drop in the dumpling batter, 1 spoonful at a time, being careful not to stir. Serve the soup with 1 or 2 knaidlach to a bowl, plus a small piece of carrot from the soup pot. Serves 6 to 8.

CHICKEN SOUP WITH KREPLACH

Prepare exactly as for Won Ton Soup, but use ground beef instead of pork in the filling.

MEXICAN FOOD

Mexican-style food is one of the most difficult to imitate because of the use of tortillas in so many of the recipes. We have developed two different tortilla recipes, neither of which is an exact substitute, but if you love Mexican food or are accustomed to eating it, you should find these recipes satisfactory. Many ingredients such as fresh or canned chilies can be bought in supermarkets these days; if you have difficulty finding them, a grocery store in a Spanish-speaking neighborhood will have them. To adapt your own favorite recipes, use our tortillas and soybeans in place of other beans.

TORTILLAS #1 (HIGH CARBOHYDRATE)

Prepare the batter as for Chinese Egg Rolls. Pour into a small lightly oiled skillet and fry on medium-low heat until set. Remove without turning. This makes a very flexible, easily handled tortilla, and can be used in recipes in which the tortilla must be folded and fried, rolled, etc. Entire recipe=2 units carbohydrate.

TORTILLAS #2 (LOW CARBOHYDRATE)

1 cup soy grits
4 eggs
¼ teaspoon salt
2½ cups water
Oil as needed

Combine the grits, eggs, salt and water in the blender; blend on medium until the grits are rather finely ground. Allow the mixture to stand 15 to 20 minutes until thickened. Heat a lightly oiled griddle or frying pan. Lower the heat to medium and pour in enough of the grits mixture to make a flat pancake about 6 inches in diameter. If the mixture is too thick, add more water as needed. The tortilla should bake in the pan, rather than fry. When able to turn, cook on the other side just until light tan. Remove and repeat, adding a little more oil as needed, until the entire batch is finished. For easier handling, place each tortilla between two sheets of wax paper. Makes about 12 tortillas.

These may be used as is or refried in hot oil. To refry: allow the tortillas to cool. Heat at least ¼ inch of oil in a pan. Drop into the hot oil and fry until golden brown. These tortillas are high in protein and low in carbohydrates. They are also extremely filling, and you'll find that you won't be able to eat more than one or two. Use them in any recipe, but especially in recipes where they don't need to be handled very much, and in meals where you plan to include some other carbohydrates. These have a flavor and texture closer to real tortillas, and for that reason as well, you may prefer to use them.

TACOS (MEAT TARTS)

Homemade Chile con Carne (*see* Casseroles) as needed
1 recipe Tortillas ※1
Peanut oil as needed
½ cup finely shredded lettuce
Canned green chili peppers
Salt to taste
Hot pepper sauce to taste

Prepare the chili, or use leftovers, heated up. Make the tortillas, cooking slightly as described in the recipe, until lightly browned. Set aside. In the frying pan, heat ¼ inch to ½ inch of oil until sizzling. Place 1 tortilla in the pan. As it fries to a crisp golden brown, gently bend it in half, forming the casing for the tart. Turn and fry on the other side. Drain, and repeat until all are fried. Fill each shell with about ½ cup of hot chili con carne, a generous amount of shredded lettuce and a chili pepper, cut into strips. Season with salt and hot pepper sauce to taste. For added protein, you could add any leftover steak or roast beef to the chili when heating it. Serves 4 to 6.

TOSTADAS (SANDWICHES)

1 recipe Tortillas ※2
1 ripe tomato, chopped
1 can tomato purée
Dash of chili powder
1 tablespoon dehydrated onion flakes
1 teaspoon dried pepper flakes
1 ¼-grain tablet saccharin
Dash of hot pepper sauce
Salt, pepper to taste
Oil as needed
1 chicken breast, cooked and shredded
1 can green chili peppers, slivered
4 ounces sharp white cheese, shredded
Shredded lettuce as needed

Prepare the tortillas according to the recipe and set aside to cool. In a saucepan, combine the tomato, tomato purée, chili powder, onion and pepper flakes, saccharin and seasonings. Cover, bring to a low boil, then simmer for 10 to 30 minutes (the longer it simmers, the better the sauce will taste). Heat ¼ inch of oil in a frying pan until very hot. Carefully slip the tortillas into the hot oil, a few at a time, until all are fried golden brown and crisp. Drain on paper towels. Make each sandwich as follows: 1 fried tortilla, then a layer of shredded chicken. Drizzle on some of the tomato sauce. Next add a few slivers of green chilies, some of the shredded cheese and a generous heap of lettuce. Top with another tortilla. This sandwich is very filling, and one will make a satisfying lunch. Be sure to use plenty of chicken on each. Serves 4 to 6.

ENCHILADAS

Ingredients are same as for Tostadas except for the following:
Substitute Tortillas ⚹1 for Tortillas ⚹2
Omit the chicken and use shredded roast beef or other leftover beef

Make the tortillas according to the recipe and spread them out to cool. Prepare the tomato sauce and the other ingredients and have them ready at hand. Heat ¼ inch to ½ inch of oil in a frying pan. Fry a tortilla briefly, just until golden brown. Remove to a paper towel. While it is still hot and flexible, place the following ingredients in the center: a little shredded meat, some of the sauce, a sliver or two of chilies, shredded cheese and a small amount of lettuce. Roll the sides of the tortilla together to form a tube, and turn the tube over so that it rests on the folded side. Repeat, making as many as you want. If you prefer, you can heat all the enchiladas again briefly in the pan until the cheese is soft. For carbohydrates, see the tortilla recipe. Serves 4 to 6.

"FRIJOLES" REFRITOS (REFRIED SOYBEANS)

2 cups yellow soybeans soaked in 6 cups cold water for 24 hours in the refrigerator
½ cup bacon drippings or oil

¼ teaspoon dried red pepper
¼ cup light cream
1 teaspoon salt or more as needed
¼ teaspoon freshly ground pepper
Dash of hot pepper sauce

Pour the beans and soaking water into a large deep pot. Bring to a boil and cover. Lower the heat, and simmer slowly for 6 hours (make sure the pot is not boiling over by checking periodically). Heat the bacon fat or oil in a large pan. Add the cooked beans, including about half of the cooking water. Add the remaining ingredients. Stir the beans, mashing them as they cook. Continue mashing and stirring, adding more water, until the mixture reaches the desired consistency, a thick paste. Serve as a side dish with additional pepper sauce, shredded cheese, or as is. These are very high in protein and can be used in tacos, tostadas, etc., as a replacement for meat. Serves 6.

"FRIJOLES" WITH CHILI

1 recipe "Frijoles" Refritos
2 tablespoons olive oil
2 cloves garlic, minced
1 large onion, diced
1 small can pimientos in water
1 cup beef broth or bouillon
1 teaspoon chili powder
Salt, pepper to taste
¼ cup vinegar
Pinch of oregano
2 ¼-grain tablets saccharin

Prepare the frijoles according to the recipe. After mashing, set aside. Heat the oil in a large frying pan and sauté the garlic and onion. Add the other ingredients including the frijoles. Cover and simmer 30 minutes to 1 hour, or until the flavors have blended and the mixture is thick again. Serves 6.

APPLE SODA

4 ounces apple juice, chilled well
Dash of liquid artificial sweetener
6 ounces club soda or Seltzer, chilled

This is a popular soft drink in Mexico. Combine the ingredients, mix and serve. This makes 10 ounces and is equal to 1 unit fruit.

MONTEZUMA PIE

1 recipe Tortillas ⚹2
Oil as needed
1 small onion, diced
1 can tomato purée
Salt to taste
2 cups cooked chicken, diced
½ pint light cream
2 or 3 canned green chilies, cut into slivers
4 ounces hard cheese, crumbled

Prepare the tortillas according to the recipe. Fry them lightly in oil until just browned, and set aside. Pour off all but 1 teaspoon of the oil. Sauté the onion and stir in the tomato purée, adding salt to taste. In a greased baking dish, make alternating layers of tortillas, tomato sauce, chicken, cream, chili peppers and cheese. Bake in a hot oven (400°) until the cheese is melted (10 or 15 minutes). Serves 3 or 4.

FLAN

1 recipe Baked Custard (see Desserts)
2 tablespoons butter
½ cup water
1 teaspoon unflavored gelatin
½ teaspoon maple flavoring
12 ¼-grain tablets saccharin

Prepare the custard according to the recipe. Bake in individual cups. When the custard is finished, remove from the oven and unmold onto individual plates. In a pan, melt the butter until it foams and turns brown. Pour in the water and sprinkle in the gelatin. Add the flavorings and heat gently over low heat, stirring, to dissolve the gelatin. Remove from the heat and set aside to cool. Chill briefly, until the sauce is thick and syrupy. Drizzle over the custards and serve immediately. This dessert is also delicious eaten cold. Serves 4; each serving=1 unit milk.

MISCELLANEOUS

SUKIYAKI

1 pound shoulder steak, frozen
2 tablespoons peanut oil
½ cup scallions, minced
2 tablespoons Kikkoman soy sauce
3 ¼-grain tablets saccharin
1 cup beef broth or Knorr-Swiss bouillon
Dash of MSG
1 can bamboo shoots, rinsed and drained

Thaw the steak slightly and slice paper thin against the grain. Cut into 4-inch strips and defrost. Drain on paper towels. Heat the oil and fry the steak and scallions, stirring, until the steak loses its pink color. Add the other ingredients. Cover and simmer 5 minutes. Serve on hot bean sprouts, braised celery or as is. Serves 2.

SHISH KEBAB

Juice of 1 lemon
1 bay leaf, crushed
¼ cup olive oil
2 pounds lamb, cut into 1-inch cubes
10 to 12 small cherry tomatoes
½ small eggplant, cut into chunks
10 to 12 tiny white onions, peeled
1 large green pepper, cut into chunks
Salt, pepper to taste

Squeeze the lemon into a large bowl. Add the bay leaf and olive oil and mix. Combine the meat and vegetables in the bowl, stirring to coat evenly. Cover and marinate in the refrigerator for several hours. Arrange on skewers, alternating meat with vegetables. Broil, basting with the marinade until the meat and vegetables are cooked. Do not broil too near the heat, and turn often. Salt and pepper to taste and serve. Serves 4.

SAUERBRATEN

2 cups water
½ cup vinegar
2 bay leaves
1 tablespoon whole peppercorns
1 clove garlic
2 tablespoons cracked ginger (*not* preserved ginger)
1 onion, chopped
10 ¼-grain tablets saccharin
½ teaspoon mustard seed
6 to 8 whole cloves
4 to 5 pound pot roast (top or bottom round)
Oat flour as needed
1 tablespoon oil
4 carrots, sliced

Combine all the ingredients except the roast, oat flour, oil and carrots. Bring to a boil and simmer 5 minutes. Cool. Place the meat in a deep pot and pour in the sauce. Refrigerate for 2 or 3 days, turning twice a day. Remove the meat from the marinade and pat dry. Rub the meat with a little oat flour, and brown in a skillet with oil until browned on all sides. Place in a roasting pan. Add the carrots and the marinade. Cover and cook in the oven at 325° for 2 to 3 hours, or until tender. Uncover for the last ½ hour for a thicker gravy. Serves 8.

MEATS

Since this is not meant to be a gourmet cookbook, we have tried to choose those dishes which would be easy to prepare and most likely to be missed by you. Some of the recipes are more adventurous in flavor than others; we hope they will give you an incentive to try adapting your own favorite meat recipes to the requirements of the diet.

In cooking meats, your objective is to obtain the most protein possible for your money. Don't try to save money with fatty or bony cuts of cheap meat; weigh your portions to make sure that you are getting enough protein at each meal, and read the unit plan occasionally to make sure that you are making the right amount. To get the most protein from any piece of meat, cook it slowly at a low temperature. It doesn't matter how low you cook it if the internal temperature is low enough to prevent the breakdown of the protein. If you are getting more gravy than meat, you are using too high a cooking temperature. A good meat thermometer is an excellent investment and will keep you from overcooking your meats. Any good cookbook will give you the suggested lengths of time for cooking various cuts; but we would suggest that you never roast or bake at a temperature higher than 325°, and preferably lower than that.

The other important rule in cooking meat or poultry is: no salt until you are almost ready to serve. Salt causes the protein-filled juices to be drained from the meat and should never be used in cooking unless you are making a soup or stew, in which case all the juices in the pan will be used. Season the meat with pepper, paprika, onion powder, garlic powder, herbs and other spices, but leave the salt off until the meat is actually served at the table.

In cooking tough or cheaper cuts of meat, you can steam or pot-roast in small amounts of liquid, as long as the liquid is used in the meal, for it will contain a great deal of the protein which has been lost from the meat. It is always best if possible to cook meat on a rack above the liquid, so the protein-rich juices will not be lost.

Many recipes for meat main dishes can be found under Foreign and Regional and Casseroles. Those recipes which don't seem to fit into either category are included in this section. We have purposely omitted recipes which can be used unchanged from any standard cookbook, such as roasted, broiled and baked meats, roasts, steaks and plain chops. These can be made as you are accustomed to making them, with an eye on the labels of your spices to make sure that you are not using any which contain sugar. Many of the recipes we give here are nothing more than suggestions which will in turn give you ideas for other meat dishes, all of which will help to increase the variety of your menus.

Roast Chicken with Stuffing
Southern Fried Chicken
Baked Chicken
Lemon-broiled Chicken
Stewed Chicken
Baked Creamed Chicken
Chicken Fricassee
Chicken Croquettes
Curried Chicken
Yorkshire Country Captain
Roast Duckling à l'Orange
Roast Turkey with Giblet
  Stuffing
Turkey Roast
Beef-chicken Fricassee
Meat Loaf
Romanian Meat Rolls
Swedish Meat Balls
Pan-broiled Meat Loaves
Deluxe Cheeseburger
Chili Meat Loaf
"Porcupines" or "Satellites"
"Octopuses" (Frankfurters for
  Children)
Nibble Sticks
Barbecued Frankfurters
Beef Fondue
Baked Steak
Yankee Pot Roast
Beef Stroganoff
Dried Beef Stroganoff
Veal Scallopini
Breaded Veal Cutlets
Stuffed Veal Chops
Veal Burgers
Dill Lamb Chops
Broiled Pork Chops
Baked Pork Chops
Oriental Pork Balls
Chinese Sweet Pork
Sausage #1
Sausage #2
Italian Sausage
Sausage Stuffing for Turkey
Scrapple
Spareribs Baked with Sauerkraut
Barbecued Spareribs
Baked Ham

Glazed Ham
Baked Ham with Jelly Glaze
Ham Steak with Fruit Sauce
Ham Loaf
Mixed Grill
Broiled Liver
Sautéed Chicken Livers
Liver and Onions

Sweet and Pungent Chicken
  Livers
Southern Fried Rabbit
Chicken Cacciatore: *see* Foreign
  and Regional
Veal Parmigiana: *see* Foreign
  and Regional

ROAST CHICKEN WITH STUFFING

1 3- to 4-pound chicken
¼ cup butter
1 thick slice homemade Oatmeal Bread (*see* Breads), crumbed
2 ribs celery, chopped in the blender
1 egg, slightly beaten
½ teaspoon salt
½ teaspoon sage
Freshly ground pepper to taste
Pinch of thyme
1 tablespoon dehydrated onion flakes
Oil as needed
Paprika as needed
Salt to taste

Wash and dry the chicken and dry the cavities. Melt the butter, and mix with the bread and celery (be sure to include the tops for added flavor). Add the egg, salt, sage, pepper, thyme and onion flakes. Mix well, adding a few drops of hot water if needed to moisten. Stuff into the cavities of the chicken. Rub the skin of the chicken lightly with oil and sprinkle generously with paprika and pepper. Do not salt. Preheat the oven to 350°; place the chicken on a rack over a roasting pan. Roast for 1 hour, then baste with the pan juices, lower the oven to 325° and roast for 1 hour or longer, until the chicken is crisp and brown, and the leg moves easily (you can also tell if the chicken is cooked by pinching the thickest part of the leg; it should yield to a light pressure). Salt and serve. Serves 4; each serving=¼ unit carbohydrate.

SOUTHERN FRIED CHICKEN

1 or 2 fryers, cut into pieces
½ cup oat flour
1 tablespoon freshly ground pepper
1 tablespoon salt
2 tablespoons paprika
2 ¼-grain tablets saccharin, crushed
¼ teaspoon MSG (optional)
Shortening as needed

Wash the chicken pieces and dry on paper towels. In a paper bag, combine the flour and seasonings. Place the chicken pieces in the bag all at once, hold the top closed and shake vigorously to coat the pieces. Remove chicken from the bag and allow to air-dry for 30 minutes. For deep frying, heat shortening in fryer; to fry in skillet, melt solid shortening to make ½ inch deep of shortening. When hot, place the chicken pieces in the hot fat; turn when brown, remove. Repeat until all pieces have been browned on all sides. Replace all the chicken in the skillet, cover and continue cooking for 30 minutes, or until tender when pierced with a fork (the larger your pan, the less time required for all pieces to cook). Turn often until all pieces are crisp and brown. Drain and serve hot or cold. Serves 4; each serving=1 unit carbohydrate.

Variations: To the basic recipe, add any of the following: sesame seeds, poppy seeds, celery seeds, onion powder, garlic powder, grated cheese, cayenne pepper, curry powder, oregano, thyme, ground nuts or chili powder.

BAKED CHICKEN

4 tablespoons butter
2 chickens, quartered
1 can sliced mushrooms
1 cup sour cream
½ envelope Knorr-Swiss onion soup and dip mix
Pinch of thyme
Water as needed

Preheat the oven to 325°. Melt the butter in a skillet and brown the chicken, turning until evenly browned. Place in a casserole with the mushrooms. Mix together the sour cream, soup mix, thyme and liquid from the mushrooms plus enough water to make it the consistency of cream. Pour over the chicken, cover and bake for 1 hour. Serves 6.

LEMON-BROILED CHICKEN

2 large chicken breasts, split
2 lemons quartered
1 tablespoon butter or oil
Pepper to taste
Salt to taste

Split the chicken breasts and place in a pan. Squeeze the lemons over the chicken. Marinate the chicken for 1 hour, turning occasionally. Transfer the chicken to a rack over a broiler pan. Rub with oil or butter, season with pepper, and broil 4 to 6 inches from the heat, basting with the remainder of the lemon juice. Turn several times to keep the skin from burning. Total broiling time should be about 15 to 20 minutes, depending on the size of the breasts. Salt to taste and serve. Serves 4.

STEWED CHICKEN

3 tablespoons butter
1 chicken, quartered
½ envelope Knorr-Swiss onion soup and dip mix
2 cups water
¼ teaspoon pepper

Melt the butter in a large skillet; brown the chicken well in the butter. Add the other ingredients, cover and simmer 20 to 30 minutes, or until tender. Remove the chicken to a serving dish and simmer uncovered until the gravy is reduced and thick. Pour over the chicken and serve as is, or over cooked mashed vegetables. Be sure to use all the sauce, as it contains much of the protein. Serves 4.

BAKED CREAMED CHICKEN

3 large chicken breasts
2 cups milk
1 Knorr-Swiss chicken bouillon cube
2 tablespoons butter
½ cup heavy cream
3 egg yolks
Salt to taste
Dash of pepper
Dash of freshly ground nutmeg
2 ounces Parmesan cheese, freshly grated

Remove the skin from the chicken; cut the breasts in half and discard the center bone. Place in a heavy pan with the milk and bouillon cube. Cover and simmer gently 20 minutes. Remove the chicken, pry the meat from the bones and discard the bones. Melt the butter in an ovenproof pan. Stir in the cream, then gradually add the egg yolks, stirring while heating. Add the milk in which the chicken was cooked and the seasonings. Continue heating and stirring until thickened. Place the chicken fillets in the pan, spoon the sauce over them and top with the grated cheese. Bake in a medium oven (350°) until the cheese melts. If you prefer the cheese to be browned rather than melted, place under the broiler until brown. Serves 6.

CHICKEN FRICASSEE

2 to 3 pounds chicken parts
4 tablespoons butter or rendered chicken fat
1 cup water
½ teaspoon salt
1 teaspoon onion powder
2 tablespoons onion flakes or 1 small onion, minced
¼ teaspoon pepper
¼ teaspoon paprika

Wash and dry the chicken pieces. Heat the butter in a large pan. Brown the chicken pieces on both sides; add the remaining ingredients. Cover and simmer over low heat for 30 minutes. Uncover and cook on low until the chicken is golden brown and tender and the pan gravy is thick. Serves 4 to 6.

CHICKEN CROQUETTES

½ cup mashed cooked carrots
1½ cups ground cooked chicken (grind well in grinder or blender)
1 slice homemade Oatmeal Bread (see Breads)
¾ cup milk
1 teaspoon salt
Pinch of sage
2 eggs, slightly beaten
1 teaspoon parsley flakes
Pinch of thyme
Oil or shortening

Mix the mashed carrots with the ground chicken. Soak the bread in the milk until soft, then combine with the other ingredients. Mix well together. Heat a small amount of oil or shortening in a skillet and scoop the chicken mixture into the skillet with an ice cream scoop. Brown the croquettes on all sides, rolling them gently as they brown. Transfer to a foil-lined baking sheet and bake at 325° for 30 minutes. Serve as is with homemade ketchup, homemade chutney or top with White Sauce (for all three see Sauces and Dressings). Serves 2; each serving=½ unit carbohydrate, ½ unit high-carbohydrate vegetable.

CURRIED CHICKEN

¼ cup oil
¼ cup butter
1 onion, diced
2 cloves garlic, minced
Pinch of ground ginger
1 tablespoon curry powder or to taste

½ teaspoon salt
Pinch of dried red peppers
¼ teaspoon coriander
2 large chicken breasts, split
1 cup plain yoghurt
1 cup chicken stock or allowed bouillon

Heat the oil and butter together in a large pan until the butter melts. Add the onion and garlic, stirring until browned. Stir in the spices. Add the chicken pieces and brown well in the mixture, turning once. Add the yoghurt and stock. Cover and simmer on low heat until the chicken is tender, turning once (about 10 minutes for each side). Remove the cover and simmer until the sauce is reduced and the chicken is golden brown. Serves 4.

YORKSHIRE COUNTRY CAPTAIN

2 to 3 pounds chicken parts
½ cup oat flour
2 tablespoons oil or butter
1 apple, peeled, cored and sliced
1 teaspoon curry powder
¼ teaspoon dry mustard
4 ¼-grain tablets saccharin
1 purple plum, chopped
¾ cup water
1 teaspoon onion powder
2 tablespoons cider vinegar
Salt to taste
1 thread saffron

Wash and dry the chicken; dredge in the flour, shaking to remove any excess. Heat the oil in a large pan and brown the chicken lightly on both sides. Add the remaining ingredients, cover and simmer until the chicken is tender (about 20 minutes). Place the chicken in a covered dish and set aside. Uncover the pan and simmer, stirring occasionally, until the gravy is reduced and thick. Pour over the chicken and serve as is or on a bed of hot bean sprouts, cooked cauliflower, etc. Serves 4; each serving=1 unit carbohydrate, ½ unit fruit.

ROAST DUCKLING À L'ORANGE

2 tablespoons butter
1 duck, thawed and wiped dry
½ teaspoon dehydrated orange peel
1 tablespoon Kikkoman soy sauce
Freshly ground pepper
1 small orange, thinly sliced
1 cup orange juice
Salt to taste

Melt the butter and brush all over the duck. Sprinkle the skin generously with the orange peel, soy sauce and pepper. Arrange the orange slices over the duck. Preheat the oven to 375°. Place on a rack in a roasting pan. Roast for 1 hour. Baste with the orange juice; lower the heat to 325° and continue roasting, basting with the pan drippings and orange juice until the skin is golden brown and the duck is tender (legs and wings can be moved easily and leg is tender when pinched). Baste frequently with a pastry brush all during roasting, and occasionally prick the skin with a fork to release some of the fat. Salt to taste when serving. Serves 3 or 4.

ROAST TURKEY WITH GIBLET STUFFING

1 large turkey, at least 18 pounds
2 tablespoons oil or melted butter
Paprika
MSG (optional)
Garlic powder
Freshly ground pepper

If using a frozen turkey, have it completely defrosted. Prepare the turkey the day *before* you plan to serve it as follows: remove the giblets and neck from the turkey and make the stuffing (see below). Wash the cavities and dry with paper towels. Stuff the turkey loosely with the giblet stuffing or any other you prefer. Set the turkey on a rack in a large roasting pan, at least ½ inch above the bottom of the pan. If you plan to serve the turkey at about six o'clock the next day, begin cooking the turkey around ten o'clock the night before. If serving earlier, begin cooking earlier (figure total cooking time will be about 20 hours). Rub the turkey all over with the oil or butter, and sprinkle with the seasonings (but *do not salt*). Preheat the oven to 325°; place the turkey uncovered in the oven and roast for 1 hour. Reduce the temperature to *180°* and continue roasting at that temperature. Use an oven thermometer if you have one to check the temperature; it should not go above 200°. When ready to serve the next night, the turkey will be tender and moist. From time to time, baste the turkey with the drippings in the pan. Salt just before serving. This method of roasting is unorthodox, but we find it is easy, makes a perfect turkey every time and eliminates shrinkage and loss of protein into the gravy. It also makes it possible for you to make a holiday meal without the pressure of preparing a turkey on the day of the holiday. Do not try cooking smaller turkeys overnight; for turkeys under 18 pounds, cook in the usual way.

GIBLET STUFFING

4 thick slices homemade Oatmeal Bread, crumbed (*see* Breads)
2 eggs, slightly beaten
½ teaspoon paprika
2 tablespoons melted butter or margarine
½ teaspoon salt
½ teaspoon sage
¼ cup chopped onion
1 cup chopped celery and tops
Pinch of thyme, parsley, marjoram

Remove the neck and organs from the cavity; set aside the liver. Place the giblets in a pan with 2 cups of water and 2 tablespoons dehydrated minced onion. Cover and simmer 1 hour. Add the liver and simmer 10 minutes more. Remove as much meat as you can from the neck and discard the bones. Chop all the meat fine. Place in a bowl and toss with the ingredients above.

TURKEY ROAST

1 2-pound turkey roast (check ingredients, as some brands contain
  sugar or dextrose)
2 tablespoons butter, softened at room temperature
½ Knorr-Swiss chicken bouillon cube
¼ teaspoon paprika

Thaw the roast in the refrigerator overnight. Remove the cover. Rub
well with the butter. Crumble the bouillon cube and sprinkle it over
the top of the turkey, then sprinkle with the paprika. Preheat the
oven and bake according to the directions on the package. Serves 4.

BEEF-CHICKEN FRICASSEE

1 pound lean ground round or sirloin
1 egg, slightly beaten
1 slice homemade bread, crumbed fine
1 tablespoon rendered chicken fat or butter
1 medium onion, diced
6 to 8 pieces chicken wings and legs
Salt, pepper to taste
½ teaspoon paprika
¼ cup water
Dash of MSG

Combine the meat, egg and bread crumbs. Mix well, then form into
meat balls. Heat the fat or butter in a large skillet, and sauté the
onion until soft, then push it to one side. Add the chicken pieces and
brown briefly on both sides. Remove, then brown the meat balls
briefly on all sides. Pour off any excess fat. Return the chicken to
the pan, add the remaining ingredients. Cover and simmer slowly
for 1 hour. Serves 3.

MEAT LOAF

3 pounds lean ground beef
1 cup tomato purée
½ cup non-fat dry milk
2 tablespoons prepared mustard
1 teaspoon salt
1 cup of any of the following: wheat germ; homemade bread, crumbed; sunflower seed meal; grated carrot; grated nuts, or a combination of any of these
1 onion, grated
2 eggs
½ teaspoon each: pepper, parsley flakes, basil
½ teaspoon dry mustard
1 onion, diced

Combine all ingredients, except the diced onion. Knead until smooth in texture, adding a little water if needed. Form into a large loaf, about 4 inches high; place in a foil-lined loaf pan. Sprinkle the diced onion onto the surface of the loaf. Bake in a preheated 325° oven for 1½ to 2 hours. Serves 4 to 6. If 1 cup wheat germ is used, each serving=1 unit carbohydrate.

ROMANIAN MEAT ROLLS

2 pounds lean ground beef
1 large onion, minced fine
1 teaspoon salt
2 eggs, beaten slightly
2 cloves of garlic, crushed
Dash of pepper
¼ cup finely chopped fresh parsley
1 teaspoon paprika or more as needed

Mix all ingredients together except the paprika. Knead until well blended. Shape into long "sausages" and roll in paprika. Place on a broiler rack over a pan and broil at least 6 inches from the heat, turning several times until cooked (about 10 or 15 minutes). Serves 4.

SWEDISH MEAT BALLS

1 pound ground beef
1 egg
1 tablespoon finely minced parsley
½ cup sour cream
¼ teaspoon freshly ground pepper
Dash of nutmeg
½ teaspoon salt
½ teaspoon onion powder

Combine the beef, egg and parsley. Mix well and roll into small meat balls, 1 inch in diameter. Place on a rack over a pan and broil briefly. Turn frequently, until meat balls are brown on all sides. Set aside. Pour ½ cup of the drippings from the broiler pan into a skillet. Add the sour cream and remaining seasonings, stirring until smooth. Add the meat balls, cover and simmer for 5 minutes. Serves 2 as a main dish; or use as an appetizer.

PAN-BROILED MEAT LOAVES

2 pounds lean ground beef
2 eggs, slightly beaten
¼ teaspoon oregano
¼ teaspoon garlic powder
½ teaspoon salt
½ cup instant oatmeal (dry)
½ cup non-fat dry milk
2 tablespoons minced onion
¼ cup finely chopped celery tops
¼ teaspoon pepper

Combine all ingredients and knead well. Allow to sit for ½ hour. Shape into 4 small loaves. Place in a Teflon-lined frying pan; brown over medium heat on one side for 5 minutes. Turn and brown on the other side for 5 minutes. Pour in 1 small can Del Monte tomato sauce. Lower the heat, cover and simmer for 20 minutes, turning occasionally. Serve with hot drained bean sprouts, mashed cauliflower, etc. Serves 4; each serving=½ unit carbohydrate.

DELUXE CHEESEBURGER

1 pound ground sirloin or round
1 tablespoon Kikkoman soy sauce
¼ teaspoon MSG
1 tablespoon onion flakes, reconstituted in 2 tablespoons water
4 ounces sharp Cheddar cheese, grated

Mix the meat with the soy sauce and MSG and knead until smooth. Form into 8 very flat patties. Divide the onion flakes into 4 portions and place in the centers of 4 of the patties. Cover with the remaining 4 patties, and press the edges to seal. Place on a broiler rack over a pan, and broil 6 to 8 inches from the heat until browned. Turn, sprinkle with the cheese and broil until the cheese is melted. Serve as is or with homemade bread. Serves 2.

CHILI MEAT LOAF

2 pounds lean ground round
1 large onion, minced
1 egg
1 teaspoon mixed Italian spices (or use oregano, basil, thyme, to total 1 teaspoon)
1 teaspoon salt
1 cup tomato purée
2 slices Thomas' Protein Bread, crumbed
1 green pepper, chopped
1 tablespoon chili powder
2 ounces green chilies, diced

Mix all ingredients together, and knead until smooth. Pat down into a square baking pan. Bake at 325° for 1 hour, or until brown and firm. Slice, serve with homemade Chili Sauce. Serves 4; each serving=½ unit carbohydrate.

"PORCUPINES" OR "SATELLITES"

2 pounds lean ground beef
1 tablespoon homemade Chili Sauce
1 thick slice homemade Oatmeal Bread, crumbed
½ teaspoon salt
1 tablespoon parsley, minced
1 egg, slightly beaten
¼ teaspoon pepper
Cheddar cheese, cut in ½-inch cubes
Sour pickles, cut in ½-inch cubes
Almonds slivers or pignolia nuts

Combine all ingredients except the cheese, pickles and nuts. Knead until smooth and form into meat balls. Press a cube of cheese or pickle into the center of each ball and re-form the ball to cover the cube completely. Stick almond slivers or whole pignolia nuts all around the ball at random. Bake on a rack in medium oven (350°) until brown, about 45 minutes. These are excellent for children's lunches or parties and can also be used as appetizers. Serves 4 adults or 6 children. Each serving=small amount of carbohydrate.

"OCTOPUSES" (FRANKFURTERS FOR CHILDREN)

1 pound sugarless hot dogs (*see* Brand Names)
2 dozen whole cloves
1 quart boiling water
1 package frozen spinach, cooked (optional)

Slice each hot dog through lengthwise up to the middle. Slice again, so that the hot dog resembles an octopus with 4 legs. Stick 2 cloves in each "head" for eyes. Place in rapidly boiling water for 5 minutes, or until the legs curl up. Sit the "octopus" up on a bed of seaweed (spinach). Serves 4 or 5.

NIBBLE STICKS

1 pound sugarless hot dogs (*see* Brand Names)

Slice each hot dog lengthwise, making two thin franks. Slice through each half lengthwise again, making 4 skinny franks. Place on a rack over a pan in the oven. Bake in a moderate oven (350° or 375°), turning occasionally. When evenly brown and rather dry, remove (about 20 to 30 minutes). Eat as is, hot or cold, dipped in mustard or other dips. Serves 2.

BARBECUED FRANKFURTERS

1 recipe Barbecue Sauce (*see* Sauces and Dressings)
1 pound sugarless hot dogs (*see* Brand Names)

Heat the sauce. Slit or slash the frankfurters and baste generously with the sauce. Place on a broiler rack over a pan. Broil, turning and basting, until brown. Serve with some of the sauce. Serves 4.

BEEF FONDUE

1½ pounds lean round or shoulder steak
Garlic powder to taste
Dash of freshly ground pepper
Oil as needed
Salt to taste

Use a better cut of steak if preferred, but it isn't really necessary. Remove all fat and gristle from the meat and cut it into bite-sized cubes. Dust lightly with garlic powder and pepper. Fill a small saucepan or fondue pot with oil and heat until bubbling. Each person should skewer a cube of beef and dip it into the hot oil for 1 minute to cook. Salt to taste and eat immediately. Repeat until all the beef has been eaten. Serve with homemade Chili Sauce, homemade Ketchup and other sauces (*see* Sauces and Dressings) and homemade relishes such as Piccalilli and Pepper Relish (*see* Preserves). Serves 3 as a main dish or 8 as an hors d'oeuvre.

BAKED STEAK

1 large can tomato purée
2 tablespoons white vinegar
1 teaspoon dry mustard
2 tablespoons Kikkoman soy sauce
1 tablespoon prepared mustard
Dash of liquid artificial sweetener
1 2- to 3-inch-thick sirloin fillet or a good London broil

Combine the tomato purée with all the condiments and seasonings. Place the steak in a shallow pan and pour on the marinade. Marinate for several hours, turning occasionally. Preheat the oven to 500°, or as hot as it will go. Place the steak on a rack over a pan and bake at 500° for 15 minutes. Turn, brush with the marinade and bake for 15 minutes more. For rare steak, remove and slice. For medium, turn off the oven and leave the pan in for 15 to 20 minutes, or until center is slightly pink when cut. Keep the marinade and use as a steak sauce, barbecue sauce, or as marinade again. Serves 4 to 6.

YANKEE POT ROAST

1 3- to 4-pound roast
Oil as needed
2 cloves garlic, minced
½ teaspoon paprika
1 can water chestnuts, drained
1 onion, diced
1 carrot, diced
1 cup tomato juice
Salt

Sear the roast on all sides in a little oil on top of the stove until all surfaces are lightly browned. Place the meat in a foil-lined roasting pan and add the other ingredients. Preheat the oven to 325°. Cover the pan tightly with aluminum foil, sealing the edges. Roast for 30 minutes; lower heat to 300° and continue cooking for 3 hours. Uncover and continue cooking until the meat is tender and brown (30 minutes to 1 hour). Salt to taste during the last stage of cooking. Serves 6.

BEEF STROGANOFF

1 small can mushrooms, drained
1 medium onion, diced
1 tablespoon butter
1½ pounds round steak, cut into slivers
1½ cups beef stock or Knorr-Swiss bouillon
2 tablespoons homemade Chili Sauce
1 teaspoon dry mustard
¾ cup sour cream
2 cups cooked homemade noodles (*see* Breads, Pasta and Noodles) or Jerusalem artichoke noodles (*see* Brand Names), or 2 cups French-style wax beans

Sauté the mushrooms and onion in the butter until the onion is transparent. Add the meat and brown, stirring. Add the broth, Chili Sauce and mustard. Cook on low heat for 25 minutes. Allow to cool slightly and gradually add the sour cream, making sure that the mixture does not bubble. Heat gently about 5 minutes, stirring. Serve over cooked noodles or wax beans. For carbohydrates, see noodles used. Serves 3 or 4.

DRIED BEEF STROGANOFF

2 tablespoons butter or margarine
1 small onion, chopped
1 jar dried beef (*see* Brand Names: check the label carefully)
8 ounces sour cream
4 ounces Gruyère cheese, diced
½ teaspoon parsley flakes
¼ teaspoon pepper
Milk if needed

Melt the butter in a skillet and sauté the onion until it is transparent. Place the dried beef in a pan of cold water and soak for 30 minutes. Drain and rinse. Drain on paper towels. Add the dried beef to the skillet and sauté until the edges curl. Add the sour cream, stirring, then the cheese and seasonings. If too thick, add a little milk. Simmer covered on low heat for 5 minutes, or until the cheese is melted. Serve on vegetables, homemade bread, sliced hard-cooked eggs or homemade noodles. Serves 2 or 3.

VEAL SCALLOPINI

3 tablespoons butter
1½ to 2 pounds thin veal fillets
½ pound fresh mushrooms
4 scallions, chopped
1 clove garlic, minced
1 pound canned tomatoes (check label)
1 teaspoon oregano
Salt, pepper to taste

Heat 1 tablespoon of the butter, and brown the veal on both sides. Remove the veal and set aside. Add the remaining butter and sauté the mushrooms, scallions and garlic. Return the veal to the pan and add the tomatoes and seasonings. Cover and simmer over low heat until tender (about 20 minutes). Serve as is, or over hot drained bean sprouts, mashed cauliflower or other vegetable. Serves 3 or 4.

Variation: Instead of veal fillets, use ground veal. Mix with 1 egg and form into small meat balls. Prepare as for Veal Scallopini.

BREADED VEAL CUTLETS

2 pounds veal cutlets, beaten flat with a tenderizing mallet
1 egg, slightly beaten
1 slice homemade bread, toasted and crumbed
¼ cup wheat germ (optional)
2 tablespoons butter
½ teaspoon salt

Pepper to taste
1 can tomato purée
1 ¼-grain tablet saccharin
1 teaspoon dehydrated green pepper flakes

Dip the veal in the egg, then coat with a combination of the bread crumbs and wheat germ (omit wheat germ for lower-carbohydrate version). Melt the butter in a large skillet, and brown the cutlets on both sides. Lower the heat and simmer covered until tender. Season the veal with salt and pepper and set aside. Pour the tomato purée and remaining ingredients into the pan in which the veal was cooked. Heat 15 minutes. Correct seasoning, pour the sauce over the cutlets and serve. Serves 4; each serving=a trace of carbohydrate.

STUFFED VEAL CHOPS

6 thick veal chops
6 slices Gruyère or Bel Paese cheese
Freshly ground pepper
2 tablespoons oil
½ cup bouillon (sugarless)
1 teaspoon onion powder
Salt

Slice each chop through the middle almost to the bone, making a pocket. Slip the cheese into the pocket. Close with toothpicks stuck through the meat. Sprinkle generously with the pepper. Heat the oil in a heavy pan and brown the chops on both sides, slipping the toothpicks through as needed. Add the bouillon and onion powder; cover and simmer until the meat is tender. If browner chops are desired, remove or tilt the cover and continue cooking until the chops are brown. Salt to taste and serve. Serves 6 for lunch or 3 for dinner.

VEAL BURGERS

1½ pounds ground veal
¼ teaspoon garlic powder
Dash of freshly ground pepper
½ teaspoon paprika
¼ teaspoon onion powder
Salt

Combine all ingredients; knead until smooth. Form into patties. Heat a Teflon-lined skillet and fry burgers on both sides until brown. Salt to taste and serve. (If preferred, these can be broiled in the broiler or barbecued.) Serves 3 or 4.

DILL LAMB CHOPS

8 large lamb chops
1 tablespoon oil or more as needed
8 ounces orange juice
1 small onion, diced
¼ teaspoon dill weed
Salt

Rub the lamb chops with oil. Place in a pan with the other ingredients except salt and marinate for 24 hours, turning occasionally. Place on a broiler rack and broil, basting often with the marinade. To make gravy, pour the pan juices into a saucepan and simmer uncovered until thickened. Pour over the broiled chops and salt to taste. Serves 4; if the gravy is served, each serving=½ unit fruit.

BROILED PORK CHOPS

2 to 3 pounds pork chops (fairly thin)
1 tablespoon oil
Dash of freshly ground pepper
½ teaspoon paprika

¼ teaspoon thyme
Salt to taste if needed

Preheat the broiler until very hot. Rub the chops on both sides with the oil. Place the chops on a broiler rack; season with pepper and paprika, then sprinkle lightly with the thyme. Broil until crisp and brown, and turn. Season again as before and broil until brown. Total broiling time should be about 20 to 30 minutes. Salt to taste and serve. Serves 4.

BAKED PORK CHOPS

4 to 6 thick lean pork chops
Oil as needed
1 large apple, peeled, cored and diced
1 onion, diced
½ cup water
Pepper to taste
2 tablespoons vinegar
1 ¼-grain tablet saccharin, crushed
½ teaspoon salt

Sear the pork chops in a little hot oil on top of the stove. Arrange them in a baking dish in a single layer. Add the remaining ingredients, tucking the apple and onions around the meat. Cover and bake at 375° for 30 minutes. Uncover and continue baking until the meat is brown, turning once or twice (about 30 to 40 minutes). Serves 2 or 3; each serving=approximately 1 unit fruit.

ORIENTAL PORK BALLS

1 pound lean ground pork
½ cup water chestnuts, drained and minced
½ teaspoon ground ginger
1 egg, beaten
1 teaspoon salt
¼ cup soy flour
Peanut oil as needed

Mix together the pork, water chestnuts, ginger, egg and salt. Form into tiny meat balls and roll in the soy flour. Heat ¼ inch of peanut oil in a skillet and fry the meat balls on all sides until crisp and brown. Serves 2 as a main dish or 4 as a side dish with other Chinese dishes.

CHINESE SWEET PORK

1 pound lean pork, cut against the grain into thin strips 1 inch by 4 inches
3 tablespoons Kikkoman soy sauce
1 teaspoon cinnamon
1 tablespoon vinegar
4 ¼-grain tablets saccharin
1 tablespoon peanut oil
¼ cup unsweetened pineapple juice

Mix all ingredients together and marinate for several hours. Bake in a moderate oven at 350° for 1 hour, basting with the marinade. Serve with Chinese vegetables. Serves 2 as a main dish or 4 as a side dish with other Chinese dishes.

SAUSAGE ⚹1

2 onions, diced
1 clove garlic
¼ cup water
3 pounds pork, ground twice
1 teaspoon freshly ground pepper
¼ teaspoon sage
1 teaspoon parsley flakes
¼ teaspoon mace
1 tablespoon salt
2 teaspoons grated lemon rind
2 teaspoons marjoram
½ teaspoon coriander or allspice

Place the onions, garlic and water in the blender. Chop, starting and stopping the blender. Mix with the pork and add the seasonings. Mix well and form into 3 rolls about 2 inches in diameter. Chill overnight to allow the flavors to blend. To cook, slice and fry slowly in a dry skillet. If preferred, sausage can be wrapped well in freezer paper and frozen; to use, thaw, slice and fry. Each roll makes about 8 to 10 slices.

SAUSAGE #2

5 pounds ground pork
2 tablespoons salt
1 tablespoon freshly ground pepper
1 tablespoon sage
1 teaspoon thyme
1 teaspoon marjoram
1 teaspoon savory

Prepare as for Sausage #1; divide into 2 or 3 rolls; wrap and freeze or refrigerate. Each roll makes about 8 to 10 slices.

ITALIAN SAUSAGE

3 pounds pork, ground twice
3 cloves garlic
1 teaspoon pepper
2 teaspoons fennel
1 teaspoon thyme
1 onion, diced
1 tablespoon salt
2 teaspoons basil
1 teaspoon oregano
1 teaspoon red peppers

Prepare as for Sausage #1; roll into 2 or 3 long narrow rolls (about 1½ inches in diameter); use with Spaghetti Sauce, etc. Each roll makes 8 to 10 slices.

SAUSAGE STUFFING FOR TURKEY

2 pounds homemade Sausage #2
1 cup finely chopped celery and tops
1 onion, diced
½ loaf homemade Oatmeal Bread
2 eggs
1 cup chicken stock or allowed chicken bouillon (*see* Brand Names)

Brown the sausage in a hot skillet, crumbling with a fork. Add the celery and onion, and sauté until soft. Slice the bread, then crumble. Toss the bread crumbs, eggs, and the sausage mixture together. Add only enough bouillon to moisten. Stuff the cavity of the turkey loosely. Or bake in a separate dish topped with a large slice of turkey skin. Makes about 6 servings of stuffing; each serving=1 unit carbohydrate.

SCRAPPLE

1 cup soy grits
3 cups beef stock or allowed bouillon
2 pounds lean pork, ground
2 teaspoons salt
1½ teaspoons sage
1 teaspoon onion powder
½ teaspoon freshly ground pepper
1 teaspoon thyme
1 egg, beaten

Soak the grits in 1 cup of the cold stock for 30 minutes. Pour the other 2 cups of the stock into a saucepan with the pork and seasonings. Bring to a boil, add the soaked grits and simmer 30 minutes. The liquid should be absorbed. Pour into a greased loaf pan and stir in the egg, mixing well. Chill until firm. Turn out of the pan, cut into ½-inch slices and fry in a skillet until crisp and brown. Serves 6 to 8.

SPARERIBS BAKED WITH SAUERKRAUT

1 large can sauerkraut
½ teaspoon onion powder
½ teaspoon salt
Dash of freshly ground pepper
½ teaspoon caraway seeds
½ bay leaf, crumbled
4 pounds spareribs

Mix the sauerkraut with the seasonings. Cover with the ribs. Cover and bake at 350° for 2 hours. If you prefer the ribs crisp, remove the cover and continue baking until done. Serves 4.

BARBECUED SPARERIBS

2 pounds spareribs or more as needed
Water as needed
6 ounces orange juice
½ teaspoon salt
1 clove garlic, mashed
4 tablespoons Kikkoman soy sauce
1 tablespoon liquid artificial sweetener
½ teaspoon imitation maple flavoring
¼ cup lemon jucie

Precook the spareribs in boiling water to cover for 10 minutes. Remove and drain. Combine the remaining ingredients for the marinade. Spread the spareribs out flat in a pan. Pour the marinade over them and let them stand overnight, turning occasionally. Broil over an outdoor barbecue or in the broiler, basting often, until crisp and brown. Serves 2.

BAKED HAM

5 pounds smoked ham (not cured)
1 tablespoon prepared yellow mustard
¼ orange, including peel, sliced paper thin
½ cup orange juice

Spread the top of the ham with the mustard. Arrange the orange slices on it. Place in a baking pan, and pour the orange juice into the pan (try to remove as much of the gelatin from the ham as possible, as it will make the juice too salty). Bake at 325° for 1½ hours, basting frequently with the pan juices. Slice the ham and serve with the pan juice as gravy. Serves 8 to 10.

GLAZED HAM

5 to 8 pounds smoked ham
8 to 10 whole cloves
¼ teaspoon ground ginger
1 teaspoon dry mustard
1 teaspoon cinnamon
½ teaspoon imitation maple flavoring
1 can Dole unsweetened pineapple slices, packed in their own juice

Score the surface of the ham with a sharp knife, making a grid or diamond-shape pattern in the skin. Imbed the cloves here and there in the ham. Place the ham, skin side up, on a low rack in a baking pan. Sprinkle with the seasonings, including the maple flavoring. Place 3 or 4 of the pineapple rings on top of the ham. Pour 1 cup of the liquid from the pineapple into the pan. Roast at 325° for 4 to 6 hours. Two pineapple rings=1 unit fruit. Serves 8 to 10.

BAKED HAM WITH JELLY GLAZE

Prepare same as Glazed Ham, but omit the pineapple and use 4 tablespoons homemade or allowed sugarless jam (*see* Preserves and Brand Names).

HAM STEAK WITH FRUIT SAUCE

1 large ham steak (smoked, not sugar-cured)
1 large apple, peeled, cored and diced
1 cup water
1 ¼-grain tablet saccharin or more to taste
1 tablespoon vinegar
Salt to taste as needed

Slash the fat around the edges of the ham steak. Heat a Teflon-lined skillet until hot. Place the ham steak in the pan and sear briefly on both sides. Lower the heat and fry until the ham is browned. Remove the ham and set aside. Add the remaining ingredients to the pan, cover and boil for 5 minutes. Remove the cover and simmer, stirring, until the sauce is reduced and thick. Return the ham to the pan and heat until cooked through. Serves 2; each serving=1 unit fruit.

HAM LOAF

3 cups ground smoked ham
½ cup gelatin from the ham can
½ cup chopped green pepper
½ cup soy flour
Pinch of salt
2 eggs
1 cup grated carrots (grate in blender)
1 tablespoon minced onion
Dash of freshly ground pepper

Combine all ingredients and mix well. Place in an oiled loaf pan. Bake at 325° for 1 hour. Serve with hot German-style mustard, boiled cabbage. Serves 4; each serving=½ unit high-carbohydrate vegetable.

MIXED GRILL

1 package Jones link sausages
8 ounces chicken livers
1 pound lamb, cut in 1-inch chunks
½ pound smoked bacon
Kikkoman soy sauce
Pepper to taste
Salt

Cut the sausage into chunks; if Jones sausage can't be found, use homemade sausage cut into chunks and rolled like meat balls. Place the meat on shish kebab skewers as follows: 1 chunk of liver, 1 piece of sausage, 1 chunk of lamb, then repeat. Wrap well with the bacon, and secure the ends with toothpicks. Brush with soy sauce and sprinkle with pepper. Broil over a fire or in the broiler on a rack, turning frequently. Remove when all the meat is cooked to your taste. Salt and serve. Serves 4.

BROILED LIVER

For superb broiled liver, purchase 6 to 8 ounces per person of thinly sliced baby beef liver or calf's liver. Place on a broiler rack over a pan. Sprinkle generously with freshly ground pepper and then lightly with artificial sweetener. Preheat the broiler and broil 2 minutes. Turn, and broil just until the surface is browned. To test, cut into the center; it should be slightly pink. Remove, salt to taste and serve.

SAUTÉED CHICKEN LIVERS

2 tablespoons butter
1 pound chicken livers

1 large can sliced mushrooms
1 tablespoon minced onion
Salt, pepper to taste

Melt the butter in a skillet. Pour in the chicken livers, including the liquid or juices in the container. Sauté the livers, stirring, until lightly browned on all sides. Add the other ingredients, including the liquid from the mushrooms and simmer 5 minutes. Correct seasoning and serve. Livers should be slightly pink in the center for best results. Serves 2.

LIVER AND ONIONS

2 pounds baby beef or calf's liver, thinly sliced and well trimmed
1 tablespoon oat flour
½ teaspoon pepper
2 tablespoons rendered chicken fat or butter
3 medium onions, sliced
Salt

Sprinkle the liver with flour and pepper. Heat the fat or butter in a large skillet. Sauté the onions, stirring, until yellow and translucent. Add the liver, adding more fat if needed. Sauté the liver until lightly browned, turn and fry briefly on other side. Test to see if the center is pinkish, and remove when still slightly pink in center. Salt to taste and serve. Serves 4.

SWEET AND PUNGENT CHICKEN LIVERS

2 tablespoons peanut oil
1 scallion, minced, including tops
1 pound chicken livers
6 ounces unsweetened pineapple juice
¼ cup cider vinegar
Dash of salt
Dash of MSG (optional)
1 can bean sprouts, rinsed, drained and squeezed dry

Heat the oil and sauté the scallions until brown. Add the chicken livers, including the juices from the container and sauté, stirring.

When the livers have lost their pink color outside, remove and set aside. Add the juice, vinegar and seasonings to the pan. Boil vigorously, stirring until the mixture is slightly thickened. Add the livers and bean sprouts, lower heat and simmer until the liver is cooked. (Color should be slightly pink in the center.) Add a little water to taste if the sauce is too strong. Serves 2; each serving=½ unit fruit.

SOUTHERN FRIED RABBIT

1 package frozen rabbit pieces

Thaw the rabbit, wash and dry. Follow the recipe for Southern Fried Chicken. Coat the rabbit pieces, and cook as for chicken, except simmer covered for 1 hour before removing the cover. Serves 4.

PRESERVES

The Preserves chapter consists of two categories of food: the pickles section, which includes relishes, and the jams and jellies. We have grouped these together because that is the way they are usually found. But unlike most cookbooks, we haven't included any instructions for actually preserving or canning these recipes. We think too many people are frightened away from home-canning by the formidable steps needed to sterilize and seal the containers. Add to that the extra time involved and the uncertainty as to whether the foods have been canned safely, and you've removed all the fun of preparing your own pickles and jams.

We suggest that you do this instead: choose the recipe you want to try. Make your "preserves" and store them in the refrigerator. Within a week, they'll be used up, and you'll be anxious to try another recipe. Simply make the recipe of your choice and store it in a clean glass container (plastic tends to absorb the flavors). All of these recipes were developed as substitutes for the most popular preserves. We have only included those pickle recipes which you are unable to buy. There are many brands of dill and sour pickles on the market that are perfectly all right to use; other ready-to-use pickles include pickled onions, peppers and pickled baby eggplants. Our pickle and preserve recipes are all of the kind that normally would use sugar. By substituting saccharin and cutting down the quantities, we have made them as safe and easy to cook as any other fruit or vegetable recipe in this book.

Sweet Pickles
Sweet Cauliflower Pickles
Bread and Butter Pickles
Sweet Dill Pickles
Piccalilli
Beet Relish
Pepper Relish
Pickle Relish
Chutney
Cranberry Relish
Pickled Pears
Pickled Peaches
Pickled Crabapples
Pickled Beets
Pickled Wax Beans

Dill Beans
Apple Butter
Instant Apple Butter
Peach Butter
Peach Preserves
Plum Butter
Apple Jelly
Pineapple Jelly
Strawberry Preserves
Strawberry Jam
Pineapple Jam
Pineapple Conserve
Orange Marmalade
Cranberry Jelly: *see* Sauces

SWEET PICKLES

2 pounds cucumbers (small)
Boiling water as needed
1 teaspoon dry mustard
½ teaspoon salt
30 to 40 ¼-grain tablets saccharin, crushed
2 tablespoons pickling spices
Pinch of ground ginger
1½ cups vinegar

Place the cucumbers in a deep pot. Cover with boiling water and place on very low heat for 15 minutes. Drain. Combine the spices with a little of the vinegar and mix to a paste. Add the rest of the vinegar and stir. Place the cucumbers in 1 or more glass jars. Strain the vinegar mixture and pour over the cucumbers. Store in the refrigerator; flavor is best after 24 hours. Makes 1 quart.

SWEET CAULIFLOWER PICKLES

1 head cauliflower
1 quart boiling salted water
2 cups vinegar

1 stick cinnamon
1 teaspoon mustard seeds
10 ¼-grain tablets saccharin
5 or 6 whole cloves

Break the cauliflower into tiny flowerettes. Set aside the core to be used for other recipes. Plunge the flowerettes into boiling salted water. Remove from the stove immediately and let stand 1 minute. Drain. Combine the other ingredients in a saucepan and simmer 15 minutes, then strain. Place the cauliflower in a large glass container and pour in the vinegar, adding water as needed to cover. Store in the refrigerator. Makes 1 quart.

BREAD AND BUTTER PICKLES

1 pound small cucumbers
Pinch of salt
¼ teaspoon celery seed
Dash of mace
Salt as needed
¼ teaspoon mustard seed
5 ¼-grain tablets saccharin, crushed
¼ teaspoon ginger
2 cups vinegar
2 cups water

Slice the cucumbers into a bowl and salt lightly. Let stand ½ hour, then drain on paper towels. Heat the spices, vinegar and water to boiling. Add the cucumbers; cover and heat on very low heat for 20 minutes. Cool and store in the refrigerator. Makes 1 pint.

SWEET DILL PICKLES

1 cup vinegar
½ cup water
30 ¼-grain tablets saccharin
2 sticks cinnamon
6 cloves
12 small dill pickles, drained

Combine the vinegar, water and spices and bring to a boil. Slice the pickles in quarters lengthwise. Add to the vinegar mixture and simmer on low heat for 30 minutes. Remove cinnamon and cloves. Cool, store in the refrigerator. Makes 1 pint.

PICCALILLI

2 large tomatoes (not very ripe)
1 green pepper
1 small onion
1 red pepper
½ cup finely chopped cabbage
½ teaspoon mustard seed
4 ¼-grain tablets saccharin
1 teaspoon pickling spice
½ cup vinegar
½ teaspoon salt

Chop all the vegetables coarsely in the blender, a few at a time, chopping and emptying into a large bowl, until all are chopped. Transfer to a saucepan, add the other ingredients and heat to boiling. Simmer for 1 minute and remove from heat. Refrigerate overnight or longer for best flavor. Store in the refrigerator in glass container. Makes 1 pint.

BEET RELISH

2 cups canned or cooked beets, drained (check label for sugar), reserve juice
¼ cup finely chopped onion
½ cup white vinegar
2 tablespoons liquid from the beet can
1 teaspoon unflavored gelatin
Pinch of salt
6 to 8 ¼-grain tablets saccharin

Chop the beets well. Mix with the onion and vinegar. Add the beet juice and sprinkle in the gelatin to soften. Heat the mixture in a saucepan to a low boil, stirring, and add the salt and saccharin.

Simmer gently, stirring, until the saccharin and gelatin are dissolved. Cool, then store in the refrigerator. Stir once or twice while chilling to mix evenly. Use sparingly; ½ cup=1 unit high-carbohydrate vegetable. Makes 1 pint.

PEPPER RELISH

3 fresh red peppers, chopped
1 large onion, chopped
½ teaspoon salt
3 green peppers, chopped
½ cup vinegar
4 to 5 ¼-grain tablets saccharin or to taste

Combine all ingredients in a saucepan. Bring to a boil. Cover, lower heat and cook slowly 10 minutes. Store in a glass container. Makes 1 pint.

PICKLE RELISH

1 recipe Sweet Pickles, including the liquid
1 green tomato, chopped
½ cup chopped green pepper
½ cup chopped onion
1 cup finely chopped cabbage
½ cup chopped celery

Prepare the Sweet Pickles, according to the recipe. Refrigerate for about 24 hours. Remove the pickles and set aside the liquid. Chop the pickles and mix with the other chopped vegetables. Heat the pickling juice to a boil and add the vegetables. Lower heat and simmer for 5 minutes. Cool and store in the refrigerator (if finished relish is too watery, drain partially). Makes 2 pints or 1 quart.

CHUTNEY

2 large ripe tomatoes, chopped
2 green and/or red peppers, chopped
1 small onion, chopped
1 tablespoon dry mustard
½ teaspoon salt
1 tablespoon curry powder
½ teaspoon dehydrated lemon rind
2 tart medium apples, peeled, cored and diced
2 purple plums, pitted and chopped
Juice of ½ lemon
½ cup vinegar
¼ teaspoon ginger
½ teaspoon cinnamon
4 ¼-grain tablets saccharin

Combine all ingredients. Cover and bring to a low boil. Lower the heat and simmer until soft (1 hour). Use sparingly for flavor, or else count toward fruit units. Makes 1 pint; entire recipe=4 units fruit.

CRANBERRY RELISH

½ orange
1 cup cranberries
½ cup walnuts, broken coarsely
1 tablespoon lemon juice
1 tablespoon grated fresh orange peel
Liquid artificial sweetener to taste

Peel the orange and place with the cranberries in a food chopper or nut chopper (they can also be chopped a few at a time in the blender, turning on and off. Just be sure to empty the blender container after each turn, so that fruit will not be puréed). Grate the orange peel. Combine all ingredients and correct sweetener to taste. Serve with any poultry, especially turkey. Makes 1 pint; ½ cup=1 unit fruit.

PICKLED PEARS

8 to 10 small Seckel pears
Water as needed
Whole cloves as needed
½ cup vinegar
2 sticks cinnamon
10 ¼-grain tablets saccharin
1 cup water

Place the pears in a pan of rapidly boiling water. Remove immediately and dip in ice water and peel. Stick 3 or 4 cloves in each pear. Combine the other ingredients in a saucepan and bring to a boil. Pour over the pears and chill. Do not use for several days for best flavor. Remove cloves if preferred before serving. Use as a side dish, but count 1 pear as 1 unit fruit. Makes 1 pint.

PICKLED PEACHES

Same as Pickled Pears, but use 4 to 5 whole peaches, firm but ripe. Peel as for pears, cut in quarters. Proceed as above. Makes 1 pint.

PICKLED CRABAPPLES

10 to 12 crabapples
Whole cloves
½ cup vinegar
1 teaspoon cassia buds
10 ¼-grain tablets saccharin or more to taste
½ cup water
1 stick cinnamon
Red food coloring as needed

Follow directions for Pickled Pears, but do not peel. Makes 1 pint.

PICKLED BEETS

2 cups cooked or canned beets (check label for sugar), including
  the liquid
1 cup vinegar
Pinch of caraway seeds
6 ¼-grain tablets saccharin
Dash of cinnamon

Combine all ingredients. Heat until the saccharin is dissolved. Cool;
refrigerate overnight before using. Use sparingly, or count as a high-
carbohydrate vegetable (½ cup=1 unit). Makes 1 pint.

PICKLED WAX BEANS

2 cups cooked or canned wax beans, including ¾ cup liquid from the
  can or cooking
¾ cup vinegar
10 ¼-grain tablets saccharin, crushed

Place the beans in a shallow dish. Add the other ingredients, being
sure that all the beans are covered. Refrigerate overnight or longer.
Makes 1 pint.

DILL BEANS

12 ounces whole green beans, canned or cooked
1 cup liquid from the beans
1 cup vinegar
Dash of salt
¼ teaspoon chopped dill weed
6 ¼-grain tablets saccharin, crushed

Combine all the ingredients in a large shallow dish. Chill overnight
or longer before serving. Makes 1 pint.

APPLE BUTTER

6 medium tart apples, peeled, cored and sliced
2 tablespoons cinnamon
1 cup cider or apple juice
1 teaspoon ground cloves
10 ¼-grain tablets saccharin

Combine all ingredients in a saucepan. Heat to a low boil; cover and simmer until the apples are soft. Mash in the pan, and continue cooking uncovered until quite thick. Pour into a container and chill. Use sparingly or count toward your fruit unit. Entire recipe=8 units fruit. Makes 1 cup or ½ pint.

INSTANT APPLE BUTTER

1 can Comstock pie-sliced apples (without sugar; *not* the apple pie filling)
1 teaspoon cinnamon
20 ¼-grain tablets saccharin

Purée all ingredients in the blender. Cook over medium heat, stirring, until reduced and thick. Chill. Makes 1 pint.

PEACH BUTTER

4 large ripe peaches
¼ teaspoon ground cloves
Saccharin to taste
½ cup water
½ teaspoon cinnamon

Plunge the peaches into boiling water, then into ice water. Peel. Cut up the peaches and discard the pits. Place all ingredients in the blender and purée. Pour into a Teflon-lined baking dish and bake in a slow oven (about 300°) for 1 hour, stirring often. Remove when thick. Store in the refrigerator. Use sparingly or count as part of your fruit unit. Entire recipe=4 units fruit. Makes 1 cup or ½ pint.

PEACH PRESERVES

Same ingredients as Peach Butter plus 1 teaspoon unflavored gelatin

Prepare the peaches and place in the blender with the other ingredients, but do not purée. Chop briefly, starting and stopping, until pieces are coarsely chopped. Sprinkle the gelatin on the peach mixture to soften. Pour it into a saucepan; heat, stirring, until the gelatin is dissolved. Chill in the refrigerator, stirring once or twice to break up the lumps. Makes 1 cup or ½ pint.

PLUM BUTTER

6 large or 10 small purple plums
1 cup water
10 ¼-grain tablets saccharin or more to taste
1 teaspoon cinnamon

Place all ingredients in a saucepan. Cover and simmer until fruit is soft and pits can easily be removed. Continue cooking uncovered on low heat. Stir often, cook until thick. Chill in refrigerator. Entire recipe=6 units fruit. Makes 1 cup or ½ pint.

APPLE JELLY

1 teaspoon unflavored gelatin
2 cups apple juice
8 to 10 ¼-grain tablets saccharin

Soften the gelatin by sprinkling over the juice. Add the saccharin and heat the mixture to a low boil, stirring. When the gelatin and saccharin are dissolved, remove from the heat. Chill in the refrigerator. Entire recipe=4 units fruit; use sparingly, or count ¼ cup jelly as 1 unit fruit. Makes 1 pint.

PINEAPPLE JELLY

Same as Apple Jelly, but use 2 cups unsweetened pineapple juice instead of apple juice. Makes 1 pint.

STRAWBERRY PRESERVES

16 ounces strawberry diet soda
1 cup mashed fresh strawberries
Saccharin to taste
1 tablespoon unflavored gelatin
1 tablespoon lemon juice
8 to 10 fresh strawberries, whole

Combine 12 ounces of the soda and the mashed strawberries. Heat until boiling and add the saccharin. Stir until dissolved. Pour 4 ounces of the soda into a bowl and sprinkle on the gelatin to soften. Add the hot soda mixture and the other ingredients. Stir well until the gelatin is dissolved. Chill, stirring once or twice to break up the lumps. Refrigerate. Entire recipe=4 units fruit. Makes 1 pint.

STRAWBERRY JAM

Same as Strawberry Preserves, but use half the amount of soda and purée in the blender before chilling. Makes 1 pint.

PINEAPPLE JAM

1 large can Dole pineapple chunks, packed without sugar in their
    own juice
1 teaspoon unflavored gelatin
6 ¼-grain tablets saccharin or to taste

Drain the liquid from the pineapple into a measuring cup, and add enough water to make the liquid total 2 cups. Pour 4 ounces of this liquid into a bowl and sprinkle in the gelatin to soften. Pour the rest into a saucepan and heat to boiling. Stir in the pineapple chunks and the saccharin and stir until dissolved. Pour over the gelatin mixture and stir until the gelatin is dissolved. Pour the entire mixture into the blender and blend, turning on and off until the pineapple is the desired consistency. Chill, stirring occasionally to break up the chunks. Use small amounts or count as fruit unit. Entire recipe=6 units fruit. Makes 1 pint.

PINEAPPLE CONSERVE

1 large can Dole crushed pineapple, packed without sugar in its own juice
½ cup flaked fresh coconut, or unsweetened coconut meal (available from health food stores)
1 small tart apple, peeled, cored and chopped
1 teaspoon grated lemon rind
Saccharin to taste
1½ teaspoons unflavored gelatin

Combine all of the fruit, including the juice from the pineapple can, and the saccharin. Sprinkle in the gelatin to soften. Heat the mixture, stirring, until the gelatin and saccharin are dissolved. Pour into a container and chill, stirring once or twice to break up the lumps. Use in small amounts or count as a fruit unit. Entire recipe=7 units fruit. Makes 1 pint.

ORANGE MARMALADE

2 small oranges
1 tablespoon unflavored gelatin
8 ounces orange juice
1 tablespoon finely chopped orange peel
10 to 15 ¼-grain tablets saccharin
2 tablespoons grated orange peel
½ teaspoon dehydrated lemon rind
Salt if needed

Peel the oranges and chop coarsely in the blender. Set aside. Sprinkle the gelatin on the juice to soften, then heat, stirring, until the gelatin is dissolved. Add the other ingredients, and stir until the saccharin is dissolved. Add a dash of salt to taste if needed. Chill, stirring once or twice. As with all the jams, use sparingly for flavor. If you use more, count as fruit. Entire recipe=4 units fruit. Makes 3 cups or 1½ pints.

SALADS

Pear Salad
Apple-cheese Salad
Cucumber-pineapple Salad
Avocado Salad
Waldorf Salad
Tomato Aspic
Creamy Salad Mold
Classic Vegetable Salad Mold
Cabbage Salad Mold
Cottage Cheese Salad
Sage Cottage Cheese
Sour Cream Salad
Caesar Salad
Green Salad with Anchovies
Cheddar Salad
"BLT" in a Bowl
Iceland Salad
Chicken Salad
Chef's Salad
Easy Crab Salad
Classic Crab Salad
Marinated Mackerel Salad
Piquant Sardine Salad

Shrimp Salad
Shrimp Cocktail
Picnic Tuna Salad
Tuna Salad
Tuna-olive Salad
Egg Salad
Pickled Pea Salad
Pickled Beets, Wax Beans or
    Cucumbers
Cauliflower Salad
Mock "Potato" Salad #1
Mock "Potato" Salad #2
Three-bean Salad
Snow Pea Salad
Summer Salad
Coleslaw #1
Coleslaw #2
Red Cabbage Slaw
Creamed Cabbage Salad
Cabbage-sprout Salad
Carrot Slaw
Antipasto: *see* Foreign and
    Regional

PEAR SALAD

2 large ripe pears
1 bottle diet ginger ale (sugarless)
1 teaspoon cinnamon
Dash of allspice
½ head iceberg lettuce
1 cup cottage cheese

Slice pears in half. Remove the seeds with a spoon and place in a baking dish. Pour in the ginger ale and sprinkle pears with cinnamon and allspice. Bake at 325° until the pears are soft, about 1 hour. Remove from oven and chill. Divide the lettuce into 4 portions, place on salad plates. Place a pear half on each, top with a ¼-cup scoop of cottage cheese and drizzle a little of the cooking liquid from the pears over each. Serves 4; each serving=½ unit fruit.

APPLE-CHEESE SALAD

¼ wedge of lemon
1 apple, unpeeled, cored and diced
1 stalk celery, sliced
2 ounces Cheddar cheese, cubed
2 large lettuce leaves
¼ cup sour cream or plain yoghurt
Dash of liquid artificial sweetener (optional)

Squeeze the lemon over the diced apple. Toss with the celery and cheese cubes. Serve on a lettuce leaf; top with sour cream or yoghurt and sprinkle with a little sweetener. Serves 2; each portion=1 unit fruit.

CUCUMBER-PINEAPPLE SALAD

Romaine, endive or other greens
1 cucumber, peeled and sliced
1 can Dole unsweetened pineapple rings, packed in their own juice
Dressing to taste (Mayonnaise, Boiled Salad Dressing; *see* Sauces
   and Dressings)

On each plate arrange greens, then cucumber slices, overlapping, in
a circle. Top with 1 pineapple ring and salad dressing of your choice.
Serves 4; each serving=½ unit fruit.

AVOCADO SALAD

1 ripe avocado
1 medium grapefruit, peeled
1 cup soft-curd cottage cheese
½ teaspoon liquid artificial sweetener
¼ cup fresh coconut, shredded (or unsweetened coconut meal from
   any health food store)

Peel and remove pit from the avocado and slice thin. Separate the
grapefruit sections gingerly, removing the membranes around each
slice. Arrange four plates as follows: slices of avocado alternating
with grapefruit sections, with a scoop of cottage cheese on the side.
Sprinkle with the sweetener, then with coconut. Serves 4; each serv-
ing=½ unit fruit.

WALDORF SALAD

1 large tart apple
1 tablespoon fresh lemon juice
½ cup coarsely broken walnut meats
2 large ribs celery, diced
¼ cup allowed or homemade Mayonnaise
4 large lettuce leaves

Halve the apple and remove core; do not peel. Dice the apple, sprinkle with lemon juice. Combine with the nuts and celery, and toss. Add the mayonnaise and mix well. Serve on the lettuce leaves. Serves 4; each serving=¼ unit fruit.

TOMATO ASPIC

3 cups tomato juice
1 Knorr-Swiss beef bouillon cube
1 small onion, finely minced
Dash of pepper
¼ teaspoon marjoram
Dash of cayenne (optional)
2 tablespoons unflavored gelatin
Juice of 1 lemon
4 large lettuce leaves

Heat the tomato juice, bouillon, onion and seasonings. Simmer until the onion is soft. Dissolve the gelatin by sprinkling over the lemon juice. Add gelatin mixture to the tomato juice mixture and stir until gelatin is dissolved. Pour into individual molds or small dessert bowls; chill until firm. To unmold, set each dish in hot water for a few seconds, then turn out on lettuce leaf. Top with homemade Mayonnaise or other dressing (*see* Sauces and Dressings). Serves 4.

CREAMY SALAD MOLD

2 tablespoons unflavored gelatin
1 cup water
1 cup sour cream
1 cup allowed mayonnaise
2 tablespoons lemon juice
1 teaspoon chopped fresh dill weed or ¼ teaspoon dried dill weed
1 teaspoon salt
1 teaspoon dehydrated minced onion
1 cup chopped celery
¼ cup chopped pimientos
¼ cup chopped green pepper
⅛ teaspoon celery seed

Sprinkle gelatin over the water to soften; cook over low heat, stirring until the gelatin is dissolved. Cool until syrupy. Fold in the remaining ingredients, stirring until evenly mixed. Pour into a mold or large bowl. Chill until firm, turn out on plate. Serves 6 to 8.

CLASSIC VEGETABLE SALAD MOLD

2 tablespoons unflavored gelatin
2 cups beef bouillon or stock, cold
2 cups mixed vegetables, canned or cooked (wax beans, peas, carrots, mushrooms, etc.)
1 teaspoon vinegar
Tiny bit of bay leaf, crushed

Soften the gelatin by sprinkling over the stock. Heat the stock, stirring until the gelatin is dissolved; add the other ingredients and simmer 5 minutes. Pour into a large mold or ring. Chill until firm and unmold. Serves 6 to 8.

CABBAGE SALAD MOLD

2 tablespoons gelatin
1 bottle diet lemon soda or diet ginger ale
2 tablespoons lemon juice
½ cup chopped celery
1 cup finely shredded cabbage
½ cup shredded carrot
½ teaspoon salt
Dash of pepper

Sprinkle gelatin over the soda to soften. Pour into a saucepan and heat, stirring until the gelatin is dissolved. Cool and chill in the refrigerator until thick and syrupy. Mix together with the remaining ingredients. Pour into a mold and chill until firm. Serves 4.

COTTAGE CHEESE SALAD

1 cup creamed cottage cheese
6 large or 12 small stuffed olives, chopped
¼ cup grated carrots
Salt to taste

Combine all ingredients. Scoop onto plates with an ice cream scoop.
Serves 4 as a side dish, or 1 as a lunch main dish.

SAGE COTTAGE CHEESE

⅔ cup cottage cheese
1 tablespoon lemon juice
½ teaspoon celery salt
⅛ teaspoon black pepper
1 teaspoon onion powder
½ teaspoon sage leaves
Chicory leaves

Combine all ingredients except the chicory. Let stand at least 15
minutes to mingle the flavors. Arrange the chicory on individual
plates, scoop half the cottage cheese mixture on each plate and serve.
Serves 2.

SOUR CREAM SALAD

1 large cucumber, peeled
1 large tomato, cut in thin wedges
1 teaspoon lemon juice
½ cup sour cream
Salt, pepper to taste
4 strips bacon, fried crisp and drained

Slice the cucumber in ¼-inch-thick slices. Place in a bowl with the tomato, lemon juice and sour cream. Toss until coated evenly. Add
salt and pepper to taste. Garnish with the bacon, crumbled. Serves 4.

CAESAR SALAD

1 can anchovy fillets, including oil
1 small head iceberg lettuce, torn into bite-sized chunks
1 cup torn chicory
1 cup torn escarole
1 small egg, slightly beaten
2 tablespoons vinegar
Dash of freshly ground pepper
Pinch of tarragon
¼ teaspoon garlic powder
Dash of liquid artificial sweetener
1 slice protein bread, toasted and cubed

Place the anchovy fillets in a dish and pound them until thoroughly mashed; set aside. Toss the greens in a salad bowl, add the egg and toss until all surfaces are coated. Add the mashed anchovies and vinegar, mix well. Mix in the seasonings, correct to taste. Add the bread cubes, toss and serve immediately. Serves 6 to 8.

GREEN SALAD WITH ANCHOVIES

¼ head lettuce
1 cup chopped watercress
¼ bunch escarole
1 can anchovy fillets
2 ounces Swiss cheese, cut in thin strips
1 recipe French Dressing

Break the greens into small pieces, toss together. Arrange the anchovies on top, a few per serving. Sprinkle evenly with the cheese strips. Pour on the dressing and serve immediately. Serves 2 to 4.

CHEDDAR SALAD

1 small head iceberg lettuce
8 radishes, sliced

2 small tomatoes, cut in thin wedges
½ sweet Spanish onion, sliced
4 ribs celery, sliced
1 small cucumber, peeled and sliced
1 cup shredded Cheddar cheese
Salad dressing

Line a salad bowl with lettuce leaves. Add the other vegetables, tossing slightly and separating the onion slices into rings. Sprinkle the cheese strips over the top. Serve with oil and vinegar, or with any dressing preferred, such as French, Russian, Roquefort. Serves 4 to 6.

"BLT" IN A BOWL

1½ cups small-curd cottage cheese
¼ teaspoon onion powder
Salt, pepper to taste
1 large ripe tomato, diced
½ head iceberg lettuce, broken into chunks
½ pound bacon (not sugar-cured), fried crisp and drained

Combine the cottage cheese, seasonings and vegetables in a bowl, and toss together. Crumble the bacon over the top and serve. Serves 2 as a main dish.

ICELAND SALAD

1 cup cottage cheese
⅓ cup peanuts, coarsely chopped
¼ cup chopped celery
¼ teaspoon onion powder
¼ teaspoon salt
4 medium tomatoes
1 recipe French Dressing

Mix together the cottage cheese, peanuts, celery, onion powder and salt. Scoop out the centers of the tomatoes and fill with the cheese mixture. Chill and serve with French Dressing. Serves 4.

CHICKEN SALAD

1½ cups ground or chopped cooked chicken
2 hard-cooked eggs, chopped
½ cup almonds, chopped or slivered
Dash of cayenne pepper
¼ teaspoon onion powder
1 tablespoon lemon juice
2 stalks celery, chopped
½ cup allowed or homemade Mayonnaise
Dash of liquid artificial sweetener
Salt to taste

Combine all ingredients, correct seasoning to taste. Chill and serve on lettuce. Serves 2 as a main dish.

CHEF'S SALAD

1 head Bibb lettuce
½ bunch curly endive
½ head iceberg lettuce
2 tomatoes, cut in wedges
4 ounces sharp cheese, cut in thin strips
1 cucumber, sliced
1 scallion, chopped, including top
1 cup thin strips of ham, chicken, turkey or roast beef
1 recipe Thousand Island Dressing

Tear the greens; toss all ingredients together, add dressing and toss again. Serves 4.

EASY CRAB SALAD

1 can crab meat, drained and flaked
½ cup finely chopped celery
2 tablespoons allowed mayonnaise
Salt, pepper to taste

Lettuce leaves as needed
Paprika

Combine first four ingredients, serve in lettuce cups. Garnish with a little paprika sprinkled lightly on top. If preferred, serve with Seafood Cocktail Sauce. Serves 2.

CLASSIC CRAB SALAD

1 can crab meat, drained and flaked
¼ cup chopped celery
1 hard-cooked egg yolk, mashed
½ cup homemade Russian Dressing
¼ cup finely chopped green pepper
2 tablespoons finely chopped onion
½ teaspoon poppy seeds
2 tablespoons lemon juice

Combine all ingredients, toss until well mixed. Serve on lettuce. Serves 2.

MARINATED MACKEREL SALAD

1 cup Pretty Pepper Dressing
1 can mackerel, drained and boned
Lettuce leaves
1 cucumber, sliced

Pour the sauce over the mackerel and marinate overnight. Line each salad bowl with lettuce and cucumber slices, and place several pieces of mackerel on each plate. Drizzle the extra dressing over the mackerel. Serves 2 to 4.

PIQUANT SARDINE SALAD

¼ Bermuda onion, sliced in rings
Iceberg lettuce, torn in chunks
1 can sardines in mustard sauce
1 tablespoon capers
1 tablespoon vinegar from the capers
1 tablespoon oil

Separate the onion rings, toss with the lettuce. Arrange in salad bowl and top with whole sardines. Combine the mustard sauce from the can with the rest of the ingredients, mix well and pour over the salad. Serves 1.

SHRIMP SALAD

2 cups diced cooked shrimp
¼ cup chopped celery
½ cup allowed mayonnaise
¼ teaspoon celery seeds
4 hard-cooked eggs, chopped
¼ cup chopped sour pickles
2 tablespoons lemon juice
¼ cup homemade Instant Ketchup

Combine all ingredients, toss to mix. Serve on greens. Serves 4.

SHRIMP COCKTAIL

½ head of lettuce
1 pound jumbo shrimp, cooked
1 lemon, quartered
1 cup homemade Seafood Cocktail Sauce

Tear the lettuce into chunks and arrange in four salad bowls. Divide the shrimp into four portions and arrange on the lettuce. Garnish with slices or wedges of lemon, serve the sauce in small cups on the side. Serves 4.

PICNIC TUNA SALAD

1 13-ounce can solid white tuna, drained
1 large pickled sweet pepper in vinegar, plus 2 tablespoons of the
    vinegar from the jar
6 to 8 small cherry tomatoes
½ small onion, chopped
½ small head iceberg lettuce, torn
2 tablespoons oil or 2 tablespoons oil from the tuna can
1 ¼-grain tablet saccharin, crushed
1 small can cut green beans, drained
½ cucumber, peeled and sliced
½ green pepper, diced
¼ teaspoon garlic powder
¼ teaspoon salt

Separate the tuna into bite-sized chunks. Sliver the pickled pepper.
Combine all ingredients, leaving the tomatoes whole. Toss all together and refrigerate to marinate about 1 hour, or pack for a picnic
and serve within the next few hours. This salad keeps well and even
improves by standing for 1 or 2 hours; it's also neat to carry in lunch
pails because of the uncut tomatoes. Serves 4 to 6.

TUNA SALAD

2 medium carrots, grated fine in blender
1 13-ounce can solid white tuna, drained
3 ribs celery, chopped
¼ teaspoon salt
1 tablespoon onion juice
¼ teaspoon paprika
½ cup allowed mayonnaise
½ teaspoon onion powder
2 ¼-grain tablets saccharin, crushed
1 tablespoon vinegar or more if needed

Grate the carrots by slicing them and adding them to the blender a
little at a time; blend them on grate or medium until all have been

grated. Flake the tuna with a fork, combine all ingredients. Correct flavoring, add a touch more vinegar if necessary. Serves 4 to 6.

TUNA-OLIVE SALAD

¾ cup tangy small-curd cottage cheese
1 teaspoon lemon juice
1 7-ounce can tuna, drained slightly
⅓ cup stuffed green olives, sliced
¼ teaspoon onion powder
Salt, pepper to taste

Combine the cottage cheese and lemon juice in the blender and blend slightly until puréed. Mix with the remaining ingredients by hand (do not blend); serve on lettuce. Serves 3.

EGG SALAD

6 hard-cooked eggs, chilled and peeled
4 ribs celery, chopped
¼ cup finely chopped onion
½ teaspoon salt
Dash of liquid artificial sweetener
1 sour pickle, chopped
1 tablespoon finely minced celery tops
1 tablespoon prepared mustard
Dash of freshly ground pepper
Dash of paprika

Chop the eggs well. Combine all ingredients and mix well. Chill and serve on lettuce, or stuff 3 hollowed-out tomatoes. Serves 3.

PICKLED PEA SALAD

1 package frozen peas
½ cup water
Pinch of chopped dill weed
1 small jar pickled cocktail onions (sugarless)

Salt to taste
1 tablespoon oil

Heat the water to boiling, add the peas. Lower heat, cover and simmer until the peas are barely cooked. Drain and cool. Combine with all ingredients, including the liquid from the jar of onions. Marinate several hours or overnight. Serve on Bibb lettuce. Serves 4. Each serving=one unit high-carbohydrate vegetable.

PICKLED BEETS, WAX BEANS OR CUCUMBERS

½ cup liquid from the canned vegetable (or ½ cup water for cucumbers)
½ cup white vinegar
4 to 6 ¼-grain tablets saccharin, crushed
1 can sliced beets (check label for sugar) or cut wax beans, or 1 large cucumber, sliced
½ small onion, sliced and separated into rings

Drain the liquid from the vegetables and set it aside. Combine the vinegar, saccharin and ½ cup liquid, and heat until the saccharin is dissolved. Pour over the vegetables, correct seasoning to taste and chill. Marinate in the refrigerator at least 1 hour, preferably longer. Serves 4.

Variations: To the beet liquid, add ⅛ teaspoon caraway seeds; to beans or cucumbers, add ¼ teaspoon chopped dill.

CAULIFLOWER SALAD

1 head cauliflower, broken into chunks
1 tablespoon oil
½ cup cider vinegar
Salt, pepper to taste
½ teaspoon celery seeds
¼ cup sliced or diced red onion
2 ¼-grain tablets saccharin, crushed

Combine all ingredients, toss well and marinate several hours or overnight. Serves 4.

MOCK "POTATO" SALAD #1

1 can water chestnuts, drained
2 ribs celery, diced
1 homemade Sweet Pickle, or 6 stuffed Spanish olives, chopped
¼ onion, chopped
⅓ cup allowed or homemade Mayonnaise
Salt to taste
¼ cup sour cream
2 tablespoons liquid from the pickles or the olives (depending on
    which was used)
3 hard-cooked eggs, sliced
¼ green pepper, chopped
1 tablespoon prepared mustard
¼ teaspoon paprika
¼ teaspoon celery seeds
Dash of freshly ground pepper

Slice the water chestnuts thinly, making about 4 pieces from each
chestnut. Combine all ingredients and chill overnight. Taste and add
more mayonnaise, salt, etc., if needed before serving. Serves 3.

MOCK "POTATO" SALAD #2

Same as #1 except: omit the water chestnuts, and add 1 head
    cauliflower

Select 1 large head cauliflower. Remove the flowerettes and set aside
for another recipe. Using just the core and branches, cut up cauliflower into 2-inch pieces. Steam, pressure cook or parboil until about
half cooked (should be firm but chewable). Drain. Dice or slice the
pieces and add remaining ingredients according to the recipe. Be
sure to chill before serving, preferably overnight. Serves 3.

THREE-BEAN SALAD

1 cup canned or cooked soybeans (*see* Vegetables)
1 can cut green beans, drained
¼ cup minced Bermuda onion
¼ cup vinegar
1 tablespoon minced fresh parsley or ¼ teaspoon dehydrated parsley
  flakes
¼ cup oil
1 can cut wax beans, drained
1 clove garlic
Dash of liquid artificial sweetener
Salt, pepper to taste

Combine all ingredients, using the liquid from the beans, but not from the green or wax beans (reserve for soups, etc.). Stick a toothpick through the garlic clove. Toss and marinate overnight in refrigerator. Remove the garlic, and correct seasoning before serving. Serves 8.

SNOW PEA SALAD

1 small can white onions
1 package frozen Chinese snow peas or pea pods
1 tablespoon oil
2 tablespoons vinegar
Salt, pepper to taste
Dash of liquid artificial sweetener

Drain the onions and pour ½ cup of the onion liquid into a saucepan. Bring to a boil, add the frozen pea pods and cover. Lower heat and simmer gently until cooked. Remove from heat and cool. Add the rest of the ingredients and marinate in refrigerator. Serves 4.

SUMMER SALAD

1 small Bermuda onion, sliced
1 head iceberg lettuce, torn
1 cup raw cauliflower flowerettes
1 tomato, diced
⅔ cup Blue Cheese Dressing or French Dressing

Separate rings of onion, toss all ingredients together. Serves 8.

COLESLAW #1

3 cups finely shredded cabbage
½ cup finely shredded red cabbage
½ cup allowed or homemade Mayonnaise
Juice of 1 small lemon
½ carrot, chopped
¼ cup finely chopped green pepper
¼ cup water
2 ¼-grain tablets saccharin, crushed
Salt, pepper to taste

Mix together all ingredients. Chill overnight, taste and correct seasoning. Add more lemon juice, sweetener or salt to taste as needed. Serves 6 to 8.

COLESLAW #2

1 recipe Boiled Coleslaw Dressing
4 cups finely shredded cabbage
1 teaspoon poppy seeds

Prepare the dressing, toss with other ingredients and chill. Correct seasoning and serve. Serves 4 to 6.

RED CABBAGE SLAW

1 small head red cabbage, shredded
2 tablespoons oil
½ cup cider vinegar
½ teaspoon prepared brown mustard
2 ¼-grain tablets saccharin, crushed
1 teaspoon salt
Dash of pepper

Sprinkle the cabbage with the oil, then toss to coat evenly. Add remaining ingredients. Toss well and chill several hours, turning occasionally. Keeps well for several days. Serves 4 to 6.

CREAMED CABBAGE SALAD

1 small head cabbage
1 medium green pepper
1 cup allowed or homemade Mayonnaise
½ cup white vinegar
½ cup evaporated milk
1 teaspoon celery seeds
4 ¼-grain tablets saccharin, crushed
Salt, pepper to taste

Chop the vegetables, being sure to chop the cabbage into tiny pieces. Blend the mayonnaise with the vinegar and milk. Add the seasonings, then mix in the vegetables. Serve immediately. Serves 4 to 6.

CABBAGE-SPROUT SALAD

2 cups shredded cabbage
⅓ cup allowed or homemade Mayonnaise
2 tablespoons vinegar
1 cup bean sprouts, raw or canned (drained)
½ cup coarsely chopped walnuts
Salt, pepper to taste

Combine all ingredients, toss well. Chill and store in refrigerator at least 1 hour. Serves 4.

CARROT SLAW

1½ cups finely shredded carrots
¼ cup salted Spanish peanuts
2 tablespoons cider vinegar
½ cup chopped celery
½ cup allowed or homemade Mayonnaise
Salt to taste

Combine all ingredients, mix well and chill. Serves 4.

SANDWICHES

Sandwiches on the diet can be made of allowed bread, such as Thomas' Protein Bread if tolerated, homemade bread or no bread at all; it depends on the carbohydrate allotment you want to use for a given meal.

If you would rather use your carbohydrate unit in the form of a dessert, there are many low-carbohydrate ways you can make a sandwich. We would define a sandwich as a high-protein filling surrounded by an edible holder. Thus a sandwich can be made by putting a filling between two crisp leaves of iceberg lettuce, or between two pancakes; even a loaf, such as a firm meat loaf or cheese loaf, can be substituted for bread in making sandwiches. Sandwiches can be cold or hot, closed or open-faced, broiled or fried like a fritter. There is almost no limitation to the combinations you can think up. And if you use homemade Soy Bread or Soy Grits Bread there is almost no limit to the amount you may have. So by all means try our suggestions, but then go ahead and see if you can invent some of your own.

COLD SANDWICHES

OPEN-FACED BROILED OR BAKED
   SANDWICHES

Chicken Reuben Sandwich
Broiled Clam Sandwich
Barbecue Sandwich

COLD PANCAKE SANDWICHES

SPREADS

Salmon Spread
Tuna Spread
Tuna-almond Spread
Peanut-butter Bacon Spread

Chicken Curry Spread
Cheese-olive Spread
Hot "Blintz-wiches"
Sardine Dip: *see* Appetizers
Clam Dip and Spread: *see* Appetizers
Bacon Spread: *see* Appetizers
Cheddar Cheese Spread: *see* Appetizers
Pickle Spread: *see* Appetizers
Chili Spread: *see* Appetizers

Olive Spread: *see* Appetizers
Basic Sweet Creamy Spread: *see* Appetizers
Turkey Pâté: *see* Appetizers
Liver Pâté: *see* Appetizers

MISCELLANEOUS

Ready-made Spreads
Hero or Submarine Sandwich
Ham and Cheese on Lettuce
Cheese on Cheese

COLD SANDWICHES

There are several ways to make a sandwich using bread:

1. Use homemade Soy Bread, Soy Grits Bread or other low-carbohydrate bread; slice thinly, use two pieces per sandwich; to toast, broil briefly on each side.

2. Using homemade high-carbohydrate bread or bought or allowed bread, use 1 slice of bread for the bottom of the sandwich, add the filling and top with a crisp flat lettuce leaf.

3. Using bought allowed bread, toast the slice in the toaster; remove and slit in half carefully using a serrated knife, making 2 very thin slices of toast. Fill; makes 1 sandwich.

A few suggestions for cold sandwiches are:
—Roast beef and coleslaw
—Ham, lettuce and tomato
—Cream cheese and olive
—Sliced cold meat loaf
—Sugarless liverwurst and Bermuda onion
—Chicken salad
—Cold sliced sugarless frankfurters
—Cold fried fish and allowed mayonnaise

OPEN-FACED BROILED OR BAKED SANDWICHES

Butter 1 slice of allowed or homemade bread. Top with sandwich filling. If using cheese, place it on last. Bake in medium oven (350°) until the cheese is runny. If broiling, place 6 to 8 inches from heat, broil at 375° until lightly browned and/or the cheese is melted. Do not burn. To barbecue, place on foil over fire and heat until filling is hot or melted, or wrap the entire sandwich lightly with foil. A few ideas for hot sandwiches are:

—Sliced turkey, tomato, bacon (precooked) and cheese
—Ham and Swiss cheese with pickle
—Sliced hot dogs, bacon and cheese
—Salmon salad and Muenster cheese
—Lobster salad and American cheese
—Cooked sausage, mustard, provolone
—Ham, hard-cooked egg slices and mayonnaise
—Ham, tomato and Wispride
—Asparagus, bacon (precooked) and cheese
—Bacon (precooked) and grated Cheddar cheese
—Crab salad and Swiss cheese
—Tuna salad, tomato and Cheddar cheese
—Sardines, mustard, onion and Swiss cheese
—Roast beef, pepper rings, American cheese
—Chili con carne and shredded sharp cheese

CHICKEN REUBEN SANDWICH

Lightly toast 1 slice bread. Spread with allowed mayonnaise. Add 2 ounces sliced cooked chicken, 1 slice Swiss cheese, ¼ cup drained sauerkraut, thinly sliced tomato. Heat until the cheese melts in the oven or under broiler. Serves 1.

BROILED CLAM SANDWICH

2 egg whites
1 7-ounce can minced clams, drained (save the liquid for soups, etc.)
¼ cup allowed mayonnaise
½ teaspoon prepared mustard
Pinch of chopped dill weed
Salt to taste
2 slices allowed or homemade bread

Beat the egg whites until fluffy but not dry. Mix the clams with the mayonnaise, mustard and dill. Add the salt if needed. Fold the clam mixture into the egg whites. Spoon onto the toast and broil about 1 minute. Serves 2; for carbohydrate units, see the bread recipe used.

BARBECUE SANDWICH

Combine ½ cup leftover chili beans with ½ cup shredded roast beef or brisket. Add 1 tablespoon finely chopped onion. Place on bread and heat in oven until warm. If the beans are too dry, add ¼ cup tomato purée and ¼ teaspoon chili powder, plus salt to taste as needed. Serves 1.

COLD PANCAKE SANDWICHES

Pancakes are good substitutes for bread in a sandwich. They can hold the sandwich filling better than most of the homemade breads and contain few carbohydrates. Use them for open-faced sandwiches topped with gravy or dressing; or use 2 pieces, trimmed to any shape or size you prefer, for a conventional sandwich. For the amount of carbohydrate, see the pancake recipe you select. An excellent recipe for sandwiches is Buttermilk Pancakes (see Breakfast Foods), but any of the others given under Breakfast Foods will do as well. You might want to add seasoning, such as onion powder, to the batter if you know in advance which filling you plan to use. Some suggestions for pancake sandwiches are:

—Peanut butter and sliced strawberries
—Butter and watercress
—Boiled ham, cream cheese
—Meat loaf and dill pickles
—Roast beef, Muenster cheese and lettuce
—Sugarless bologna, allowed mayonnaise and homemade Sweet Pickles
—Whipped cream cheese and chopped salted peanuts
—Farmer cheese and anchovies
—American cheese and apple butter
—Salmon, cream cheese and Bermuda onion

SPREADS

Sandwich spreads can be used with homemade bread, with unlimited amounts of Soy Bread, with pancakes or other allowed breads. Also, you might want to make a "sandwich" using a spread on a slice of cheese, roast beef, ham or cold meat loaf, and topped with a piece of lettuce. Following are some of the ideas you can try, but we're sure you can invent some of your own as well, using leftovers from other recipes.

SALMON SPREAD

1 cup red salmon, drained
1 tablespoon finely chopped pickle
Pinch of celery seeds
1 hard-cooked egg, riced or mashed
Pinch of salt
Dash of paprika
Allowed or homemade Mayonnaise as needed

Combine ingredients, adding enough mayonnaise to moisten to spreading consistency. Serves 3.

TUNA SPREAD

1 7-ounce can chunk tuna, drained
¼ cup finely chopped celery
2 tablespoons allowed or homemade Mayonnaise
Dash of liquid artificial sweetener
2 hard-cooked eggs, riced or mashed
1 teaspoon lemon juice
¼ teaspoon onion powder

Flake the tuna well; combine with other ingredients and mash until smooth. Serves 3.

TUNA-ALMOND SPREAD

1 7-ounce can tuna, drained
¼ cup allowed or homemade Mayonnaise
Salt, pepper to taste as needed
4 blanched almonds
1 tablespoon lemon juice

Combine all ingredients in the blender. Blend until smooth, pushing the mixture with a rubber spatula to free the blades. Serves 3.

PEANUT-BUTTER BACON SPREAD

3 or 4 slices bacon (not sugar-cured)
½ cup allowed peanut butter

Fry the bacon until crisp; drain well and crumble. Mix into the peanut butter. Serves 3.

CHICKEN CURRY SPREAD

¾ cup finely chopped or ground cooked chicken
¼ cup finely chopped celery
½ teaspoon instant minced onion

1 tablespoon lemon juice
Salt, pepper to taste
¼ cup pecan halves, chopped fine
2 tablespoons allowed or homemade Mayonnaise
½ teaspoon curry powder

Mash together all ingredients until smooth. Serves 3.

CHEESE-OLIVE SPREAD

1 cup grated sharp Cheddar cheese
¼ cup allowed or homemade Mayonnaise
1 scallion, minced very fine
¼ cup stuffed Spanish olives, chopped fine

Mash together the cheese and mayonnaise until smooth. Add the remaining ingredients and mix well. Serves 4.

HOT "BLINTZ-WICHES"

A blintz consists of a pancake-like outer wrapping rolled around a filling. The classic blintz appears in the chapter Foreign and Regional; similar sandwiches are found all around the world—the Mexican enchilada and tostada are similar, and also the Chinese egg roll, to name just a few. We give here some variations, all of them using a filling wrapped in a pancake and fried. We call them "blintz-wiches."

Basic directions:
Make 6 thin Almond Pancakes. Set aside on a plate and cover with a cloth. Fill each pancake with any of the following fillings; fold and seal the edges with brushed egg white. Place apart on foil and bake at 400° until brown; or fry in hot butter in a skillet, turning once.

Fillings:

1. 1 cup diced cooked ham, ¼ cup diced Swiss cheese, 2 tablespoons finely chopped green pepper
2. 1 cup drained and flaked chunk tuna, ¼ cup mayonnaise, 4 large stuffed olives, chopped

3. 3 hard-cooked eggs, ¼ cup cubed Swiss cheese, ¼ cup mayonnaise, 2 teaspoons minced pickles

4. 1 cup diced cooked chicken, ¼ cup mayonnaise, ¼ cup chopped celery, 4 black olives, sliced

Variation ⚹*1:* Use same batter and one of the fillings above, but place small amount of filling on the left side of the pancake; fold the right side over the left to form a small pie. Seal edges with egg white; fry.

Variation ⚹*2:* Make the pancakes as above, but fry until crisp and golden on both sides. Sprinkle filling over 1 pancake, top with another pancake. Heat in a medium oven until the filling melts and runs.

Variation ⚹*3:* Fry 1 pancake, add filling in the center; fold, continue frying, holding the pancake closed with spatula; sprinkle with hot pepper sauce.

MISCELLANEOUS

READY-MADE SPREADS

Some ready-made sandwich spreads which you can buy are:

Wispride cold pack cheese food
Pimiento cheese
Chive cheese
Sugarless peanut butter

HERO OR SUBMARINE SANDWICH

1 small loaf homemade Soy Bread
4 slices provolone cheese
8 ounces assorted meats, including sugarless bologna and salami if
    available
½ tomato, sliced paper thin
¼ onion, thinly sliced
½ cup finely shredded lettuce

6 to 8 hot cherry peppers (remove seeds)
½ teaspoon olive oil
1 teaspoon cider vinegar
¼ teaspoon oregano
Salt, pepper to taste

Split the bread in half lengthwise; use one half for the sandwich. Split the half loaf in half lengthwise again, making it resemble a large Italian roll. Spread the cheese over the two halves of bread, then the meats, then the sliced tomato. Next sprinkle the onions on, then the shredded lettuce. Top with the cherry peppers, distributing evenly. Drizzle the oil and vinegar over all, season with the oregano, salt and pepper. Carefully fold the two halves together. Allow the flavors to mingle a few minutes before eating (for crisper bread, toast the bread in the oven for a few minutes before making the sandwich). Makes 1 large sandwich, but can be eaten by two people for lunch.

HAM AND CHEESE ON LETTUCE

Peel a large leaf off a crisp head of iceberg lettuce. Place a large (1½- to 2-ounce) slice of Muenster cheese on top, then top with several slices of ham. Spread the ham lightly with mustard. Fold the entire stack in half, so that the lettuce is outside, replacing bread, to form a sandwich.

CHEESE ON CHEESE

Use a bland firm cheese, such as provolone or Gouda. Spread with Wispride or homemade sharp cheese spread; cover with another slice of the first cheese. Eat as a sandwich.

SAUCES AND DRESSINGS

Basic White Sauce
Mushroom White Sauce
Hollandaise Sauce
Cheese Sauce
Rarebit Sauce
Clam Sauce
Lemon Butter Sauce
Garlic Butter Sauce
Herb Butter
Roquefort Butter
Spaghetti Sauce
Instant Ketchup
Barbecue Sauce
Deluxe Barbecue Sauce or
  Ketchup
Chili Sauce #1
Chili Sauce #2
Seafood Cocktail Sauce #1
Seafood Cocktail Sauce #2
Mayonnaise
Green Mayonnaise
Swedish Mayonnaise
Horseradish Mayonnaise
Seafood Mayonnaise
Tartar Sauce

Russian Dressing
Thousand Island Dressing
Green Goddess Dressing #1
Green Goddess Dressing #2
Boiled Coleslaw Dressing
Italian Dressing
French Dressing
Garlic French Dressing
Tomato French Dressing
Mustard Dressing
Pretty Pepper Dressing
Chive Cheese Dressing
Roquefort Dressing
Cheddar Cheese Dressing
Yankee Salad Dressing
Yoghurt Dressing
Chinese Mustard
Chinese Duck Sauce (Plum
  Sauce)
Cranberry Sauce
Strawberry Sauce
Strawberry Butter
Maple "Syrup"
Apple Syrup

BASIC WHITE SAUCE

2 tablespoons butter
2 tablespoons soy flour
1 cup half and half or evaporated milk
1 egg yolk, beaten
Dash of white pepper
Salt to taste

Melt the butter in the top of a double boiler. Blend in the soy flour, mixing to a paste. Add the milk slowly, stirring with a whisk to avoid lumps. Add the egg yolk and seasonings, and heat, stirring frequently. Do not boil. Continue cooking until the desired thickness is reached. If necessary, thin with milk. Makes 1 cup.

MUSHROOM WHITE SAUCE

3 tablespoons butter
¼ pound fresh mushrooms, chopped
2 tablespoons soy flour
½ cup non-fat dry milk
1 cup milk
1 small or ½ large allowed bouillon cube (*see* Brand Names)
Dash of freshly ground pepper
Salt to taste

Melt the butter in the skillet and sauté the mushrooms until brown. Add the flour and dry milk and mix over medium heat. Slowly add the milk, stirring to make a paste, then adding the rest of the milk. Add the bouillon, pepper and salt to taste if needed. Heat until warm, stirring frequently. For a smoother sauce, place all ingredients in the blender and blend on low for a few seconds. Use with cooked vegetables, leftovers, meats, etc. Makes 2 cups.

HOLLANDAISE SAUCE

½ cup butter at room temperature
2 tablespoons lemon juice
½ teaspoon salt
Dash of cayenne (optional)
3 egg yolks
Dash of paprika
Pinch of garlic powder
¼ cup boiling water

Combine all the ingredients except the water in the blender. Blend on low, then on medium, until well blended. Continue to blend and gradually add the boiling water. Pour immediately into the top of a double boiler, over a small amount of boiling water. Cook 5 minutes, stirring, or until the sauce is smooth and as thick as custard. Serve over poached eggs, asparagus, broccoli, etc. Makes 1 cup.

CHEESE SAUCE

¼ cup butter
¼ medium onion, minced
½ cup evaporated milk
4 ounces Cheddar cheese, diced
Hot milk as needed
Dash of Tabasco sauce or cayenne
Salt, pepper to taste

Melt the butter and sauté the onion until soft. Add the evaporated milk, and heat. Transfer to the blender with the cheese. Blend until smooth, adding a little hot milk if needed to blend. Add seasonings to taste. Serve over vegetables, etc. Or use as a base for casseroles using leftover meat and vegetables. Makes 1 cup.

RAREBIT SAUCE

8 ounces Velveeta processed cheese
½ cup non-fat dry milk
1 teaspoon vinegar
Salt, pepper to taste
¼ cup cream or evaporated milk
½ cup milk plus more as needed
¼ teaspoon dry mustard

Cut the cheese into small pieces. Combine all ingredients, mixing over low heat until the cheese melts, stirring often. For thinner sauce add more milk until the desired consistency is reached. Pour over homemade bread, polenta, cold sliced meat, vegetables, etc. Makes 1½ cups.

CLAM SAUCE

2 tablespoons olive oil
2 cloves garlic, minced fine
2 8-ounce cans minced clams, including juice
Salt to taste
Dash of freshly ground pepper

Heat the oil in a pan and brown the garlic, stirring. Add the clams, clam broth and seasonings. Cook over medium heat until the clams are heated through (about 3 minutes). Serve over bean sprouts or homemade noodles. Makes 2 cups.

LEMON BUTTER SAUCE

¼ cup salt butter
1 tablespoon lemon juice
2 tablespoons water

Melt the butter, and stir in the juice and water. Mix well, heat and pour over vegetables (asparagus, Brussels sprouts, broccoli, etc.) or use with seafood such as lobster and shrimp. Makes ⅓ cup.

GARLIC BUTTER SAUCE

¼ cup butter
1 clove garlic, minced fine

Melt the butter and sauté the garlic until soft. Pour over vegetables, seafood, etc. Makes ⅓ cup.

HERB BUTTER

1 cup heavy cream or ¼ pound melted butter (unsalted)
½ teaspoon salt
¼ teaspoon each of: parsley, thyme and oregano
Dash of paprika

Combine all ingredients in the blender. Blend on low until the cream turns into butter. Use as a spread on bread, toast, sandwiches, etc., or dot on hot vegetables; also can be brushed on fish before broiling.

Variation: Substitute chives, parsley and chervil for the herbs. Makes 1 cup.

ROQUEFORT BUTTER

¼ cup sweet butter (½ stick)
4 tablespoons Roquefort cheese
1 teaspoon milk
Salt to taste if needed

Combine all ingredients and blend until smooth. Use as a spread or on vegetables. Makes ½ cup.

SPAGHETTI SAUCE

2 tablespoons olive oil
1 clove garlic, finely chopped
1 medium onion, chopped
4 to 6 fresh mushrooms, sliced thin
¼ green pepper, chopped
1 large can tomato purée
1 pound whole ripe tomatoes
½ teaspoon finely chopped basil
½ teaspoon finely chopped parsley
½ teaspoon salt
¼ teaspoon pepper
1 ¼-grain tablet saccharin

Heat the olive oil in a large skillet. Add the garlic, onions, mushrooms and green pepper. Cook over medium heat until the onion is translucent. Add the tomato purée, whole tomatoes and seasonings. Cook on low heat for 1 hour. Makes 6 cups.

INSTANT KETCHUP

2 cups tomato purée
6 ¼-grain tablets saccharin
Dash of cinnamon
2 tablespoons cider vinegar
Pinch of salt
Dash of onion powder

Mix together all ingredients. Heat over medium heat, stirring. Remove from the heat and chill. Correct the seasoning to taste when cool. For emergencies, this can be made even more quickly by combining all ingredients, mixing well and serving as is without cooking. Makes about 2 cups.

BARBECUE SAUCE

2 cups tomato purée
2 tablespoons lemon juice plus more as needed
½ teaspoon salt
1 tablespoon dehydrated minced onion
1 tablespoon vinegar
2 ¼-grain tablets saccharin
½ teaspoon dry mustard
Dash of hot red pepper

Combine all ingredients and heat for 10 minutes. Serve hot; brush on frankfurters, spare ribs or any other meat to be broiled or barbecued. Makes about 2 cups.

DELUXE BARBECUE SAUCE OR KETCHUP

1 46-ounce can tomato juice
½ cup cider vinegar
½ teaspoon pepper
Pinch of ground cloves
Pinch of curry powder
Pinch of ginger
½ teaspoon paprika
½ medium onion, grated
4 ¼-grain tablets saccharin
Pinch of allspice
Pinch of cinnamon
1 teaspoon dry mustard
½ teaspoon salt

Combine all ingredients in a large pan and bring to a boil. Reduce heat, and simmer uncovered on low for 3 hours, or until very thick (stir often). Spoon into a clean jar or plastic squeeze bottle. Chill. Makes about 12 ounces. Brush on spare ribs, steak, frankfurters.

Variation: Deluxe Ketchup: omit the vinegar, substitute 2 tablespoons lemon juice.

CHILI SAUCE #1

2 cups tomato purée
1 small onion, chopped
2 tablespoons peanut oil
1 teaspoon salt or to taste
½ teaspoon basil
2 red chili peppers, fresh or canned
1 clove garlic
1 ¼-grain tablet saccharin or to taste
½ teaspoon black pepper
½ teaspoon parsley flakes

Combine all ingredients in a saucepan and bring to a boil. Reduce the heat and simmer 15 minutes. Remove the garlic, and mash or remove the chili peppers. Chill before serving. Makes about 2 cups.

CHILI SAUCE #2

3 pounds ripe tomatoes
¾ cup chopped onion
1 green pepper, chopped
2 ¼-grain tablets saccharin or to taste
2 red chili peppers, finely chopped
¼ teaspoon celery seed
¼ cup cider vinegar
Salt to taste

Skin the tomatoes by dipping briefly in boiling water. Cut into eighths. Pour all ingredients into a saucepan and bring to a boil. Simmer over low heat uncovered for 1 hour or longer, until desired consistency is reached. Use hot or cold. Makes 1½ to 2 cups.

SEAFOOD COCKTAIL SAUCE #1

½ cup tomato purée
Juice of 1 small lemon
Salt to taste
3 tablespoons prepared white horseradish
1 ¼-grain tablet saccharin, crushed

Combine all ingredients and mix well. Chill, then correct seasoning to taste. Serve with boiled shrimp, crab, etc. Makes ½ cup.

SEAFOOD COCKTAIL SAUCE #2

½ cup homemade Instant Ketchup or Deluxe Barbecue Sauce
2 tablespoons prepared white horseradish
¼ teaspoon salt or to taste if needed
2 tablespoons lemon juice
1 tablespoon grated onion

Combine all ingredients and mix well. Chill and serve with seafood. Makes about ½ cup.

MAYONNAISE

1 large egg
½ teaspoon salt
¼ teaspoon paprika
½ tablespoon white vinegar
1 tablespoon lemon juice
½ teaspoon dry mustard
1 cup vegetable oil

In the blender combine all ingredients except the oil. Make sure the oil is very fresh and light in taste (do not use heavy-flavored oil such as olive oil). Blend on low until mixed. *Keep the blender running continuously* on medium until the recipe is finished. With the blender running, begin adding the oil very slowly, one drop at a time, then in a steady drip; as the mixture begins to thicken, stir slightly with a rubber spatula so that it will not stop moving. Continue dripping and blending until the mixture is the thickness of mayonnaise. Remember, the mayonnaise is going to be getting thicker as you add more oil, not thinner. Don't panic if it doesn't seem to be getting thick. If the mayonnaise is still not thick enough for your taste after all the oil has been added, add a small amount more of oil, remembering to continue blending. Store mayonnaise in the refrigerator. Makes 1¼ cups.

GREEN MAYONNAISE

1 cup homemade Mayonnaise
1 teaspoon chopped chives
Dash liquid artificial sweetener
1 tablespoon vinegar
1 teaspoon chervil

Combine in blender and blend until smooth. Chill overnight or for several hours to blend the flavors. Makes 1 cup.

SWEDISH MAYONNAISE

1 cup homemade Mayonnaise
1 teaspoon chopped dill weed
4 to 6 capers
1 tablespoon lemon juice

Combine all ingredients, mix and chill. Makes 1 cup.

HORSERADISH MAYONNAISE

½ cup homemade Mayonnaise
1 teaspoon prepared white or red horseradish
1 teaspoon onion powder

Combine all ingredients. Mix well, serve with cold roast beef, veal, etc. Makes ½ cup.

SEAFOOD MAYONNAISE

½ cup homemade Mayonnaise
½ teaspoon prepared white horseradish
1 tablespoon prepared yellow mustard

Combine ingredients, mix well. Serve with sardines, smoked fish, etc. Makes ½ cup.

TARTAR SAUCE

1 homemade Sweet Pickle (*see* Preserves) or 1 small sour pickle
1 tablespoon dehydrated onion flakes
2 tablespoons juice from the pickles used
½ cup allowed or homemade Mayonnaise

Mince the pickle fine. Sprinkle the onion flakes into the pickle juice to reconstitute for 5 minutes. Mix in the mayonnaise and chill. Serve with hot or cold fish, fish cakes, salad, etc. Makes about ½ cup.

RUSSIAN DRESSING

½ cup allowed or homemade Mayonnaise
¼ cup homemade Instant Ketchup or Deluxe Barbecue Sauce
1 tablespoon lemon juice
2 ¼-grain tablets saccharin, crushed

Combine all ingredients and mix well. Serve with salad or use as a sandwich spread with turkey, Swiss cheese, etc. Makes ¾ cup.

THOUSAND ISLAND DRESSING

¾ cup allowed or homemade Mayonnaise
½ cup homemade Instant Ketchup or Deluxe Barbecue Sauce
½ small onion, minced fine
½ teaspoon paprika

1 tablespoon vinegar
1 sour pickle, minced fine
2 tablespoons finely minced green pepper
Dash liquid artificial sweetener

Combine all ingredients. Chill, serve with salad, hearts of lettuce,
etc. Makes 1¼ cups.

GREEN GODDESS DRESSING #1

½ cup allowed or homemade Mayonnaise
1 tablespoon lemon juice
½ cup chopped fresh parsley
1 teaspoon capers
½ cup sour cream
¼ teaspoon garlic powder
½ teaspoon tarragon
¼ teaspoon salt

Place all ingredients in the blender and blend on low, stirring with a
rubber spatula if needed to free the blades. Correct the seasoning
if necessary. Makes 1¼ cups.

GREEN GODDESS DRESSING #2

1 cup allowed or homemade Mayonnaise
¼ cup chopped fresh parsley
½ teaspoon garlic powder
Dash of tarragon
½ cup sour cream
1 tablespoon lemon juice
4 scallions, chopped, including tops
1 tablespoon tarragon vinegar
½ teaspoon salt
Dash of freshly ground pepper
1 or 2 anchovy fillets

Combine all ingredients in the blender and blend until smooth.
Makes 1¾ cups.

BOILED COLESLAW DRESSING

1 cup sour cream
1 egg
1 teaspoon salt
Dash of white pepper
¼ cup vinegar
¼ cup lemon juice
4 to 6 ¼-grain tablets saccharin

Blend all ingredients together until smooth. Heat in the top of a double boiler, stirring, until thickened. Use as dressing for coleslaw or other raw vegetables. Makes 1½ cups.

ITALIAN DRESSING

¾ cup salad oil
¼ teaspoon salt
¼ teaspoon onion powder
Pinch of basil
2 ¼-grain tablets saccharin
¼ cup white vinegar
Dash of freshly ground pepper
¼ teaspoon oregano
¼ teaspoon garlic powder

Place all ingredients in shaker or blender. Shake or blend until mixed. Serve on tossed salad, mixed greens, raw spinach or any other salad. Makes 1 cup.

FRENCH DRESSING

½ cup salad oil
¼ cup water
1 teaspoon paprika
¼ teaspoon white pepper
¼ cup tarragon or cider vinegar

½ teaspoon dry mustard
¼ teaspoon salt or to taste
2 ¼-grain tablets saccharin

Place all ingredients in the blender and blend until liquefied. Serve immediately, or else chill and blend or shake vigorously before serving. Makes 1 cup.

GARLIC FRENCH DRESSING

Same as French Dressing plus 1 clove garlic. Makes 1 cup.

TOMATO FRENCH DRESSING

½ cup salad oil
½ cup tomato juice
½ teaspoon dry mustard
Dash of freshly ground pepper
2 tablespoons lemon juice
¾ teaspoon salt
1 teaspoon onion powder
1 ¼-grain tablet saccharin

Combine all ingredients in the blender and blend until smooth. Makes 1 cup.

MUSTARD DRESSING

½ cup salad oil
1 tablespoon white vinegar
½ teaspoon salt
1 ¼-grain tablet saccharin
½ cup evaporated milk
2 tablespoons prepared mustard
Dash of pepper

Blend until smooth. Serve with cold meats, cheese, etc. Makes 1 cup.

PRETTY PEPPER DRESSING

½ cup pimientos or roasted sweet peppers, drained
2 large pickled peppers (California wonder peppers, packed in vinegar)
¼ cup vinegar from the pepper jar
¼ teaspoon garlic powder
Salt to taste
2 ¼-grain tablets saccharin
½ teaspoon onion powder

Combine all ingredients in the blender. Blend until liquefied. Correct seasoning to taste. Serve with salads, greens, sardines and other canned fish, etc. Makes 1 cup.

CHIVE CHEESE DRESSING

1 cup cottage cheese
¼ teaspoon salt
⅓ cup water
2 tablespoons chopped fresh or freeze-dried chives

Combine all ingredients except the chives in the blender. Blend until smooth. Toss in the chives and stir lightly to mix. Chill until the flavors have blended. Spoon over tomatoes, cucumbers, salads, cold poached salmon, etc. Makes 1⅓ cups.

ROQUEFORT DRESSING

1 cup sour cream
4 ounces Roquefort cheese, crumbled
¼ cup milk
¼ teaspoon salt
Dash of garlic powder

Combine all ingredients in the blender. Blend on low until smooth. Serve on salad. Makes 1½ cups.

CHEDDAR CHEESE DRESSING

½ cup evaporated milk or light cream
¼ cup oil
½ teaspoon salt
1 teaspoon prepared brown mustard
4 ounces sharp white Cheddar cheese, cubed
1 egg yolk
¼ cup cider vinegar
Dash of cayenne pepper
1 ¼-grain tablet saccharin

Combine all ingredients in the blender and blend until smooth. For a thicker consistency use less milk and blend longer. Use like mayonnaise on salads, fish, etc., or on cold cooked vegetables, such as asparagus. Makes 1¼ cups.

YANKEE SALAD DRESSING

6 strips bacon, fried crisp and drained
2 eggs
¼ cup light cream
Dash of pepper
¼ cup white vinegar
2 ¼-grain tablets saccharin, crushed
Salt to taste

Set the bacon aside. Beat the other ingredients together. Add to the hot bacon fat, and cook, stirring constantly until thick. Serve warm on cucumbers, raw onions and other raw vegetables. Also on cabbage, celery, spinach and other cooked vegetables. Makes ¾ cup.

YOGHURT DRESSING

1 cup plain yoghurt
½ teaspoon chopped chives
½ teaspoon paprika
2 teaspoons lemon juice
½ teaspoon dry mustard
¼ teaspoon salt

Mix or blend. Serve on cooked or raw greens, other vegetables. Makes 1¼ cups.

CHINESE MUSTARD

2 tablespoons dry mustard
2 tablespoons heavy cream
¼ teaspoon salt
1 or 2 ¼-grain tablets saccharin, crushed
1 drop of water if needed

Mix all ingredients together, adding water if needed. Serve fresh and make sure the dry mustard is fresh also. This mustard is meant to be extremely hot and does not keep well. Use with Chinese Egg Roll (*see* Foreign and Regional), and other Chinese foods. Makes ¼ cup.

CHINESE DUCK SAUCE (PLUM SAUCE)

2 tart plums
2 apricots
Water as needed
¼ cup white vinegar
1 teaspoon ground ginger
Dash of salt
1 tablespoon lemon juice
½ teaspoon cinnamon
4 ¼-grain tablets saccharin

Cut the fruit into chunks, discarding the pits. Place in a saucepan with ½ inch of water. Cover and cook slowly, stirring often, until soft. Purée in blender until smooth. Chill, serve with Chinese Egg Roll, duck, etc. One fourth of recipe=1 unit fruit. Makes 1 cup.

CRANBERRY SAUCE

1 pound fresh cranberries (1 box)
1 cup water
10 ¼-grain tablets saccharin
1 tablespoon unflavored gelatin

Place the berries and ¾ of the water in a saucepan. Simmer gently until the skins "pop." Stir in the sweetener and continue heating. Soften the gelatin in the remaining ¼ cup of water, then stir into the berries until dissolved. Pour into a mold and chill until firm. Makes 2 cups, or 4 units fruit; ½ cup sauce=1 unit fruit.

Variation: To make cranberry jelly, prepare as above, then purée in the blender before chilling.

STRAWBERRY SAUCE

2 cups strawberries, chopped (fresh or loose-frozen berries, slightly thawed)
¾ cup strawberry diet soda
4 ¼-grain tablets saccharin or to taste

Place all ingredients in the blender. Blend on low until puréed. Pour over cake, ice cream, etc. Serve immediately. If keeping, refrigerate and blend again just before serving. Makes 3 cups; 1 cup=1 unit fruit.

STRAWBERRY BUTTER

½ cup strawberries, fresh or loose-frozen without sugar
¾ cup heavy cream
Dash of salt
2 to 4 ¼-grain tablets saccharin

If using frozen strawberries, thaw slightly. Combine all ingredients in the blender. Blend on medium until the cream is just beginning to turn into butter. Stop blending as soon as the butter forms, or the mixture will separate and become runny. Serve with pancakes, breakfast cake, toast, etc. Entire recipe=1 unit fruit. Makes 1 cup.

MAPLE "SYRUP"

4 tablespoons sweet butter (½ stick)
6 ¼-grain tablets saccharin or more to taste
½ teaspoon imitation maple flavoring
½ cup water

Melt the butter in a small saucepan. Add the remaining ingredients and heat. Serve hot on French toast, pancakes, etc. (*See* Breakfast Foods.) Makes ¾ cup.

APPLE SYRUP

1 small apple, peeled, cored and chopped
1 tablespoon butter
1 cup apple juice (unsweetened)

Combine in a saucepan. Bring to a rolling boil, then simmer until the apple is soft. Thin with water if desired or use as is. Entire recipe=3 units fruit. Pour over ice cream, pancakes, etc. Makes about 1¼ cups.

SEAFOOD

One of the best-tasting, cheapest and most versatile sources of protein on the diet is seafood. Any fresh, canned or frozen (un-breaded) fish can be used, as well as shellfish. They can be eaten in salads, soups, chowders, casseroles and, perhaps the most delicious and easiest way of all, just plain unadorned fresh fish brushed with a little oil or melted butter and whisked under the broiler for a few minutes.

Many of your favorite fish recipes can be duplicated by substituting our bread crumb substitutes for the flour and bread crumbs called for in your recipe, and by using homemade cream soups and cream sauces in place of the canned soups often called for in seafood recipes. As far as we know there are no prepared fish cakes, frozen or freshly made which are safe for us to eat; all of them contain flour, starch or sugar. It is these ready-to-eat fish products that today's busy housewife will miss the most. We have concentrated on substitutes for these convenience foods in this chapter, and we think you'll find them as good as the manufactured products, and not too difficult to make.

Fried Fish Fillets
Baked Fillet of Sole
Fillet of Sole Amandine
Poached Fish Fillets
Broiled Fish Fillets
Cheese-crusted Turbot
Portuguese Haddock
Haddock Veracruzana
Baked Halibut Tarragon
Cod au Gratin

Flounder Mousse
Salmon Mousse
Hot Tuna Salad
Tuna à la King
Instant Tuna à la King
Tomato Herring
Skewered Scallops
Shrimp Cocktail
Ginger Shrimp
Shrimp Creole

Fried Shrimp
Barbecued Oysters
Oysters in Jackets
Deviled Clams
Deviled Crab
Fish Cakes
Codfish Cakes
Salmon Croquettes
Tuna Salad: *see* Salads

Picnic Tuna Salad: *see* Salads
New England Clam Chowder:
   see Soups
Manhattan Clam Chowder: *see*
   Soups
Oyster Stew: *see* Soups
Winter's Night Oyster Stew: *see*
   Soups
Bouillabaisse: *see* Soups

FRIED FISH FILLETS

½ cup of any of the following, or a mixture of several: wheat germ;
   homemade bread, toasted and crumbed fine in the blender;
   sesame seeds; dry grated American cheese; ground nuts; soy flour;
   pumpkin seed meal
1 pound fish fillets (sole, flounder, etc.)
½ teaspoon paprika
½ teaspoon salt
Oil or solid shortening as needed (Crisco, etc.)
Fresh parsley as needed

Combine the bread crumbs or bread crumb substitutes in a paper
bag. Dry the fillets on a paper towel and place in the bag. Shake the
bag vigorously until all pieces are coated. Spread out the fillets and
season generously on both sides. Heat ⅛ inch of oil or shortening in
a large frying pan. Slip the fish into the hot pan and fry for 5 minutes; turn gently and fry until the fish flakes easily with a fork (1 or
2 minutes). Do not overcook. Garnish with fresh parsley and serve
with lemon wedges or sugarless mayonnaise. If you use wheat germ
or high-carbohydrate bread crumbs, be sure to count them as part of
your carbohydrate unit for the meal. Serves 3.

BAKED FILLET OF SOLE

1 pound fillets of sole (or flounder, cod, haddock, etc.)
2 tablespoons butter
½ teaspoon parsley flakes

1 teaspoon sesame seeds or wheat germ
¼ teaspoon freshly ground pepper
Dash of paprika
Salt

Place the fillets in a well-greased baking dish and dot with the butter. Place the parsley flakes in the palm of your hand and mash them well to release the flavor. Sprinkle over the fish, along with the other ingredients except salt. Place in a preheated 375° oven and bake 25 to 35 minutes, or until the fish is opaque and flakes easily. Remove from the oven and salt to taste just before serving. Serves 3.

FILLET OF SOLE AMANDINE

Same ingredients as Baked Fillet of Sole, but omit the sesame seeds and add 1 ounce slivered almonds.

Melt the butter in a frying pan; sprinkle the fish with the other ingredients and brown briefly on both sides. Transfer carefully to a baking dish and bake at 375° for 20 minutes, or until the fish flakes easily. Serves 3.

POACHED FISH FILLETS

Same as Baked Fillet of Sole, plus ¼ inch of milk.

Just before baking, pour the milk around the fish to approximately ¼ inch deep. Cover and bake at 375° until fish flakes easily (about 25 minutes). Serves 3.

BROILED FISH FILLETS

1 pound fish fillets or 2 pounds whole fish, cleaned and trimmed
¼ cup melted butter
Paprika
Dash of onion powder
Freshly ground pepper
Salt to taste

Place the fish on an oiled broiler rack over a broiler pan. Brush generously with melted butter and sprinkle with paprika and onion powder. Place in the broiler 5 or 6 inches from the heat. Broil 3 minutes for fillets, 5 minutes for whole fish. Turn, season with paprika, onion and pepper on the other side. Continue broiling until the fish flakes easily (1 or 2 minutes for fillets, 3 minutes for whole fish). If you find the odor of fish unpleasant, try removing the skin before broiling, and broiling 6 to 8 inches from the heat. This eliminates most of the fat and the "fishy" smell. Salt to taste and serve. Serves 3.

CHEESE-CRUSTED TURBOT

1 pound frozen turbot fillets (or other fillets)
¼ teaspoon paprika
Freshly ground pepper
¼ cup grated Parmesan or American cheese (dry grated type)
Salt to taste

Thaw the fillets slightly, just enough to separate them (about 5 minutes under cold running water). Separate them and place on an oiled rack over a broiler pan. Sprinkle generously with paprika and pepper. Broil 6 to 8 inches from the heat until the top is brown and crisp. Turn. Sprinkle with the cheese, then with paprika and pepper. Broil until the fish is opaque and white all through and flakes easily. Topping will be crusty and brown. Salt and serve. Serves 3.

PORTUGUESE HADDOCK

¼ cup vinegar
1 clove garlic, chopped fine
½ teaspoon paprika
1 cup tomato juice
1 bay leaf, crumbled
¼ teaspoon red peppers
1 pound fillet of haddock (or other fillets, such as cod, flounder, etc.)
Salt to taste

Combine all ingredients except the fish and salt. Place in a saucepan and heat to boiling. Lower the heat and simmer for 10 minutes.

Allow the mixture to cool. After it is cool, place the fish in a shallow pan, pour the liquid over the fish and marinate overnight. Transfer the fish to a greased baking pan, spoon in ¼ of the marinade and bake at 375° for 30 minutes, or until the fish flakes easily. Salt to taste and serve. Serves 3.

HADDOCK VERACRUZANA

2 tablespoons oil
2 cloves garlic, chopped
1 onion, sliced
3 large ripe tomatoes, sliced
Salt to taste
1 tablespoon finely minced fresh parsley
2 packages frozen haddock or 1½ pounds fresh haddock (or red snapper fillets)
4 thin slices lemon
2 yellow or green chilies, cut in strips

Heat the oil in a frying pan, and sauté the garlic and onion until browned, stirring. Add the tomatoes to the pan with the salt and parsley, and cook 5 minutes. Arrange the fish in a greased baking dish and pour the tomato mixture over the fish. Top with the lemon slices and strips of chili peppers. Bake at 350° for 30 minutes, or until the fish flakes easily. Serves 4.

BAKED HALIBUT TARRAGON

¼ cup melted butter
1 teaspoon dry mustard
1 teaspoon tarragon
1 large halibut steak (about 1½ pounds) or any other fish steak

Melt the butter and mix in the spices. Arrange the fish in a large shallow baking dish. Pour or brush the butter sauce over the fish. Bake at 375° for about 25 minutes, or until the fish flakes easily with a fork. Serves 4.

COD AU GRATIN

1½ pounds cod fillets
2 ounces butter
1 leek or 2 scallions, sliced thin
1½ cups milk
Dash of paprika
½ teaspoon salt
½ cup grated cheese (preferably Gruyère)

Place the cod fillets in a single layer in a greased casserole and set aside. In a small saucepan melt the butter and cook the leek or scallions for 5 minutes. Pour over the fish and add the milk and seasonings. Cover the casserole and bake at 375° until the fish flakes easily (about 20 minutes). Uncover and sprinkle with the grated cheese; bake in the oven at 425° until the cheese is melted and browned (10 minutes). Serves 4.

FLOUNDER MOUSSE

1 pound flounder fillets (or sole, halibut, etc.)
1 cup cream or evaporated milk
1 slice homemade high-carbohydrate bread
Dash of cayenne pepper
½ teaspoon salt
Pinch of chopped dill weed
2 eggs, separated
4 tablespoons butter

Place the fish fillets and half the cream together in a bowl. Chop, then mash them with a fork until smoothly blended to a thick paste. Blender crumb the bread; mix into the fish. Add the seasonings. Beat the egg whites until stiff. Fold gently into the fish mixture. Pour into a greased loaf pan or fish-shaped mold. Cover lightly with aluminum foil and place in a pan of hot water. Bake at 325° for 1 hour, or until firm. Remove from the oven and allow to stand for 10 minutes. Carefully unmold on a serving plate. Make the sauce as follows: melt the butter and beat together the egg yolks, salt and the rest of the cream. Stir into the butter, and heat. Remove from the heat and pour over the mousse. Serves 4; each serving=¼ unit carbohydrate.

SALMON MOUSSE

1 1-pound can red salmon, drained slightly
2 eggs, separated
½ cup cream or evaporated milk
Dash of cayenne pepper
½ teaspoon onion powder
¼ teaspoon parsley flakes
Salt to taste

Place the salmon in a bowl with the egg yolks, cream and seasonings. Flake with a fork, then mash until smooth. Beat the egg whites until stiff. Fold gently into the salmon mixture. Pour into a well-greased mold or loaf pan. Set the pan in a pan of hot water (about 1 inch) and bake in a preheated 350° oven for 30 minutes. Remove from the oven and allow to cool slightly before unmolding. Serves 3.

HOT TUNA SALAD

2 tablespoons butter
1 slice homemade Oatmeal Bread
3 cups Tuna Salad (see Salads)
6 to 8 large stuffed Spanish olives, sliced

Melt the butter in a small saucepan. Toast the bread in the broiler, then cube it. Add the toast cubes to the butter and toss until all the butter is absorbed. Place the tuna salad in a well-greased casserole, top with the bread cubes and garnish with the sliced olives. Place in a moderate oven (325°) and bake for 30 to 40 minutes, or until hot and browned. Entire recipe=1 unit carbohydrate. Serves 3 or 4.

TUNA À LA KING

1 tablespoon butter
¼ cup finely chopped green pepper
½ small onion, minced fine
1 cup milk
⅓ cup non-fat dry milk
1 package frozen peas and carrots
1 cube Knorr-Swiss chicken bouillon
6 to 8 large stuffed Spanish olives, sliced
1 13-ounce can solid white meat tuna, separated into chunks

Melt the butter in a large pan, and add the pepper and onion. Sauté until soft, stirring. Do not brown. Add the milk and stir in the dry milk. Heat, stirring, until smooth. Add the frozen vegetables, cover and simmer for 5 minutes. Add the remaining ingredients, crumbling the bouillon cube between your fingers before adding it. (For extra flavor, do not drain the tuna.) Lower the heat, cover and simmer gently until heated through. Garnish with a few more olive slices before serving. Serves 3.

INSTANT TUNA À LA KING

1 13-ounce can chunk light meat tuna, drained slightly
2 cups leftover cream soup (see Soups)
¼ cup salad olives, chopped

Combine the ingredients; simmer until heated through (about 10 minutes). Serves 3.

TOMATO HERRING

½ cup Pretty Pepper Dressing (see Sauces and Dressings)
½ cup tomato purée
1 large can mackerel, drained

Combine the dressing and the tomato purée and mix well. Pour over the mackerel and marinate in the refrigerator for several hours or overnight. Serve cold on a bed of lettuce. Serves 3.

SKEWERED SCALLOPS

1½ pounds fresh or frozen scallops (if frozen, thaw)
Juice of 1 large lemon
¼ cup oil or melted butter

Spread the scallops in a pan; squeeze the lemon juice over them
and marinate for 10 minutes. Place the scallops on shish kebab
skewers. Brush with oil or melted butter, and drizzle the remaining
lemon juice over them again. Broil 3 to 5 minutes, turning several
times, until cooked through. Serves 3.

SHRIMP COCKTAIL

Water as needed
1 pound frozen shelled extra large or jumbo shrimp
Lettuce as desired

Heat about 1 inch of water in a large deep pot. When boiling
vigorously, toss in the frozen shrimp. Return to a full boil, cover
and remove the pot from the heat. Allow to sit for 5 minutes.
Shrimp should be pinkish white and opaque. Drain, chill. When
cold, transfer to a serving plate with lettuce. Serve with lemon
wedges and Seafood Cocktail Sauce (see Sauces and Dressings).
Serves 4.

GINGER SHRIMP

2 tablespoons peanut oil
2 stalks celery, sliced thin
¼ cup minced scallions
1½ pounds raw shrimp, shelled (if frozen, thaw partially)
1 bottle diet ginger ale, sugarless
1 tablespoon Kikkoman soy sauce
1 can bean sprouts, rinsed and drained
Minced scallion tops as needed

Heat the oil in a large pan. Sauté the celery and scallions. Slice the
shrimp in half lengthwise and add to the pan. Stir and fry until the

shrimp are beginning to turn opaque. Add the ginger ale and soy sauce, cover and simmer about 5 minutes, or until the shrimp are cooked. Drain the bean sprouts and squeeze all the moisture out of them. Add to the pan and heat 5 minutes. Stir in a small amount of scallion tops as a garnish and serve. Serves 3.

SHRIMP CREOLE

1 large green pepper, diced
2 1-pound cans tomatoes (check label)
½ package frozen sliced okra (slice the package in half with a serrated knife)
2 ¼-grain tablets saccharin
Pinch of thyme
1 stalk celery, diced
½ cup tomato purée
Salt to taste
Pinch of parsley flakes
1½ pounds small raw shrimp, shelled and deveined

Combine all ingredients except the shrimp in a large pot. Simmer covered for 5 minutes. Set the cover slightly ajar and simmer 30 minutes, or until the sauce is thickened. Add the shrimp, cover and simmer 5 minutes, or until the shrimp are cooked. Serves 4.

FRIED SHRIMP

1 egg, slightly beaten
¼ cup oat flour
½ teaspoon salt
½ teaspoon paprika
Evaporated milk as needed
1 pound extra large shrimp, peeled and deveined (if frozen, thaw and drain)
Shortening as needed

Beat the egg and gradually stir in the flour, mixing to a paste. Add the seasonings, then add a few drops of evaporated milk, until the mixture resembles pancake batter (not too thin, or it won't coat the shrimp properly). Dip the shrimp in the batter, stirring to coat well. Leave in the batter until ready to fry. In a skillet or deep-fat fryer, heat enough shortening to cover the shrimp, at least 1 inch. When the fat is very hot, drop the shrimp a few at a time into the pan and fry until crisp and brown outside (shrimp will tend to float when done). Drain, repeat until all the shrimp are fried. Serve hot with homemade Tartar Sauce (*see* Sauces and Dressings). Entire recipe=2 units carbohydrate. Serves 2.

BARBECUED OYSTERS

12 raw oysters on half shell
1 tablespoon butter
Salt, pepper to taste
½ slice homemade bread
Homemade Instant Ketchup (*see* Sauces and Dressings)

Place the oysters on half shell on a broiler rack. Dot each oyster with a small dab of butter, then season to taste. Toast the bread and crumb in the blender. Sprinkle the crumbs on the oysters, and top each with a dab (½ teaspoon) of the ketchup. Place in the broiler 4 to 6 inches from the heat and broil for just a few minutes. Serve with lemon wedges. If high-carbohydrate bread is used, entire recipe—1 unit carbohydrate. Serves 2.

OYSTERS IN JACKETS

12 raw oysters, shelled
6 slices smoked bacon, half cooked

Wrap each oyster with half a bacon slice. Secure with a toothpick. Place on a rack in a shallow pan and bake at 400° for 30 minutes, or until the bacon is crisp. Serve with the drippings from the pan. Serves 2.

DEVILED CLAMS

2 dozen raw cherrystone clams
4 tablespoons butter
½ cup chopped celery
1 small onion, chopped
¼ cup chopped green pepper
1 tablespoon oat flour
¾ cup milk
1 thick slice homemade Oatmeal Bread
1 teaspoon salt
½ teaspoon dehydrated parsley flakes
½ teaspoon thyme
¼ teaspoon pepper

Steam the clams (or buy them already steamed if you prefer). Wash the shells and set them aside. Chop the clams and set aside. Melt the butter in a saucepan; add the vegetables and sauté until soft. Add the flour and mix, then gradually add the milk and stir until smooth. Toast the bread and crumb in the blender. Add the bread crumbs, clams and seasoning to the vegetables. Cook for 5 minutes. Place the clam shells on a rack and fill with the clam mixture (or fill a greased muffin tin if you prefer). Broil for 10 minutes, until brown and bubbly. Or bake at 400° for 15 to 20 minutes. Entire recipe=1 unit carbohydrate. Serves 3.

DEVILED CRAB

2 tablespoons butter
1 small onion, minced fine
1 thick slice homemade Oatmeal Bread
1 pound crab meat, flaked
2 tablespoons heavy cream
2 tablespoons soy flour
Dash of cayenne pepper
¼ teaspoon paprika
Pinch of thyme

1 egg, slightly beaten
½ teaspoon dry mustard
½ teaspoon salt
Dash of freshly ground pepper
Oil as needed

Melt the butter, add the onion and sauté until soft. Crumb the bread in the blender. Mix together all the ingredients except oil, and correct seasoning to taste. Shape into cakes. Heat ⅛ inch of oil in a heavy skillet and fry the cakes briefly until browned on both sides. Transfer to a preheated 350° oven and bake until puffy and brown (30 minutes). Makes approximately 8 cakes. Entire recipe=1 unit carbohydrate. Serves 4.

FISH CAKES

½ cup water
1 cup frozen sliced carrots
1 pound white fish fillets (sole, flounder, cod, etc.)
1 extra large egg
½ cup cream or evaporated milk
¼ cup soy flour
1 tablespoon butter
1 tablespoon minced onion
½ teaspoon salt
Dash of nutmeg
Dash of freshly ground pepper
1 thick slice homemade Oatmeal Bread, crumbed fine in the blender
Oil as needed

Heat the water and cook the carrots, covered, until soft enough to mash. Remove the carrots and set aside. Add a little more water to the pan if needed and cook the fish, covered, for 5 minutes, or until fish can be flaked with a fork. Set aside. In the blender, combine the egg, cream, flour, butter and seasonings. Blend and add to the cooked fish. Add the carrots and half of the bread crumbs. Mash the entire mixture well with a fork, until thoroughly mixed. Chill until the mixture is fairly stiff. Form into patties or croquettes of the desired shape. Roll carefully in the rest of the bread crumbs. Fry in ¼ inch of hot fat until evenly browned. Remove and drain on paper towels. Serves 4; each serving=a trace of carbohydrate, ½ unit high-carbohydrate vegetable.

CODFISH CAKES

1 pound cod fillets
½ cup water
½ cup soy flour
1 egg, slightly beaten
¼ cup heavy cream
2 tablespoons finely minced fresh parsley
¼ cup oat flour
2 to 4 scallions, finely chopped
½ teaspoon salt
Dash of freshly ground pepper
Oil as needed

Place the cod fillets and water in a saucepan; cover and simmer until the fish flakes easily with a fork (about 10 minutes). Add the other ingredients except oil and mix well. Form into balls or patties. Fry in an oiled skillet (about ⅛ inch of oil) until brown on all sides. Serves 4; each serving=½ unit carbohydrate.

SALMON CROQUETTES

2 slices homemade Oatmeal Bread
2 eggs
1 medium onion, quartered
1 1-pound can red salmon, drained
½ teaspoon paprika
½ teaspoon salt
Dash of freshly ground pepper
Oil or shortening as needed

Crumb the bread in the blender and transfer to a large bowl. Place the eggs and onion in the blender and blend by turning the blender on and off until the onion is grated, but not liquefied. Pour the mixture into the bowl with the crumbs. Flake the salmon with a fork and add to the onion mixture. Season and mix well.

Heat shortening in a deep-fat fryer or melt ¼ inch of shortening or oil in a frying pan. When the fat is hot, scoop the salmon mixture into the pan using an ice-cream scoop. This should make about 8 croquettes. If the mixture is too runny, add 1 tablespoon oat flour. Fry until evenly browned. Remove and drain on paper towels. Serves 4; each serving=½ unit carbohydrate.

SOUPS

Can there be anything better than hot homemade soup in the winter? Soup is so easy to make, we are always amazed at how few people make their own. If you have always made your own soups, you will find that many of your favorite recipes can be used almost unchanged. You will have to leave out the potatoes, barley, rice and noodles, and find substitutes such as are used in the following recipes. Many fine recipes can be found in any classic cookbook. We have given a variety of recipes to show how you can adapt any soup recipe to fit your needs.

The main purpose of this chapter though is to give you a substitute for that familiar red and white can of instant condensed soup, without which we are lost. There are so many recipes that begin with: "Take a can of condensed cream of mushroom soup . . ." Is it possible to cook without these time savers? And what do we do without that winter stand-by, the canned soup-and-sandwich lunch?

This is why we have concentrated on quick, easily made soups (five to ten minutes' preparation time) and "instant" soups (five minutes' preparation time, five minutes' cooking time). These can be used as soups, or as the basis for sauces, dips and gravies, just as your prepared soups were used. All unnecessary steps and utensils have been eliminated. Some of these soups can be prepared in five to ten minutes in the morning and forgotten until suppertime.

Do they taste the same as canned soups? Some will taste better, others will be just as good, but all are designed to make life on a low-carbohydrate diet just a little bit easier.

ALLOWED PREPARED SOUPS

GARNISHES

Basic Beef Stock
Basic Chicken Stock
Instant Chicken and "Rice"
  Soup
Vegetable Soup
Instant Vegetarian Vegetable
  Soup
Blender Vegetable Soup
Turkey Vegetable Soup
Italian Ham Soup
Gazpacho
Three-vegetable Soup
Steak Bone Soup
Meat Loaf Soup
Cabbage Soup
Bean Soup
Tomato Soup
Cream of Tomato Soup
Mushroom Broth
Instant Cream of Mushroom
  Soup
Double-rich Cream of Mushroom
  Soup

Easy Manhattan Clam Chowder
Instant Clam Chowder
New England Clam Chowder
Bouillabaisse
Oyster Stew
Winter's Night Oyster Stew
Cream of Vegetable Soup
Mock Split Pea Soup
Cheese Soup
Cream of Spinach Soup
Cream of Asparagus Soup
Mock Cream of Potato Soup
Vichyssoise
Cream of Turkey Soup
Instant Cream of Chicken Soup
Golden Chicken Soup with
  "Knaidlach" (Dumplings):
  see Foreign and Regional
Golden Chicken Soup with
  Kreplach: see Foreign and
  Regional
Won Ton Soup: see Foreign and
  Regional
Egg Drop Soup: see Foreign and
  Regional
Minestrone: see Foreign and
  Regional

ALLOWED PREPARED SOUPS

These are a few of the soups which we've found to be free of sugar and starches.

The formulas may change, so check the label each time you buy them:

Campbell's Frozen Oyster Stew
Clear Bouillon: Knorr-Swiss Chicken and Beef (large cubes, makes 2 cups of soup); Barnet Bouillon cubes (small, each makes 1 cup)

Canned Soup: College Inn Chicken Broth; Shop-Rite Chicken Broth; some of the Progresso and S. S. Pierce soups: read the labels carefully

Knorr-Swiss Dry Onion Soup and Dip Mix (comes in foil envelope)

GARNISHES

Slivered pork
Cooked chicken, shredded
Minced scallion tops
Minced celery tops
Dehydrated parsley flakes
French toast, cubed (*see* Breakfast Foods)
Homemade dumplings or noodles (*see* Breads, Pasta and Noodles)
Toasted minced onion
Toasted almond slivers
Grated Parmesan cheese
Hard-cooked egg yolks, riced
Sprigs of fresh parsley

BASIC BEEF STOCK

(*Step 1*). Collect the bones, drippings and trimmings from your roasts and steaks in a bag in the freezer (also, gravy and those nice crusty drippings which you can save easily if you line your pans with aluminum foil). Add some marrowbones from your butcher and leftover meat and meat loaf.

(*Step 2*). When you have enough to fill a large (5-quart) pot, add 2 to 4 quarts of water, ¼ cup of white vinegar, 1 large onion and 1 tablespoon salt. Cover, simmer 2 to 3 hours and set aside to cool. (The vinegar helps to draw the calcium out of the bones and into the water. By the time the soup is finished the vinegar odor and flavor will have disappeared.)

(*Step 3*). Chill in the refrigerator until the fat congeals on top. Remove the bones and most of the fat. Shred the meat and return it, with ¼ cup of the fat to the pot. Heat until the fat is melted. Use in any recipe, or freeze in 1- and 2-cup containers for future use.

Variations:

1. Use a veal knuckle and veal bones, along with the other meat.
2. Prepare as above, adding 1 clove garlic, I bay leaf and a sprig of parsley.
3. For richer broth, use an inexpensive roast or meaty shin bone, in addition to the drippings, etc.
4. Use a combination of beef, veal and ham bone.
5. After chilling, remove all fat. Serve as jellied consommé.
6. Prepare as above, plus 1 quart of tomato juice.
7. For quick stock: place your beef, bones and trimmings in a pressure cooker with 4 cups of water. Add the onion, vinegar and seasonings. Cook for ½ hour, then allow the pressure to fall by itself (½ hour more). Pour into individual ice molds or ½-cup containers and freeze. This makes a highly concentrated stock, and should be diluted when used. Use whenever bouillon is called for.

BASIC CHICKEN STOCK

(*Step 1*). Place 1 roasting chicken, including the neck, in a large pot. Cover with water. Add 1 tablespoon salt, ¼ cup vinegar and 1 large onion. (The vinegar draws the calcium out of the bones and into the soup. By the time the soup is finished the flavor and odor is gone. If you prefer, you can also use lemon juice.) Cover and simmer for at least 3 hours.

(*Step 2*). Remove the chicken. Discard the bones and skin. Strip off all the meat and set it aside. Chill the soup. When the fat is congealed, remove all but ¼ cup of it. Return the meat to the soup.

(*Step 3*). Return the soup to the stove. Tie together 1 small bunch of parsley and 1 small bunch of dill weed. Place in the soup, along with 1 large carrot (whole), 1 large onion or leek, 1 large parsnip (whole) and 4 stalks of celery, including the tops (do not peel or cut the vegetables). Cover and simmer until the vegetables are cooked through. Remove from the heat and steep for 1 hour. Remove the herbs; serve as is or pour the soup into containers to freeze. Be sure to taste and correct seasoning before serving. You will probably want to dilute the soup further with water, and if so, you can add salt, pepper and some more of the fat which was removed in *Step 2*.

Variations:

1. Make as above, but use only 1½ quarts of water. Pour into ice-cube molds. To use, add 1 cup of water to 1 cube of frozen soup.

2. Make according to the directions. Dice the meat and vegetables and mince the parsley and dill weed before adding to the soup. Serve with a generous helping of meat and vegetables in each bowl.

3. Make the soup according to the directions. Chill and remove all fat. Serve cold as jellied consommé.

INSTANT CHICKEN AND "RICE" SOUP

4 to 6 cups College Inn Chicken Broth or Knorr-Swiss Chicken
    Bouillon
½ teaspoon dehydrated celery flakes
½ teaspoon dehydrated parsley flakes
1 teaspoon minced onion flakes
Dash of pepper
Salt to taste if needed
½ cup H-O quick oatmeal (not instant)

Combine the ingredients and bring to a boil. Reduce heat and cover. Simmer for 1 minute. Serves 2 to 4. Entire recipe=2 units carbohydrate.

VEGETABLE SOUP

1 large pot Basic Beef Stock
1 package frozen peas and carrots
1 cup cooked soybeans or 1 can plain cooked soybeans
4 stalks celery, sliced, plus the tops
1 large onion, diced
½ teaspoon basil
Dash of thyme
1 large can tomatoes
1 package frozen French-style green beans
1 green pepper, diced
1 sprig parsley
Salt, pepper to taste

Prepare the stock according to the directions. Add the rest of the ingredients. Cover and simmer slowly until the vegetables are tender, but not mushy. Correct seasoning and serve. Serves 8 to 10.

INSTANT VEGETARIAN VEGETABLE SOUP

4 cups water
1 package frozen peas and carrots
1 tablespoon instant onion flakes
1 teaspoon dehydrated celery flakes
½ teaspoon onion powder
Pinch of parsley or thyme
2 cups tomato juice
2 tablespoons dehydrated soup vegetables
Dash of liquid artificial sweetener
1 tablespoon dehydrated green pepper flakes
Dash of freshly ground pepper
Salt to taste

Combine all ingredients; cover and simmer on low until the vegetables are just tender. Total time: 10 minutes. Serves 4; each serving= 1 unit high-carbohydrate vegetable.

BLENDER VEGETABLE SOUP

1 large raw carrot, sliced
½ large Bermuda onion, cubed
1 parsnip, sliced
1 green pepper, cubed
2 stalks celery, sliced
1 quart water
1 quart tomato juice
2 Knorr-Swiss bouillon cubes
Salt, pepper to taste
2 tablespoons dehydrated soup vegetables
½ teaspoon parsley flakes

Place the vegetables, a few pieces at a time, in the blender. Add some of the water. Blend until grated. Pour into a saucepan and continue adding vegetables and liquid until all the vegetables are grated. Combine all ingredients in the saucepan. Cover and simmer for 15 to 30 minutes, or until the vegetables are cooked and the flavors blended. This makes a light creamy soup, and can be served also as a hot beverage. Serves 6; entire recipe=1 unit high-carbohydrate vegetable.

TURKEY VEGETABLE SOUP

Bones, carcass, skin, leftover gravy and leftover stuffing from a roast turkey
Water to cover
1 tablespoon lemon juice
1 tablespoon salt
2 large ribs celery, chopped, with tops
1 parsnip, diced
1 package frozen peas
Dash of thyme
1 onion, diced
½ bay leaf
Water as needed

Break up the turkey carcass. Place the bones, meat and all leftovers in a pressure cooker. Cover with water and add the lemon juice and salt. Be sure not to fill more than two thirds full. Cook for 15 minutes. Remove from the stove and let the pressure fall by itself. (If you don't use a pressure cooker, place in a large pot, cover and simmer over medium low heat for 2 to 3 hours.) Strain the broth into a large pot. Add the other ingredients to the broth, plus water to taste. Cover and simmer until the vegetables are cooked, but not mushy. Remove any pieces of turkey from the discarded carcass, dice and add to soup. Serves about 6; each serving=⅔ unit high-carbohydrate vegetable.

ITALIAN HAM SOUP

1 tablespoon butter
1 thick slice of smoked ham, diced
1 medium zucchini, chopped
2 large leeks, sliced thin
2 carrots, diced
1½ quarts stock or Knorr-Swiss bouillon
Salt, pepper to taste
Grated Parmesan cheese

Melt the butter in a pan. Add the ham and vegetables, stirring until the onions are soft. Add the stock and simmer for 45 minutes. Serve topped with Parmesan cheese. Serves 4.

GAZPACHO

3 thick slices homemade Oatmeal Bread
¼ cup white vinegar
½ teaspoon thyme
¼ cup olive oil
3 pieces pimiento
2 hard-cooked eggs, peeled
Salt, pepper to taste
3 cups water plus more as needed
1 1-pound can of tomatoes or 4 medium tomatoes
½ teaspoon oregano
1 clove garlic, crushed
½ Bermuda onion, chopped
½ cucumber, peeled and sliced

Place all ingredients in the blender (reserve a few slices of cucumber). Blend well. Pour into a bowl and refrigerate. Serve cold and garnish with cucumber slices. Serves 3; each serving=1 unit carbohydrate.

THREE-VEGETABLE SOUP

12 ounces tomato juice
4 cups water plus more if needed
1 Knorr-Swiss chicken bouillon cube
½ cup thinly sliced mushrooms
1 teaspoon dehydrated celery tops
1 small zucchini, cubed
2 cups small chunks raw cauliflower
2 ¼-grain tablets saccharin
1 tablespoon dehydrated minced onion
Salt, pepper to taste

Combine all ingredients. Cover and simmer gently until the vegetables are cooked. Serves 4.

STEAK BONE SOUP

Bones, fat, pan drippings and meat leftover from 2 broiled steaks
    (save in the freezer until you have enough to make a really rich
    soup)
6 cups water
2 tablespoons lemon juice
1 Knorr-Swiss beef bouillon cube
1 onion, chopped fine
1 package frozen peas and carrots
Dash of garlic powder
⅛ teaspoon sherry flavoring

Place the bones, fat, etc., from the steaks in the bottom of a pressure cooker. Add 2 cups of the water, the lemon juice and bouillon cube. Pressure cook for 15 minutes (or simmer in a covered pot for 1½ to 2 hours). Reduce the pressure and strain the liquid off into a large pot. Add the rest of the ingredients, cover and simmer until the vegetables are cooked (about 10 minutes). Skim off the excess fat and correct the seasoning. If there is any lean meat left in the pressure cooker, trim it and add to the soup. This makes a rich brown soup. Try making it right after a steak meal while cleaning up, then serve it the next day as a soup course or part of a protein snack. Serves 4; each serving=1 unit high-carbohydrate vegetable.

MEAT LOAF SOUP

1 cup leftover meat loaf (or more)
2 cups water plus more to taste
1 package frozen peas and carrots
1 cup gravy or pan drippings and fat from the meat loaf
2 cups tomato juice
1 large can French-style green beans
Salt, pepper to taste

Crumble the meat loaf with your fingers. Combine with the rest of the ingredients, and cover. Bring to a low boil. Simmer gently until the vegetables are cooked (about 10 to 15 minutes). Correct seasoning and serve. If this is too greasy, skim, or add 1 cup homemade Soy Noodles. Serves 4; each serving=1 unit high-carbohydrate vegetables.

CABBAGE SOUP

2 to 3 quarts water
1 pound beef flanken
1 beef marrowbone
1 tablespoon salt
1 small head cabbage, shredded
1 large onion, diced
1 large carrot, whole
Juice of 1 small lemon
2 ¼-grain tablets saccharin plus more if needed

Heat the water to boiling. Add the meat, bone and salt. Cover and simmer on low for 2 hours. Add the remaining ingredients and simmer 1 hour. Add more lemon if needed, and correct the other seasonings. Makes about 2½ quarts.

BEAN SOUP

1 cup yellow soybeans
1 quart water plus more as needed
2 ounces salt pork
1 teaspoon salt or to taste
2 cups milk
1 large onion, sliced
½ teaspoon pepper

Soak the beans in the water overnight. Pour into a deep pot and add another quart of water. Cover and simmer 4 to 6 hours, until the beans are soft. Add the other ingredients and simmer 1 to 2 hours. If you have a ham bone or any leftover ham, bacon, etc., they can be added to the soup during the last stage of cooking. Serves 4 to 6. With ham this can be served as a main dish.

TOMATO SOUP

1 46-ounce can tomato juice
1 tablespoon minced onion or ½ small onion, chopped
¼ teaspoon ground cloves
Dash of freshly ground pepper
Salt to taste
2 cups beef broth or Knorr-Swiss bouillon
½ bay leaf
1 sprig fresh parsley, minced fine
1 ¼-grain tablet saccharin

Combine all ingredients. Bring to a low boil and simmer for 5 minutes. If the flavor is too strong, dilute with water. Serves 4 to 6.

CREAM OF TOMATO SOUP

Same as Tomato Soup, plus ½ cup non-fat dry milk, ½ cup evaporated milk and 1 tablespoon butter.

MUSHROOM BROTH

2 tablespoons butter
3 carrots, minced fine
1 leek (or ½ Bermuda onion), minced
2 stalks celery, minced fine
1 pound mushrooms
2 quarts water
1 teaspoon chopped fresh parsley
1 bay leaf
¼ teaspoon thyme
Salt, pepper to taste

Melt the butter in a large pot. Add the carrots, leek and celery to the pot and sauté without browning over low heat. Slice the mushrooms lengthwise, including the stems. Add to the pot. Add the water and seasonings. Cover and simmer for 1 hour. Serves 6.

INSTANT CREAM OF MUSHROOM SOUP

1 large can mushrooms
½ cup light cream
½ Knorr-Swiss chicken bouillon cube
⅓ cup non-fat dry milk
1½ cups milk
Dash of parsley flakes

Combine all ingredients in the blender. Blend on low until puréed. Pour into a saucepan, cover and simmer. Cook over low heat, stirring occasionally, until hot but not boiling. Serves 2; each serving=1 unit milk.

DOUBLE-RICH CREAM OF MUSHROOM SOUP

¼ cup butter
½ pound fresh mushrooms, sliced
3 cups Basic Chicken Stock or chicken bouillon (*see* Brand Names)
3 egg yolks
1 tablespoon finely minced fresh parsley
Dash of freshly grated nutmeg
Salt, pepper to taste
½ cup cream
⅓ cup non-fat dry milk

Melt the butter in a saucepan. Add the mushrooms and sauté until cooked, about 5 minutes. Pour all but a few mushrooms into a blender container, add the broth and egg yolks. Blend until smooth. Stir in the parsley and nutmeg and correct the seasoning. Return to the heat, and stir in the cream and dry milk. Heat gently, stirring until thick and hot. Do not boil. Pour into individual soup bowls and garnish with the remaining mushrooms. Serves 2 or 3; each serving= ½ unit milk.

EASY MANHATTAN CLAM CHOWDER

2 cups tomato juice
2 cups water
1 can cut green beans, including liquid
1 small zucchini
¼ cup dehydrated soup vegetables
1 teaspoon thyme
1 cup finely chopped celery (including tops)
2 tablespoons dehydrated minced onion
½ teaspoon parsley flakes
Dash of cayenne pepper
Salt to taste
Dash of liquid artificial sweetener
1 10-ounce can minced or baby clams, including liquid
1 bottle clam broth

Heat the tomato juice and water. Add the vegetables, herbs, seasonings, sweetener, and cover. Simmer until the vegetables are just tender, but not mushy. Add the clams and broth. Heat through and serve. Serves 4. To serve as a main dish, add another can of clams.

INSTANT CLAM CHOWDER

Same as Easy Manhattan Clam Chowder, but omit 1 cup of the water and the zucchini and celery. Serves 4.

NEW ENGLAND CLAM CHOWDER

The core of a fresh cauliflower (not the flowerettes)
⅔ cup non-fat dry milk
2 cups beef stock, bouillon or water
1 10-ounce can clams and broth
1 tablespoon butter
1 tablespoon minced onion
2 cups milk
1 sprig or ½ teaspoon minced parsley
Salt to taste

Dice the cauliflower. Heat the milk and stock together. Add the cauliflower. Simmer uncovered for 10 minutes, or until the cauliflower is the consistency of cooked potato. Add the other ingredients and heat through Serves 4; each serving=1 unit milk.

BOUILLABAISSE

2 tablespoons olive oil
2 leeks, chopped
1 onion, chopped
2 16-ounce cans tomatoes
2 cloves garlic, chopped
½ teaspoon salt
¼ teaspoon each: thyme, parsley, celery seed, pepper
1 bay leaf, crumbled
2 pounds fish fillets, cut into bite-sized chunks
2 dozen shellfish
1 pound lobster meat
1 can crab meat
4 cups tomato juice or water

Heat the oil in a large pot. Add the vegetables, seasonings and fish. Cool for 5 minutes. Add the shellfish, lobster and crab. Add tomato juice or water, cover and cook over low heat for 45 minutes. Correct seasoning as needed. This is a great soup for company, and can be used as a main dish for an easy meal. Serves 8 to 10.

OYSTER STEW

2 tablespoons butter
1 quart fresh or frozen shelled oysters (including liquid in container, if any)
1 cup cold water
1 quart milk, scalded
2 teaspoons salt
Dash of paprika
¼ teaspoon pepper

Melt the butter in a skillet. Add the oysters and oyster liquid and water. Bring to a low boil. Remove the oysters with a slotted spoon and place in the heated milk; set them aside. Add the seasoning to the oyster liquid and boil 1 minute. Stir into the milk and top with

an additional dash of paprika and additional butter if desired. Serves
4; each serving=1 unit milk.

WINTER'S NIGHT OYSTER STEW

1 can Campbell's frozen oyster stew
1 medium can asparagus, including juice
Salt, pepper to taste if needed
½ teaspoon chopped chives
1 tablespoon butter

Prepare the oyster stew according to the directions on the package.
Add the remaining ingredients and simmer slowly for 5 minutes, or
until heated through (do not boil). Serves 2 or 3. Each serving=1
unit milk.

CREAM OF VEGETABLE SOUP

2 stalks celery
1 leek
3 carrots
1 small onion
3 quarts Basic Beef Stock or water
1 clove garlic, crushed
¼ teaspon fennel
Salt, pepper to taste
3 sprigs parsley
¼ teaspoon thyme
½ bay leaf
1 cup tomato purée
1 cup non-fat dry milk
1 tablespoon butter

Chop the vegetables and place in the blender with 2 cups of the
stock. Blend until liquefied. Add the garlic and herbs. Pour into a
large pot with the rest of the liquid and simmer over low heat for 1
hour, or until the flavors are blended, stirring occasionally. Scoop
about 1 cup of the soup into a bowl. Mix in the dry milk until smooth,

and add to the soup. Cook until creamy. Add butter, correct the
seasonings and serve. Serves 6; each serving=½ unit milk.

MOCK SPLIT PEA SOUP

3 slices smoked bacon
1 package frozen peas
1½ cups water
2 cups milk
1 cup light cream
Dash of freshly ground pepper
½ teaspoon salt

Sauté the bacon until soft. Add the peas and water. Bring to a boil,
cover and lower the heat. Simmer until the peas are soft. Pour into
the blender and blend on low until puréed. Return to the heat, add
the remaining ingredients and seasonings. Cook uncovered, stirring,
until heated. Serves 4; 1 serving=1 unit limited vegetable, ½ unit
milk.

CHEESE SOUP

4 cups Basic Beef Broth or bouillon (see Brand Names)
1 carrot, diced
2 large ribs celery, including tops, minced
1 small onion, diced
1 cup milk
1 cup non-fat dry milk
6 ounces American cheese, diced
1 sprig parsley
Pinch of nutmeg
Salt, pepper to taste

Combine the stock and vegetables in a saucepan. Cover and simmer
for 30 minutes. In a bowl combine the milk and dry milk. Mix
thoroughly and add to the soup. Heat but do not boil. Add the
cheese and seasoning. Stir until the cheese melts. Pour into the
blender and blend until the vegetables are puréed, but not liquefied.
This is a very rich cream of vegetable soup; you will not be able to

tell it has been made with cheese, the flavor is so unusual. Serves 4; each serving=1 unit milk.

CREAM OF SPINACH SOUP

2 cups water
1 package frozen chopped spinach
⅔ cup non-fat dry milk
2 cups milk
Pinch of nutmeg
1 Knorr-Swiss chicken bouillon cube
Salt, pepper to taste
1 tablespoon butter

Heat the water, add the spinach and cook until tender. Pour into the blender. Add the dry milk. Blend until the spinach is puréed. Return to the pan, add the other ingredients, and simmer until heated through. Serves 4; each serving=1 unit milk.

CREAM OF ASPARAGUS SOUP

1 package frozen or 1 pound fresh asparagus, trimmed
3 cups water
½ cup cubed ham
1 tablespoon butter
1 tablespoon dehydrated onion flakes
⅓ cup non-fat dry milk
3 cups milk
1 tablespoon minced parsley
Salt to taste

Cook the asparagus in the water until the stalks are tender, but not soft. Place in the blender with the rest of the ingredients. Blend until puréed. Return to the stove. Heat, but do not boil. Correct seasoning to taste, and add more water if needed. Serves 4; each serving=1 unit milk.

MOCK CREAM OF POTATO SOUP

1 small head cauliflower
1 tablespoon butter
¼ teaspoon pepper
6 cups milk
2 cups water
1 teaspoon salt
½ teaspoon parsley flakes

Break the cauliflower into tiny flowerettes. Chop the core and branches into small pieces. Combine all ingredients in a pan. Cover and heat almost to the boiling point. Lower the heat and simmer until the cauliflower is very soft. Correct the seasoning, and serve. For a creamier soup, blend in the blender untill puréed. This soup makes an excellent sauce and can be used as a base for casseroles. Serves 6; each serving=1 unit milk.

VICHYSSOISE

Same as Mock Cream of Potato, plus 2 large leeks, sautéed in butter before adding the other ingredients. After blending, chill and serve cold. Garnish with chopped chives. Serves 6.

CREAM OF TURKEY SOUP

Bones, carcass, skin, leftover gravy and stuffing from a roast turkey
6 cups water
1 tablespoon lemon juice
1 tablespoon salt
½ cup evaporated milk
1 cup non-fat dry milk
2 stalks celery, including the tops, minced fine
1 large carrot, blended until grated
Pepper to taste

Break up the turkey carcass. Place the bones, meat, etc., in a large pot. Cover with water. Add the lemon juice and salt. Cover the pot and simmer for several hours. Strain the broth into another pot. Add the remaining ingredients and simmer for 30 minutes. Serves 4; each serving=1 unit milk.

INSTANT CREAM OF CHICKEN SOUP

4 cups milk
1 tablespoon butter
Salt, pepper to taste
2 Knorr-Swiss chicken bouillon cubes
⅔ cup non-fat dry milk
1 tablespoon dehydrated onion flakes
1 or 2 cups cooked chicken
4 cups water

Combine ingredients in the blender (leave out some of the milk if necessary). Blend until smooth and creamy. Transfer to a saucepan and heat, stirring. Correct seasoning. Serve immediately. Serves 6; each serving=1 unit milk.

VEGETABLES

If you were to make a list of the most popular American vegetables, french-fried potatoes would lead the list, followed by baked potatoes, baked beans and perhaps corn on the cob. These dishes, besides being delicious, have one thing in common: they're not allowed on the hypoglycemic's diet. Nor are most of the canned and prepared vegetables available in supermarkets and restaurants.

It's true that there are many vegetables we *are* allowed to have, but many of these will be new to you, and people tend to avoid eating new foods. Also, many people have an aversion to vegetables, perhaps because they have never had them in a palatable form. You should try to use a new recipe every week until your range of foods is enlarged. This diet is going to become extremely boring unless it is varied as much as possible. So pick out the recipe which sounds like the food you miss the most, and keep an open mind until you try it.

Included in this section you will find excellent substitutes for mashed potatoes (Mashed Cauliflower), french fries (French-fried Parsnips), baked beans (Baked Soybeans) and many others which will help to satisfy your craving for the starchier foods. We have also included many basic recipes and cooking instructions, on the assumption that some of the vegetables will be new to you, and therefore you may not know how to prepare them.

The amounts of vegetables allowed and not allowed were given earlier. Since this is a lot of information to keep looking up, we have included a listing here of the vegetables allowed with their suggested amounts and percentages of carbohydrate.

An easy way to remember amounts is: 3 to 6 per cent carbohydrate vegetables, eat in large amounts; 10 per cent carbohydrate vegetables, eat in small to medium amounts; and 15 per cent carbohydrate vegetables, limit to small amounts, and try to have little or no other carbohydrate at that meal. To help you at first, weigh your portions on a small postage scale, or measure in a half-cup measure. If you find the amounts suggested are still too high for you, cut them back; if you find you can tolerate a little more, add a bit more.

Following is a list of allowed vegetables, in order of use in the diet:

VEGETABLES ALLOWED

3 to 6 per cent carbohydrate: suggested portion, 4 to 10 ounces at lunch and supper

Asparagus
Bamboo shoots
Bean sprouts
Beet greens
Broccoli
Cabbage, raw
Cauliflower
Celery
Chard (Swiss chard)
Chicory
Chinese cabbage
Chives
Collard greens, raw
Cucumbers
Dandelion greens
Eggplant
Endive
Escarole
Fennel
Kale
Leeks
Lettuce
Mustard greens
Mushrooms

Okra
Olives, green and black
Onions, cooked
Parsley
Pea pods (snow peas)
Peppers
Pickles (sour, half-sour, dill)
Pimientos
Radishes
Rhubarb
Sauerkraut
Scallions
Spinach
String beans, French-style only
Summer squash (yellow, crookneck)
Tomatoes (fresh, canned without sugar)
Turnips, white
Turnip greens
Water chestnuts
Watercress
Wax beans, French-style only
Zucchini, fresh or frozen

10 per cent carbohydrate: suggested portion, 4 ounces or ½ cup at lunch or supper

Artichoke
Brussels sprouts
Cabbage, cooked
Carrots (fresh, frozen or
    sugarless canned)
Celeriac
Collard greens, cooked

Chervil
Green beans (string beans)
Kohlrabi
Onions, raw
Rutabaga (yellow turnip)
Tomato purée

15 per cent carbohydrate: limit to a total of 4 ounces or ½ cup at supper, and cut down on other carbohydrates

Beets
Jerusalem artichokes
Parsnips
Peas (fresh, frozen or dietetic
    canned)
Pumpkin

Salsify
Soybeans (unless tolerated in
    larger amounts)
Squash, winter (hubbard, acorn,
    butternut)

Stuffed Artichokes Hearts
Artichokes with Garlic Butter
Marinated Artichoke Hearts
Yoga Asparagus
Baked Asparagus
Cheese-topped Asparagus
Braised Asparagus
Bacon-baked Asparagus
Asparagus Amandine
Asparagus with Hollandaise
    Sauce
Simple Bamboo Shoots
Bamboo Shoots Oriental
Buttered "Rice" (Bean Sprouts)
Baked Bean Sprouts
Sautéed Bean Sprouts

Brown Sprouts
Bean Sprout "Spaghetti"
Spanish "Rice"
Wilted Beet Greens
Harvard Beets
Stuffed Beets
Spiced Beets
Broccoli with Hollandaise Sauce
Broccoli with Lemon Butter
Broccoli au Gratin
Creamed Broccoli
Broccoli Soufflé
Scalloped Brussels Sprouts
Caraway Cabbage
Baked Sweet and Sour Cabbage
Unstuffed Cabbage

Scalloped Cabbage
Skillet Cabbage
Baked Cabbage
Cabbage Sticks
Minted Carrots
Carrots Amandine
Baked Carrots
Carrot Soufflé
Candied Carrots
Creamed Carrots
Carrot Ring
Mock "Mashed Potatoes"
   (Mashed Cauliflower)
Cheese-baked Cauliflower ⅜1
Cheese-baked Cauliflower ⅜2
Cauliflower Puffs
Scalloped Cauliflower
Braised Celery
Sautéed Celery
Creamed Celery
Marinated Cucumbers
Braised Cucumbers
Dandelion Greens
French Eggplant
French-fried Eggplant
Eggplant Fritters
Baked Eggplant
Jerusalem Artichokes
Baked Jerusalem Artichokes
Scalloped Jerusalem Artichokes
Creamed Kale
Baked Leeks
Sautéed Mushrooms
Baked Stuffed Mushrooms
Oriental Mushrooms
Mushrooms in Sour Cream
Cooked Okra
Baked Okra
Creamed Onions
Onion Pie

Fried Onion Rings
Mashed Parsnips
Baked Parsnips
French-fried Parsnips
Parsnip Pancakes
Creamed Parsnips
Candied Parsnips
Peas Parmesan
Peas with Pimientos
Peas and Mushrooms
Creamed Peas
French Peas
Cooked Pea Pods
Chinese Pea Pods
German-style Pea Pods
Stuffed Peppers
Fried Peppers
Stewed Peppers
Peppers and Eggplant
Fried Pimientos
Jiffy Pimientos
Buttered Pumpkin
Pumpkin Custard
   Turnip)
Yellow Turnip Croquettes
Mashed Rutabaga (Yellow
Baked Sauerkraut
Hot Spicy Kraut
Instant Sweet and Sour
   "Cabbage"
Sauerkraut and Apples with
   Pork Roast
Soybeans: An Introduction
Soybeans: Basic Cooking
   Instructions
Cooked Soybeans
"Baked Beans"
Boston "Baked Beans"
Spicy Barbecue Beans

MISCELLANEOUS

Chili con Carne: *see* Casseroles
"Frijoles" Refritos: *see* Foreign
   and Regional
Dill String Beans: *see* Preserves

Mock "Potato" Salad: *see*
   Salads
Wax Bean Lasagna: *see*
   Casseroles

ARTICHOKES: 10 per cent carbohydrate (medium)

STUFFED ARTICHOKE HEARTS

1 can artichoke hearts
2 tablespoons butter
¼ pound mushrooms, chopped fine
1 small onion, minced fine
Salt, pepper to taste
2 tablespoons grated Parmesan cheese

Heat the artichoke hearts and drain. Melt the butter in a frying pan and sauté the mushrooms and the onion. Stuff the mushroom mixture into the leaves of the artichokes, heaping the excess in mounds on top. Season and sprinkle with the cheese. Broil briefly until the cheese melts and browns slightly. Serves 4; 2 to 3 hearts=approximately 1 unit medium-carbohydrate vegetable.

ARTICHOKES WITH GARLIC BUTTER

1 whole artichoke
1 teaspoon to 1 tablespoon garlic powder to taste
¼ to ½ cup salt butter, melted

Cook the artichokes on a rack in a pressure cooker until tender (2 to 3 minutes). (To cook without a pressure cooker, steam on a rack in a covered pan with 1 cup water for 30 minutes, or until the leaves pull out easily.) Drain upside down. Stir the garlic powder into the melted butter. Serve with side cups of the garlic butter; eat by removing the leaves and dipping the ends into the seasoned butter. Serves 1; 1 artichoke=½ unit medium-carbohydrate vegetable.

MARINATED ARTICHOKE HEARTS

1 can artichoke hearts, drained
Dash of liquid artificial sweetener
½ cup white vinegar
Pinch of tarragon

Combine all ingredients. Marinate in the refrigerator overnight. Serve cold. Serves 4; 2 or 3 hearts=1 unit medium-carbohydrate vegetable.

ASPARAGUS: 3 to 6 per cent carbohydrate (low)

YOGA ASPARAGUS

1 pound fresh asparagus, washed and trimmed
Outer leaves of 1 head of lettuce
1 tablespoon water
Juice of ½ lemon
Salt to taste

Lay the lettuce leaves in an oiled skillet or Teflon-lined frying pan until the bottom is covered. Trim the bottoms off the asparagus and place on the lettuce leaves. Cover the pan tightly and steam over low heat until the asparagus is tender. Add more water if necessary to prevent burning. Asparagus should be firm but tender. Squeeze lemon over asparagus. Salt to taste and serve. Serves 4.

BAKED ASPARAGUS

1 15-ounce can asparagus spears
½ cup mayonnaise (homemade or sugarless)
1 tablespoon lemon juice
Pimiento strips as needed
Salt to taste

Drain the asparagus and place the spears in an oiled casserole. In a bowl, combine the mayonnaise and lemon juice; pour over the asparagus. Garnish with strips of pimiento. Bake at 325° until heated through (about 20 minutes). Salt to taste. Serves 3 or 4.

CHEESE-TOPPED ASPARAGUS

1 medium can asparagus spears, drained
2 slices Swiss cheese
Dash of paprika
Dash of onion salt

Spread the asparagus spears, touching, on heavy aluminum foil. Top with the cheese and seasonings. Broil 6 inches from the heat until the cheese is brown and bubbly. Serves 2.

BRAISED ASPARAGUS

1 pound fresh asparagus, washed and trimmed
2 tablespoons butter
½ onion, minced
½ cup beef stock or sugarless bouillon

Cut the asparagus tips into 3-inch lengths and cut the stalks into ½-inch pieces. Melt the butter and sauté the onion until soft. Add the asparagus and sauté for 5 minutes. Lower the heat, add the stock and cover. Simmer until tender (about 5 to 10 minutes). Serves 4.

BACON-BAKED ASPARAGUS

1 pound cooked or canned asparagus, drained
½ pound smoked bacon, fried until soft and translucent

Place the asparagus in a casserole. Spread the bacon over it in a single layer. Bake at 400° until the bacon is crisp. Serves 4.

ASPARAGUS AMANDINE

2 tablespoons butter
¼ cup slivered almonds
1 15-ounce can asparagus, drained

Melt the butter and sauté the almonds until brown. Add the asparagus, cover and heat. Serves 3 or 4.

ASPARAGUS WITH HOLLANDAISE SAUCE

Prepare Hollandaise Sauce (see Sauces and Dressings). Serve over hot cooked or canned asparagus.

BAMBOO SHOOTS: 3 to 6 per cent carbohydrate (low)

SIMPLE BAMBOO SHOOTS

½ cup water
½ Knorr-Swiss beef bouillon cube
1 tablespoon Kikkoman soy sauce
Dash of garlic powder
1 can sliced bamboo shoots, drained

Heat the water to boiling; add the bouillon cube and stir until dissolved. Add the seasonings and bamboo shoots and heat briefly. Serves 3.

BAMBOO SHOOTS ORIENTAL

1 tablespoon peanut oil
¼ cup minced scallions
½ cup chopped celery

1 can sliced bamboo shoots, drained
Dash of garlic powder
Pinch of MSG (optional)
2 tablespoons Kikkoman soy sauce
Salt to taste as needed
Minced scallion tops

Heat the oil, stir in the scallions and celery and fry until crisply cooked. Add remaining ingredients except scallion tops, and stir until heated through. Serve hot; garnish with minced scallion tops. Serves 4.

BEAN SPROUTS: 3 to 6 per cent carbohydrate (low)

BUTTERED "RICE" (BEAN SPROUTS)

1 can bean sprouts, drained
Butter and salt to taste

Chop the sprouts into rice-sized pieces. Plunge into boiling water and stir to heat. Remove from heat and drain immediately. Toss with butter and salt. Serve hot. Serves 3.

BAKED BEAN SPROUTS

1 small onion, minced fine
1 teaspoon butter
1 can bean sprouts, drained
1 cup beef stock (include any leftover gravy, bits of meat, etc.)
Salt to taste
Pinch of saffron
Freshly ground pepper

Sauté the onion in the butter until yellow. Combine the rest of the ingredients. Place in a casserole and bake in a slow oven (300°) until the sprouts are golden (about 30 to 45 minutes). Serves 3.

SAUTÉED BEAN SPROUTS

1 tablespoon oil or butter
2 cups fresh or 1 can bean sprouts, drained
Salt to taste

Heat the oil in a Teflon-lined pan. Add the sprouts and stir over medium heat until the sprouts are limp and lightly browned. Salt to taste and serve. Serves 3.

BROWN SPROUTS

1 can bean sprouts, drained
½ cup beef stock or gravy

Freshen the sprouts by rinsing with cold water and drain again. Squeeze the sprouts to remove the excess liquid. Heat the beef stock and add the sprouts. Cover and heat 5 minutes, then set the cover slightly off to allow the steam to escape. Continue heating until the liquid is nearly gone and the sprouts are light brown. Serves 3.

BEAN SPROUT "SPAGHETTI"

1 can bean sprouts, drained
1 teaspoon olive oil
1 cup tomato sauce (Aunt Millie's, Del Monte or homemade)
1 teaspoon dehydrated pepper flakes
Dash of liquid artificial sweetener
1 tablespoon onion flakes
Grated Romano cheese

Drain the sprouts, freshen in cold water and drain again. Squeeze between paper towels to remove the excess moisture. Heat the oil in a frying pan and add the sauce and seasonings, including onion flakes. When the sauce is hot, add the sprouts. Cover and remove from the heat. Let stand for a few minutes to heat through and serve with the grated cheese. Serves 3.

SPANISH "RICE"

2 tablespoons oil
½ onion or 2 scallions, minced
¼ green pepper, diced
¼ can red pepper, diced
1 ripe tomato, chopped
1 can bean sprouts, drained
¼ teaspoon salt
Pinch of saffron

Heat the oil and sauté the onion and peppers until soft. Add the tomato, cover and simmer for 5 minutes. Freshen the sprouts in cold water and drain on a paper towel. Chop the sprouts into rice-sized pieces, and add to the pan with the seasoning. Heat, stirring, until well mixed. Serves 3.

BEET GREENS: 3 to 6 per cent carbohydrate (low)

WILTED BEET GREENS

Place beet greens in a Teflon-lined pan. Add ¼ cup of water. Cook over low heat until the greens are wilted. Toss with butter, add salt and pepper to taste and serve.

BEETS: 15 per cent carbohydrate (high, limited vegetable)

HARVARD BEETS

1 egg yolk, beaten
½ cup white vinegar
½ cup liquid from the beets
2 tablespoons butter
2 ¼-grain tablets saccharin
2 cups cooked or canned beets, diced and drained
Salt to taste

Beat the egg yolk, stir in the vinegar and beet juice. Heat over a double boiler, stirring. Add the butter and saccharin and continue cooking until slightly thickened. Add the beets and cook until they are heated. Serve hot and salt to taste. Serves 4; each serving=1 unit high-carbohydrate vegetable.

STUFFED BEETS

6 medium beets
½ cup water
1 cup leftover mashed vegetables (any kind)
2 tablespoons butter

Leave the beets whole, with 1 inch of stem still attached. Steam on a rack over the water, or cook in a pressure cooker until the beets are tender. Remove the skins and stems. Slice off the root end and scoop out a cavity from each beet, reserving the scooped beets for another meal. Prepare mashed vegetables and fill the cavities. Top each with a small pat of butter. Serves 6; each serving, minus stuffing=½ unit high-carbohydrate vegetable.

SPICED BEETS

1 8-ounce can sliced beets
1 tablespoon butter
¼ teaspoon cinnamon
Dash of ginger
1 ¼-grain tablet saccharin
Dash of allspice

Drain the liquid from the beets into a small saucepan and add the butter and spices. Heat to boiling. Add the beets, lower the heat and cook for 5 minutes. Serve hot or cold. Serves 2; each serving=1 unit high-carbohydrate vegetable.

BROCCOLI: 3 to 6 per cent carbohydrate (low)

BROCCOLI WITH HOLLANDAISE SAUCE

1 head of broccoli
½ cup water
Salt to taste
1 recipe Hollandaise Sauce

Cut the flowerettes 1 inch from the stalks. Peel the tough outer fiber from the stalks and cut them into 2- to 3-inch lengths. Place on a rack in pressure cooker with the water. Add the flowerettes on top of the stalks. Cook for 1 to 2 minutes; reduce pressure and remove from the cooker. (If you do not use a pressure cooker, steam in a covered pan on a rack until just tender—do not overcook.) Salt to taste. Prepare the sauce according to the directions in the recipe. Drizzle the sauce on individual portions of the broccoli. Serves 4.

BROCCOLI WITH LEMON BUTTER

Prepare the broccoli as above. Melt 2 tablespoons of butter; add 2 tablespoons freshly squeezed lemon juice. Toss with the broccoli, salt to taste and serve. Serves 4.

BROCCOLI AU GRATIN

Same as Broccoli with Hollandaise Sauce: use Cheese Sauce instead (*see* Sauces and Dressings). Serves 4.

CREAMED BROCCOLI

1 recipe Instant Cream of Mushroom Soup (*see* Soups)
1 package frozen broccoli
Pinch of parsley

Prepare the soup according to the directions, but use 1 cup of milk, instead of the 1½ cups which the recipe calls for. Heat the soup in a saucepan, add the frozen broccoli and cover. After a few minutes, separate the broccoli with a fork. Cover and continue cooking over low heat until the broccoli is tender (to thicken the sauce, tilt the cover while cooking). Serves 3.

BROCCOLI SOUFFLÉ

3 eggs, separated
1 cup grated Swiss or Gruyère cheese
1 cup milk
1 package frozen chopped broccoli, slightly thawed
Salt, pepper to taste
Dash of allspice

Place the egg yolks, cheese, milk, broccoli and seasonings in the blender. Blend until well chopped on low, then purée on medium. Pour into a bowl. Beat the egg whites with a mixer until stiff. Fold the whites into the broccoli mixture. Pour into a buttered casserole or soufflé dish. Bake in a preheated 350° oven for 45 minutes to 1 hour. Serve immediately. Serves 3 as a main dish for lunch.

BRUSSELS SPROUTS: 10 per cent carbohydrate
(medium)

SCALLOPED BRUSSELS SPROUTS

½ cup water
1 package frozen Brussels sprouts
1 cup evaporated milk
Salt, pepper to taste
4 ounces white American cheese, grated
¼ cup finely chopped filberts

Heat the water. Add the frozen Brussels sprouts, cover and simmer until partially cooked (5 minutes). Transfer with the cooking liquid to a deep casserole. Pour in the evaporated milk and seasonings.

Spread the cheese on top, then sprinkle with the chopped nuts. Bake at 350° for 30 minutes, or until the cheese is completely melted. Serves 4; each serving=½ unit milk.

CABBAGE: cooked cabbage: 10 per cent carbohydrate; raw cabbage: 3 to 6 per cent carbohydrate

CARAWAY CABBAGE

1 medium head of cabbage
½ cup water
¼ teaspoon caraway seeds
1 tablespoon butter
Salt, pepper to taste

Cut the cabbage into eighths. Place with the water on a rack in a pressure cooker (or steam in a pan on a rack) and sprinkle with the seeds. Cook 3 to 4 minutes, or until the cabbage is tender. Remove to a serving dish. Drizzle the cooking liquid over the cabbage, toss with the butter and add seasonings to taste. Serves 6 to 8.

BAKED SWEET AND SOUR CABBAGE

1 head of red cabbage, shredded
1 baking apple, sliced thin
1 small onion, sliced thin
4 ¼-grain tablets saccharin, crushed
½ cup white vinegar
¾ cup water
1 tablespoon butter
1 teaspoon salt

Combine all ingredients in a casserole in layers. Cover and bake at 350° for 1 hour, or until tender (may also be simmered in a covered pan on top of the stove until tender). Serves 4 to 6; each serving= ½ unit fruit.

UNSTUFFED CABBAGE

½ head of cabbage
8 ounces lean ground beef
4 ¼-grain tablets saccharin
2 tablespoons vinegar
2 cups tomato juice
Juice of 1 lemon
Salt as needed
½ teaspoon onion powder

Parboil the cabbage in a little boiling water, covered, until tender enough to separate the leaves. Remove and separate. Brown the beef in a deep saucepan, stirring with a fork to break up the pieces. When the meat has lost its pink color and is crumbly, add the remaining ingredients. Stir well, pushing the cabbage leaves down until covered by the sauce. Cover and simmer over a low heat for 1 hour, or until tender. For thicker sauce, tilt the lid slightly during the last ½ hour of cooking. Correct seasoning: flavor should be sweet and sour. Serves 4 as a side dish. To serve as a main dish, increase beef to 1 pound.

SCALLOPED CABBAGE

1 small head of cabbage, cut in eighths
½ cup water
1 cup light cream or evaporated milk
Salt as needed
1 tablespoon butter
4 ounces sliced American cheese or Velveeta

Cook the cabbage in the water until tender, but not limp. Pour into a casserole. Add the cream or milk and salt. Dot with butter. Spread the cheese on top. Bake at 325° for about 30 minutes, or until the cheese is melted and bubbly. Serves 4; if evaporated milk is used, each serving=½ unit milk. Serve as a main dish for lunch.

SKILLET CABBAGE

3 or 4 strips bacon
½ large carrot, grated
½ head of cabbage, shredded
½ to 1 cup hot water
Salt to taste

Fry the bacon in a large skillet until crisp. Remove, drain and crumble the bacon; set aside. Pour off all but 2 tablespoons of the bacon fat. Add the vegetables to the hot skillet, stirring to coat evenly. Add the water, lower the heat and cover. Simmer until the vegetables are tender, adding more water if needed. Season; toss in the crumbled bacon, and serve hot. Serves 3.

BAKED CABBAGE

½ head of cabbage, shredded
½ cup water
2 tablespoons cider vinegar
Salt as needed
1 tablespoon onion flakes
4 sugarless frankfurters, split lengthwise

Combine the shredded cabbage, liquids and seasonings in a casserole; toss to mix. Lay the split franks on top, cut side down. Cover and bake in a slow oven for 45 to 60 minutes; for browner franks, uncover and continue baking for 15 minutes. Serves 4.

CABBAGE STICKS

Cut a head of cabbage in half. Cut out the center of heart. Save the rest of the cabbage for another recipe. Cut the cabbage heart into 3- to 4-inch sticks. Serve with dips (*see* Appetizers).

CARROTS: 10 per cent carbohydrate (medium)

MINTED CARROTS

½ cup water
1 package frozen sliced carrots
1 tablespoon butter
2 ¼-grain tablets saccharin
1 teaspoon chopped mint leaves
¼ teaspoon salt

Heat the water in a saucepan and add the carrots. Cover and simmer 5 minutes. Add the other ingredients, and more water if needed. Cook gently 5 minutes, or until the carrots are tender. Serves 4; each serving=1 unit medium-carbohydrate vegetable.

CARROTS AMANDINE

1 package frozen carrots
½ cup water
1 tablespoon butter
½ teaspoon almond extract
2 ¼-grain tablets saccharin
¼ cup slivered almonds

Cook the carrots in the water until tender. Mash well with a fork. Mix in the butter, extract and saccharin, and mash together. Top with the almonds and toast under the broiler until the almonds are lightly singed. Serves 4; each serving=1 unit medium-carbohydrate vegetable.

BAKED CARROTS

4 large carrots
½ cup orange juice

1 tablespoon butter
Pinch of salt

Scrub and quarter the carrots. Place in a 1-quart casserole. Pour in the juice and dot with butter. Cover and bake at 325° for 1 hour, or until carrots are tender. Salt to taste before serving. Serves 4; each serving=1 unit medium-carbohydrate vegetable.

CARROT SOUFFLÉ

1½ cups chopped cooked carrots
2 eggs, beaten
1 ¼-grain tablet saccharin, crushed
¼ teaspoon dehydrated orange peel
1 cup milk
½ cup cream or evaporated milk
Pinch of salt
Dash of nutmeg

Combine all ingredients in the blender and blend on low until puréed. Pour into a greased 1-quart casserole and bake at 325° for 1 hour. Serves 4; if evaporated milk is used, each serving=1 unit medium-carbohydrate vegetable, ½ unit milk.

CANDIED CARROTS

1 package frozen carrot slices
2 ¼-grain tablets saccharin
½ teaspoon maple flavoring
1 tablespoon butter
Pinch of salt
¼ cup water

Combine all ingredients in a 1-quart casserole. Cover and bake at 325° until tender (30 minutes); uncover and continue baking until the liquid is almost completely evaporated. Serves 4; each serving= 1 unit medium-carbohydrate vegetable.

CREAMED CARROTS

1 package frozen carrot slices
1 teaspoon butter
1 cup half and half
Salt, pepper to taste

Combine all ingredients in a saucepan. Cover and simmer until the carrots are tender. Uncover and continue cooking for 5 minutes, stirring, until the sauce is reduced. Serves 4; each serving=1 unit medium-carbohydrate vegetable.

CARROT RING

Prepare Creamed Carrots. Mash carrots and sauce together. Pour into a ring mold and place in a pan with 1 inch of hot water. Bake at 375° until set (about 30 minutes). Turn out and serve hot. (For a firmer ring, mix in an egg.) Serves 4.

CAULIFLOWER: 3 to 6 per cent carbohydrate (low)

MOCK "MASHED POTATOES" (MASHED CAULIFLOWER)

1 head cauliflower (about 2 pounds)
1 cup water
1 tablespoon butter
Salt, pepper to taste

Break the cauliflower into flowerettes. Cut the stem into 2-inch pieces. Place on a rack in a pan or pressure cooker. Add the water, cover and steam until tender (or pressure-cook for 2 minutes). Remove from the pan, reserving the cooking liquid for soups, etc. Mash the cauliflower until smooth. Dot with butter and seasonings. Serves 4.

Variation: For Mock "Whipped Potatoes," prepare as above, then add ¼ cup light cream or evaporated milk, and beat until fluffy.

CHEESE-BAKED CAULIFLOWER #1

1 package frozen cauliflower
½ cup water
4 ounces Swiss cheese, shredded
Salt to taste

Cook the cauliflower in the water (without salt) according to the package directions. Drain, reserving the liquid for soups, etc. Transfer the cauliflower to a greased shallow pan. Sprinkle in the cheese, and broil 6 to 8 inches from the heat until the cheese is brown and bubbly. Serves 3.

CHEESE-BAKED CAULIFLOWER #2

1 package frozen cauliflower
¼ cup water
2 teaspoons butter
½ cup grated Cheddar cheese
Salt to taste

Place the cauliflower and water in a 1-quart casserole. Dot with butter and cover with the grated cheese. Cover and bake at 375° until the cauliflower is tender (about 45 minutes). Serves 3.

CAULIFLOWER PUFFS

1 package frozen or ½ head raw cauliflower, cooked
1 teaspoon butter
Salt, pepper to taste
½ teaspoon onion powder
¼ cup light cream or evaporated milk
2 eggs, separated

Cook the cauliflower according to the directions for Mock "Mashed Potatoes." Place the cooked cauliflower, butter, seasonings, cream and egg yolks in the blender. Blend on medium until puréed. Beat the egg whites with an electric mixer until they are stiff. Fold the whites into the cauliflower mixture. Gently pour into greased muffin tins, heaping the mixture in peaks. Bake at 350° until puffy and brown (about 30 minutes). Serves 4.

SCALLOPED CAULIFLOWER

1 small head cauliflower, separated into flowerettes (slice stalk into 1-inch pieces)
1 cup milk
2 tablespoons butter
½ cup grated American cheese (dry type)
Salt to taste
¼ teaspoon paprika

Place cauliflower in a deep casserole. Pour in the milk. Dot with butter and sprinkle with the grated cheese and seasonings. Cover and bake at 375° for 30 to 40 minutes. Serves 4.

CELERY: 3 to 6 per cent carbohydrate (low)

BRAISED CELERY

1 tablespoon butter
6 large ribs celery, sliced ½ inch thick
½ cup chicken stock or sugarless bouillon

Melt the butter in a pan and sauté the celery until slightly translucent. Add the stock, cover and simmer briefly until just tender (about 5 minutes). Serves 3.

SAUTÉED CELERY

2 tablespoons peanut oil
1 scallion or ¼ small onion, minced
6 to 8 ribs celery
Salt to taste

Heat the oil in a frying pan. Add the scallion or onion and celery. Sauté, stirring, until the vegetables are cooked but still slightly crisp. Salt and serve. Serves 3 or 4.

CREAMED CELERY

2 tablespoons butter
6 ribs celery, sliced in 2-inch pieces
2 leeks, sliced thin
1 tablespoon celery tops, minced fine
½ cup milk
½ cup cream or evaporated milk
Pinch of curry powder
Salt, pepper to taste

Heat the butter and sauté the vegetables until they are translucent. Add the milk, cover and simmer over low heat until tender. Add the cream and seasonings, and simmer uncovered, stirring, until thickened. Serves 3 to 4.

CUCUMBERS: 3 to 6 per cent carbohydrate (low)

MARINATED CUCUMBERS

1 medium cucumber, peeled
½ small onion, finely sliced
½ cup white vinegar
2 ¼-grain tablets saccharin, crushed
Pinch of chopped dill weed
¼ cup water
¼ teaspoon salt

Slice the cucumber into paper-thin slices. Place in a deep bowl with the onion slices. Pour the other ingredients over the vegetables. Marinate in the refrigerator at least 1 hour before serving (preferably longer). Serves 3.

BRAISED CUCUMBERS

2 or 3 small cucumbers, peeled
2 teaspoons butter
½ tablespoon boiling water
½ Knorr-Swiss chicken bouillon cube

Slice the cucumbers into ¼-inch-thick pieces. Melt the butter in a frying pan and brown the cucumber slices on both sides. Pour the boiling water into the pan and add the bouillon cube. Cover and simmer until the cucumbers are tender (about 5 to 10 minutes). Serves 4.

DANDELION GREENS: 3 to 6 per cent
carbohydrate (low)

DANDELION GREENS

2 ounces salt pork
2 cups water
1 pound tender young dandelion greens
Salt to taste

Cut the pork into thin strips. Place it in a deep kettle with the water. Cover and boil gently for 30 minutes. Add the greens and cook, pushing them down into the water as they wilt. Cook over low heat until the greens are tender. Remove greens with a slotted spoon and salt to taste. This recipe may also be used for beet greens, kale and turnip greens. Serves 3.

EGGPLANT: 3 to 6 per cent carbohydrate (low)

FRENCH EGGPLANT

2 to 4 tablespoons olive oil
1 medium eggplant, peeled and sliced into ½-inch-thick pieces
1 clove garlic, minced
1 large green pepper, sliced thin
1 onion, diced
1 small can mushrooms, drained
1 large can tomatoes
½ teaspoon each: basil and oregano
Salt, pepper
¼ pound Cheddar cheese, shredded

Heat the oil in a large skillet and sauté the eggplant, garlic, peppers, onion and mushrooms, stirring, until softened and slightly browned. Place in a casserole. Pour in the canned tomatoes, add the spices and top with the shredded cheese. Bake uncovered at 375° for 45 minutes. Serves 4 to 6.

FRENCH-FRIED EGGPLANT

1 small eggplant
2 eggs, beaten
2 tablespoons soy flour
Oil or shortening as needed
Salt to taste

Peel the eggplant, then cut into strips resembling french-fried potatoes. Beat the eggs and mix with the flour. Dip the eggplant strips in the egg mixture, then fry in deep fat until golden brown; if you do not have a deep fat fryer, use a frying pan with ¾ inch fat. Fry a few at a time, removing to a paper towel when crisp. Salt and serve hot. Serves 4.

EGGPLANT FRITTERS

Shortening as needed
¼ large unpeeled eggplant, chopped in the blender
2 eggs
½ teaspoon oregano
Dash of freshly ground pepper
1 teaspoon onion powder
2 tablespoons soy flour
Salt to taste

Mix together all ingredients. Heat 1 inch solid shortening (such as Crisco, etc.) in a frying pan, or heat fat in a deep-fat fryer. Drop the eggplant mixture with a small scoop or soup spoon into the hot fat, a few at a time, and fry until crisp and brown (make sure the fat is hot enough or the eggplant will absorb it). Drain on paper towels; repeat until all the mixture has been used. Serves 3.

BAKED EGGPLANT

1 medium unpeeled eggplant, sliced into ¼-inch-thick pieces
½ cup water
1 onion, peeled
2 cups tomato juice
1 teaspoon dehydrated pepper flakes
Salt to taste
Freshly grated pepper to taste
¼ cup grated American cheese (dry type)

Parboil the eggplant slices in the water, covered, until slightly soft. Drain; grate the onion, or if you prefer, place the onion in the blender container with the tomato juice and grate in the blender. Combine the grated onion and tomato juice with the pepper flakes, salt and pepper. Place the eggplant slices in a casserole and pour in the tomato sauce. Top with the grated cheese. Bake at 325° for 1 hour, or until the eggplant is tender and the sauce is thick. Serves 4.

JERUSALEM ARTICHOKE: 15 per cent
carbohydrate (high)

JERUSALEM ARTICHOKES

Peel the Jerusalem artichokes like potatoes; slice. Place in boiling water for 10 to 12 minutes. Drain. Serve with butter, parsley, salt and pepper. Serve 1 artichoke per person. Each artichoke=1 unit high-carbohydrate vegetable.

BAKED JERUSALEM ARTICHOKES

2 to 4 Jerusalem artichokes, peeled and grated
1 egg, slightly beaten
½ teaspoon onion powder
1 cup milk
Salt, pepper

Grate the artichokes. Combine all ingredients and pour into a greased casserole. Bake at 325° until cooked (about ½ hour). Serves 3; each serving=1 unit high-carbohydrate vegetable.

SCALLOPED JERUSALEM ARTICHOKES

1 pound Jersusalem artichokes, peeled and diced
1 recipe Basic White Sauce
1 cup grated cheese (Swiss, Muenster or mild American)

Parboil the artichokes by placing them in boiling water for 5 minutes. Drain. Place in a greased casserole, cover with the Basic White Sauce and sprinkle generously with the cheese. Cover and bake at 325° until the vegetables are tender. Serves 4; each serving=1 unit high-carbohydrate vegetable.

KALE: 3 to 6 per cent carbohydrate (low)

CREAMED KALE

1 8-ounce can white onions
1 package frozen kale
½ cup evaporated milk
½ cup non-fat dry milk
1 tablespoon butter
Salt, pepper

Drain the liquid from the onions into a saucepan. Heat, add the kale. Cover and lower the heat. Simmer until the kale is tender (about 15 minutes), stirring occasionally. In a cup, combine the evaporated milk and the dry milk, and mix until smooth. Add to the kale, stirring, along with the other ingredients. Heat, stirring, until the sauce is thick. Serves 4; each serving=½ unit milk.

LEEKS: 3 to 6 per cent carbohydrate (low)

BAKED LEEKS

4 to 6 large leeks
1 Knorr-Swiss chicken bouillon cube
1 cup milk, heated

Clean the leeks and cut into 3-inch pieces. Dissolve the bouillon cube in the hot milk and pour over the leeks. Bake uncovered at 350° for 1 hour or until tender. Serves 3.

MUSHROOMS: 3 to 6 per cent carbohydrate (low)

SAUTÉED MUSHROOMS

2 tablespoons oil
½ pound mushrooms
½ teaspoon onion powder
Salt to taste
¼ teaspoon garlic powder

Heat the oil. Slice the mushrooms lengthwise with the stems on, making several thin slices for each mushroom. Add the mushrooms to the hot oil and sauté, stirring. When the mushrooms have turned slightly brown, add seasonings, stir to mix and serve. Serves 2 or 3.

BAKED STUFFED MUSHROOMS

8 large mushrooms
2 tablespoons lemon juice
1 tablespoon butter
½ cup chicken stock or water
2 tablespoons toasted wheat germ (if tolerated: if not, use chopped almonds)

Separate the stems from the mushroom caps. Squeeze the lemon juice over the mushroom caps and set the caps aside, with the cupped side up. Chop the stems well. Melt the butter and sauté the caps. Mix in the bouillon and stir until cooked. Stuff into the mushroom caps, heaping the excess mixture on top. Sprinkle with wheat germ or almonds. Carefully place the stuffed mushrooms in a baking dish; pour the rest of the bouillon into the dish. Bake at 375° for 30 minutes. Serves 2 to 4.

ORIENTAL MUSHROOMS

2 tablespoons peanut oil
½ pound small mushrooms, sliced in half lengthwise
1 scallion, sliced, including top
1 tablespoon Kikkoman soy sauce
Salt to taste
Dash of MSG
Pinch of garlic powder

Heat the oil in a skillet. Add the vegetables; stir and fry until browned but still crisp. Season, stir a few seconds more and serve. Serves 2 or 3.

MUSHROOMS IN SOUR CREAM

½ pound mushrooms, sliced
1 small onion, diced
2 tablespoons butter
¼ cup sour cream
½ teaspoon celery salt
1 sprig of fresh parsley, minced fine
Salt to taste

Sauté the mushrooms and onion in the butter until tender. Lower the heat, add the remaining ingredients except salt and stir. Heat gently for a few minutes and serve, adding salt to taste. Serves 2 or 3.

OKRA: 3 to 6 per cent carbohydrate (low)

COOKED OKRA

2 strips bacon
1 package frozen sliced okra
1 ¼-grain tablet saccharin

1 cup tomato juice
1 tablespoon minced onion
Salt, pepper to taste

Fry the bacon until translucent. Add the remaining ingredients. Cover and simmer until the okra is tender (about 5 minutes). Uncover and continue simmering until the sauce is thickened and reduced. Serves 3.

BAKED OKRA

1 tablespoon butter
1 small onion, minced
1 package frozen okra
Salt to taste
1 small can tomatoes
Dash of freshly ground pepper

Melt the butter and sauté the onion until brown. Combine with the rest of the ingredients. Pour into a 1-quart casserole, and bake at 350° for 1 hour. Serves 3.

ONIONS: 10 per cent carbohydrate (medium)

CREAMED ONIONS

½ cup water
1 pound small white onions, peeled
¼ cup evaporated milk
½ cup non-fat dry milk
1 Knorr-Swiss bouillon cube
Dash of cayenne or paprika

Boil the water and add the onions. Cover, lower the heat and simmer 10 minutes, or until tender. Drain the liquid into the blender and add the evaporated milk and the dry milk. Blend until smooth. Pour over the onions, and add the bouillon cube and a little water if needed. Heat, stirring, until thickened. Add a dash of cayenne or paprika to taste. Serves 4.

ONION PIE

3 strips smoked bacon
3 large Bermuda onions, sliced
1 egg
1 cup milk
½ cup sour cream
Dash of nutmeg
Salt, pepper to taste
¼ cup grated Swiss cheese

Sauté the bacon until crisp. Remove and drain. Slip the onion slices into the hot bacon fat and sauté without stirring. When the onion slices are translucent, remove and place in a greased pie plate. Beat together the egg, milk and sour cream and pour over the onions. Add the seasonings and sprinkle on the cheese. Top with the crumbled bacon. Bake at 325° until firm (about 1 hour). For a different effect, blend the onions with the eggs and milk; bake as above. Serves 6; each serving=1 unit medium-carbohydrate vegetable.

FRIED ONION RINGS

1 egg
1 tablespoon oil
4 tablespoons water
½ cup evaporated milk
¼ cup oat flour
¼ cup soy flour
½ teaspoon salt
1 large Bermuda onion, sliced ¼ inch thick
Oil as needed
Salt to taste

Prepare the batter by beating together the egg and oil. Add the water and evaporated milk, then mix in the flours and salt, stirring until smooth. Separate the onion slices into rings. Dip the rings into the batter, coating thickly. Set aside on wax paper until all are coated and air-dried slightly. Heat 1 inch of fat in a frying pan. Drop the rings a few at a time into the hot fat. Fry until golden. Drain on paper towels and salt to taste. If any are not eaten while hot, refrigerate, then reheat by spreading on a cookie sheet in a slow oven until warm again. Serves 4 to 6; each serving=½ unit carbohydrate and 1 unit medium-carbohydrate vegetable.

PARSNIPS: 15 per cent carbohydrate (high)

MASHED PARSNIPS

½ cup water
1 pound parsnips, peeled and sliced
2 tablespoons cream
Salt to taste
1 tablespoon butter

Heat the water and add the parsnips. Cover, lower the heat and simmer until the parsnips are soft (about 15 minutes). Remove from the pan and mash, including the cooking liquid. Add the remaining ingredients and mash well. Serve with meat and pan gravy. Serves 4; each serving=1 unit high-carbohydrate vegetable.

BAKED PARSNIPS

1 pound parsnips, peeled and cut into sticks
½ cup orange juice
1 ¼-grain tablet saccharin, crushed
Salt to taste
1 tablespoon butter

Place the parsnips in a baking dish. Pour in the juice, season and dot with butter. Cover and bake at 375° until the parsnips are tender (about 1 hour). Serves 4; each serving=1 unit high-carbohydrate vegetable.

FRENCH-FRIED PARSNIPS

1 pound parsnips, peeled
Fat as needed to cover

Cut each parsnip into 8 slivers the size of thin french-fried potatoes. Fry in deep fat until crisp. Drain and serve hot. Serves 4; each serving=1 unit high-carbohydrate vegetable.

PARSNIP PANCAKES

4 large parsnips, peeled and grated in the blender (makes about 1½ cups)
2 eggs, slightly beaten
¼ cup soy flour
½ cup grated onion
Salt to taste
Oil as needed

Combine all ingredients except oil. Drop by heaping spoonfuls into a pan containing ¼ inch of hot fat or oil. Fry until brown on both sides. Serves 6. Each serving=½ unit high-carbohydrate vegetable.

CREAMED PARSNIPS

½ cup water
½ pound parsnips, peeled and sliced
¼ cup evaporated milk
¼ cup cream
1 tablespoon butter
1 ¼-grain tablet saccharin
Salt to taste

Heat the water to boiling and add the parsnips. Cover and simmer on low heat until the parsnips are tender. Drain the liquid into a dish. Add the remaining ingredients and stir until the butter and saccharin are dissolved. Pour over the parsnips, heat for a few seconds and serve. Serves 2; each serving=1 unit high-carbohydrate vegetable.

CANDIED PARSNIPS

1 pound parsnips, cut into eighths
Dash of freshly ground nutmeg
1 small can Dole unsweetened pineapple chunks, packed in their own juice
1 tablespoon butter
2 ¼-grain tablets saccharin, crushed
1 drop each of red and yellow food coloring

Combine all ingredients and pour into a 1-quart casserole. Bake uncovered at 325° for 1 hour, or covered at 375° for 30 minutes. Serves 4; each serving=1 unit high-carbohydrate vegetable.

PEAS: 15 per cent carbohydrate (high)

PEAS PARMESAN

½ cup water
1 package frozen peas
2 eggs
½ cup evaporated milk
½ cup milk
1 ¼-grain tablet saccharin
Salt
4 ounces Parmesan cheese, freshly grated

Heat the water and pour in the peas. Cover, lower the heat and simmer for 5 minutes, or until the peas are barely cooked. Beat together the eggs and milks. Add the seasonings. Pour into the blender with the peas and cooking water, and purée until smooth. Pour into a well-greased 1-quart casserole. Sprinkle with grated cheese, and bake at 300° for 1 hour. Serves 4; each serving=1 unit high-carbohydrate vegetable.

PEAS WITH PIMIENTOS

1 can dietetic canned peas
Dash of liquid artificial sweetener
2 tablespoons finely minced pimiento
Pinch of salt

Combine all ingredients in a saucepan. Heat over medium heat briefly, until hot. Serves 3; each serving=½ unit high-carbohydrate vegetable.

PEAS AND MUSHROOMS

1 small can mushroom pieces
1 package frozen peas
Pinch of salt
Dash of onion powder

Drain the liquid from the mushrooms into a saucepan. Add the peas and seasonings. Cover, lower the heat and simmer until the peas are cooked (about 5 minutes). Add the mushrooms, heat and serve. Serves 4; each serving=1 unit high-carbohydrate vegetable.

CREAMED PEAS

1 can dietetic canned peas
¼ cup evaporated milk
¼ cup non-fat dry milk
Dash of salt
Dash of paprika
1 teaspoon butter

Drain the liquid from the peas into a saucepan. Mix in the evaporated milk and the dry milk. Heat, add the peas and the remaining ingredients and heat, stirring, until the sauce is thick. Serves 3; each serving =½ unit high-carbohydrate vegetable, ½ unit milk.

FRENCH PEAS

1 tablespoon butter
1 package frozen peas, shaken loose
¼ cup thinly sliced onion
¼ teaspoon salt
2 tablespoons water
Dash of parsley flakes

Melt the butter. Add the peas and onion. Stir over low heat until the onion is soft. Add the remaining ingredients, cover tightly and steam over low heat until the peas are just tender (about 2 to 3 minutes). Serves 4; each serving=1 unit high-carbohydrate vegetable.

PEA PODS (SNOW PEAS): 3 to 6 per cent carbohydrate (low)

COOKED PEA PODS

1 tablespoon oil
1 package frozen pea pods (snow peas)
¼ teaspoon salt
¼ cup water

Heat the oil and stir in the pea pods. Add the salt and water, and cover. Simmer over low heat for 5 minutes, or until just tender. Serves 3.

CHINESE PEA PODS

2 tablespoons peanut oil
1 package frozen pea pods (snow peas)
1 rib celery, sliced ½ inch thick
2 scallions, sliced
1 small clove garlic, chopped fine
¼ teaspoon salt
¼ teaspoon Kikkoman soy sauce
Dash of freshly ground pepper

Heat the oil in a skillet. Add the vegetables and fry, stirring, until the pea pods and celery are tender, but still slightly crisp. Add the seasonings and serve. Serves 4.

GERMAN-STYLE PEA PODS

½ cup milk
1 package frozen pea pods (snow peas)
¼ cup heavy cream
Salt, pepper to taste
1 teaspoon butter

Heat the milk and add the pea pods. Cover tightly and simmer over low heat for 10 to 15 minutes. Remove from the heat and add the other ingredients. Stir until the butter is melted and serve. Serves 3 or 4.

PEPPERS: 3 to 6 per cent carbohydrate (low)

STUFFED PEPPERS

4 large green peppers
Boiling water
2 cups any creamed, mashed or au gratin vegetable, or any casserole
    leftovers
Wheat germ or grated cheese (optional)

Cut a slice from the stem end of each pepper, and remove the seeds. Plunge the peppers into rapidly boiling water for 1 to 2 minutes; remove and drain. Fill with desired filling. Place the stuffed pepper in a buttered baking dish. Bake at 375° for 30 minutes, or longer, until soft. If a crisp topping is desired, sprinkle with a little wheat germ or grated cheese before baking. Serves 4.

Suggestions for fillings:
—Creamed Cauliflower
—Leftover Eggplant Parmigiana
—Leftover Hamburger Stew
—Leftover Broccoli au Gratin
—Mashed Baked Butternut Squash
—Leftover "Succotash"

Also:

—Chicken-stuffed Peppers: *see* Casseroles
—Beef-stuffed Peppers: *see* Casseroles
—Cheese-stuffed Peppers: *see* Casseroles

FRIED PEPPERS

1 pound sweet frying peppers
2 tablespoons olive oil
1 large scallion, minced
1 clove garlic, minced
Salt, pepper to taste

Slice the peppers in half lengthwise and remove the seeds and stems. Slice again lengthwise. Heat the oil and add the scallions, garlic and peppers. Sauté, stirring until the vegetables are soft. Add seasonings to taste and serve. Serves 3.

STEWED PEPPERS

1 large red pepper
2 large green peppers
1 tablespoon oil
1 cup tomato juice
Salt to taste

Cut the peppers into 1-inch chunks, discarding the stems and seeds. Heat the oil in a pan and sauté peppers briefly until slightly softened. Add the juice. Cover and cook over low heat until the peppers are soft. To thicken, remove the cover and simmer until the sauce is reduced. Salt to taste. Serves 2 or 3.

PEPPERS AND EGGPLANT

3 large green peppers, cut into thin strips
1 medium eggplant, peeled and cubed
1 teaspoon capers
1 tablespoon onion flakes
½ teaspoon salt
1 large can Del Monte tomato sauce
1 tablespoon olive oil
½ teaspoon minced garlic flakes
Pinch each of basil and oregano

Combine all ingredients in a shallow casserole and mix well. Bake at 375° for 45 minutes, or at 325° for 1 hour and 15 minutes. Serves 6.

FRIED PIMIENTOS

1 tablespoon olive oil
¼ small onion, minced
1 clove garlic, finely minced
1 jar pimientos, drained and sliced (about ½ cup)
Salt to taste

Heat the olive oil. Sauté the onion and garlic until soft. Stir the pimiento slices into the pan. Stir until hot and beginning to brown. Season and serve. Serves 2.

JIFFY PIMIENTOS

Heat 1 jar of pimientos. Drain and season lightly with garlic powder, onion powder, salt and a pinch of oregano. Serve hot as a vegetable, or cold as a relish. Serves 2.

PUMPKIN: 15 per cent carbohydrate (high)

BUTTERED PUMPKIN

1 small pie pumpkin, split open, with seeds and pulp removed
¼ cup butter, melted
1 teaspoon liquid artificial sweetener

Brush the edges and cavity of the pumpkin with the melted butter. Sprinkle with the sweetener. Place on foil-lined baking pan in a hot (400°) oven until tender. Remove from the oven, scoop out the pumpkin and serve it in chunks with the butter as a sauce. Serves 8; each serving=1 unit high-carbohydrate vegetable.

PUMPKIN CUSTARD

2 eggs, slightly beaten
1 medium can pumpkin (1½ cups)
1 cup evaporated milk or light cream
4 ¼-grain tablets saccharin
¼ teaspoon maple flavoring
¼ teaspoon ground cloves
Pinch of salt
¼ teaspoon vanilla extract
1 teaspoon cinnamon
Dash of nutmeg

Beat the eggs and add the other ingredients. Beat well until smooth. Pour into individual custard dishes or a shallow casserole. Bake at 350° for 45 minutes or longer, until set and brown. Serve as a side dish with game or poultry, or as dessert if you prefer. Serves 4; each serving=1 unit high-carbohydrate vegetable, ½ unit milk.

RUTABAGA (YELLOW TURNIP): 10 per cent carbohydrate (medium)

MASHED RUTABAGA (YELLOW TURNIP)

1 rutabaga
Water as needed
1 tablespoon butter
Milk or cream to taste
Salt, pepper to taste

Peel the rutabaga and cut into chunks. Cook in boiling water to cover until tender. Mash with 1 tablespoon butter, a little milk or cream and salt and pepper to taste. If you prefer, beat or whip until fluffy. Serves 4; each serving=1 unit medium-carbohydrate vegetable.

YELLOW TURNIP CROQUETTES

Prepare Mashed Rutabaga. Add 1 beaten egg to the mixture. Heat 1 tablespoon oil in a heavy skillet. Spoon the mixture into the hot oil. Fry until brown. Turn and repeat until crisp and brown on both sides. Serves 4; each serving=1 unit medium-carbohydrate vegetable.

SAUERKRAUT: 3 to 6 per cent carbohydrate (low)

BAKED SAUERKRAUT

1 large can sauerkraut, drained
1 tablespoon prepared mustard
½ cup tomato juice
3 or 4 strips smoked bacon

Combine the sauerkraut, mustard and tomato juice in a small casserole. Mix well. Lay the bacon strips on top. Bake uncovered at

375° for 30 minutes or longer, until the bacon is brown. Serves
4 to 6.

HOT SPICY KRAUT

1 pound fresh or "new" sauerkraut
1 teaspoon dry mustard
¼ teaspoon dehydrated horseradish
Dash of freshly ground pepper

Combine all ingredients in a saucepan. Heat until steaming, about 10
minutes. Serves 4.

INSTANT SWEET AND SOUR "CABBAGE"

2 large cans sauerkraut, drained
1½ cups tomato juice
3 or 4 ¼-grain tablets saccharin
2 tablespoons white vinegar
1 Knorr-Swiss beef bouillon cube
Juice of ½ lemon
¼ teaspoon ground ginger

Drain the sauerkraut and squeeze it dry. Combine all ingredients in
a saucepan. Cover and heat on low heat for 1 to 2 hours. Add
more lemon juice or sweetener to suit your taste. For a thicker sauce,
leave the cover ajar for the last ½ hour. This recipe is called "instant"
because even though it should cook for a long time, it can also made
by simply heating and serving immediately. Serves 8 to 10.

SAUERKRAUT AND APPLES WITH PORK ROAST

1 large tart apple, peeled and sliced
1 large can sauerkraut, drained well
1 pork roast

Mix the apple slices and sauerkraut together. Place in the bottom
of the pan surrounding an uncooked pork roast, so that it will be

cooking in the pan drippings. Bake at 325° for 40 minutes per pound. Drain slightly to remove the excess fat and serve as a side dish with the pork. Entire recipe contains 2 units fruit. Serves 4; each serving=½ unit fruit.

SOYBEANS: 10 per cent carbohydrate (if tolerated, you can use more because of their high protein content)

SOYBEANS: AN INTRODUCTION

If this is your first experience cooking and eating soybeans, you will need to know something about them. Soybeans are a staple food on this diet because their high protein content allows them to be used as a meat substitute. Soybeans contain four times the amount of protein of other beans, and are delicious when prepared well. They may be used as a vegetable, a protein snack or a bread substitute. Anyone accustomed to eating starchier beans will find soybeans satisfy their yen for beans. They can be used in Mexican, southern, Spanish and Indian dishes without affecting the flavor very much. For information on where to buy soybeans and soybean products, see Where to Buy Hard-to-Find Ingredients. Fresh soybeans, or green soybeans, are almost impossible to come by, unless you grow your own. The kind usually for sale in the health food stores are dried or yellow soybeans. These are similar to pea beans when cooked. Soy flour is made from ground soybeans, with some of the oil removed. Soy grits are chopped raw soybeans, and are similar to soybeans in flavor, but do not need to be presoaked, and cook in a very short time. Roasted soybeans, which can be bought salted, unsalted and even garlic-flavored, are ready-to-eat, yellow nut-like beans, and may be eaten as is, or with milk as cereal.

Soy flour and soy powder are good substitutes for flour and dry milk. They are not as high in carbohydrates as flour and milk and contain many times more protein. Soy grits make an excellent substitute for corn meal. They should be ground in the blender, then cooked, using twice as much liquid as your favorite corn meal recipe calls for. Soy products can be difficult to digest and should be cooked long and slowly for best results.

SOYBEANS: BASIC COOKING INSTRUCTIONS

1. Soak beans in cold water for 24 hours in the refrigerator.
2. (Optional): Transfer the beans and soaking water to ice trays and freeze solid. This aids in the softening process, but if pressed for time, you can skip this step.
3. Place the soaked (or frozen) beans in a large pot with additional water. Cover and simmer for 4 to 6 hours, or until tender.
4. Add fats, meat, stock, vegetables, seasonings, tomato paste, etc., or whatever the recipe calls for. Cover and continue to simmer for 4 to 5 more hours. To reduce the cooking liquid, tilt the lid during the last hour.

or,

4. Place the beans and liquid in a deep casserole. Add the fat, seasonings, etc. Cover and bake 4 to 6 hours in a slow oven. Beans can also be "baked" in a heavy covered pot on top of the stove over a very low heat for about 12 hours.

Double recipe when preparing cooked beans. After step 3, freeze half the beans until needed; or, continue cooking or baking, add seasonings according to recipe, then freeze half.

COOKED SOYBEANS

1 cup yellow soybeans
3 cups cold water
3 cups hot water
2 tablespoons butter
1 large onion, diced
Salt to taste as needed
1 Knorr-Swiss bouillon cube

Soak the beans in the cold water overnight (*see* Basic Cooking Instructions). Freeze if desired. Pour the beans and soaking water into a large pot. Add the hot water and cover. Simmer 4 to 6 hours. Add the butter, onion and seasonings and simmer for at least 2 hours more, or until beans have developed full flavor. Makes about

3 cups beans. For all practical purposes, you will be better off to
double this recipe, then freeze half when finished. This is true of
all the bean recipes in this section. Serves 4 to 6.

"BAKED BEANS"

1 cup yellow soybeans
3 cups water
3 cups tomato juice
¼ pound salt pork
¼ teaspoon pepper
1 tablespoon prepared mustard
½ Knorr-Swiss bouillon cube
2 medium onions, diced
1 teaspoon salt
2 ¼-grain tablets saccharin
1 tablespoon vinegar

Presoak the beans in the water overnight. Combine with the tomato
juice and simmer for 6 hours. Pour into a deep casserole and add
the other ingredients. Cover and bake at 300° for at least 4
hours, stirring occasionally, adding more juice if needed. For a
crusty effect, leave the cover off for the last ½ hour. Double the
recipe and freeze half if you can. Serves 4 to 6.

BOSTON "BAKED BEANS"

1 cup yellow soybeans
¼ pound salt pork
½ teaspoon imitation maple flavoring
¼ teaspoon pepper
1 tablespoon dry mustard
4 cups water
1 cup orange juice
4 ¼-grain tablets saccharin
2 tablespoons dehydrated onion flakes
1 teaspoon salt

Prepare exactly the same as for "Baked Beans." Serves 4 to 6.

SPICY BARBECUE BEANS

1 cup yellow soybeans
3 cups water
3 cups tomato juice
½ pound sugarless hot dogs, sliced ¼ inch thick
2 ¼-grain tablets saccharin
Dash of cayenne pepper
1 teaspoon chili powder or to taste
1 tablespoon prepared white horseradish
½ cup chopped onion
2 tablespoons chopped green pepper
½ teaspoon freshly ground pepper
1 teaspoon salt
1 tablespoon dry mustard
1 Knorr-Swiss beef bouillon cube

Soak the beans overnight in the water. Add the tomato juice and simmer for 6 hours. Remove 1 cup of the beans to a bowl and mash well. Pour the mashed beans in with the rest of the beans. Pour, with all the other ingredients, into a deep casserole. Bake covered in a slow (300°) oven for 4 to 6 hours. Leave the cover off for the last hour. Double recipe and freeze half if you can. Serves 4 to 6.

SOUTHERN-STYLE BEANS WITH HAM BONE

1 cup yellow soybeans, soaked overnight in 3 cups water
3 cups hot water
1 large ham bone, including the fat and as much of the ham (smoked)
   as possible
Salt to taste
4 ¼-grain tablets saccharin
½ teaspoon freshly ground pepper

Combine the soybeans with the hot water in a deep pot. Cover and simmer 6 hours. Add the other ingredients, cover and simmer over low heat for 4 to 6 hours more, adding more water as needed. Serves 4 to 6.

CHILI BEANS

1 can cooked soybeans (*see* Brand Names) or 2 cups Cooked Soybeans
1 small can tomato purée
¼ teaspoon salt
¼ teaspoon chili powder
Dash of garlic powder
1 tablespoon onion flakes
¼ teaspoon freshly ground pepper
1 tablespoon bacon drippings or butter
Dash or liquid artificial sweetener

Combine all ingredients in a saucepan. Bring to a slow boil, then
simmer, stirring occasionally, for 30 minutes, or until the sauce
is thick. Serves 4.

SOYBEAN BURGERS

1 can cooked soybeans or 2 cups cooked soybeans (any recipe
   above)
1 egg, slightly beaten
1 teaspoon dehydrated parsley flakes
1 tablespoon Kikkoman soy sauce
Salt to taste as needed
Homemade Instant Ketchup or Chili Sauce

Mash the soybeans and add the other ingredients (except the Ketchup
or Chili Sauce). Mash well together. Form the mixture into patties.
Fry in a well-oiled skillet until crisp and brown, adding a little bacon
drippings or butter if desired. Serve with homemade Ketchup or
Chili Sauce to taste. Serves 3.

COOKED SOY GRITS

1 cup soy grits
3 cups stock or gravy (cold)

Combine the grits with the liquid and soak for 30 minutes. Pour into a skillet and simmer 10 minutes. The longer the grits are cooked, the less they will have of a "bean" flavor. If you want them as a substitute for wild rice, kasha, etc., cook very slowly for 1 to 2 hours in a well-flavored rich stock or beef gravy. Serves 4.

SPINACH: 3 to 6 per cent carbohydrate (low)

EASY CREAMED SPINACH

1 cup water
1 package frozen chopped spinach
1 teaspoon butter
Dash of nutmeg
½ cup non-fat dry milk
½ teaspoon salt

Heat the water to boiling; add the spinach. Lower the heat, cover and simmer, occasionally stirring with a fork, to break up the block into chunks. Simmer until just tender. Do not overcook. Pour into the blender (including the cooking liquid). Add the rest of the ingredients. Cover and purée until smooth. Serve immediately or reheat. Serves 3 or 4.

DELUXE CREAMED SPINACH

1 cup milk
1 package frozen chopped spinach
¼ cup heavy cream
1 tablespoon butter
Salt, pepper to taste
⅓ cup non-fat dry milk
1 egg yolk
Dash of freshly ground nutmeg

Heat the milk, add the spinach. Cover and simmer gently over low heat until the spinach is cooked. Pour into the blender. Add the rest of the ingredients and purée until smooth. Return to the pan and cook gently, stirring, until thick and hot. Serves 4; each serving=½ unit milk.

SPINACH SOUFFLÉ

Prepare Deluxe Creamed Spinach as above. After puréeing in the blender, stir in 3 eggs, beaten well. Pour into a greased casserole and bake at 325° until set (about 45 minutes to 1 hour). Serves 4; each serving=½ unit milk.

SPINACH AU GRATIN

1 package frozen spinach
½ cup water
1 recipe Cheese Sauce (*see* Sauces and Dressings)
2 to 4 slices Jones smoked bacon, fried crisp and drained on paper towels

Cook the spinach in the water until tender. Drain, saving the liquid for soup or using it as part of the liquid in the sauce. Prepare Cheese Sauce according to the recipe. Pour over the spinach, top with the bacon strips. Serves 4.

SPINACH IN SOUR CREAM SAUCE

1 package frozen chopped spinach
1 tablespoon butter
½ cup sour cream
Salt, pepper

Thaw the spinach slightly to separate it. Heat the butter in a saucepan. Add the spinach and cover. Simmer gently on low heat until the spinach is soft. Add the sour cream and season to taste. Stir until well mixed and serve. Serves 3 or 4.

STRING BEANS (GREEN BEANS): 10 per cent carbohydrate (medium)

FANCY FRENCH STRING BEANS

3 tablespoons butter
¼ medium onion, minced
4 to 6 mushrooms, sliced
1 package frozen French-style string beans
½ cup water
Pinch of marjoram
Salt to taste
3 pimientos, chopped
Riced egg yolk or grated Parmesan cheese (optional)

Melt the butter. Sauté the onion and mushrooms. Add the beans, stirring to coat with butter. Add the water and seasonings; cover and simmer until just tender. Add the pimientos and stir to heat and serve. Garnish with egg yolk or Parmesan cheese if desired. Serves 3 or 4.

SUPER STRING BEANS

2 slices bacon, diced
¼ cup chopped green pepper
2 cups cooked or canned green beans
½ teaspoon onion powder
Dash of pepper
½ cup cream
Salt to taste as needed
Dash of nutmeg

Fry the bacon until nearly done. Add the green pepper and cook until soft. Add the remaining ingredients. Heat through, serve hot. Serves 4.

BAKED STRING BEANS

1 package frozen French-style green beans
¼ cup water
¼ teaspoon salt
1 tablespoon butter
¼ cup grated sharp Cheddar cheese

Place the frozen beans in a small deep casserole. Add the water and salt. Dot with the butter and sprinkle with the grated cheese. Cover and bake at 350° for 30 minutes, or until the beans are tender. Serves 3 or 4.

STRING BEANS AMANDINE

1 tablespoon butter
¼ cup slivered almonds
1 large can cut green beans
Dash of freshly ground pepper

Melt the butter in a saucepan. Add the almonds and fry until golden. Drain the beans and add to the pan. Toss until the beans are heated through, add pepper and serve. Serves 3 or 4.

SAVORY STRING BEANS

1 cup leftover smoked ham (include fat)
1 cup water
1 pound whole fresh green beans
Pinch of parsley flakes
½ cup evaporated milk
1 small onion, diced
½ teaspoon savory
Salt, pepper to taste

Mince the ham and fat. Place in a pot with the water. Cover and simmer 30 minutes. Add the other ingredients. Simmer covered, until the beans are tender, adding a little more water if needed. Serves 6.

STRING BEANS IN TOMATO SAUCE

1 large can string beans, including liquid
½ cup non-fat dry milk
1 6-ounce can tomato paste (*see* Brand Names)
2 ounces Cheddar cheese, grated
½ teaspoon onion powder
½ teaspoon celery salt

Drain the liquid from the beans into a saucepan. Add the dry milk and tomato paste, and stir until mixed. Sprinkle in the cheese and seasonings and heat until the cheese melts. Add the beans. Heat through and serve. Serves 4.

SUMMER SQUASH: 3 to 6 per cent carbohydrate (low)

SUMMER SQUASH MEDLEY

2 tablespoons oil or bacon drippings
1 yellow crookneck squash, diced
1 small zucchini, diced
1 rib celery, sliced
1 clove garlic, minced fine
2 tablespoons onion flakes
2 tablespoons water

Heat the oil in a skillet and sauté the vegetables until slightly browned. Add the rest of the ingredients. Cover tightly and simmer over low heat until the vegetables are tender. Serves 4.

"CREAMED CORN" (YELLOW SQUASH)

2 small yellow crookneck squash
½ cup milk
1 teaspoon butter
Salt to taste
Dash of liquid artificial sweetener

Dice the squash into small pieces the size of corn kernels. Heat the milk. Add the rest of the ingredients. Cover, lower heat and simmer 2 to 4 minutes until the squash is cooked. Do not overcook; pieces should be almost crunchy. Serves 3.

PAN-FRIED YELLOW SQUASH

2 tablespoons oil
1 yellow crookneck squash, thinly sliced
2 scallions, thinly sliced
Salt as needed

Heat the oil. Sauté the vegetables, stirring occasionally, until lightly browned and tender. Salt to taste and serve. Serves 1 or 2.

WINTER SQUASH: 15 per cent carbohydrate (high); also hubbard, acorn, butternut, etc.

BAKED WINTER SQUASH

Split the squash in half and remove the seeds and pulp. Place the squash, cut side down, on an aluminum foil-lined pan in a hot (400°) oven. Bake for 1 to 1½ hours, or until the squash is easily pierced with a fork. Scoop out the squash, dot with butter and sprinkle lightly with salt and liquid artificial sweetener. Makes about 2 cups, or 4 servings; each serving=1 unit high-carbohydrate vegetable.

MOCK "CANDIED SWEET POTATOES" (WINTER SQUASH)

1 recipe Baked Winter Squash
2 tablespoons butter
2 or 3 ¼-grain tablets saccharin, crushed and dissolved in ¼ cup hot water
½ teaspoon maple flavoring

Bake the squash according to recipe. Remove from the oven when just tender, but not mushy. Scoop out the squash in chunks with a spoon. Transfer the chunks to a greased baking dish. Dot with the butter. Mix together the sweetener and flavoring and sprinkle over the squash. Bake at 375° for 30 minutes, or until the syrup is thick. Serves 4; each serving=1 unit high-carbohydrate vegetable.

MOCK "SWEET POTATO" PUDDING (WINTER SQUASH)

1 package frozen puréed squash
½ cup water
1 tablespoon butter
1 egg
⅓ cup unsweetened pineapple juice
4 ¼-grain tablets saccharin
¼ cup evaporated milk or light cream
⅓ cup non-fat dry milk

Combine the squash, water and butter in a saucepan. Cover and simmer over low heat until the squash is soft. Pour into the blender, along with the other ingredients, and mix. Pour into a greased 1-quart casserole. Bake at 350° until set (about 30 to 45 minutes). Serves 4; each serving=1 unit high-carbohydrate vegetable.

MOCK "SWEET POTATO" CASSEROLE (WINTER SQUASH)

1 egg, beaten
1 cup light cream
3 cups baked butternut squash (*see* Baked Winter Squash)
Dash of salt
1 can Dole crushed unsweetened pineapple, packed in its own juice
½ teaspoon vanilla extract

Beat the egg and cream together. Mash the cooked squash and mix all the ingredients together until smooth (include the juice from the pineapple). Pour into a shallow casserole and bake in a moderate (350°) oven until set (about 45 minutes). Serves 6; each serving=1 unit high-carbohydrate vegetable, 1 unit fruit.

BAKED SQUASH WITH ORANGE FILLING

1 large acorn squash
1 tablespoon butter
½ cup orange juice
⅔ cup sour cream
½ teaspoon grated orange peel
Pinch of salt
¼ teaspoon pumpkin pie spice
4 ¼-grain tablets saccharin, crushed
¼ teaspoon nutmeg
1 small orange, peeled and diced

Bake the squash according to the directions given for Baked Winter Squash. Turn the baked squash so that the cut side is facing up. Brush the cut edges and cavity with butter and orange juice, and continue baking, brushing often, until the squash is very soft (about 20 minutes). In a bowl combine the remaining ingredients. Mix well. Remove the squash from the oven and spoon the filling into the two cavities. Serve immediately. Serves 4; each serving=1 unit high-carbohydrate vegetable, ½ unit fruit.

TOMATOES: 3 to 6 per cent carbohydrate (low)

BROILED TOMATOES

2 large ripe tomatoes
Oil
Pinch of thyme
Salt, pepper
Grated Parmesan cheese

Slice the tomatoes in half across the middle. Place cut side up on the broiling rack. Brush cut side with the oil. Sprinkle lightly with the seasonings, then with the grated cheese. Broil 6 inches from the heat until the cheese is lightly browned (about 10 to 15 minutes; do not allow the tomatoes to get too soft). Serves 4.

STEWED TOMATOES

1 16-ounce can whole tomatoes
½ teaspoon onion powder
1 slice homemade bread, crumbed
¼ green pepper, diced
1 ¼-grain tablet saccharin
Salt, pepper to taste

Slice the tomatoes. Place all ingredients in a saucepan. Simmer on low heat for 10 minutes. Entire recipe=1 unit carbohydrate if using high-carbohydrate bread. Serves 3.

STUFFED TOMATOES

4 medium tomatoes
2 tablespoons oil
½ pound mushrooms, sliced
Pinch of basil
Pinch of parsley flakes
Salt, pepper to taste
1 slice homemade Soy Bread, crumbled

Cut a slice off the top of each tomato. Remove the pulp and set aside. In a pan, heat the oil. Add the mushrooms and sauté until brown. Add the pulp from the tomatoes and the seasonings. Simmer for 10 minutes. Mix in the bread crumbs and spoon into the tomatoes. Serves 4.

SCALLOPED TOMATOES

2 or 3 large ripe tomatoes
¼ teaspoon salt
6 to 8 slices processed American cheese
¼ cup wheat germ or ground nuts

Slice the tomatoes. In a greased casserole, place a single layer of tomato slices. Salt lightly and cover with the sliced cheese. Repeat until all are used up. Sprinkle the wheat germ on top (if tolerated; if not, use ground nuts). Bake at 325° until the cheese is melted and bubbly, and the topping is browned. Serves 4; each serving contains small amount of carbohydrate.

TOMATOES IN HERB SAUCE

2 tablespoons butter
½ onion, minced
6 small whole tomatoes, peeled
1½ cups milk
Dash of freshly ground pepper

1 tablespoon prepared mustard
½ teaspoon salt
½ teaspoon each: dill, tarragon, chervil

Melt the butter in a saucepan. Sauté the onion until soft. Add the other ingredients. Cover and simmer until the tomatoes are soft. Serves 4.

MARINATED TOMATOES

2 ripe tomatoes
2 tablespoons olive oil
¼ cup cider vinegar
Pinch of chopped dill weed
Salt to taste

Slice the tomatoes ¼ inch thick, or cut into thick wedges. Arrange on a serving plate. Drizzle evenly with the oil, then the vinegar. Sprinkle generously with the dill, then lightly with the salt. Set aside for at least 1 hour to marinate. Serve cold. Serves 3.

WHITE TURNIPS: 3 to 6 per cent carbohydrate (low)

CREAMED TURNIPS

Peel the turnips and cut into bite-sized chunks. Add boiling water to cover. Cook until tender. Drain and toss with butter; salt and pepper to taste. Add a small amount of evaporated milk or light cream, and toss until evenly coated. Correct seasoning and serve hot.

MASHED TURNIPS

Prepare same as for Creamed Turnips. After adding the cream, mash well. Garnish with a dash of paprika, and serve immediately.

WATER CHESTNUTS: 3 to 6 per cent carbohydrate (low)

WATER CHESTNUT "HOME FRIES"

¼ cup bacon drippings
1 small onion, diced
1 can water chestnuts, drained and diced
Paprika to taste
Salt, pepper to taste

Heat the bacon fat. Add the onion, water chestnuts and seasonings. Fry until brown and crisp. Correct seasonings, drain slightly on paper towels and serve. Serves 3.

BAKED WATER CHESTNUTS (WITH ROAST BEEF)

Drain a can of water chestnuts. Prepare your roast and place on a rack in the oven. Roast for 1 hour, or until there are drippings in the pan. Arrange the water chestnuts around the roast in the bottom of the pan so that they are cooking in the drippings. Continue roasting, turning the water chestnuts, several times. Sprinkle them lightly with paprika ½ hour before the roast is finished, and do not turn again. This can also be done with pot roast or any other roast, or with meat loaf. Serves 3.

WAX BEANS: 3 to 6 per cent carbohydrate (low)

WAX BEAN SUCCOTASH

¾ cup milk
1 package frozen wax beans
Salt, pepper to taste

½ package frozen peas
1 tablespoon butter

Heat the milk. Add the other ingredients. Cover and lower heat. Cook until the vegetables are soft. Remove some of the peas and mash to thicken the sauce. Return to the pan and correct seasoning. Serves 4; each serving=½ unit high-carbohydrate vegetable.

WAX BEAN "MACARONI"

1 package frozen French-style wax beans, slightly thawed to separate
½ cup milk
Salt, pepper to taste
4 ounces American cheese slices
2 tablespoons dry grated American cheese

Thaw the beans just enough to separate them. Spread in a single layer in a small greased casserole. Add the milk and seasonings, and spread the cheese slices on top (for a fancy effect, cut the cheese into diamonds or triangles and separate slightly). Sprinkle the top with the grated cheese. Cover and bake at 325° until the cheese is melted and the topping is brown (about 45 minutes to 1 hour). Serves 4.

ZUCCHINI: 3 to 6 per cent carbohydrate (low)

BRAISED ZUCCHINI

2 tablespoons butter
3 or 4 tiny zucchini, sliced
1 scallion, minced, including tops
¼ cup water
Salt, pepper to taste

Melt the butter and sauté the vegetables until browned. Lower the heat; add water and cover tightly. Simmer until the zucchini are tender (about 5 minutes). Add more water if needed. Season with salt and pepper and serve. Serves 3.

ITALIAN-STYLE ZUCCHINI

2 tablespoons olive oil
½ medium onion, diced
1 clove garlic, minced
1 large zucchini, cubed (about 3 cups)
1 8-ounce can Del Monte tomato sauce
Dash of oregano
¼ cup grated Romano cheese
Dash of pepper

Heat the oil. Sauté the onion and garlic until soft. Add the zucchini and stir until the zucchini is slightly browned at the edges. Lower the heat and add the sauce and oregano. Cover and simmer until the zucchini are tender. Add the grated cheese and pepper, simmer 5 minutes and serve. Serves 4.

STUFFED ZUCCHINI

2 large zucchini
½ pound lean ground beef
1 egg, slightly beaten
1 teaspoon capers
½ teaspoon garlic powder
Dash of basil
2 tablespoons minced onions
Salt, pepper to taste
1½ cups tomato sauce or tomato purée
4 ounces mozzarella cheese, shredded (or Muenster)

Slice the zucchini in half lengthwise. Scoop out the seeds and pulp, forming "boats." Combine the beef, egg, capers and seasonings in a bowl. Add 1 cup of the chopped pulp and mix well. Stuff into the hollowed-out zucchini, heaping the extra on top. Place in a greased shallow baking dish. Pour in the tomato sauce, drizzling some on the zucchini, the rest around it. Bake in a slow (325°) oven for 1 hour.

Sprinkle the cheese on top, return to the oven and bake at 425° until the cheese is melted and bubbly (10 minutes). Serves 4 as a side dish, or 2 as a main dish.

MISCELLANEOUS

VEGETABLE STEW

2 tablespoons butter
½ small rutabaga, peeled and diced
1 package frozen green beans
1 yellow squash, diced
1 green pepper, diced
1 carrot, sliced
1 onion, diced
1 16-ounce can tomatoes
Dash of basil
Salt, pepper to taste

Heat the butter and sauté the vegetables, stirring, until softened. Add the canned tomatoes, season and cover. Place in the oven at 325°. Bake for 1 hour, or until the vegetables are cooked. Serves 6.

CHINESE VEGETABLES

2 tablespoons peanut oil
2 scallions, minced
3 ribs celery, sliced diagonally
2 ribs Chinese cabbage, in slivers
6 to 8 fresh mushrooms, sliced
½ Knorr-Swiss beef bouillon cube
2 tablespoons Kikkoman soy sauce
Dash of MSG
½ cup water
1 can bean sprouts, drained

Prepare the vegetables and set aside. Heat the oil in a frying pan or a wok, if you have one. Fry the scallions, celery, Chinese cabbage and mushrooms, stirring, over high heat. After 5 minutes add the bouillon cube, soy sauce, MSG and water. Lower heat and cover. Simmer for about 5 minutes, or until the vegetables are tender but crisp. Rinse the bean sprouts in cold water and drain well. Squeeze the excess moisture out in a dish towel. Add the sprouts to the mixture. Stir until heated through and serve. Serves 4.

VEGETABLE TZIMMES

2 tablespoons rendered chicken fat
½ pound stew beef, cubed
1 teaspoon salt
2 cups water
6 medium carrots, sliced
2 parsnips, peeled and sliced
1 medium onion, diced
1 large apple, peeled, cored and sliced
1 teaspoon salt
Dash of freshly ground pepper
½ teaspoon paprika
1 ¼-grain tablet saccharin

Heat the chicken fat in a deep pot; add the meat and sear, stirring, until brown. Add the salt and water. Cover tightly and simmer on low heat for 1 hour. Add the remaining ingredients, cover and simmer at least 1 hour on low heat until the flavors are well blended. To reduce the liquid to a thick sauce, tilt the lid, and simmer another 30 minutes. Serves 4; each serving=½ unit fruit, 1 unit high-carbohydrate vegetable.

"SUCCOTASH"

1 package frozen peas
½ cup milk
1 medium yellow squash
1 tablespoon butter
1 tablespoon minced onion
⅓ cup non-fat dry milk
Salt to taste

Place the peas and milk in a large saucepan. Cover and simmer over low heat until able to break the peas up with a fork. Cut the squash into small pieces, the size of corn kernels. Add to the pan, along with the butter and minced onion. Cover and cook gently until the vegetables are tender, but still slightly chewy. Stir in the dry milk, and heat uncovered, stirring occasionally until thickened. Salt to taste. Serves 4 to 6; each serving=1 unit high-carbohydrate vegetable.

MUSHROOM STEW

1 tablespoon butter or oil
½ pound raw mushrooms, sliced (include stems)
1 small onion, diced
1 cup rich beef broth or sugarless bouillon
Dash of garlic powder
1 can bean sprouts, drained and squeezed dry

Heat the butter or oil in a saucepan. Sauté the mushrooms and onion, stirring, until the onion is translucent. Add the other ingredients. Cover the pan and simmer on low for 15 minutes. Serves 4.

SPROUTS AND ONIONS

1 can bean sprouts
1 cup beef gravy from pot roast, or roast beef drippings plus water
    to equal 1 cup
2 onions, sliced in rings

Drain the sprouts, freshen with cold water and drain again. Squeeze between towels. Combine all ingredients in a saucepan. Cover and simmer over low heat until the onions are soft (about 15 to 20 minutes) or bake at 325° for 30 minutes. Serves 4.

RECIPE INDEX